BRADMAN

The Illustrated Biography

BRADMAN
The Illustrated Biography

by Michael Page
USING THE PRIVATE POSSESSIONS OF
SIR DONALD BRADMAN

SUN BOOKS

First published 1983 by
THE MACMILLAN COMPANY OF AUSTRALIA PTY LTD
107 Moray Street, South Melbourne 3205
6 Clarke Street, Crows Nest 2065
Reprinted 1987, 1990 , 1994

Associated companies in
London and Basingstoke, England
Auckland Dallas Delhi Hong Kong
Johannesburg Lagos Manzini Nairobi
New York Singapore Tokyo Washington Zaria

National Library of Australia
cataloguing in publication data

Page, Michael F. (Michael Fitzgerald), 1922- .
  Bradman, the illustrated biography.

  Includes index.
  ISBN 0 7251 0498 8.

  1. Bradman, Sir Donald, 1908-   . 2. Cricket
  players — Australia — Biography. I. Title.

796.35′8′0924

Set in Times and Stymie by Savage Type, Brisbane
Printed in Hong Kong

CONTENTS

INTRODUCTION:
A NOTE OF THANKS

I first met Sir Donald Bradman about twelve years ago, when he was chairman of directors of the Adelaide company which employed me. Of course I knew something of his story, and I had been conscious of his name ever since I was an eight-year-old urchin in England. Like most pre-war schoolboys I collected cigarette cards, including the Test Cricketers series which Player's Navy Cut cigarettes gave away in 1930. In that year, Don Bradman's meteoric appearance in English cricketing skies greatly increased his value in cigarette card currency, so that one had to trade two Jack Hobbs to obtain one Don Bradman.

English schoolboys have always been among Don Bradman's most ardent fans, and so I was fully aware of his spectacular domination of the Test arena during the 1930s. He was part of my knowledge of the world. But I certainly never expected to meet this living legend, and so it was quite astonishing when I was introduced to him.

It was at an evening function, and I was impressed by his attitude of simple friendship towards everyone in that assembly. Early newspaper reports often commented upon the young Don Bradman's 'absence of swelled head', and it was obvious that more than half-a-century of massive adulation and publicity had not corrupted his innate modesty.

As the years passed I met Sir Donald on a number of occasions, in the ways that a middle-management executive will encounter the chairman of directors. As a man, I found him to be friendly and forthright. As a businessman, he was obviously shrewd, meticulous, honourable, and excellently well-informed. His ability to absorb complex information, and compute it into prompt decisions, must surely be one of the reasons for his brilliance as a batsman and cricket captain.

Shortly after my retirement, the Macmillan Company of Australia gave me some exciting news. They had been asking Sir Donald to write a new complete autobiography and, although he had neither the time nor the inclination to do so, he had consented to make available to them his personal records and memorabilia which could form the basis of a biography. And, since he was acquainted with me, he had accepted Macmillan's suggestion that I should write and compile the book.

They offered me the commission, and of course I seized the opportunity to write the life story of the most famous living Australian. I had only one misgiving. I knew from experience that Sir Donald is reluctant to talk about his achievements, and I feared he might want to limit the scope of the biography.

But, like many other people over the years, I had underestimated Sir Donald. He had agreed to the project, and he never enters into any agreement without seeing it through to the end.

In early discussions, he made it clear to me that he was concerned only about the factual accuracy of the book. He did not want to guide my hand or influence my opinions in any way. But, to ensure this accuracy, he asked for the right to check my manuscript as I proceeded with the work and told me that he would answer all my questions as fully as possible. Naturally I accepted these conditions with relief and gratitude.

I think we were a trifle wary of each other to begin with. For my part I was a little overawed. After all I was talking to a segment of living history, and I was keenly aware of my responsibility to tell his story correctly. As for Sir Donald, he has long experience of writers of many breeds — including those influenced by jealousy, or malicious gossip, or editorial pressure for a sensational story. Perhaps he wondered what angle I would be seeking.

But as we came to know each other better I found I could not have asked for a more patient and sympathetic subject. I had been entrusted with a carload of his priceless archival material — the letters, documents, photographs, scrapbooks, and press cutting books, accumulated during a long lifetime — and my task of piecing this enormous jigsaw together would have been much more difficult without his guidance through the maze. At the same time, he set me right on many points of cricketing history, personalities, technique and terminology.

When he read my first drafts of the text, I discovered one of his dominant characteristics. It is an almost fierce honesty, which demands absolute truth, accuracy, and justice. Also he has a formidable memory, apparently capable of recalling every ball of every significant match; and a love of the English language which caused him often to debate the finer shades of meaning in a word or phrase.

These qualities often provided me with invaluable help and guidance, by ensuring that I wrote the exact facts about every incident — even if it was one which concerned a less successful moment in his career. As a result, I am able to feel that the narrative is a totally accurate interpretation of Sir Donald's story and of his attitude towards life.

I was also deeply impressed by the integral decency of a man who would not overlook any comment which seemed to reflect unfairly, even if unintentionally, upon an old cricketing associate or antagonist. Nor did he take kindly to revelations which might hurt or embarrass anyone still alive. During his lifetime he has suffered so many assaults on his privacy, and so many misinterpretations and misrepresentations, that he is unwilling to subject other men to the same hurtful experience.

Apart from my working relationship with Sir Donald, I feel a particular pride and pleasure in my association with him. The English cricketer Arthur Gilligan once described him as 'one of the truest gentlemen who ever wore flannels' and I find it easy to understand why. He is one of those remarkable men whose personalities seem to radiate complete confidence, and a warmth, sympathy, and sensitivity which evoke trust and confidence in return. These qualities, complemented as they are by the charm and serenity of Lady Bradman, make me deeply grateful not only for Sir Donald's assistance with this book but also for the privilege of knowing one of the great men of our time.

Michael Page

1

THE BOWRAL WONDER

The ancient game of cricket arrived in Australia in December 1803, when the officers of the ship *Calcutta* played the first game in Sydney. Colonial-born youngsters took eagerly to the sport, and successive waves of immigrants nourished the cricketing spirit with skills learnt on English village greens. Many of the immigrants were young farmhands from the English countryside, where village lads invented the game at least four centuries ago. In 1852, they included nineteen-year-old Charles Bradman from the county of Suffolk. Nobody knows whether he was a cricketer, but cricket was played so vigorously in south-eastern England, including Suffolk's neighbouring county of Cambridge, that it would be strange if he had not handled a crude bat and ball during his childhood.

Charles Bradman settled first in the Southern Highlands of New South Wales: the high fertile country which in those days lay about four days' journey to the south of Sydney. John Oxley had opened the district only twenty-six years earlier, but the townships of Bowral, Berrima, Moss Vale, Mittagong, Exeter, and Wingello had been established and the region was flourishing.

Young Charles Bradman found a rewarding new life among the rolling tree-clad hills of the highlands. After eleven years of working for others he had saved enough money to buy land for himself. With his young wife Elizabeth Biffen of Mittagong, whom he married when she was fifteen, he moved west to Jindalee in the Cootamundra district. The railway had reached Bowral in 1867, on its way to Melbourne, and so they could make the move in comparative comfort.

Charles and Elizabeth brought up a family of six children on their Jindalee farm. The youngest, George Bradman, continued the link with the Southern Highlands when he married a Mittagong girl, Emily Whatman, in 1893. He was only seventeen when he met twenty-two-year-old Emily, who was visiting friends in Cootamundra.

George took up land near Yeo Yeo, a tiny farming community on the line running west towards Hay. He was a tall, strong young man, disciplined since childhood in the gruellingly hard work of a family farm. Apart from the seasonal work of sowing and harvesting, shearing and dipping, he had to carry out all the mechanical and maintenance work around the property, and he became a skilled self-taught mechanic and carpenter.

Youngest of the family. Don Bradman while his family were still living at Yeo Yeo in New South Wales

But even farmers can find time to relax, and he followed the English-Australian tradition of amateur cricket by playing for Cootamundra. The town's situation on the railway line meant that teams could come from neighbouring townships to play the great game.

When Emily's children began to arrive, she took the train to Cootamundra so that they might be delivered in Mrs Scholz's nursing home. In August 1908, when the family comprised Victor, Islet, Lilian, and Elizabeth May, she made the trip to Cootamundra for the birth of her youngest son. He was born on 27 August 1908, and George and Emily named him Donald George.

The new baby was toddling and talking when his parents made a long-discussed decision. The heat of the inland plains, and the toilsome isolation of a farmer's wife, had never really suited Emily Bradman. Her health was suffering, and George decided to take her back to the hills of her girlhood. There would be other advantages, too. The educational facilities were better in Bowral, and the move seemed to offer better prospects for every member of the family. As for himself, he would give up farming and set himself up as a carpenter. The family link with the Bowral district, where Emily's brothers George and Richard Whatman were dairy farmers, told him that there was plenty of work for a good carpenter. Alf Stephens, who owned the town's joinery works and did much of its building, could find more than enough to occupy a skilled tradesman.

The family moved to Bowral early in 1911. George bought a weatherboard house in Shepherd Street, Victor and the girls went to school, and young Donald flourished in the new environment.

Bowral was the classic Australian small town of that period: a self-contained community that supplied most of its population's simple needs. The main industries were quarrying and the Wingecarribee Butter Factory, which took some of the Whatman brothers' milk production. There were two district newspapers, four hotels, two banks, a gasworks, primary and secondary State schools and a Church of England girls grammar school, a School of Arts, a hospital, and a number of stores.

Many of the population earned their modest livelihood by working for themselves. George Harvey was listed simply as a 'horseshoer'; John McCann as 'fruiterer, billposter, and bellman'. K. Drescher and his son were the watchmakers. The ladies of the district could use the services of several dressmakers. A surprising number of music teachers, including Colin Ferguson who taught violin and Mrs Ingoldsby who taught piano, trained the youngsters of Bowral in the gentle art of making music for themselves. There were no radios or cassette players, and very few phonographs, to provide music at the touch of a switch.

Gregory's Livery Stables provided horses to ride or drive (and metamorphosed into Gregory's Garage, Bong Bong Street, a few years later). Delamont the blacksmith worked in a sooty cavern; Gowrie Ruthven was the leading stock salesman and auctioneer; Oxley the solicitor took care of wills and conveyancing.

The difference between Bowral and many other small towns was the summer climate. The height, of 674 metres above sea level, ensured a comparatively cool summer. In those days before air conditioning it attracted many refugees from steamy-summer Sydney, only 132 kilometres to the north, and the hotels and boarding houses prospered in the summer months.

Wealthier Sydney folk built themselves summer homes in the Bowral district. Some, like Anthony Hordern and Sir Samuel Hordern, owned extensive properties. Their 'hobby farms' of Milton Park and Retford Park were local show-places. Other summer homes, in that expansive era, were almost as palatial as the Hordern residences. The building and maintenance of such retreats provided George Bradman with some of his work, and the seasonal visitors contributed to Bowral's prosperity.

Summer sophistication faded away when the cold west winds began to blow and the town settled into its winter routine. Winters are cold in Bowral, and Sir Donald Bradman remembers the frost still lying thickly under the trees in the middle of winter days.

Boyhood for young Donald was much the same as that for any small town boy of that era. He was a little too young to be much affected by the intense excitement of 1914, when the young horsemen and infantrymen trained under the compulsory service scheme were fare-welled at the railway station; but consciousness of the faraway battles dawned as patriotic rallies, children's games, magazine illustrations, and the sad or excited talk of adults maintained a background of half-understood drama. There were many other things to occupy a child's mind. Choir practice, school lessons in which he did best at arithmetic, his sister Lilian teaching him to play the piano, household chores, and all the homely closewoven texture of small-town life made more sense than the ominous names of Gallipoli or Passchendaele. The sight of a Light Horseman swaggering along the street was exciting to a little boy, but somehow not as significant as the Saturday cricket matches in which Alf Stephens captained the side, father sometimes umpired, and Uncle George and Uncle Dick showed their paces.

Nobody knows who introduced cricket to the Southern Highlands: whether it was English settlers like Charles Bradman or their Australian descendants. By the time Charles Bradman's youngest grandson was conscious of the game it was well established in the area. There was a local cricket association, Berrima District, and its members competed as earnestly for the trophy donated by a local identity, the Tom Mack Cup, as New South Wales did for the Sheffield Shield. Towns within a radius of about 50 kilometres around Bowral jousted every Saturday in the season, under a local rule which restricted an afternoon's play to four hours but allowed the final match of the season to continue on successive Saturdays until it was finished. This rule sometimes meant that cricket was still being played after the football season had started, and it was eventually to give Bradman his first burst of publicity.

There was no water to spare for turf pitches, and nobody who knew anything about looking after turf. The wickets were fast and hard, with pitches consisting of concrete strips covered with matting. It is no wonder that Donald Bradman never felt very comfortable on a sticky wicket during his cricketing career. In those days when people had few other distractions, there was hot spectator support for each of the community teams and a degree of partisanship which would rival that of barrackers on the Hill at Sydney Cricket Ground. The feats of local cricketers were discussed as ardently as those of Test champions.

Don Bradman's youngest sister, May, photographed during the early Bowral days. Apart from Sir Donald Bradman she is the only survivor of the five children of George and Emily Bradman

Don Bradman grew up in this cricketing atmosphere, and heard the game discussed within his own family. His own opportunity to participate was slow in arriving. He began school when he was five, but there was very little in the way of organised sport and certainly no attempt to coach youngsters in such games as cricket. All he could do was watch the games of schoolyard cricket played by the bigger boys. A fence divided the school playground into two sections, one for the primary school and one for the high school, and he stood at the gate in this fence observing the noisy games played by the high-school youngsters during recess.

This schoolyard cricket had a close resemblance to the seminal games of cricket in the English countryside. Like the shepherd lads of old, the Bowral schoolboys fashioned their bats from any handily-shaped tree limb. Their wicket was chalked on the foot of the bell post which stood in the schoolyard, and their balls were the despised 'compo'. Nobody coached them, and what they knew of the game had been passed on in a kind of folklore or imitated from Saturday matches in Bowral's Glebe Park; but they played with as much zest and argument as did their Elizabethan ancestors.

As young Donald grew older the high-school boys occasionally invited him into the game, but these momentary tastes of handling the bat and ball were far from sufficient for one who was just beginning to sense a lifelong addiction to competitive sport. He would have enjoyed a continuation of this schoolyard cricket at weekends or in the evenings, but none of the other boys lived close enough to the Bradman house to provide him with partners. There was no organisation for junior teams, and his parents would not allow him to roam away from home in search of playmates. Consequently he invented games in which he was his own opponent.

He played tennis by hitting a ball against the garage door, football by kicking a ball around in the paddock, and cricket with a stump and a golf ball.

A cylindrical rainwater tank, set on a round brick stand, stood behind the Bradman home in an area covered by the verandah roof and with a concrete floor. A laundry projected from the house, so that the tank, the laundry and the house wall made a covered area, open on one side, in which he could play in any weather.

Using the laundry door as a wicket, he threw the golf ball at the tank stand. The curved brick surface made it rebound at high speed and constantly varying angles, but he set himself to hit it before it struck the laundry wall or door.

It is quite difficult to hit a cricket ball with a stump, and far harder to hit a golf ball, but constant practice made young Bradman proficient at his solitary game. He invented a system of ways in which to be caught out and to score boundaries, and determined that the open side of his playing area should correspond to the on-side of a cricket field. This absolved him from chasing the ball for any shots on the off-side.

He had to move with split-second speed and accuracy: holding the stump in his left hand, throwing the ball with his right hand, and then switching the stump to both hands in time to hit the ball as it bounced back at him. Sometimes he pretended he was a left-handed batsman and used the stump with his left hand.

To give his game more interest he invented two 'sides', comprising

Don Bradman the choirboy, aged about nine

Left: Young Don with the family dog Teddy

Above: Don Bradman's sister Lilian, who taught him to play the piano and subsequently became a professional music teacher

such well-known cricketing names of the period as Taylor, Gregory, and Collins, and played for each of them in turn. He kept the score in his head and built up great excitement as the hard springy ball bounced back at him countless times and he hit it back at the tank stand. No doubt his family became inured to the endless tock-tock-tock of ball against brick or ball against stump, although Emily Bradman frequently 'declared' an important Test Match when dinner was on the table.

Bradman played this game without any particular thought of the future. It was simply an enjoyable way of passing the time, and increasing proficiency imparted the pleasure which any athlete feels at his own expertise. Unconsciously, perhaps, he was learning the basic truth which every sportsman knows: that success on the field depends on perpetual practice.

By way of varying his amusements, he often took the golf ball into the nearby paddock and threw it about ten metres at the bottom rail of the dividing fence. If he missed the rail, and the ball hit the palings, he had to run in to pick it up. Consequently he made sure that he hit the rail more often than not, and as the ball bounced back at erratic angles he leapt or ran to catch it and throw it back again.

The image of a solitary youngster disciplining himself with these games is thought-provoking. Like most boys of his age at that time, and indeed most males of the Australian countryside in that era, he had a dedicated interest in cricket and he knew about the great figures of the cricketing world, but he could not have guessed that his continuous practice would help to make him one of the cricketing giants of the future. As he wrote in 1950, 'I can understand how it must have developed the co-ordination of brain, eye and muscle which was to serve me so well in important matches later on.'

In 1949, the great Indian cricketer Maharajkumar Duleepsinhji wrote of him: 'What is the secret of his success? Cricket sense, extra quickness of eye, foot-work, suppleness of wrist, looseness of shoulders and correct timing. The highly-developed cricket sense helps him make up his mind in a split second to decide on a stroke soon after the ball has left the bowler's hand. Bradman is seldom at fault in judging the correct stroke. The quickness of foot-work gives him the correct position to play the stroke he intends to play. The suppleness of wrists, looseness of shoulders and correct timing have given his strokes the great speed with which he despatches the ball to all corners of the field.'

All these qualities must owe much to the self-imposed training of those childhood years, added of course to that intangible quality which, like the ability of any genius, comes from a mysterious combination of inheritance, willpower, concentration, and flair.

His lonely practice obviously showed its effects on his schoolyard cricket, because the older boys were sufficiently impressed to invite him into a more formal match. It was played on the recreation ground in Glebe Park, but the schoolboy cricketers were not allowed to use the adult pitch. They used a fiery wicket on the football field, more earth and dust than grass.

An artist's impression, from the Sydney *Referee* of 1931, of Don Bradman playing schoolboy cricket in Bowral

Bradman's captain won the toss and went in to bat. A left-handed bowler promptly dismissed the first two batsmen for ducks, and young Bradman then found himself facing the demon bowler. He wrote in 1930: 'It is a trait in my make-up which it is quite impossible to explain, that I am almost a total stranger to that species of nervousness common to most people whenever involved in an unusual happening'; and he displayed this coolness when the first ball whistled towards him over the dusty pitch.

He played it as he was to play countless thousands during the next thirty-odd years: with the correct response calculated in a split second. The bowler's chance of a hat-trick was foiled, and young Bradman carried his bat for 55 runs.

This demonstration virtually ensured his place in future matches. He was selected to play against Mittagong High School, who were the deadly rivals of the Bowral school. For the first time, he played on a 'real' pitch, of concrete covered with matting.

Perhaps the Mittagong bowlers thought the twelve-year-old youngster would be 'easy meat'. If so, they were sadly disappointed when he punished their bowling to such effect that he made his first century. He made 115 not out, out of a total of 156.

Bowral were the victors, but his pardonable pride was dampened on the following morning. When the school was lined up in the playground, the headmaster announced: 'I understand that there is a certain boy among you who scored a century yesterday against Mittagong. Well, that is no reason or excuse why you should have left a bat behind.'

In that cricket season after his twelfth birthday he had the opportunity to play regularly in the 'scratch' matches, played on one afternoon a week between two and four-thirty. If the first side to bat had not been dismissed by three-thirty, they had to declare the innings

The school at Bowral. The portion of the schoolyard in which Don Bradman played his earliest games of cricket is just out of the photograph to the left

closed at that time and give the others a turn at the wicket.

His father and uncles began to take a more serious interest in his self-taught cricketing skills, and his Uncle George delighted the boy by inviting him to act as scorer for the Bowral team during the 1920–21 season. He spent his Saturday afternoons on the Bowral oval, or travelling with the team on its cricketing forays around the Berrima District. Most of them rode in the back of a truck shod with solid tyres, which gave them a bumpy ride over the unsealed roads. Sitting on a kerosene box among his elders, some of them men in their forties, young Donald listened intently to their discussions of cricket lore and legend. The first Test Series after the first world war was about to be played in Australia and the names of such men as Arthur Mailey, C. G. Macartney and Johnny Taylor were on the lips of every cricket lover.

One Saturday the team rode to Moss Vale but found themselves short of the eleventh man. Uncle George pressed his nephew into service, and with mingled awe and excitement the boy went in to bat at the fall of the eighth wicket. Wielding a full-size bat, he handled the bowling to the tune of 37 not out. When the match continued on the following Saturday he went in as first man, to score 29 not out.

Sidney Cupitt of the Bowral team rewarded this debut in senior cricket with the gift of an old bat. It was dented and cracked but it was a real bat with a splice. George Bradman sawed three inches off the bottom and rounded it off at the foot, and his son ran into the paddock and played imaginary shots until the light failed. It was as though Leonardo da Vinci had been given his first paint brush.

The next cricketing adventure came when George Bradman decided to take a couple of days off work to watch some of the fifth Test of that record 1920–21 series. For the first and only time, Australia was to make a clean sweep of the English team by winning all five Tests. The googly bowler Arthur Mailey had spun out nine Englishmen in one innings at Melbourne and he was to take 36 wickets during the series.

Donald begged his father to take him along, and on a February day they took the train to Sydney. For the first time, Donald Bradman saw the classic splendour of the Sydney Cricket Ground, with its huge grandstands and famous Hill surrounding the flawless turf. It was an awe-inspiring experience for a boy beginning to sense that cricket would play some part in his future.

He sat among one of the enormous crowds which first-class cricket attracted in those days and watched a brilliant display, although his heart sank when he saw his cricketing hero, Johnny Taylor, caught by Patsy Hendren.

During one of the intervals George Bradman took his son for a walk around the ground, and smiled 'with affectionate tolerance' when Donald said fervently, 'I shall never be satisfied until I play on this ground'. Perhaps the father thought it was an understandable but impossible ambition.

They returned to the less glamorous cricketing life of Bowral, with the boy's mind full of the virtuoso exhibition he had witnessed. Again and again he pictured Macartney's delicate leg glances, the smooth rhythm of Ted McDonald, and Woolley's beautiful strokes.

Cricket was only one of the sports to attract Bradman's interest. He gravitated naturally into tennis, partly because his Uncle Dick had a court on which he could play at any time. His nimble footwork, un-

Don's mother, Mrs Emily Bradman, in the garden of their Bowral home

erring eye and lightning reactions made him an antagonist to be feared across the net. In winter he played for the school rugby team, and in the school sports he won the 100-yards, 200-yards, quarter-mile and half-mile events for boys of his age group.

Childhood ended with the final years at school, amidst the friendly and familiar surroundings of the little hills township. There was always something to do. His father was helping to build a new house for the family, and there were odd jobs for Donald on the building site. They moved into the new home, opposite Glebe Park and a very short distance from what is now known as Bradman Oval, in 1924.

On some weekends he went fishing in the rivers and creeks or rabbit-shooting in the hills. There were occasional visits to Weedon's Picture Show, to see Douglas Fairbanks or Charlie Chaplin, concerts in the church hall, and piano practice to develop his growing pleasure in music.

Below: Emily Bradman copied out this horoscope which was relevant to her son's birth on 27 August 1908. Most appropriately, it reads 'This day's children are ambitious, keen and hard working and they often make a real mark in the world.

'They are kind and generous and win the good esteem of all with whom they come in contact. They should take care of their health, however, and should spend as much time as possible in the open air. They will travel a lot through their work. Since they are so intent on making a success of life, love will probably come rather late to this day's folk. Their lucky day is Tuesday, their lucky number 10.'

TRUE AND FALSE

The first of the millions of words to be printed about Sir Donald Bradman's cricket career appeared in a now defunct Sydney journal, *Smith's Weekly.*

The paper printed 'pars' submitted by contributors around the countryside, and during Bradman's school-days a writer who signed himself 'John' sent in the following:

'*Bounding Ball.* Saw a curious thing at a junior cricket match at Bowral (New South Wales) recently.

'Don Bradman (crack "bat") sent a ball over the boundary fence. It struck half a brick, rebounded onto a fence post, poised there for an appreciable time, and ran along the top of the palings the whole length of a panel of fencing before descending outside the boundary.'

At least the story is true, which is more than may be said about some other Bradman stories.

One canard, still told oc-casionally, concerns his first appearance before the Sheffield Shield selectors.

It depicts him as such a raw country lad that he took his place at the nets with his flannels held up by black braces.

Nobody knows who invented this absurd yarn, which gained considerable credence among those jealous of Bradman's rise to fame.

The fact, of course, is that he had been playing country cricket for some years and was well acquainted with the regulation garb.

Irving Rosenwater, in the biography *Sir Donald Bradman* published in 1978, says that Lady Bradman, née Jessie Menzies, is the daughter of a Bowral bank manager.

Sir Donald points out that Lady Bradman is one of the daughters of a Glenquarry farmer, and that his only knowledge of Bowral bankers may have been on his application for an overdraft!

The Bradman home in Bowral, built in 1924 and still standing opposite what is now the Bradman Oval

He passed his intermediate examination and left school at the end of 1922, to begin work in the real estate agency owned by Mr Percy Westbrook. The estate agent proved to be a sympathetic employer, always ready to give his young clerk time off to play sport on Saturdays although that was their busiest day of the week.

To Donald Bradman's contemporaries, who included a farmer's daughter named Jessie Menzies, it must have seemed that the conventional life of a small-town youngster lay ahead of the trim athletic teenager with his easy smile and friendly personality. He would work his way up in the business, marry a local girl, and settle down to a life of contented obscurity.

For a time he even abandoned cricket. He became more interested in tennis, and during the season of 1923–24 he did not put on the pads for the Bowral side. In the following season he played tennis for most of the summer until he took part in two or three of the last cricket matches of the year. If he had any dreams of emulating Macartney they evaporated when he was dismissed by the first ball of the first game, but he recovered his form when Bowral played the semi-final of the competition against Wingello. He made a total of 66, the top score for Bowral.

The headmaster's report when Don Bradman left Bowral school in 1922. It reads: 'Don Bradman has been a pupil of this school under my personal tuition for the past 18 months. He is truthful, honest and industrious, and an unusually bright lad. He is specially good at Mathematics and French. P.S. He will, when the results appear, be found to have done very creditably at the recent Inter. Certif. Examn.'

Left: The young real estate clerk, in about 1924. As an employee of Percy Westbrook's real estate agency, young Don Bradman kept the books and learnt to drive in order to take clients out to inspect properties

Above: Jessie Menzies, now Lady Bradman, photographed at about the time Don Bradman first played cricket in Sydney

At the beginning of the 1925–26 season he enrolled as a regular member of the Bowral Town Club, although he still made time for tennis. At seventeen he was the youngest of the Bowral team, which included his brother Victor, and he felt himself rather privileged to play with, or against, the Berrima District heroes of the concrete and matting pitches.

The first few games of the season passed undramatically until Bowral was drawn to play Wingello. This town, about forty kilometres south of Bowral, was the proud possessor of a demon bowler named Bill O'Reilly. He had been largely instrumental in Wingello's capture of the Tom Mack Cup during the previous season.

Local cricketers tended to speak of O'Reilly's prowess in hushed tones, especially of his ability to turn a leg break with speed. He was a medium-paced bowler who could make a ball turn either way on a matting wicket, and his local fame eventually led to his selection for a Sheffield Shield team.

On a Saturday afternoon early in 1926, David in the form of seventeen-year-old Don Bradman faced Goliath in the shape of Bill O'Reilly. Bradman was unperturbed by the dire prophecies of what would happen when he faced O'Reilly's bowling, and it was to be his first demonstration of the fact that he usually performed best when opposed to bowlers acclaimed for their speed and cunning.

His team mates watched with growing astonishment as he smacked O'Reilly's most dangerous balls all over the Bowral ground, in a display of batting which would not have disgraced the Sydney Cricket Ground. During two and three-quarter hours he scored 234, including four sixes and six fours as part of the last 50 runs. But O'Reilly had his revenge on the following Saturday, when he took Bradman's wicket with his first ball.

The 234 runs broke the Berrima District record, and he was to break it again during the final match of the season. It was played against Bowral's deadliest cricketing rivals: Moss Vale. The match attracted eager partisans from both sides, and Emily Bradman promised her son a new cricket bat if he scored a century against Bowral's enemies.

George Whatman won the toss and sent his nephew in first — perhaps walking to the wicket with that slow, deliberate pace which was to become his hallmark on the classic cricket grounds of the world.

Moss Vale had the frustration of seeing Don Bradman and his partner, O. Prior, play for most of the afternoon before Prior was dismissed. Bradman scored 80 not out. The game recommenced on the following Saturday, with Bradman partnered by Uncle George. By the end of the afternoon George Whatman had scored 119 not out, Bradman's score was up to 279, and Bowral was still at the wicket.

On the third Saturday, Bradman continued batting until he was caught by Prigg, bowled Ryder. When Prigg snatched the ball out of the air, Bradman's score was 300 — the second record for the Berrima District.

This quartet of Bowral district schoolgirls includes Jessie Menzies (second from left). The Bradman and Menzies families were old friends and Jessie boarded in the Bradman home during her first year at school. On 30 April 1932 she became Mrs Don Bradman

Don Bradman's parents, George and Emily Bradman, photographed in about 1930

The match was still far from over, and it was beginning to attract attention from as far away as Sydney. It ran for five Saturday afternoons, with a victory for Bowral, and the Sydney *Sun* wrote: 'At last! Yes, it is really over. The final match in the Berrima District Cricket Competition has been brought to a conclusion . . . It was the easiest win in the history of the Berrima District cricket, but it took Bowral five weeks to vanquish their persevering rivals.'

After the game, Bradman suggested to his mother that she owed him three new bats, but settled for one. It was the first new bat he had ever owned.

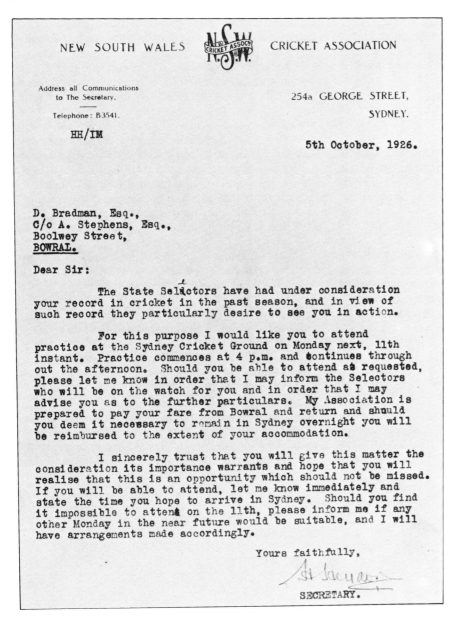

The letter from the New South Wales Cricket Association, of 5 October 1926, which invited young Don Bradman to attend practice in Sydney and virtually launched him upon his cricketing career. The letter was sent in care of Alf Stephens because the NSWCA did not know Bradman's address and Stephens was well known as an official of the Bowral Cricket Club

During that spectacular season he had made 1318 runs, averaging 94.14 over 23 innings, and he had been not out nine times. He was naturally pleased with his performance and he began to think that he might progress towards first-class cricket. For the time being, however,

WHAT THE PAPERS SAID

Even though the Sheffield Shield selectors did not choose Bradman for the New South Wales side against Queensland in the 1926–27 season, the cricket writers who watched the trial match were greatly impressed by his performance.

The *Daily Telegraph* reporter said: 'With the exception of D. Bradman, the other batsmen shaped poorly against the bowling of McNamee and Campbell. Bradman was very slow, but he showed that he has the ability, for his experience on turf wickets has been limited, and to come straight off matting wickets in the country and score 37 runs without losing his wicket was a fine performance. There should be plenty of opportunities for Bradman to show his worth in first-class company in the near future.'

The *Sydney Morning Herald* called him 'One of the successes of the day', in his stand at the wicket for 97 minutes with a not-out score of 37. The newspaper remarked: 'Bradman's success was all the more gratifying when it is considered that he was making his match debut against first-class bowling. Although a trifle on the slow side, Bradman showed supreme confidence and the further he went the better he shaped. He was one of the few batsmen to leave his crease to the slow deliveries of Campbell, whom he played well at a period when that bowler was meeting with considerable success.'

The *Guardian* commented that he had made his 37 runs 'rather defensively', but that he was batting against Campbell at a time when 'the young Gordon bosie bowler looked like going through the side. Bradman afterwards fielded excellently, and sent down two overs, the first of which justified the claim that he is an all-rounder worth encouraging.'

The *Sun* wrote: 'Great interest was taken in the young Bowral player, Don Bradman, and there was a round of applause when he hooked one from Campbell to the square-leg fence. He showed fine defence, too, and covered his wicket well when he had to play "scotch" to McNamee.'

Twenty-seven players took part in the trial match, which was dubbed the 'Probables' against the 'Possibles'. Bradman played for the 'Possibles'.

The 'Probables' contained at least two players who were later to make their names. The captain was Alan Kippax, who scored 58 before he was bowled by Nicholls, and Archie Jackson scored 53 before he retired.

Many years later, Bradman wrote that Jackson's untimely death robbed Australia of one of her greatest Test batsmen: a man who, in fact, might have rivalled Bradman himself.

After the 'Probables v. Possibles' match, a Sydney newspaper wrote: 'The chief feature was the brilliant batting of A. Jackson, the Balmain colt.

'Jackson, who is only 17 years of age, has been showing great form in club cricket, and his appearance at headquarters yesterday gained him many admirers. There appears to be little doubt that Jackson is destined to be an Australian XI player of the future, his stand at the wicket greatly resembles that of Kippax, and he makes his strokes with perfect freedom, and seemingly without effort.

'This young player possesses all the strokes of a first-class batsman; drives with equal power on both sides of the wicket, and his late cuts are a treat to watch . . . One cannot speak too highly of his stylish ability.'

Jackson and Bradman played together in the 1928–29 Test Series in Australia. During their partnership in the Fourth Test, Jackson scored 164 and became the youngest player in history to make a Test century.

Jackson, then 19, had opened the batting and within half-an-hour had seen Woodfull, Hendry and Kippax dismissed with the score totalling only 19. Sir Donald later wrote: 'Undaunted by this setback, Jackson proceeded to play an innings which from the point of view of stroke execution, elegance and sheer artistry held the spectators as few innings in history have done.'

Only four years later, Archie Jackson died of tuberculosis and Donald Bradman was one of the pall-bearers at his funeral.

his ambitions reached no higher than inclusion in the Southern Country Cricket Week team. He hoped that he might be selected for one of the eight teams, each assembled from different areas of New South Wales, which would battle for the championship on various Sydney cricket grounds. After a series of matches, the pick of the players would play against a city team on the Sydney Cricket Ground. Inclusion in a Country Week team was a big step upward for a small-town cricketer and the Sydney visit would be a memorable experience.

But the reports of his achievements in Berrima District games had attracted even more attention than he realised. On 5 October 1926, the secretary of the New South Wales Cricket Association wrote to him in care of the Bowral cricket captain. The letter invited him to take part in practice on the Sydney Cricket Ground, so that the State selectors might see him in action.

The selectors were mainly interested in choosing bowlers for the Sheffield Shield team to play Queensland, but they had a keen eye for all new talent. George Bradman accompanied his son to Sydney, where the eighteen-year-old batsman stepped confidently to the nets. Selectors, cricket writers, representatives of suburban clubs, and other spectators had assembled to watch about forty young bowlers and batsmen show their styles. One of the journalists wrote for his newspaper: 'Great interest was shown in the knock of the Bowral wonder, Don Bradman. He was quite undismayed by the size of the gallery, and undoubtedly has talent. On the short side, he uses a short-handled bat, but makes powerful strokes all around the wicket.'

Another wrote: 'Perhaps the most surprising feature about yesterday — although not the least unexpected — was that the practice, which was designed primarily for the benefit of bowlers, produced a batsman.

A cricket match on the Bowral Oval, with George Bradman umpiring. It was on this pitch that Bradman encountered the bowler Bill O'Reilly early in 1926 and first broke the Berrima District record, with his score of 234 runs

The *Smith's Weekly* strip cartoon 'The Dead Finish' of 10 June 1926 based on the prolonged cricket final between Moss Vale and Bowral which helped to bring Don Bradman into public prominence

And a batsman from the country, too. Don Bradman is a lad 18 years of age, who resides in Bowral. Last year he made 1318 runs, his highest score being 300. His batting created a most favourable impression among onlookers. Though he is not polished by any means, yet he makes most of his scoring strokes correctly and bats with plenty of freedom. He gets across to the ball nicely and watches it well. His footwork is exact but clumsy — a fault associated with most country players who bat on hard wickets. But with a little tuition he should develop into a batsman of class.'

The spectators included men from the Central Cumberland club, who were so impressed by the young batsman that they invited him to play for them. But they could not afford to pay his fares and other expenses and he had to decline.

Bradman returned to Bowral, where he showed that his previous season's performance had not been a fluke by scoring 170 (retired) in a match against Exeter. The next approach from the big city came with an invitation to play in an all-day trial match on the Sydney Cricket Ground, to help the selectors choose the Sheffield Shield side. He scored 37 not out, insufficient to influence the selectors; but their interest in him may have played a part in his selection for the Country Week team.

He was chosen for a trial match at Goulburn, where he scored 62 not out and took four wickets. The cricket writer of the Goulburn newspaper said: 'The Goulburn representatives, assisted materially by young Don Bradman of Bowral, a young batsman with, I should say, an International future, completely overshadowed the South Coast team in the Southern Districts Country Week Test Match on Saturday.'

Later, the same man wrote: 'Young Bradman never had a lesson in batting in his life, and has had to think out the strokes for himself, and besides possessing unique natural policy he has developed his play marvellously all around the wicket . . . not even Jack Hobbs, in his more brilliant days, used his feet better to get to a slow ball, and it was glorious to watch this Bowral youngster step out yards like a flash of lightning and play a perfect off or cover drive.'

When the selectors invited Bradman to join the Country Week team he found himself in a dilemma. His cricketing successes had not distracted him from his enjoyment of tennis, and he still played for Bowral in the local competitions. A Country Tennis Week had been organised in much the same way as the Cricket Week, and its selectors invited Bradman to join the team for the area. If he accepted then he would need two weeks in Sydney: one for cricket and one for tennis.

He decided to accept both invitations, and asked Percy Westbrook for leave to spend the two weeks in Sydney. But Westbrook placed Bradman at the turning point of his career by saying 'Don, you can have only one week in Sydney. You can have the tennis week or the cricket week, but you can't have both'.

Bradman was not entirely sure whether he enjoyed cricket more than tennis, or vice versa, but he had to make the decision. If he had chosen to attend the Country Tennis Week, then the future course of his life might have been entirely different. By a narrow margin he chose cricket — perhaps for no better reason than that Cricket Week preceded Tennis Week. The 'Boy from Bowral' was on his way.

'THE DADDY OF THEM ALL'

Don Bradman's first great batting exploit, a score of 234 in the Berrima District Association, is all the more creditable when gauged against the quality of the bowler who tried hard to dismiss him.

When Bowral played Wingello, in that historic game which first made cricketers' ears prick up at the name of Bradman, the young batsman was seventeen. His opponent, William Joseph O'Reilly, was a student teacher of twenty. He was over six feet tall, and when he began his run-up to the wicket his arms and legs seemed to whirl like aircraft propellers.

He launched the ball with deadly ferocity and it ricocheted off the matting wicket as though it would take off the batsman's legs. Bradman wrote later that he survived the first few overs more by good luck than good judgment, and after that it became a battle of youthful giants. Bradman was beginning to display the calmly calculating aggression which later broke every batting record in the book.

He wrote later of O'Reilly that he 'never gave the batsman any respite. He was always aggressive, had great stamina and courage. To hit him for four would usually arouse a belligerent ferocity which made you sorry. It was almost like disturbing a hive of bees. He seemed to attack from all directions.'

O'Reilly was a left-handed batsman but he bowled right-arm, with unrelenting accuracy and hostility. Bradman remarks that he 'did not hold the ball in his fingers quite like the orthodox leg-spinner. It was held more towards the palm of the hand. He was advised by certain "experts" to change his grip, but fortunately refused to be advised. This grip did not enable him to spin the ball very much, but it did enable him to achieve phenomenal accuracy plus *sufficient* spin.

'His stock ball was the leg-break, but now and then he would bowl a very well concealed googly or an overspin with a delightfully delicate change of pace and for good measure an occasional fast one.

'This slower ball would often be played uppishly by batsmen because in addition to the deceptive flight O'Reilly's great height gave it much lift from the pitch.'

The New South Wales selectors picked O'Reilly for Shield cricket but the switch to turf wickets seemed to puzzle him for a while until the 1931–32 season, when he took 25 wickets in five matches.

This opened the door to his first Test opportunity, against the South Africans in the same season. He played in the fourth and fifth Tests and in the second innings of the latter he helped to devastate South Africa by taking three wickets for 19.

From then on his Test future was assured. Under the apt nickname of 'Tiger' he soared to fame during the 1930s and took 102 English wickets in four consecutive Test series from 1932–33 to 1938. As Bradman wrote in 1950: 'No other player can approach such a performance.'

Altogether, between his first South African Test and his final Test, when he toured New Zealand in 1945–46, he took 144 Test wickets for an average of 22.59. In first-class cricket he dismissed 774 batsmen at 16.60. In his first-grade career with St George he took 766 wickets for an average of 8.7, a performance unapproached by any other player.

In Don Bradman's book *Farewell to Cricket* he describes the action and abilities of various bowlers he has known and he classifies O'Reilly as 'The Daddy of Them All', with the comment that O'Reilly and Sidney Barnes (1873–1967) 'were the two greatest bowlers who ever lived, and that each was undoubtedly the greatest of his time'.

The 1926 confrontation between Bradman and O'Reilly set the pattern for the future. When Don Bradman moved to Adelaide he played Sheffield Shield cricket for South Australia while O'Reilly appeared for New South Wales. The two old friends from the Southern Highlands delighted the spectators with a number of thrilling duels.

2

A MODEST HERO

The cricketer A. G. Moyes, one of the Sheffield Shield selectors of that period and later to be one of Bradman's mentors and friends, remembered his first sight of the young batsman when he wrote his book *Bradman*, published in 1948. He wrote: 'One day in 1926 a quiet knock sounded on the door of my office in Sydney. It opened to admit a fair-haired, keen-eyed, intelligent youth of lithe physique.

''"I'm Don Bradman," he said with a shy grin, as he entered the room and sat down.'

Alf Stephens, a Bowral builder, played an important part in the Bradman family fortunes. He employed George Bradman as a carpenter when the Bradmans moved to Bowral from Cootamundra, and as a keen local cricketer he did much to help and encourage the cricketing talent of young Bradman. The photograph shows Alf Stephens' business premises, with George Bradman in the centre of the trio in the foreground

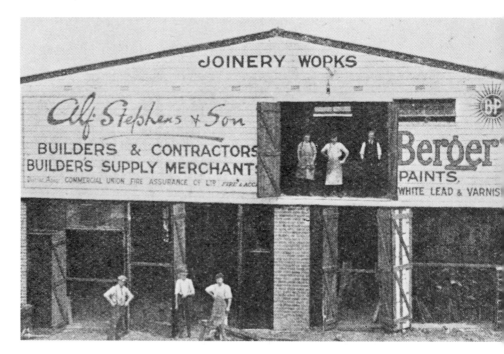

Moyes was not the only man to remark upon the unassuming attitude of the country youth: his deference towards his seniors, willingness to learn, and readiness to accept criticism. They were qualities with a particular appeal to cricket lovers of that era. Australia had inherited not only the game of cricket from England but also the ethos which saw it as the essence of good sportsmanship — a kind of white-flannelled miniature of life itself, in which a real man should accept triumph and disaster with equal modesty, courage and good humour. The phrase 'It's not cricket' was commonly used as a comment upon tricky behaviour in any activity, with the implication that the noble game provided a model for society as a whole. The game was still very largely a trial of skill for dedicated amateurs untainted by big-money publicity, and a player was expected to disguise any pride in his own expertise. Cricket fans kept a keen eye open for any signs of 'swelled head', and would have hooted with derision at the hugging and kissing which now celebrate a momentary triumph on the field.

Bradman's first appearance before a Sydney crowd was on 22 November 1926, as a member of the Southern team playing Riverina in Country Cricket Week. The press reported that Eric Weissel, the Rugby star and all-round athlete who was the pride of the Riverina, 'magnificently caught and bowled Don Bradman, the Bowral colt who excelled in the recent State trial, at a time when Bradman was set for big runs. Bradman's driving was surprisingly vigorous'.

He had made 43 when Weissel dismissed him. Later in the week, a headline proclaimed 'Bradman's Debut Stamps Him as Man of Promise', above a photograph of him hitting a ball from Cameron, of Newcastle, to the fence.

Before the end of Country Cricket Week, he was approached by R. L. (Dick) Jones, another of the State selectors and president of St George Cricket Club in the south-eastern suburbs of Sydney. Jones asked Bradman if he would play regularly for St George if the club

Alf Stephens on the Bowral Oval

paid his fares from Bowral and other expenses, and after a little discussion the young batsman agreed. On the Saturday of that week he took the field with St George's first-grade side, and justified Dick Jones's selection by scoring 110. Using the bat which his mother had given him, he had scored his first century on a turf wicket.

On the following Monday he came close to another century. The selectors had picked him for the country side which was to play a team

Don Bradman wearing the cap of St George Cricket Club in about 1927. Bradman played first-grade cricket for St George, a Sydney suburban cricket club, from November 1926 until he moved to North Sydney in 1932

of city cricketers, captained by none other than the redoubtable Charlie Macartney. Bradman played a sparkling innings, and Macartney himself took over the bowling in an attempt to dismiss him. The crowd held its breath as the runs mounted steadily towards the century, which seemed certain when Bradman had scored 98, but then groaned when he was snapped up in the slips off a slow bowler.

The Goulburn newspaper reported that 'Old international representatives expressed delight at the confidence and brilliance of the Bowral colt', and Macartney was generous with his praise. Writing for the *Evening News*, he said: 'The Countrymen's best performer with the bat was Bradman. He played a fine innings, using his feet nicely to the first grade slow bowler Morris, and playing the other types with easy confidence. He is rather weak on the on-side, however, and had a bad habit of walking away from the wicket when playing defensive strokes. The latter fault is a common hard-wicket player's error.

'Bradman has every probability of being a State player in the near future and, provided he overcomes these faults, will be a very classy one.'

Bradman on the Bowral pitch with Alf Stephens, mayor of Bowral, at about the time when Bradman returned home for the inauguration of a turf wicket on the Bowral ground

Country Cricket Week preceded the busiest period in Bradman's young life. He had to rise at five a.m. every Saturday to catch the early train to Sydney, in order to play for St George, and it was nearly midnight before he found his bed again. His work in the real estate agency demanded careful attention, so he had to find time to practise cricket after work. Practising on a hard wicket on weekdays, sometimes at the home of Alf Stephens who had laid a concrete wicket in his garden, and playing on a turf wicket on Saturdays, was an odd experience. He still found time for an occasional game of tennis, and for a new love: motoring.

Towards the end of 1926, Moyes and Dick Jones and their fellow

A GOLD WATCH AND CHAIN

Alf Stephens, the mayor of Bowral and one of its leading businessmen, also was one of the district's most ardent cricketers. He was several times captain of the Bowral Cricket Club, and he continuously backed and encouraged Bradman in his early years. One of Stephens' ambitions was that of a turf wicket for Bowral, and he eventually persuaded the council to lay one in Loseby Park.

The wicket was ready early in 1928. Stephens asked Bradman to bring a team from Sydney to play an inaugural match in Loseby Park, but Bradman was too modest to ask his friends to make the trip. Instead, he broached the subject with Dick Jones.

Jones, a renowned cricketer in his own right, was one of the New South Wales selectors in 1926 and an official of the St George Cricket Club. As one of those who watched Bradman among the young batsmen's trials in Sydney, he had invited Bradman to join St George.

He delighted Stephens by arranging for a team consisting largely of St George players, including Kippax and Bradman and captained by Vic Richardson, to visit Bowral and face the local side in an inaugural game.

Bowral folk seized the opportunity to honour the young man who was making the town famous. They took up a collection to present Don Bradman with a gold watch and chain, to be given to him during a reception held for the visitors.

The local newspaper reported: 'Such a tribute of respect and admiration has seldom been paid to a resident in these districts and Don might have been pardoned had he shown some little sign of swelled head. But his greetings of old friends and his reply to the speeches made in his praise was marked by a modesty of demeanour that explains the rapid progress he has made in the affections of his new associates in the game.'

The evening began with dancing 'to the strains of Mr Beavan's orchestra', followed by Mayor Stephens' introduction of the visitors to the guests. He explained that Kippax would not arrive until the following day because he was being married that evening.

The audience applauded when he said: 'The great wish of Bowral folk is to see Don Bradman in an Australian team.' When Arthur Mailey spoke, he said that Don was 'undoubtedly a coming international'.

Bradman's employer, Percy Westbrook, said he 'did not think they should wait until a man was dead before they told him how much they admired his good qualities. He would rather endorse the sentiment of the legend which greeted the return of the wanderer to his own land with the words "We love you and we tell you so".'

He said that 'whether it was keeping books, driving a car, playing tennis, or wielding a bat, the smartest man of his age I know is Don Bradman . . . he is undoubtedly one of the greatest cricketers in the State'.

Audience and orchestra broke into 'For He's a Jolly Good Fellow' when Stephens presented Bradman with the watch and chain and asked him to say a few words. The newspaper reported that he was 'evidently overcome by the extreme cordiality of his reception'.

His speech consisted mainly of thanks to Alf Stephens, 'who had given him the chance to have a knock in Sydney', to Percy Westbrook for giving him time off to play cricket, and to the president and secretary of St George. He concluded by 'thanking his audience from the bottom of his heart and hoping he would never do anything to make them regret they had given him their present'.

The evening concluded when 'an excellent supper was served by the ladies'.

Alf Stephens continued to be one of Don Bradman's most constant admirers, and in the 1930s he made a special trip to England to watch 'The Don' play in a Test match.

selector 'Mudgee' Cranney chose Bradman for his first appearance in interstate cricket; he played for the New South Wales Second Eleven against the Victorian Second Eleven in a match which opened on New Year's Day 1927. *Truth* reported: 'The home batsmen failed miserably, only Bradman and Seddon showing anything like form.' Bradman was bowled for 43 in his first innings, in a performance described as 'entirely devoid of nerves', but in his second innings, after making only 8 runs, he had the misfortune to tread on his stumps in pulling a ball to the boundary.

The people of Berrima District were as proud of 'our Don' as were the Bowral folk. Reg Tickner, secretary of the Moss Vale club which

was one of Bowral's keenest opponents in the local association, wrote him a congratulatory letter on behalf of Moss Vale early in 1927. A list of 71 averages of first-grade batsmen, published at about the same time, showed Bradman fifth from the top, with only Alan Kippax, Salmon, Archie Jackson and Gray above him. Bradman showed an average of 69 for three innings.

But Moss Vale's magnanimous attitude changed after Bradman played against them in the final for a local trophy, the Pickard Cup. It was a 'needle match', with the neighbouring townships eager to see one another driven to defeat, but Moss Vale's ambitions evaporated soon after Bradman faced the bowling for Bowral. The local newspaper reported: 'Getting his eye in quickly, Don commenced to pepper the bowling, and was not long in reaching his century. Never before has Moss Vale bowling received such an unmerciful flogging; good and bad were treated alike, the balls whizzing to every part of the field, and only those who attempted to stop them knew how much ginger was behind them.'

Bradman broke his own local record, with a score of 320 not out including six sixes and 43 fours. City newspapers picked up the story and one commented: 'This is a great performance in any company. Bradman is scarcely a stylist, but that he has cricket in him is undoubted. The rough edges will soon wear off in good company, and with his eye and temperament he should develop into a champion.'

Above: The young Bowral batsman in 1926, when his exploits in Berrima District brought him to the attention of the State selectors

Left: Alf Stephens, the Bowral businessman who did much to encourage young Don Bradman in his early cricketing years, on the concrete pitch at his Bowral home

BRADMAN'S GRIP

The cricketer A. G. Moyes, one of the New South Wales selectors in 1926, was among the earliest men to spot Bradman's potential. He and his fellow selectors had heard about Bradman's cricketing exploits in the Berrima District Association, and they arranged for him to come from Bowral for a trial at the nets.

They and other observers noticed his quick eye and speedy footwork, and Moyes also noticed the peculiarity of his grip.

In Moyes's book *Bradman*, published in 1948, he wrote: 'With most players, the handle runs across the palm of the hand and *rests* against the ball of the thumb. With Bradman, the hand is turned over so far that the handle *presses* against the ball of the thumb. As the grip tightens, the pressure becomes more intense. The left hand is turned so that the wrist is behind the handle. This means that whether he is attacking or defending, danger to the fingers and back of the hand from a ball that lifts unexpectedly is reduced to a minimum. The combined result is that the bat slopes at an angle of about forty-five degrees from the ground, and so keeps the ball down, ensuring that in both the hook and the cut the blade is automatically turned over the ball.

'Some noticed this freakish grip and advised a change. Bradman would not hear of it. It had served him well and would, he believed, continue to do so.'

Moss Vale licked their wounds, and their defeat may have influenced a ruling by the Berrima District association that first-grade players would not be allowed to play in future local contests.

St George enjoyed a record season in 1926–27 and attracted large crowds to Hurstville Oval, with Bradman averaging 48.16. St George players and officials regarded him as a quiet, modest but businesslike cricketer and he was happy with his new cricketing friends — apart from the need to make those long Saturday journeys. He began to think that his future might lie in cricket and that he should move from Bowral to Sydney, but this would have meant a surrender of the job with Percy Westbrook, which he enjoyed very much, and a search for some other way to support himself.

Another step forward came in December 1927. J. M. Gregory and H. S. Love could not accept the selectors' invitation to join the Sheffield Shield team to play the southern States, and they chose Bradman and Albert Scanes, both of St George, to travel instead of the two better-known cricketers. Scanes had played one season in Shield cricket and so Bradman was to be twelfth man; but his selection was still a resounding knock from opportunity on his doorway to first-class cricket.

The Bowral newspaper applauded the selectors' decision and remarked: 'Judging by city press reports, Donald has not contracted swelled head, the most deadly disease that waylays a youngster in any branch of sport, and his steady devotion to the game is bound to take him far. Good luck to him!'

Macartney, who would normally have led the team, had just decided to retire from cricket. The selectors appointed Alan Kippax in his place, and the team also included Bradman's friend Archie Jackson. The manager was Dr F. V. McAdam.

They took a roundabout way to the southern States by travelling via Broken Hill, to play a fixture with the Barrier team on the Jubilee Oval. Young Don Bradman, only four months past his nineteenth birthday, was full of resolution as he boarded the train. His selection for a Shield team was the first step of a ladder which might lead anywhere — even to a place in a Test team. As the train climbed through the Blue Mountains he could see himself attaining the Mecca of cricketers and taking his place at the wicket at Lord's. These daydreams were heightened by the excitement of his first long trip away from home. People did not travel as easily and casually then as now, and a journey across south-eastern Australia, in a train with sleeping carriages, seemed to the Bowral boy the summit of sophistication.

But he found it was almost impossible to sleep in the jolting train, the carriage was hot and stuffy in the summer night, and he tried to cool down by turning the compartment fan onto his head and shoulders. When the team reached Broken Hill he felt dopy and listless and had a cold in one eye. Archie Jackson had developed a boil on his knee, and the two youngsters had to suffer the indignity of being sent to bed for the day by Dr McAdam.

On the following day, the visitors took the field on a pitch which would have made Bowral Oval look like Sydney Cricket Ground. In those days, water was almost as precious in Broken Hill as the ore from the mines. Little rain had fallen for about two years and the Jubilee Oval consisted of hard-baked red earth and thick red dust. The wicket,

The young batsman as he appeared during his early days in Sydney

of course, was concrete, and Bradman noticed the novel sight of a concrete 'launching pad' for the bowlers. McAdam would not allow their fast bowler to play on it for fear of injury.

Archie Jackson's boil meant that Bradman, the twelfth man, made his first appearance with a Shield side in such unpromising conditions. Sprigged cricket boots were useless and the visitors played in sandshoes or ordinary walking shoes. To make matters worse, a dust storm blew up during the one-day match, but it did not deter a large crowd from turning out to see a Barrier side tackle the Shield team. They gave the visitors a hard battle for victory.

At the end of the game Bradman managed to secure the ball for a souvenir. It was a ball of the 'old' rules, larger and heavier than the modern type which was just coming into use at that time, and it is still in Sir Donald's cricket collection. In those days a ball might measure between 9 and 9¼ inches in circumference and weigh between 5½ and 5¾ ounces, but the new rules restricted the circumference to a minimum of 8¹³⁄₁₆ inches and a maximum of 9 inches.

Jackson's knee was still troubling him when the team arrived in Adelaide, and Bradman was suffering from a finger badly bruised during the Barrier match, but Dr McAdam decided that he was better fitted to play than Jackson. On 16 December 1927 he walked for the first time onto the beautiful Adelaide Oval with its world-famous back-drop of St Peter's Cathedral rising above parkland trees — 'the cathedral end'.

South Australians had heard something of 'the Bowral wonder' and they watched keenly to see how he would perform against their own cricketing phenomenon: the bowler Clarrie Grimmett. Bradman showed them how when he went in just before tea on the first day, and promptly hit two fours off Grimmett in his first over. He reached 50 in 67 minutes. After one and three-quarter hours at the wicket he had scored 65 not out.

Above: A car was a proud possession in the 1920s, as Vic Bradman shows in this photograph taken while he was polishing his new Ford

Right: George Bradman sits on the running-board of Vic Bradman's car, with Victor in the background

The next morning dawned as a typical Adelaide summer day, with a cloudless blue sky radiating intense heat. The temperature seemed likely to reach the century before any of the batsmen did, and the heat affected Kippax so much that he had to retire twice during his first innings. But Bradman seemed unperturbed. He delighted the crowd with a calm confidence and flashing brilliance, and took his score up to 118 before he was caught by Williams, off the fast bowler Jack Scott, just before lunch. He was the twentieth Australian batsman to make his century during a debut in first-class cricket, and the seventh New South Wales batsman to score the magic number in a first appearance against South Australia.

Telegrams of congratulation from friends and relations poured into Bradman's hotel, and the press was ecstatic. One report, headed 'Bradman's Brilliant Debut', commented: 'If some of the so-called champions only used their feet to slow bowlers as this youngster does, cricket would have a larger public following.

'When nearing the century, he did not potter about for singles in order to claim the coveted honour of making a century in his first Sheffield Shield match, but smacked boundaries with a delightful abandon and received an ovation on getting three figures.

'The only bad stroke he made was the one which got him out.'

Another newspaper remarked: 'Don Bradman's success in his initial effort in interstate cricket is yet another instance of the opportunities which await persistent effort in this sunny land ... Bradman has attained his present position without fortuitous aid and it is the hope of all his friends that he may ultimately reach to higher honours.'

In his second innings he fell victim to Grimmett. He made 33 in 64 minutes before being bowled off his pads soon after lunch.

New South Wales lost the match by one wicket, and boarded the Overland Express for Melbourne with their heads slightly bloodied but still unbowed. In Melbourne, they faced a formidable team of Victorians, including Ponsford and Woodfull as batsmen and Blackie

The ball used in Don Bradman's first match for New South Wales, against Broken Hill in December 1927

Don Bradman's elder brother Vic photographed sometime during the 1920s astride his motorbike

and Ironmonger as bowlers. Only a few days earlier, Ponsford had set a new world record with a score of 437.

The young man whom various observers described, then and later, as 'a cordial kid', 'a happy, smiling boy', and 'a bright-faced boy', faced the Victorian bowling as confidently as though he were playing against Moss Vale. Arthur Mailey reported to the Sydney press: 'When Bradman came in Blackie was bowling remarkably well, and there might have been serious results had Andrews not been at the wickets. A tribute to Bradman's confidence was illustrated in his first over at Blackie. Andrews was intentionally kept down at Morton's end, with the object of allowing Blackie to attack Bradman. It was a case of age and experience against youth and innocence.

'Woodfull came up to silly point, and Blackie pitched his first delivery well up. Bradman jumped down the wicket and drove the ball like lightning to the off boundary. Although Blackie tried to tempt him into a false stroke, the Bowral lad went along in quite a natural manner, and put together 31 in excellent style.'

Don Bradman's father George Bradman was noted for his meticulous handiwork and craftsmanship — a trait which he undoubtedly passed on to his son. His children were so proud of this fence, which he built single-handed along the frontage of a Bowral property, that they called it 'Dad's fence'

Hartkopf dismissed him lbw in his first innings, and Blackie yorked him for five on the last afternoon, but he felt he had gained a great deal from the experience of playing Victoria. He had had the opportunity to observe the master batsmen Ponsford and Woodfull at close quarters, and to field against a side of extremely high calibre. New South Wales lost the match but that was no disgrace against such a redoubtable team.

On that first tour, the youngster whom the older men called 'Braddles' founded some permanent friendships and attracted keen attention from many observers. Patsy Hendren, then coach for the South Australian Cricket Association, was favourably impressed. Umpire George Hele, who was later to umpire the 'bodyline Test' in Adelaide, felt confident that Bradman had a future as a Test champion and took particular note of the speed and accuracy of his fielding — a dividend of those long hours of throwing the golf ball at fence rails. Grimmett invited him to his home one evening, spun yarns of Test trips to England, and fascinated the young cricketer with a demonstration of spinning a small rubber ball on a table. Bradman, who later described Grimmett as the greatest slow bowler of them all, found it was impossible to tell where or how the ball was going to break.

In 1930, Bradman wrote: 'It is characteristic of the make-up of most top-flight cricketers that they are always ready and willing to give a word in season to a young player, provided he is keen and anxious to learn . . . in my experience no elder player has ever declined to give me advice when I asked for it.' He learned a lot by watching and asking other players during that first Shield tour, even though some of the older players still did not take him very seriously. Apart from Archie Jackson he was the youngest of the travellers and, like any other young man in male company, he was the butt of practical jokes and tall stories. The veteran cricketers had seen many flashes in the cricketing pan and they remembered that a century scored in a first-class debut is by no means a guarantee of future fame.

Vic Bradman bore little resemblance to his famous brother. Physically he was a larger man, but he had nothing like the sporting ability of Don Bradman. He lived a comparatively obscure life, as the owner of a menswear store in Bowral, and died at the age of fifty-five. This photograph of him was taken in about 1930

FROM ONE OF THE POTTED OPINIONS

The following description of Don Bradman comes from a press cutting of which the source is now unknown. Printed in about 1928, it appears to be one of a number of 'potted biographies' of cricketers in that period. It says:

D. BRADMAN (New South Wales). Bradman is a country man who has played for his club and district, and who, in his first inter-State match, against South Australia, made a century. He is a right-handed batsman, short in build, fairly strong and very active. There is nothing stodgy about either the man or his play. He is a good starter, has plenty of confidence and pluck, is a quick scorer, and puts lots of power into his shots; indeed, one wonders where all the power comes from. He must have a very quick eye, for he is very fleet of foot, and walks down the pitch with great daring to make splendid strokes off deliveries which might otherwise prove difficult propositions even to play. His style is somewhat similar to that of Clem Hill, and, like the famous left-hander, he impresses with the idea that he is thoroughly enjoying himself. He is a most likeable chap and altogether a good type of cricketer.

At the end of 1927, the Sheffield Shield team played Queensland in Sydney and Bradman's performance may have made some of those veteran players shake their heads. Going in on the second morning, at 467 for six, he joined Kippax who was playing the slow bowler H. J. Gough. Kippax gently pushed the first ball to mid-on, and they made a single run. Bradman then faced Gough and he decided to emulate Kippax's stroke, but he had forgotten that Kippax had been batting for some time and was accustomed to the wicket and to Gough's technique. Bradman had expected another slow and turning ball, but it came through straight and fast and whipped out his middle stump. It was a lesson in not deciding how to play a ball until it was actually in flight. 'Sneaked out for a blob', Macartney wrote.

But on the last day of the match, with only 74 minutes left to play, he took the field with New South Wales at 60 for six. It was essential to preserve wickets, and he showed cautious skill in dealing with the bowling of Hurwood and Nothling. In partnership with the New South Wales wicket-keeper, H. S. Love, he played a straight bat against a fusillade of balls. He had to play an unusually defensive game, instead of the aggressive tactics in which he delighted; but he learned quickly to gauge the state of the pitch before attempting to hit across the flight of the ball.

Tension increased as thunder grumbled on the horizon and gathering rain clouds dulled the light, but he played steadily on until a ball from Nothling caught the shoulder of his bat and went into the hands of the Queensland wicket-keeper, O'Connor. Reporting the game, Macartney wrote: 'It was the colt, Bradman, and wicket-keeper Love, who saved New South Wales, for they kept together in an eighth wicket partnership until six minutes before the end.'

This game was followed by another match against the South Australians, also in Sydney. In his first innings he executed 'a dreadful shot' against a full toss from Dr Douglas McKay. It was swinging away to the off, and he tried to turn it to the on-side. The ball skied off the edge of the bat back into the hands of the Adelaide doctor.

He showed better form in the next innings, when he used the attacking style of play which was becoming his trademark. He stepped well out of the crease to punish the bowling, until crafty Clarrie Grimmett got his measure and left him standing some yards down the pitch. He was dismissed for 73 and he had learned yet another lesson: to judge the bowling more carefully before leaving his crease for it.

The final Shield match of that season, against Victoria in Sydney, again showed him at his best in a crisis. The Victorians were attacking hard and they were in fact to carry away the Shield for that season, but he stood up to Blackie and Ironmonger for 225 minutes and scored 134. It was his first century on the Sydney Cricket Ground, where his father had smiled when he said he would 'never be satisfied' until he stood on its hallowed turf. A crowd of 30 386, a record for a Shield match until that time, watched the Bowral wonder live up to everything that had been written and said about him.

Despite the duck in the Queensland match he had completed his first Shield season with a respectable result: a total of 416 runs in ten innings, one not-out. He hoped that he might be chosen for the team which Vic Richardson, Hugh Trumble and Tom Howard were selecting for a New Zealand tour, but they named him only as reserve batsman in case a player dropped out before departure. This did not happen and he was never to tour New Zealand.

He accompanied a team captained by Vic Richardson, and consisting mainly of St George players, to open the new turf wicket at Loseby Park in Bowral, and then joined Arthur Mailey's team, the Bohemians, on a tour which took them to Canberra and various New South Wales country centres. It was second-class cricket but there were still lessons to be learned from it — including the fact that a promising young cricketer could be dismissed for one run when he played in his birthplace, Cootamundra, and have his stumps scattered for a duck at Canowindra. The game of cricket has a habit of humbling its devotees.

He ended that country tour with an aggregate of only 77 runs for seven completed innings. In thinking back over this performance, he began to realise that he could give of his best only when he had to rise to the dangers and difficulties of severe opposition. Then, and only then, did his ability and willpower concentrate themselves into a diamond-hard performance.

His belief in himself was unshaken, and with the 1927–28 season

'Three musketeers' of cricket, photographed in about 1929. Don Bradman (left) poses with Alan Fairfax and Archie Jackson. Sir Donald is now the only survivor of the trio. Jackson died from tuberculosis in 1933, and Fairfax at the age of forty-nine in 1955

behind him he began to think very seriously about the future. The 'baby of the team' was now reasonably certain that he could make a career in cricket, but he doubted whether he could do so while he was based in Bowral. He had to be 'where the action was', and that meant moving to Sydney.

This was easier said than done. In those days, proper parents did not surrender the physical and moral responsibility for their children until they were twenty-one, and Don Bradman honoured his father and mother too much to battle against their reluctance to let him live alone in the big city. Also he could not support himself with his bat alone, and would have to have the backing of steady employment.

His sympathetic and sports-loving employer, Percy Westbrook, solved one of these problems. He had recently opened a new Sydney real estate company, known as Deer & Westbrook Ltd, and he offered Bradman the position of secretary of the new venture. Another friend, G. H. Pearce, helped Bradman to win his parents over to the idea of a move. Pearce, a country traveller for a Sydney insurance company, invited the young cricketer to stay in his home for his first few months in Sydney.

Bradman's move to Sydney, in September 1928, did not go unnoticed by the cricketing world. The Northern District Cricket Club heard about it and invited him to join them, but he was happy with his St George associations and decided to stay with that club.

He had now had experience of playing on some of the finest turf wickets in Australia. He had learnt the vital differences between the matting wickets of his boyhood and the turf of first-class cricket, but he had always had to return to practise on concrete and matting. For the first time, he was able to practise regularly on turf, and he set

THOSE MATTING WICKETS

Nobody knows which cricket team first used a 'matting wicket'. Probably it was in England. The cricketers may have used a length of matting to prevent the batsmen from bogging down in a pitch softened by English rains, to provide a smooth surface on a crumbling pitch, or simply to protect the surface of a pitch during practice games.

The matting, of closely-woven jute or coconut fibre, was usually known as 'coconut matting'. Naturally it provided a very smooth fast wicket.

In the early days of Australian cricket, turf wickets were virtually unknown. Visiting English teams wrote of playing on pitches that were 'more dust and earth than grass'. Reticulated water did not reach Australian cities until the second half of last century, and in many country towns there was no mains supply until the fairly recent past. People relied on rainwater tanks, wells or bores. They had nothing to spare for watering cricket pitches, and nobody knew anything about the establishment and care of suitable turf.

Consequently a matting wicket, at first laid straight onto the eroded soil and then onto a strip of concrete, was a great step forward from 'dust and earth'. In Don Bradman's youth, most country clubs and many suburban clubs played on the fast, hard concrete and matting wickets. To some degree they were more predictable than turf wickets and they tended to create a batting style of their own. When Don Bradman first went to Sydney, observers quickly remarked that he had a background of matting wickets.

But the rock-hard wickets may have been a useful initiation for his later appearances in Melbourne. In 1950 he wrote: 'The hardest of our grounds, both to play on and in actual fact, was Melbourne. Very few players can stand a whole day on the Melbourne wicket or ground without noticing the extreme hardness of the surface . . . Yet somehow I always liked batting in Melbourne and was more successful there in Test cricket than on any other Australian ground. Perhaps the wicket suited me.'

In New South Wales cap and blazer, the 'boy from Bowral' poses for a photograph in the backyard of his old home

himself to hone a sharp edge onto his game. His first foray into Sheffield Shield cricket had awakened great ambitions. He knew that he enjoyed nothing better than playing cricket, he revelled in the company of the cricketing fraternity, and he believed that 'his future lay in his bat'. He knew it could be an uncertain future, and that cricketers, like entertainers, may be the idols of the crowd one year and ignored the next, but all the hopeful confidence of youth was on his side.

Cricket lovers were looking forward to one of the most exciting Test series of the post-war world. England had recovered from her shameful defeat of 1920–21, and men like Jardine, Larwood, Hobbs, Hammond, Leyland and Sutcliffe were rising to the zenith of their fame. Sixteen of England's finest, captained by A. P. F. Chapman, would arrive in Australia aboard the liner *Otranto* in October 1928, and twenty-year-old Don Bradman saw no reason why he should not be among the Australians to defy them.

Of these four New South Wales 'colts' photographed in 1929, two went on to international cricketing fame. From left, they are Arthur Allsopp, Don Bradman, Stan McCabe, and Charlie Andrews. McCabe and Bradman played together in all the Test series against England in the 1930s

He started the new season well with a score of 106 not out, on the first day of a match for St George against Gordon. The selectors picked him for a trial match in Melbourne, Australia v The Rest of Australia, which would help them in their arduous task of choosing those to face the Englishmen. Bradman played for The Rest, captained by Vic Richardson, against a team led by Bill Woodfull.

His performance was a shocking disappointment to himself and his friends, although perhaps no worse than the rest of his side. He scored only 14 and 5 in his two innings, and his only consolation — if there was one — was that none of The Rest did much better. The top scorer in the first innings made only 31. Bradman could not even tell himself that he had not risen to the occasion because his opponents were not good enough to bring out the best in him. He had to acknowledge that Grimmett and Oxenham had simply bowled too well.

But only a week later he made up for this downturn by a sparkling performance against Queensland. He scored 131 in the first innings and 133 not out in the second, and felt that his chances of Test selection had been restored.

With renewed hopes, he found himself selected to play for New South Wales against the M.C.C. on Sydney Cricket Ground, on 9 November 1928. The Australian selectors, Warren Bardsley of New South Wales, Dr C. E. Dolling of South Australia, J. S. Hutcheon of Queensland, and E. E. Bean of Victoria, all of them former first-class cricketers, were in the pavilion to watch the game, and a crowd of more than 43,000 crammed the ground. The slim youngster from Bowral perhaps felt some of his usual confidence a little shaken by the prospect of taking the field against Hammond, Freeman, Jardine and Hendren. Jack Hobbs, the English veteran with the massive credit balance of 50,000 runs, had stood down for this game because of a strenuous series of matches against State sides, thus robbing Bradman of a hope to see him in action at close quarters.

The New South Wales team in which Don Bradman played a Sheffield Shield match against Queensland, in October 1928. His scores of 131 in the first innings and 133 not out in the second began a long list of high scores in his Shield matches against Queensland, and helped to secure his selection in the 1928–29 Test series against England

Walter Hammond later wrote in his book *Cricket My Destiny* that, during this match, he was batting with Hendren when 'the ball was tossed to a slim, shortish boy with a grim nervous face whom I had never seen before and whose name was unfamiliar to me. He looked about nineteen and not very formidable.'

Hammond and Hendren thought that Bradman's bowling was not much to be feared, until Hendren was caught off a ball from the young Australian. Hammond, in partnership with Leyland, continued to punish Bradman's bowling and took 24 off the next over. Bradman was then withdrawn to mid-off, and soon after that Leyland called for a quick single. But Bradman returned the ball with flashing accuracy, and Hammond was surprised to find himself run out. He decided that the 'slim, shortish boy' was a fieldsman to be reckoned with.

Hammond's comment about Bradman's 'grim nervous' expression is in considerable contrast to those other reports of the period which portray him as a 'smiling kid'. It may show how seriously he took this crucial game.

When he went in to bat, the M.C.C. had scored 734 for seven declared, the highest total that he had fielded through in his life. Three of the best New South Wales batsmen had been dismissed for a mere 20-odd runs. The time was ten minutes to six, and the light was fading, but he stood up to the bowling until close of play and on the next day he took his score to 87.

In the second innings, he displayed his full potential against the Englishmen. Hammond quickly realised that the 'slim, shortish boy' was a powerful and aggressive batsman who showed every sign of dominating the game. He wrote later that 'young Bradman looked as if he could stay in for ever', and Bradman's score of 132 not out made the visitors look more closely at this new opponent.

He felt he had done well enough to be considered seriously by the selectors, and his name was tossed around freely during the innumerable arguments in pubs and clubs, lunchbreaks and smoke-ohs, when Australians canvassed the likely composition of their team for the Test Series which was to begin in Brisbane. But yet another trial lay ahead.

The Australians played another match against the M.C.C., again on the Sydney Cricket Ground, and Bradman had one of the hardest battles of his career up to that time. He had to face the tantalising accuracy of Jack 'Farmer' White's slow bowling, the wicket was softer than he liked, and he took three hours and twenty minutes to knock up 58 not out. On his second innings he made only 18.

But he still felt that his two centuries against Queensland, and that against the M.C.C., gave him some hope of inclusion in the Test team. There was nothing to do but wait for the selectors to make up their minds.

The Sydney radio station 2FC had announced that it would broadcast the names of the Australian side immediately they were released by the selectors. By that time, Bradman was still living in the Pearces' home, and on the appointed night he sat by the family radio. When the scheduled time came the announcer could say only that the selectors were still deliberating. After another tense delay, he announced that the four selectors were still deadlocked.

Bradman had waited long enough. He had to go to work in the morning, and he told himself that whatever he felt or hoped would make no difference now. His fate was in the hands of other men. He told Mrs Pearce 'I shall find out whether I'm in or not when the news-papers come in the morning. I'm off to bed now. Good-night.'

He went to his room, but Mrs Pearce kept the radio on and Bradman could still hear it as he prepared for bed. About ten minutes after he got into bed he heard the announcer read the Test names in alphabetical order. Bradman was first on the list.

He felt satisfied, but not particularly excited. It was as though he had set himself to a task in which he had been reasonably sure of success, and now it was completed he could relax. He closed his eyes and slept so soundly that he was late for work on the following morning.

Don Bradman, third from right, during a kangaroo shoot on a country property while touring inland New South Wales with a NSW Cricket Association team

The Bohemians, a team assembled by Arthur Mailey (kneeling, second from left) to play New South Wales country cricket clubs early in 1928. Bradman is kneeling on Mailey's left. Claude Spencer, who was to play an important part in Bradman's future, is standing first on right. Fourth from right is Jim Bancks, creator of the immortal Ginger Meggs

3

THE FIRST TESTS

D. BRADMAN,
who provided the brightest and most stylish batting of the match in scoring 131 for New South Wales. He did not give a chance.

This 1928 cartoon from a Sydney newspaper (possibly the *Referee*) was perhaps the first of countless cartoons of the great batsman to appear in Australian and overseas newspapers during the next twenty years

In hindsight, it is tempting to feel that Bradman's first twenty years comprised a series of fortuitous turning points, each providing another step towards success. If his father had not moved from Yeo Yeo to Bowral, then he might have played cricket for Cootamundra; but it is unlikely that the chain of events which led to his invitation by the selectors would have been linked together. If his employer had not been a cricket lover, then he could not have obtained regular time off for cricket. If other boys had lived near to the first Bradman home in Bowral, he would not have invented the game which helped to sharpen his mental and physical reflexes. If Archie Jackson had not suffered a boil on the knee, then Bradman would not have been able to play his first Shield match in Adelaide. And so on.

And, if one accepted the theory that a benign fate was somehow aiding his progress in the game, it would be dramatically satisfying to record that his first appearance in a Test match was crowned with dazzling success. Instead, it was to be a dismaying baptism of fire.

At first, all went smoothly. The radio announcement was followed by a telegram from W. H. Jeanes, secretary of the Australian Board of Control for International Cricket, saying: 'Confirm your selection in twelve from whom first Test team will be chosen necessary arrive Brisbane twentyseventh letter following.'

The promised letter asked Bradman to arrive in Brisbane on 27 November 1928, told him to apply to the New South Wales Cricket Association for his travel expenses, and informed him that the allowance for the match was £30 plus rail fares and thirty shillings a day for expenses. The players had to make their own arrangements for board and lodging.

The Test, on the Exhibition Ground, was to be the first ever played in Brisbane and the only Test against England ever played on the Exhibition Ground. The Queenslanders mounted an excited welcome for the two teams and the newspapers made great play with the fact that Bradman was the 'baby' of the Australians. Some writers hinted that a few of the Australians were a little 'long in the tooth' for international cricket. Jack Ryder, the captain, was thirty-nine, Grimmett was thirty-six and Ironmonger was forty-one.

But these minor grumbles did not perturb the Australians as they prepared for the match. The Governor of Queensland entertained both teams at dinner, reporters besieged them, and on 30 November they took their places on the Exhibition Ground.

Bradman found that the conditions were totally different from anything he had ever known. Summer in Brisbane is a time of heavy humid heat and frequent rains, and the turf was strangely soft beneath his cricket boots. It seemed that these conditions affected the rest of the Australians also. When he went in on the third morning the wickets were falling thick and fast, with the score only 71 for five. Australian spectators watched hopefully as the Bowral wonder took his stance.

He began well, by hitting four fours in 33 minutes, but he made only 18 when Tate sent down a ball that he tried to place behind the square-leg umpire, thinking it would miss the leg stump. Instead, he found himself out, lbw.

In the second innings, he played for the first time in his life on a sticky wicket. He had never even seen one before then. Cautious and uneasy, he watched 'Farmer' White make his run-up and scored one off the first ball. On the second, he was caught by Percy Chapman.

These disasters seemed typical of Australia's misfortunes in that first Test of the season. Kelleway could not play in the second innings because of a stomach upset, and had to lie in his hotel room and listen to radio commentators tell the sad tale of Australia's collapse. Jack Gregory, whom Bradman has described as 'one of the greatest of all Australia's fast bowlers, the greatest slip fieldsman I ever saw, and, when in the mood, a magnificent hitter', was crippled by a knee injury when he fell heavily while attempting a catch. He limped into the dressing room with his knee heavily bandaged, and with tears in his eyes said 'Boys, I'm through, I've played my last game'.

The visitors dismissed the Australians for 122 in the first innings and 66 in the second. And the Englishmen played a very peculiar game when they were batting.

They seemed to be determined to pile up the maximum number of runs without taking any chances: to stonewall their way through to a

This strip cartoon of unknown origin, extracted from one of Sir Donald Bradman's scrapbooks, was yet another of the many newspaper cartoons to portray him, or mention his name, during his years of batting dominance

Relaxation on a rest day during the first Test, Brisbane 1928. A local cricket supporter (far left) had invited members of the Australian and English teams to spend the day at the beach. Bradman is third from left and the other cricketers are Patsy Hendren, Wally Hammond, George Duckworth, and George Geary. The names of the 1920s bathing beauties are now unknown

devastating victory. In 1941, the famous cricket writer Neville Cardus wrote in *The Globe*: 'Even when England was six hundred runs ahead at Brisbane in this mockery of the summer game, no risks were taken by the batsmen, no chivalrous strokes were seen . . . England won by 675, and in England our satisfaction was just a little tinctured with a sense of uneasiness: was Test cricket coming to this, a mechanical process designed utterly to achieve gain and to avoid loss?'

Bradman's fielding compensated for his difficulties at the wicket. He caught Tate in his second innings, and ran out Hobbs, the master-judge of a run who rarely lost his wicket in this way, by a remarkable throw from the boundary. Hobbs obviously under-estimated the speed and accuracy of Bradman's throw. Even Bradman's brief appearance in the first innings had displayed batting of a quality which enthused the cricket writers. But his team mates, exhausted by the gruelling battle against the stonewalling Englishmen and lacerated by Australia's greatest-ever Test defeat, were less enthusiastic. In the post mortems after the game, Kelleway said unkindly that Bradman was 'not up to Test standard'. To some of his admirers, including A. G. Moyes who had written newspaper articles urging his inclusion in the team, it seemed that his meteoric career might be burning out.

But one newspaper asked 'Is the youthful New South Wales cricket star, Don Bradman, to be sacrificed because, like many other players, he failed with the bat in the first Test match in Brisbane?

'Bradman saved many runs in the field at Brisbane, and he is too great a colt to be dropped like a hot coal after his first experience in Test cricket. He should be given a chance to make good in the match commencing at the Sydney Cricket Ground to-morrow.'

But the selectors did not quite agree. On the morning of the second Test, played in Sydney on 14–20 December, he found himself relegated to twelfth man. He would have had to sit out the game if, on the first day, a ball from Larwood had not broken a bone in Ponsford's left hand. Bradman had to field throughout the English innings, another long-drawn-out battle of attrition in which the visitors amassed 636 runs and Australia lost the match by eight wickets.

The twelve men selected for the second Test against England, 14–20 December 1928. Bradman was twelfth man, but fielded because Ponsford suffered a hand injury. The cricketers are (standing, from left) Bill Woodfull, Bill Ponsford, Bert Ironmonger, Don Blackie, Otto Nothling, 'Stork' Hendry; (seated) Vic Richardson, Clarrie Grimmett, Jack Ryder, Don Bradman, Bert Oldfield, Alan Kippax

The Sheffield Shield selectors showed more faith in Bradman's potential. They picked him to play for New South Wales against Victoria, in Melbourne, in the match fixed for 22–27 December. This would be followed almost immediately by the third Test, on Melbourne Cricket Ground.

Perhaps even Bradman's most loyal supporters may have felt that the 'colt' was, after all, not going to live up to his early shining promise. In the first innings of the Shield match, Hendry dismissed him in three minutes for a single run.

But in the second innings he displayed a sudden return to form. On the last morning of the game he scored 71 not out in 103 minutes, and his admirers could breathe again.

They were relieved to see his name listed in the Australian Eleven for the third Test, and his return to form continued during his first innings. He went in late on the first day, at first in partnership with Ted a'Beckett and later with Ron Oxenham. On that afternoon, and on the following day, he played determinedly against 223 balls from England's finest bowlers, for a score of 79 including nine fours.

And then at last, in his second innings, he displayed the kind of 'Bradmanesque' Test performance that his fans had anticipated. He went in at noon on the fifth day, made a slow start, and took 143 minutes to reach 50. But then he began suddenly to jump out at the balls and he made his second 50 in 83 minutes. In one of the mighty strokes which brought him his first Test century he split his bat.

Still eight months short of his twenty-first birthday, he was at that time the youngest player ever to score a century in a Test match — and he had made it with only eleven first-class matches behind him.

The crowd and the players gave him a tremendous ovation. In Sydney, cricket lovers had been watching scoreboards erected outside the newspaper offices. As the steadily mounting score was telegraphed from Melbourne, homegoing crowds crammed the streets outside the offices and ignored the trams waiting to take them home. Soon after five-thirty the triumphant figure appeared on the board and they greeted it with a roar of acclaim. A. G. Moyes, who watched the crowds jammed into Martin Place outside the *Sun* office, wrote: 'One could see nothing but a mass of hats, umbrellas, and handkerchiefs in the air, while their owners jumped up and down, clapping and yelling with joy.' The *Evening News* said that the scene outside its office made all previous public demonstrations in Australia pale into insignificance. The newspaper rhapsodised: 'Some pictures on life's canvas are quickly obliterated. Others, like this one, are unforgettable.'

Bradman's stand at the wicket continued until he had scored 112 and was caught by Duckworth. If he had not broken his bat, and been forced to play on with a bat which was heavier than he liked, he might have done even better.

Ponsford, who was reporting the match for the *Sydney Morning Herald*, wrote: 'The more I consider young Bradman's performance the brighter his future seems. On the occasion of the opening of both his hands he had to stop the possibility of an Australian rot. Larwood had the new ball in the first innings, and had just captured Kippax's wicket.

'It was a crisis in the game, but young Bradman turned the scale in our favour. Then again in the second innings he came in when an Australian collapse was a distinct possibility. Kippax and Ryder were both out in a few minutes of play yesterday, and we were striving for another start. Anything might have happened, but Bradman stuck beside Woodfull, and saw us through. Earlier in the season I picked an Australian eleven and omitted Bradman, principally because I did not consider he had the necessary experience in big cricket. I am convinced now that my judgment was sadly astray.'

A spate of telegrams poured into the Melbourne Cricket Ground and the Windsor Hotel, where the Australians were staying. Many were from friends and relations; others from strangers. The staff of the Rosemount Military Hospital, Brisbane, and the Minister for Labour in Canberra, were among those who felt impelled to congratulate the 'hope of Australia'. One telegram, addressed to 'Bonzer Baby Bradman, Cricket Ground, Melbourne', said cryptically: 'Bush builds best Batsman Bowral boys beauty Bexley banks bakers barbers buses butchers.'

Rumours about Bradman's future filled cricketing conversations, and Sydney folk were horrified by one which claimed that he planned a move to Brisbane to manage a sports store. Moyes dispelled this fear in an article revealing that Bradman had accepted an offer from Mick Simmons Ltd, a firm of sporting goods distributors in Sydney, to work with them from 1 February 1929.

Despite Bradman's triumph in the third Test, Australia still lost by three wickets and so England had won the rubber and retained the Ashes. But the fourth and fifth Tests were still to be played, in Adelaide and Melbourne, and Australians hoped that the 'Bowral colt', whom they were beginning to call 'The Century Maker', would restore some of the nation's tarnished cricketing glory.

Before the fourth Test, he played in Shield matches against South

The bat which Don Bradman used to score his first Test century, when he made 112 against England in January 1929

Australia, in Adelaide, and against Victoria on the Sydney Cricket Ground. The first of these games incorporated a disastrous experiment. Bradman had always rather fancied the idea of opening the batting, but when he went in as first man on 11 January 1929 he was caught at square-leg after ten minutes with a score of five. On 14 January, in the second innings, he opened the batting again and was bowled in the first over, with the score at two. It was one of only two matches in his career in which he was dismissed twice for single figures.

Shortly before the Shield team met Victoria, the firm of Wm. Sykes Ltd, a leading manufacturer of cricket equipment, approached Bradman for permission to use his name on their bats. Their approach may have been made easier by the fact that the first new bat which Bradman owned and chose for himself, the one given to him by his mother, was a Sykes product.

Negotiations concluded just before the match opened, and the firm gave him a new bat to celebrate the agreement. Bradman took the virgin bat onto the field without oiling or preparing it in any way, and began an innings which lasted from shortly before lunch on the first day until New South Wales declared at five o'clock on the following afternoon.

One newspaper report said: 'He literally flayed the attack with strokes all round the wicket, never being in trouble to any bowler. And always, while he despatched deliveries to the fine leg, straight drive, square, and back-cut boundary, he wore a cheerful grin.'

It was a virtuoso performance of staggering power, confidence and endurance. He was at the wicket for eight hours and eight minutes, while the awed spectators watched him break one record after another. The newspapers almost ran out of superlatives in their attempts to describe the glory of his innings. One said he had 'won the right to have his name inscribed with those of Australia's mightiest batsmen'.

When New South Wales declared, he had scored 340 and brought his total in first-class cricket for that season up to 1207, only 39 short of Victor Trumper's total for a first-class season.

The 340 was then the highest score ever made on the Sydney Cricket Ground, and remained the record until Bradman later broke it for himself. It remains the highest score ever made by a New South Wales player against Victoria. It was the record New South Wales innings in Sheffield Shield contests — until Bradman broke this record also — and it remained the record innings in first-class cricket, by a player under twenty-one, until 1974.

Moyes wrote: 'Raise your hat to Donald Bradman, of Bowral, who, in less than two cricket seasons, has come close to breaking all existing cricket records in this State . . . his extraordinary effort of yesterday, which excelled in runs scored the best knocks of Trumper and Armstrong, will long be remembered, and though the bowling was not all that it might have been, nothing can detract from the merit of the achievement.'

The firm of Wm. Sykes was delighted. They asked him to return the bat he had carried during that triumphant day, and displayed it in Sydney. The bat was never used again and it remains a part of Sir Donald Bradman's cricket memorabilia.

Journalists who had earlier commented upon the mature ages of most of the Australian Test players now began to laud the 'Test

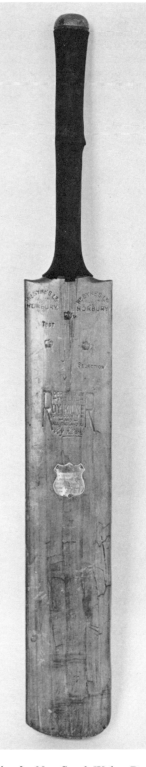

Playing for New South Wales, Don Bradman used this bat to score 340 not out against Victoria in January 1929. His score was then the highest ever made on the Sydney Cricket Ground

The great English batsman Jack
Hobbs took this snapshot of Don
Bradman at Adelaide during the
1928–29 Test series. At that time,
neither man could have guessed
that Bradman would outclass
Hobbs' achievements in Test
matches. (Hobbs: 61 Tests, 5410
runs at 56.94, 15 centuries.
Bradman: 52 Tests, 6996 runs at
99.94, 29 centuries)

Babies': Archie Jackson who was nineteen, Don Bradman twenty, and Ted a'Beckett twenty-one. Of this youthful triumvirate, Bradman was the only one still playing first-class cricket a few years later. The demands of a'Beckett's legal practice made him retire early from the game, and Jackson, whom Bradman later called 'this gloriously talented youngster', died untimely in 1933.

When the fourth Test of the 1928-29 series opened in Adelaide, there were those who felt that Jackson, the 'boy from Balmain', would rival if not surpass the 'boy from Bowral'. He was a batsman of supreme style, subtlety and elegance. A sportswriter of the period, comparing Bradman and Jackson, said that the former had 'forced his way to the top by sheer natural ability, a straight bat, cool cheerful temperament, determination, and enterprise', whereas Jackson was 'the finished batsman, the batsman who knows the one stroke for every ball, and executes that stroke with an artistry that has no parallel in the present day — at 19!'

At Adelaide, between 1–9 February 1929, South Australians had the privilege of watching this young cricketing genius make his first Test century, in a score of 164 in his first innings before he was bowled by White. He was then the youngest player in history to make a Test century.

Bradman made a useful 40 before Larwood caught him off a ball from Tate.

The first innings ended with Australia at 369 against England at 334. The second innings developed extreme tension in a narrowly fought contest. When Bradman was at the wicket, in partnership with a'Beckett, Oxenham and Oldfield, the crowd watched in breathless silence as he faced the cunning slow left-arm bowling of 'Farmer' White. Bradman was playing aggressively, and each time the *crack!* of willow against leather resounded across the field it triggered a great roar of applause, as the crowd released its tension and sank into silence again.

He was batting with what one newspaper described as 'supreme assurance', and had scored 58, when Oldfield cover-drove a ball towards Hobbs. Oldfield shouted 'Yes!' and began to run, although Bradman could see that Hobbs was virtually certain to have the ball in the wicket-keeper's hands before the run was completed.

He faced the split-second dilemma of calling 'No!' and leaving Oldfield stranded out of his crease, or of attempting the run. He chose the latter and was run out.

The correctness of that run-out decision remains open to question. Duckworth had his back to the umpire, who therefore was not in a position to see whether the ball was in Duckworth's gloves as he removed the bails. Bradman later said: 'I certainly was out of my ground but the ball fell out of Duckworth's gloves before he broke the wicket.'

But for Oldfield's foolhardy call, Don Bradman's batting would almost certainly have saved the game. The rot set in very quickly after his dismissal, but even so the visitors won by only twelve runs.

Both teams made the long overland journey back to Sydney, where New South Wales was to play a fixture against the M.C.C. The match, on 16, 18, and 19 February, was ruined by rain and ended in a draw. On a difficult wicket, Bradman went in at 45 for three and played for only twenty minutes before giving an easy catch to square-leg.

The first 'Don Bradman Bat', manufactured by Wm. Sykes Ltd, ever used in Australia. In the 1929 season Don Bradman used this bat to make what was then the record score for the St George Cricket Club

After a brief respite, Bradman then played for his home State in a match against South Australia on the Sydney Cricket Ground. Spectators who watched the four-day game were thrilled by a demonstration of 'The Don' at his brilliant best. In his second innings, on the third afternoon, he went in at 65 for one and was 125 not out at close of play. On the following morning he added another 50 to this score before being caught at the wicket.

But the grim challenge of the fifth Test still lay ahead, and the Australians boarded the train for Melbourne with the dire responsibility of saving their country from a five-Test defeat. The idea of losing every match in the series was almost unendurable, and the selectors had given anxious thought to the composition of the team to meet the victorious Englishmen in this last contest of the season. They had heeded the criticisms about 'old' players, and the twelve Australians included Bradman, Jackson, a'Beckett, 'Tim' Wall who was then twenty-five, twenty-three-year-old Alan Fairfax, and Percy Hornibrook, thirty.

The crowd which packed the amphitheatre of the Melbourne Cricket Ground saw England win the toss and elect to go in first, which made the pundits shake their heads because Australia would have to take the fourth innings.

Jack Hobbs, the old master himself, seemed to demonstrate that age had nothing to do with success in cricket. Then aged forty-seven, he made his twelfth century against Australia, and his fifth on the Melbourne ground, in a superb display of batting which ended only when Ryder dismissed him lbw.

The Yorkshireman Maurice Leyland thumped the Australian bowling for another century, and the bad luck which dogged the Australians in that season decreed that their best slow bowler, Clarrie Grimmett, should injure his knee and have to withdraw on the second day.

The English innings ended with a score of 519. Pessimists now freely predicted a fifth Australian defeat, and the Englishmen seemed determined to fulfil this prediction. With the bowling concentrated in the hands of Larwood, Tate, Geary, White and Hammond, they attacked with tremendous energy and élan. George Geary, the big powerful fast-medium bowler, had had his nose broken by a ball earlier in the season but this did not deter him from a remarkable feat of bowling endurance. He bowled 81 overs, of which 36 were maidens, and took five wickets for 105.

But Bill Woodfull set the style for Australia, and justified his nicknames of 'The Rock' and 'The Unbowlable' by standing confidently up to the assault for three and a half hours and scoring 102, before Geary caught him off a ball from Larwood. He and Ryder made a splendid stand, although the newspapers criticised them for 'stodgy defence and complete lack of initiative', and the score was 203 for four when Bradman and Alan Fairfax came together at 2.23 p.m.

From then until stumps were drawn at 5.42 p.m., after two appeals against the light, they played in a magnificent partnership. The visitors changed the bowling again and again, but the two colts were equal to everything from White's tricky bowling to Larwood's explosive deliveries. With Bradman as the aggressor and Fairfax as the stonewaller, they seemed set to play interminably.

One newspaper reported: 'It was Bradman who provided the fireworks by trouncing every bowler brought against him . . . He

Clarrie Grimmett (left) and Don Bradman on the tennis court in the late 1920s. Bradman was an admirer of the slow bowler, whom he played against in a number of Sheffield Shield matches and played with on the 1930 and 1934 tours of England

jumped straight into the bowling as though he were out for a practice knock instead of having to save Australia from collapse.

'First he hit Larwood practically off his length; then to Tate he showed wonderful skill in driving and turning.

'To White he used his feet, often going a couple of yards down the pitch to meet him, and hit him hard, either straight or through the covers. Impishly he dragged the slow bowler round to the on — a spot to which he is rarely played.'

At 46, the crowd held its breath when Geary leapt for one of Bradman's strikes to mid-on. But the ball was travelling like a rocket and it was too hot for Geary to hold. That narrow escape was the closest that England came to dismissing Bradman during the afternoon.

He reached his first 50 in 71 minutes, and after that played steadily towards the century. With the Australian score at 312, Larwood replaced Tate in yet another attempt to dismiss the young batsman. Bradman welcomed him back by hitting nine off the first three balls, with cuts for four and two and a pull for three.

The *Daily Pictorial* wrote: 'Barrackers rose to hoarse shouts of glee as the batsmen smacked Larwood in all directions, and hit the imperturbable White to the boundary with gusto. This was real cricket.

'Never were such heroes in flannels. The 20,000 barrackers were now staring at the crease, as if they individually were playing each ball, gasping or cheering as occasion dictated.

'At tea, when Bradman, 62 and Fairfax, 23 walked in, Great Pompey in his passage of Rome had nothing on them. The crowd yelled until old Yarra must have trembled in her banks.

'When the partnership yielded 100, of which every stroke after tea was applauded, there was another ovation.

'The fifth wicket record went by the board, and then came the great triumphal moment when Bradman's century was hoisted and the cheering became ecstatic.

'Some men were so hoarse they could yell no more and, leaping up in their seats, they were crouching like bookmakers before the last race on Melbourne Cup Day.

'At stumps, 20,000 pressed madly to greet the two colts as they left the wickets, cheering round after round rolling away in great waves of sound, while hats waved in the air with parasols and handkerchiefs.'

The journalist concluded his piece with a phrase which might stand as an epigraph on the great monolith of Don Bradman's career: *Such hero worship comes to few men in their time*.

On the following morning the two colts continued their partnership until they had added 183, in three hours thirty-three minutes. Bradman was then caught at short-leg, but the Australian score was 386 for five and there was a substantial chance of winning the fifth Test after all.

When Australia's turn came to renew the attack they found that some of the fighting spirit had gone out of the Englishmen — perhaps because of the arduous weather conditions with a hot north wind gusting across the ground. Young Tim Wall showed his mettle by taking out Jardine, Larwood, Tyldesley and White, with no more than 56 runs between them. A catch by Fairfax off Grimmett dismissed Hobbs for 65. By the end of the innings the Englishmen were all out for 257 and Australian hopes were high. They thought that, with a little bit of

Don Bradman, the businessman, as he would have appeared in the late 1920s when he had moved to Sydney as secretary of the real estate firm Deer & Westbrook Ltd. His employer, Percy Westbrook, said in a 1964 speech to the Moss Vale Rotary Club that when Bradman worked for him 'he kept his books clearly written, neatly ruled, and without a trace of a blot or smudge'

luck, it should be possible to tip the balance in favour of Australia.

In *Don Bradman's Book*, published in 1930, he recalled the last minutes of that crucial game. 'Our score rose steadily until an Australian victory was in sight, and it was a real pleasure to me to be at the wicket with my captain, Jack Ryder, when the winning runs were made.

'When I realized that we were bound to win, my one desire was to see Ryder make the winning hit, for he had been a wonderful fellow in the previous matches, and my wish that he should get the winning hit was shared by everybody. The runs which gave Australia her one victory in the series, however, were byes.

'Before these came, Ryder had hit a ball towards the boundary, and Maurice Tate was so sure that it was a four that he grabbed a couple of stumps so as to add to his score of souvenirs. Tate just roared when he saw that the ball had not reached the boundary, and to the accompaniment of much good-humoured banter, restored the stumps.

'When the match was won the crowd gave themselves up to unbounded enthusiasm. Jack Ryder had got hold of two stumps as souvenirs. For myself I had no thought or mind for mementoes. I ran for all I was worth to the pavilion. My happiness that at last Australia had won was enough.'

The crowd grabbed Ryder and carried him shoulder-high to the pavilion, and then refused to leave the ground before they had done due honour to all the Australians. Fairfax, Jackson, Kippax and Bradman had to catch the train back to Sydney, but when they had showered and changed they still had to fight their way through the crowd. As soon as they emerged the mob surrounded them with a clamour for autographs and yells of congratulation, pushing them apart so that the four youngsters were separated. Bradman was carrying a cricket bag and suitcase, and before he could protest some wellwisher snatched his bag and insisted on carrying it for him. Bradman was afraid that it would be 'souvenired' and struggled to keep him in sight as he fought through the crowd.

Tousled and breathless, the four cricketers eventually managed to rendezvous at the kerb where a car should have been waiting for them. But it was nowhere in sight, all the taxis had gone, and the minutes were ticking away to train-time.

At last they saw an ancient hansom cab and hailed it in desperation. Two of them squeezed inside with the luggage, another perched on the dicky seat with the driver, and the fourth stood on the rear step 'hanging on like grim death'. In this somewhat undignified manner the four young batsmen departed from the Melbourne Cricket Ground for the railway station.

Sydney cricket lovers gave him a rapturous welcome: not simply because he and Fairfax had saved the game in Melbourne but also because he had set yet another series of records. One newspaper wrote: 'With his 37 not out on Saturday the Bowral boy, Don Bradman, is on a pinnacle never reached by any other Australian cricketer not yet 21 years of age, and paralleled only by the immortal W. G. Grace of England.'

With an aggregate for the season of 1690 he had surpassed by 156 runs the previous best seasonal aggregate in Australia, set by the South African G. A. Faulkner in the season of 1910–11.

Don Bradman hit this ball with resounding effect when he scored his first Test century (112 runs) in the third Test against England at Melbourne in January 1929

The fifth wicket stand of 183 was then a record for Australia in any Test Match. The previous fifth-wicket partnership record had been set by Joe Darling and Syd Gregory in 1894, with a score of 142.

He had recorded the highest average for the season, 93.88, ahead of Hammond's average of 92.06, and he had made seven centuries in first-class cricket during the season. This was a unique achievement in Australia.

He had scored more runs in a series of Tests before he was twenty-one (468) than any other cricketer. The previous record holder, Clem Hill, aggregated 452 for eight completed innings in 1897–98 — and Hill had had previous Test experience.

Men who had said such things as 'Bradman is not up to Test standard' were beginning to think again, although there were those who remained sceptical. Percy Fender, the renowned English cricketer who was in Australia to report the Test series for a London newspaper, later wrote a book about the 1928–29 Test series and remarked that Bradman was 'one of the most curious mixtures of good and bad batting I have ever seen . . . If practice, experience, and hard work enable him to eradicate the faults and still retain the rest of his ability, he may well become a very great player; and if he does this, he will always be in the category of the brilliant, if unsound, ones. Promise there is in Bradman in plenty, though watching him does not inspire one with any confidence that he desires to take the only course which will lead him to a fulfilment of that promise. He makes a mistake, then makes it again and again; he does not correct it, or look as if he were trying to do so. He seems to live for the exuberance of the moment.'

Big extrovert 'Chub' Tate put it more pithily. He advised young Bradman: 'You'll have to learn to play with a straighter bat before you come to England.'

THE BOWRAL CONNECTION

Don Bradman never received any formal cricket coaching (which may be just as well, because it might have affected his unique natural style and inborn instinct for the game) but he did enjoy the advantages of a family and community dedicated to cricket and vigorously supportive in every other way.

His father, George Bradman, was a 'useful all-rounder' in country matches, although he never achieved a match total of more than 77, and young Donald heard cricket discussed in the family circle from the very earliest years. His mother, Emily Bradman, not only enjoyed the game as a spectator but also played it with her children, bowling left-handed at Donald with a kerosene tin as a wicket. She could offer cogent opinions on the local cricketers, and her family valued such opinions as they did her guidance in all aspects of life.

George was plagued by repetitive bouts of sciatica and he eventually abandoned the more active side of cricket in favour of umpiring, which helped his son to appreciate the finer points of the game.

As a self-taught cricketer, who learned by practice and observation, Donald must have inherited his father's ability to teach himself. George left school at eleven but he developed an excellent practical command of English and a precise usage of the spoken and written word — a trait certainly inherited by Donald Bradman. Brought up as a farmer, he taught himself to be an admirable craftsman in wood and metal. He took pride in the meticulous completion of any task to which he set himself, and his children were equally proud of his abilities. When he built a fence around a local property, doing every part of the work himself from digging the postholes to painting the posts and rails, the family was so proud of his handiwork that they named it 'Dad's Fence'.

Bowral folk named him 'Pop' Bradman, in affectionate tribute to his paternal interest in local affairs and his support for Bowral sporting activities. He shot regularly for the Bowral Rifle Club, with an accuracy of eye also inherited by his son Donald.

Emily Bradman's brothers, George and Richard Whatman (Uncle George and Uncle Dick), played a substantial part in the development of their nephew's cricketing potential. Uncle George was an opening batsman and an exceptional wicket-keeper. He captained the Bowral Cricket Club for a number of years. Uncle Dick, another all-rounder, captained the cricket club at Glenquarry, about ten kilometres from Bowral. Sir Donald Bradman recalls that the two brothers played for local sides against visiting English teams.

Uncle Dick's dictum 'You've got to practise at least an hour a day to become a good cricketer' was well and truly absorbed by his nephew.

As in most country towns, a large part of Bowral's social life revolved around its various sporting activities. When Donald Bradman left school and began to play regularly in the local cricket and tennis teams, he became even more closely integrated into the comfortable and homely texture of small-town life, in which everyone knows everyone else at least by sight. It is restrictive in some ways, perhaps, but it imparts a 'sense of place' much deeper and more supportive than one may absorb in the asphalt and concrete wilderness of a city. When young Donald began to take his first giant steps to cricketing fame, the people of Bowral — and indeed of much of the Berrima district — felt a much closer link with him than a mere abstract admiration of a popular hero. They knew everything about him from childhood onward. They had played with him or against him in local contests, discussed him with his family, chatted about his future. Each, in some small way, felt he had played a part in the creation of the local hero.

Donald Bradman's love of music dates back to his Bowral days, and may well be inherited from both sides of the family. George Bradman played the violin; Emily played the piano and the accordion — both by ear, because she had not been taught how to play. Donald's sister Lilian, who later became a professional music teacher, taught him to play the piano and discovered that he had a natural ear. Uncle George and Uncle Dick, and Donald's cousin Hector Whatman, were all violinists.

The family love of music flowed naturally into regular enjoyment of the popular pastime of that era when 'canned music' was virtually unknown: the 'musical evening'. Bradmans, Whatmans and

Bowral, like most other country towns, boasted of a brass band and a bandstand. In the days before 'canned music' the brass band gave regular performances, and played on such ceremonial occasions as that of Don Bradman's homecoming after his overseas Test triumphs

their friends would gather around the piano and sing together, or enjoy renditions by one or another of the company. In these days one may perhaps smile a little at such rustic amusements, but they imparted a sense of togetherness which our more sophisticated society has lost.

The Bradman connection with the little farming community of Glenquarry extended even further than the link with the Whatman family. In 1877, when Don Bradman's mother Emily Whatman first went to school, another of the new entrants on that same day was a little boy named James Menzies. His father was a Scottish stonemason who had emigrated to Sydney as one of the builders of Sydney University, induced by the colonial government's promise of a grant of land when the work was done.

The land was at Glenquarry, where young James grew up to take over the family farm. His family included three daughters, of whom the eldest was Jessie Menzies.

There were no school buses in 1921, the year when Jessie Menzies first attended Bowral school. The distance was too far for a little girl to travel each day by herself, but the Menzies-Whatman-Bradman connection soon solved the problem. Jessie would stay with the Bradmans during the week and return home at weekends.

Jessie was a pretty, lively little girl, with blue eyes and wavy auburn hair, about a year younger than Don Bradman. She settled easily into the Bradman home and she and young Donald were occasional playmates.

After a year, Jessie's two sisters were old enough to go to school. She returned to her own home, and drove them to school and back in a buggy every

Jessie Menzies (right) with a friend from the
Commonwealth Bank in Sydney about 1930

Jessie Menzies (right) in ski gear of the 1920s, on a snow
holiday at Mount Kosciusko

day. The horse-oriented community saw nothing strange about the sight of three little girls in a buggy driven by one of them. Some other youngsters rode their own horses to school.

Bowral, like most other small towns, could not offer a very promising future for young people unless they worked on a family farm or in a family business, or, like fourteen-year-old Don Bradman, found a billet in a local firm. Many of them joined the drift to the cities, either to continue their education or to look for a job. James Menzies settled the matter for his teenage daughters by purchasing a house in the Sydney suburb of Burwood. His wife and family moved there in 1926, and he joined them whenever he could get away from the farm.

Jessie went to business college in Sydney, and when she graduated she found a job with the Com-

monwealth Bank. An uncle, James Kell, had been the second governor of the bank.

When Don Bradman made his own move to Sydney in 1928, the Menzies girls had been living there since 1926. Burwood lies immediately south of Concord, the suburb in which Bradman lived at the home of his friend G. H. Pearce, and the Menzies home was within easy distance of the Pearces. Naturally the young cricketer knew that his childhood playmate and family friend was living in Burwood, and he soon became a frequent visitor.

The long friendship between the two young people blossomed into romance, and a courtship which lasted until 30 April 1932, when they were married in St Paul's Church, Burwood, New South Wales.

4

'THE RUN-MAKING MACHINE'

Don Bradman's first employer, Percy Westbrook, had originally been a minister. He had left the church, and established his real estate agency in Bowral, because he found the demands upon a country parson to be too much for him. His agency flourished and he was able to give young Donald a good grounding in business practice, both in the office and in the field. By the time Bradman made his move to Sydney, Westbrook was sending him out in the firm's car to show properties to prospective clients. The personable young man proved himself to be a meticulous bookkeeper and a reliable representative, and these early experiences gave him a useful background in dealing with the public. Young as he was, he was not by any means the raw country lad that some people believed him to be, even though the newspapers persisted in calling him the 'colt from Bowral' for more than a year after he had first made his mark in Test cricket. As the saying goes, he 'knew how to handle himself' in any kind of company.

When Westbrook smoothed his way to the city by transferring him to the new Sydney real estate agency, Deer & Westbrook, Donald Bradman quickly fitted himself into the new operation; and despite the demands of cricket he worked hard at the job. Both Deer and Westbrook were aficionados of cricket and they never hesitated to give him the time he needed for practice or playing — perhaps with a realisation that his increasing reputation had a certain amount of publicity value.

When Bradman moved to Sydney, Australia was still riding the crest of the post-war boom. It was an expansive period, even though it rested upon the fragile foundations of massive overseas borrowings and the number of unemployed rarely fell below eight per cent. Real estate dealings flourished, as they usually do in a buoyant economy; but the tremors of the Great Depression reached Australia at just about the same time as Percy Chapman's team of English cricketers played their first game in Perth, in October 1928. Real estate was among the first activities to feel the sudden downturn in business, and that of Deer & Westbrook rapidly declined. Their young secretary might well have found himself out of a job.

Fortunately, his increasing reputation had attracted the attention of Mr Oscar Lawson, who handled advertising and public relations activities for the prestigious firm of Mick Simmons Ltd. This business had various facets, but in the sporting world of New South Wales it was known principally as a distributor of sports goods. If you purchased a fishing rod, cricket bat, football, baseball bat, golf club, tennis racket or boxing glove anywhere in New South Wales, it could have passed through the hands of Mick Simmons Ltd. The firm, which still flourishes, was then about sixty years old.

In February 1929, during the fourth Test, Lawson invited Bradman to join the organisation. Bradman accepted, and spent his first day in the firm's George Street headquarters, in the Haymarket, Sydney, as soon as he could find time during the matches of that season. Naturally it was understood that he should have time off for cricket. The more that Bradman appeared on the cricket pitch the better he would serve Mick Simmons Ltd. As a part of his public relations activities he ran coaching classes for schoolboys, and coached teams of boys on the Domain. They played a team led by young Stan McCabe, who was later to play with Bradman in Test teams.

In the autumn of 1929 the New South Wales Cricket Association asked him to join a team, consisting largely of Shield players, which

ALL ABOARD THE IRON HORSE

In these jet-propelled days it is difficult to realise that a cricketer of Don Bradman's vintage spent a great deal of his time simply in getting from one place to another. There were no aircraft capable of carrying the thirteen men of a Sheffield Shield group until Australian National Airways introduced Douglas airliners in 1936 — and soon lost one without trace in Bass Strait. Shield and Test teams did not travel by air until after the second world war. Until then, they went everywhere by train. The problems of travel across and around the 'big country' meant that Tasmania and Western Australia rarely played against all the other States. A return rail journey from Perth to Sydney took ten days, and the only easy way to reach Tasmania was by sea.

It was possible to make a leisurely sea voyage between the State capitals, or a gruelling journey by automobile over roads on which long stretches were still unsealed; but the railways were the only means of public transport with a regular daily schedule.

Even so, each train journey tended to be an endurance test. When the New South Wales eleven played their series of Sheffield Shield 'away' matches in the 1929–30 season, Don Bradman and his team-mates spent a total of about 118 hours in the train. The shortest rail journey between capitals was the sixteen-hour trip from Sydney to Melbourne. Sydney to Brisbane took seventeen hours, and Sydney to Adelaide thirty-two hours plus a day in Melbourne between trains.

Some States had different track gauges, so that passengers from Sydney to Melbourne had to change at Albury. A trip to Perth meant five changes: at Albury, Melbourne, Adelaide, Terowie, and Kalgoorlie.

Many people now cherish a nostalgia for 'the great days of steam', but those days were far from romantic for passengers who endured them. There was no air-conditioning even in the first-class carriages. The teams always travelled in summer, with the temperature often over the century on the Fahrenheit thermometer, and passengers had a choice of sweltering with the blinds and windows closed or opening them to the hot winds and the smoke and smuts from the coal-burning locomotive.

Train travel was jolting and noisy, with frequent stops for the locomotive to take on water and occasional unscheduled stops because of 'hot boxes'. A man needed to be a sound sleeper to enjoy a full night's rest. There was no dining car on trains between Adelaide and Melbourne, and the hungry or thirsty traveller had to turn out at the refreshment stop at Murray Bridge or join the throng seeking breakfast at Ballarat.

The mainline expresses were luxurious compared with the trains to country towns, and a journey to almost any part of Australia served by the railways took at least twice as long as one would now expect for a road journey to the same places.

Travelling teams always took a day's rest when they arrived at their destination, before playing on the following day. They needed it to recover from the fatigues of the rail journey.

was to make a kind of educational tour of country centres. The policy of the NSWCA was to encourage young country players in their cricketing ambitions, and to urge country clubs to upgrade their wickets from concrete to turf, with the aim of creating a reservoir of promising State and even international players. The 'educational' team was to play a number of fixtures with country sides, in which they would not necessarily strive to win but rather concentrate on giving the colts an example of first-class cricket, and smoothing off their rough edges.

The travellers played in a number of inland towns, and attracted many spectators who seized this chance of seeing star State cricketers in action. At Singleton, with the concrete wicket grilling in a temperature of 42 degrees, they had the unusual experience of watching the first four batsmen make a century apiece, and the fifth make a duck, and then the innings was closed.

At Maitland, Bradman opened the innings for the visitors. In the first over of the day, he endeavoured to glance to leg a ball going away on the leg side. The ball hit his pad and rebounded towards square leg. He called for a run, but saw the umpire signalling that he was out lbw — for a duck.

Don Bradman recalled the incident when he wrote in *Don Bradman's Book*: 'As I was making my way to the pavilion, a gentleman full seventy years of age stopped me. His face was all wry, and half a glance told me he was filled with some sorrow. He unburdened himself by telling me that he had travelled sixty miles that morning just to see me bat. I shared his regret, for instinct told me that the old fellow had set apart this day on which he had hoped to make a cricketing feast, and see all the Test cricketers make at least a few runs each.'

Bradman's work with Mick Simmons Ltd was partly to help in the store and partly to make trips with country representatives to the cities and larger towns inland and up and down the coast. His appointment created wonderful publicity for Mick Simmons, and Lawson made the most of it. Retailers were delighted to meet the young batsman, pump him about his Test experiences, and ask his advice about cricket equipment. In Sydney, his presence in George Street was a valuable creator of 'store traffic'. Both in the city and suburbs and on the country trips, Lawson arranged for him to give cricket talks and demonstrations to schoolboys not much younger than he had been when he first batted in Sydney.

He spent most of the winter of 1929 on familiarisation tours of the Mick Simmons territory. When he returned to Sydney he appeared frequently at the Menzies home in Burwood, where the three daughters and their two brothers welcomed him as an old Bowral friend. The 'musical evenings' of Bowral were repeated in somewhat more elaborate form when the six young people formed their own small orchestra and tackled everything from jazz to popular classics.

Apart from spending his time on work, music and cricket, he enjoyed himself much like any other young man of the same age. His association with the St George Cricket Club had given him a wide circle of friends. There were occasional visits to that new phenomenon, the 'talkies', in the magnificent movie theatres of Sydney, and to his favourite games of tennis and cricket he had added a new one: golf. He played occasional games with Will Corry, the professional golfer

At the age of twenty, Don Bradman faces the camera for the first time in the green-and-gold blazer of an Australia XI. The photograph shows him as young, calm, and innocent, but he was to give some nasty shocks to the English players

attached to Mick Simmons Ltd. He spent quite a long time at this sport before he achieved anything like mastery, but in the meantime he found it to be a challenging and enjoyable relaxation which gave him something different to think about.

Naturally cricket was never far from his mind. He had made such an impact upon the Test scene that he could be reasonably sure of inclusion in the Australian tour of Britain in 1930, but nothing is certain in cricket.

Even before the 1929–30 season opened he was off on a NSWCA tour of the far north of the State, in an eleven captained by Alan Kippax. They visited Taree, Moree and Wauchope, and some of them, including Bradman, joined kangaroo shoots organised by local sportsmen.

His scores in the cricket matches did not ring up any records in second-class cricket: bowled for seven at Taree, caught for 37 at Wauchope, 13 not out in one innings at Moree and caught for 96 in the next. Some country cricketers must have felt a flush of pride at these dismissals of the 'Bowral wonder'.

He was to play 21 second-class matches during that season, a number of them for the NSWCA but also for such sides as the Sydney *Sun* against the Theatricals and Gladesville against the *Sydney Morning Herald*. The NSWCA matches included a tour of western centres. They played five matches in Orange, Dubbo, Parkes and Bathurst, and attracted enormous crowds — for that part of the world. For example, 3500 cricket lovers flocked to the Parkes Oval from the town and the surrounding countryside to watch a match against Far West.

The phenomenon which Bradman had previously noted, that he was sometimes unable to give of his best against comparatively inexpert opposition, certainly applied in some of the second-class matches. But when he walked onto the pitch for his first grade match of the season, St George v. Glebe at the Glebe Jubilee Oval on 28 September and 5 October 1929, the sportswriters quickly noted that he was in peak form. One wrote: 'The brilliant Don Bradman gave the spectators a further demonstration of his prowess with the bat. After an early ''life'', he quickly rattled together 32 runs in 23 minutes, making his unfinished score 180.'

The first Shield match of the season, New South Wales v Queensland, followed a month later. The New South Wales team included the Test stars Bert Oldfield (as captain), Archie Jackson, Alan Fairfax and Don Bradman, together with a young batsman of sparkling promise: eighteen-year-old Stan McCabe. New South Wales batted first, on the Exhibition Ground at Brisbane, and Bradman went in at 72 for one. He hit up 48 in sixty-six minutes before being run out.

In his second innings, the 'Bradman Touch' seemed to be unusually absent. One reporter wrote: 'Bradman played like a man under restraint, his usual strong forcing shots not being in evidence. He was well set, and looked likely to stay a long time, when he was given out caught behind the wicket. Though his energy in the field would not encourage such an idea, his restrained batting would cause one to feel he may have been somewhat off colour physically.' It was indeed a remarkably sober performance for the hardhitting young batsman. He took 209 minutes to score 66 before O'Connor caught him off a ball from Brew.

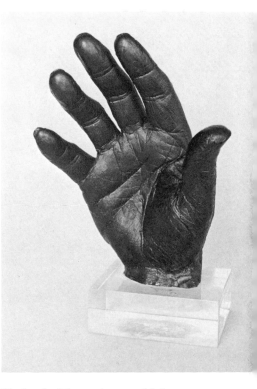

The hand of the master, moulded in plastic as a bronze-like replica by K. P. Polis in 1973

New South Wales squeaked a win by 23 runs, and none of the star batsmen performed particularly well. But on 13 November, on their way home from Brisbane, they tackled Newcastle on that team's home ground and 'gave them a day of leather hunting'. Bradman began quietly but then opened out and scored his century in ninety minutes. He was caught after adding 11 more in fifteen minutes.

A more formidable challenge awaited the State players on their home ground. An M.C.C. team captained by Harold Gilligan was touring the mainland capitals *en route* to New Zealand, and it included Eddie Dawson, Fred Barratt, Maurice Allom, Frank Woolley and Kumar Duleepsinhji. The match, on Sydney Cricket Ground on 21–26 November, was in fact a kind of 'mini-Test', with the New South Wales side including Fairfax, Kippax, Oldfield and Bradman.

Bradman went in on the first morning and immediately sprang into life with a magnificent display of batting expertise. If any of the English players had listened to such reports from their compatriots as 'Bradman plays with a cross bat', they were speedily disillusioned. With the advantage of a perfect wicket, he flogged the English bowling all over the ground and 'rattled the pickets with repeated boundaries'.

He kept the scorers busy during 175 whirlwind minutes at the crease. He recorded almost a run a minute and was up to the century in 103 minutes. Because of his batting, New South Wales was scoring at terrific speed and 200 appeared on the board after only 132 minutes.

One report said: 'He was very crisp on both sides of the wicket and behind as well as in front of the sticks. He used his feet to the slows, and altogether played a very high-class innings, timing perfectly in clean, forceful, well-paced strokes.'

He was up to 157 when Stan Worthington dismissed him. The crowd applauded vigorously as he walked back to the pavilion, and the opinion was 'He's a certainty for England'.

While the M.C.C. was batting, Bradman enjoyed the chance to observe the techniques of men like Woolley and Duleepsinhji. He classified the Indian as 'a giant batsman'. Woolley scored 219 in his last match on Sydney Cricket Ground. Don Bradman remembered his performance so well that he said many years later: 'It remains one of the most majestic and classical innings I have seen, with every stroke in the book played with supreme ease.'

The game developed into a close-fought struggle and ended in a draw. Ten days later, on 6 December 1929, Bradman again walked onto the Sydney Cricket Ground, which he has described as 'The ideal batsman's wicket . . . Perfectly true, and easy-paced, it is a batsman's Paradise.' He was to take part in a crucial game, arranged by the Test selectors to aid their task of choosing the 1930 travellers to England.

The very cream of Australian cricket in that period, from youngsters like Bradman, Jackson and McCabe to veterans like Blackie and Ryder, had been divided into two elevens captained by Bill Woodfull and Jack Ryder. Bradman played for Woodfull's eleven in a five-day contest which the selectors watched like Roman emperors: preparing to give the thumbs-up sign which meant inclusion in the tour of England, or the thumbs-down sign which meant relegation to the cricketers left behind.

The tension obviously affected some of the star batsmen in Woodfull's eleven, who fell like ninepins before Oxenham's deadly

deliveries. But Bradman, as so often, showed himself at his best on a stricken field. The sportswriters said that he and Keith Rigg, of Victoria, were the only bright spots of 'Woodfull's unhappy eleven'. Bradman 'treated all the bowlers with the greatest disrespect' in his first innings, and scored a brilliant 124 before he was caught by Jackson off Oxenham.

In the second innings, on a day of stifling heat with a duststorm in the late afternoon, Bradman performed in a way which made the sportswriter George Thatcher describe him, probably for the first time, as a 'Run-scoring Machine'. The tag was to be attached to him many times over the years.

Thatcher wrote: 'Hats off to Don Bradman, greatest Australian run-getter since the war! Bradman made Australian cricket history at the Sydney Cricket Ground yesterday, in the third day's play of the Australian XI's trial game. The Bowral youth batted five and a half hours, scored 273 runs during the day, and followed his first innings score of 124 with a brilliantly compiled 205 not out. Bradman is . . . the first cricketer to score a century in his first innings and 200 in the second in a first-class match at the Sydney Cricket Ground.'

This cartoon of Don Bradman appeared in a Sydney newspaper after the sportswriter George Thatcher called him a 'Run-scoring machine', when he scored a century in the first innings and a double century in the second innings of the Test trial match in December 1929

On 4 and 6 January 1930, Don Bradman set himself deliberately to beat Bill Ponsford's previous world record score of 437. Using this bat, he succeeded by scoring 452 not out for New South Wales against Queensland

The five-day game developed into an epic match; 1704 runs were scored for 39 wickets, and Ryder's eleven eventually won, after an exciting finish, by one wicket. Bradman ended his second innings with 225, but some critics made the strange comment that he concluded by playing 'a defensive game'.

Soon after setting these new records, Bradman was in the Shield team, captained by Kippax, which boarded the train for the gruelling thirty-two-hour journey to Adelaide. They were to play South Australia from 19–24 December, and Victoria in Melbourne, which meant Christmas away from home.

For Bradman and his fans, the match was a letdown after his dazzling performance in the Test trial. In his first innings he was run out after five minutes, for two. When he opened his second innings, in partnership with Jackson, the Sydney *Sunday Guardian* reported: 'Jackson and Bradman staged a glorious partnership . . . each making over 80.' But Bradman had to face his 'friendly antagonist', Clarrie Grimmett.

In *Don Bradman's Book*, he wrote: 'In our second innings, Grimmett bowled with tremendous effect. Some of the balls he sent down to me were the most difficult I had ever been called upon to play; I was absolutely tied up and made to look like a schoolboy. I never had such a bad time, but somehow I remained to make 84, and then Grimmett, as he should have done long before, got me out l.b.w.'

Fortune did not favour the visitors. Their only slow bowler, Campbell, had a finger badly broken when he was batting. Bradman wrote wryly: 'Being the only other slow bowler on our side, I was called upon to bowl — perhaps that is why we did not do very well.' Sir Donald Bradman freely admits that he rarely made the bails fly as a bowler, and it would perhaps be too much to ask that he should have bowled as splendidly as he batted and fielded.

New South Wales lost the match by five wickets, and with tails between their legs they travelled eastward again, to play Victoria in Melbourne. In the first innings, neither side scored particularly well. For Victoria, Ryder, Ironmonger and Alexander were all dismissed for ducks, and even the mighty Ponsford made only 65. Bradman later felt that Ryder's failure in this innings led to his omission from the 1930 Test team. For New South Wales, Fairfax was caught for two. Bradman displayed better form when he went in at eight for one and compiled 85 not out by lunch. After that he delighted the spectators with a display of the unique Bradman style. Of one stroke, a reporter wrote: 'Never has a batsman taken the liberties that Bradman took when facing Alexander. Long before the ball pitched he walked confidently across to the off and hooked the fast-rising ball. For sheer audacity it has never been matched. While the crowd was still applauding the success of the venture it brought about his undoing, Alexander shattering his stumps with a ball pitched further up.'

Apart from the Bradman fireworks the spectators found it rather a dull match, which ended with a draw on 31 December.

Almost immediately after the New South Wales men returned home, Bradman was on the Sydney Cricket Ground again for the Sheffield Shield fixture with Queensland. It opened on 3 January 1930, with no hint that it was to be a fateful match — and the start of a fateful cricketing year — for the young batsman.

He opened the first innings for New South Wales, but made an unpromising start when wicket-keeper Leeson caught him, off a ball from Hurwood, after only seven minutes and three runs. The two sides completed their first innings almost neck-and-neck: 235 for the home side, 227 for the visitors.

Perhaps the spectators and sportswriters who turned up on the second day, a Saturday, felt that the rest of the match was hardly likely to excite them — that it would simply be another pleasant spectacle of accomplished cricketers performing their summer ritual; white figures against green turf in the classic configurations of the game. If so, they must have opened their eyes when Bradman began his second innings.

Playing in successive partnerships with Fairfax, Kippax and McCabe, he scored almost a run a minute: 50 in fifty-one minutes, and then 100 in 104 minutes. By close of play, he was 205 not out after 195 minutes at the wicket. During his partnership with McCabe he hit 11 in an over off Brew, and then with two more runs off Rowe he reached a total of 1000 for the season. It was the second time that he had done so, thus ranking himself with Ponsford and Kippax, and the crowd gave him an ovation when the score went up on the board.

The Sunday newspapers proclaimed 'Don Bradman the Wonder Cricketer of the Season'. One wrote: 'Some of Bradman's drives were immense, revealing perfect timing. The wicket was such that the ball came through truly and soon lost all vestige of nip . . . One of Bradman's most furious and fruitful strokes was a square drive. Repeatedly he stepped back and crashed the ball back past Brew, who was impotent to prevent a four.'

During that Saturday night, which Bradman spent quietly with some friends, and on the Sunday, he conceived a new ambition. In the past, his records had simply been part of the game, and he had enjoyed them

Bradman starting to run after cutting Hurwood during his historic innings against Queensland

HOT LINE TO DON BRADMAN

A twelve-word telegram cost only the equivalent of ten cents in 1930, and admirers deluged Don Bradman with telegrams after each of his record-breaking achievements. A few of those sent after he scored 452 against Queensland said:

'Give Don huge embrace unique performance behalf Taralga girl admirers.'

'Heartiest congratulations brilliant achievement beg you express bat used to us advertising propaganda purposes. Sykes.'

'Congratulations to Don Bradman from a blind soldier at Kurnell.'

'Congratulations Wyong is proud of you.'

'Congratulations from a boy admirer.'

'Congratulations from Heaths Cafe Bathurst.'

'NSW State Soccer League congratulate your splendid performance world record.'

'Promising colt average six offers thirty bob your ticket England. Secretary Mugs Cricket Club Barellan.'

'Congrats citizens of Mittagong upon breaking world's record. Terry Mayor Mittagong.'

Some telegrams were from friends and relations. Many others were from admirers unknown to him, and a number came from cricket clubs and associations in many parts of Australia.

only because they helped his side to win. Now, for the first time, he determined to make a definite attempt at a record-breaking stand. He would go all out to secure the highest individual score in first-class cricket, and demolish Ponsford's record of 437.

On the Monday morning he went calmly out to the wicket at that slow and deliberate pace which, for some reason, was beginning to annoy his critics. Some were later to call it 'theatrical'. He took his stance, and faced Alec Hurwood, the tall medium-pace bowler who had tried desperately hard to dismiss him on the Saturday. Both men were refreshed by the day's rest, and Bradman watched the Queenslander keenly as he began his run-up.

Any hopes the visitors nourished that Hurwood and their other prime bowlers, Brew, Gough, and Rowe, would rid them of this turbulent batsman, soon evaporated as the 'run-scoring machine' sent the ball rocketing to every quarter of the field. The bowlers dismissed McCabe, then Marks, then Allsopp, but Bradman survived one over after another. Hurwood was his most dangerous opponent, with a stamina and determination which matched Don Bradman's. The young batsman played him carefully, but still punished his bowling as cruelly as he did that of lesser men.

The runs mounted steadily, at a rate of better than one a minute. Bradman reached his third century after 288 minutes at the wicket, and his fourth after 377 minutes. During the next half-hour the tension was almost palpable. Both spectators and cricketers now realised that Bradman was aiming at Ponsford's record. Staid elderly gentlemen in the Members Stand rose to their feet, staring fixedly at the apparently impregnable batsman, and the crowd watched in hushed silence as the runs mounted inexorably on the board. Suddenly all the spectators burst into a roar of acclaim, and the Queenslanders applauded, when he made the record-shattering stroke.

He raised his cap to the plaudits, and then continued to bat as coolly as though he had just opened his innings: still perfectly calm, still calculating the exact stroke to deal with every ball. He seemed to be set at the wicket until the end of the match, but Kippax declared for New South Wales when Bradman reached 452.

One of Mick Simmons' travellers, who had been watching the game, immediately leapt the fence and ran to Bradman in an attempt to carry him off the ground. He tried to lift Bradman onto his shoulder, but the young man was too heavy for him and they fell with Bradman across his chest. Four Queenslanders picked Bradman up and shouldered him off the ground.

His performance had rewritten the record books. His score of 452 included 49 fours: the highest number of boundaries ever hit in a Shield match and the most runs scored in boundaries. He had made the highest first-class score, his match aggregate of 455 was the highest on record, he was the only New South Wales batsman twice to make a score over 300, he was the youngest batsman ever to score 400, his time for reaching 400 was the fastest on record, and for reaching 300 it was the fastest for New South Wales. His partnership with Kippax for the third wicket was the record for matches between New South Wales and Queensland, and for any match against Queensland.

One newspaper wrote: 'To-day, he can, with safety, pack his bag and label it: D. Bradman, Australian Eleven, England.'

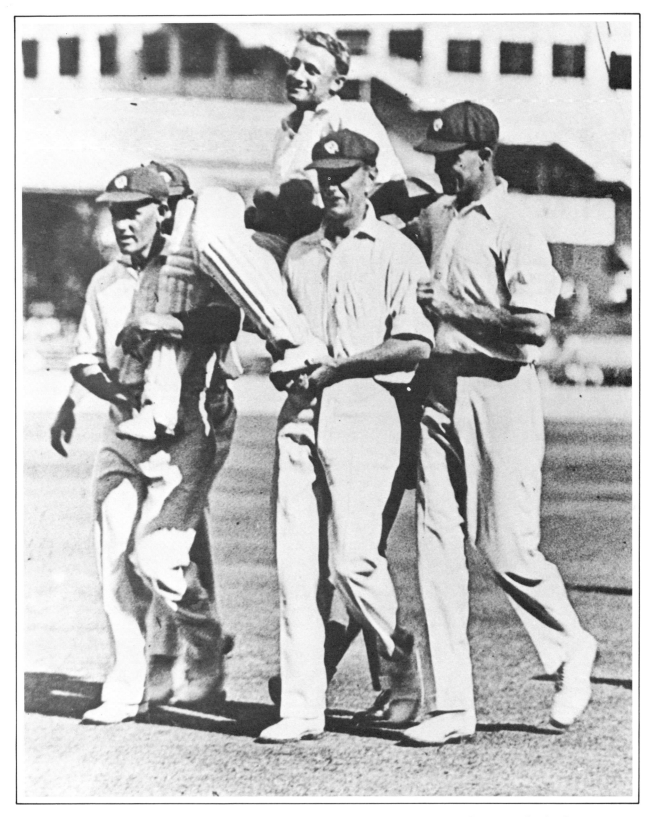

Queensland cricketers 'chair' an embarrassed young Don Bradman off the Sydney Cricket Ground in January 1930, after he made his record-breaking 452 not out in the Sheffield Shield match against Queensland. His performance brought enormous acclaim and virtually guaranteed his inclusion in the 1930 Test tour of England

Ponsford telegraphed from Melbourne: 'Congratulations on your great feat player your ability deserves the honour.'

Mick Simmons Ltd, 'The Leaders in Outdoor Sport and Home Entertainment', placed advertisements reviewing Don Bradman's achievements and concluding: 'Come along and meet this unassuming young man. His charming personality, his happy smile and expert advice are at your service.'

The newspapers dealt with the record-breaking stand in every conceivable manner, from printing a photograph of 'Conductor C. Tighe, who for 12 years has worked the tram switchway at the Cricket Ground', because his badge number 452 corresponded with Bradman's score, to comparing the batsman with young cricketing giants of the past.

The ABC invited him and some other players to speak on Radio 2FC, and on 10 January 1930 he faced the microphone for the first time. He said 'Good-evening, everybody. Don Bradman speaking. This is a new experience for me to-night — broadcasting. I just want to thank the cricket followers of Australia for their wonderful tribute to me in connection with my efforts at Sydney Cricket Ground on Monday last. You will all understand how impossible it is for me to answer all your telegrams and letters personally.

'Playing cricket for New South Wales all day makes the night seem quite short enough for a good rest, so you can see that I have very little time left for writing letters. I was very glad, however, to seize the chance of thanking you through Radio 2FC, when the Australian Broadcasting Company offered me this opportunity of really speaking to each and every one of you who were so kind in sending me messages of congratulation.

'When I look at the bundle of telegrams and letters, it strikes me there is hardly time to read the messages themselves . . . To all you good kind friends, I send my thanks. Perhaps I might be excused if I make special mention of the message from Taralga which reads "Give Don Huge Embrace Unique Performance Behalf Taralga Girl Admirers." The thought strikes me that perhaps my luck is out that I am not up at Taralga instead of speaking by wireless.

'Now, I think the time for my share of to-night's programme is finished, as I know a lot of you will want to listen to Bert Oldfield. There are numbers of people that I would like to write to personally, but I must ask you to take the will for the deed. I feel very proud that so many friends have remembered me and I can assure you that I appreciate their goodwill very much indeed.

'Possibly, I will never have the opportunity of meeting many of you, but you can rest assured that I do very much appreciate all your kindness. Again, thank you very much. Good-night, everybody.'

The radio talk was characteristic of the 'public face' of young Don Bradman: modest, well-organised, good-humoured. If he had been a different type of personality, he could very easily have 'contracted swelled head'. The press continued to blazon his name in every way from editorials to letters to the editor. One magazine article, on 'Heroes', said 'already he has acquired a fame comparable to that which enshrines the greatest heroes of the past'. A Mr A. E. Shearston asked 'What about a bob-in fund for Bradman now that he has broken all previous records and the aggregate for big cricket? It is up to us to

Journalists seeking for more ways to dramatise Bradman's 452 against Queensland photographed tram conductor C. Tighe, who worked the tram switchway at the Cricket Ground, because his badge number was 452

recognise him in some way, and I suggest a bob in for Bradman. For a colt so young, his is a marvellous feat.'

One admirer, signing himself 'Isis', launched into a fifty-three line verse concluding:

> *'Twas on the Cricket Ground*
> *With bobbites all around*
> *That Don the bat did wield*
> *Till Queensland wilted in the heat*
> *And bowlers swore he'd got them beat,*
> *And cursed the panting field.*
> *But on he goes from strength to strength*
> *And knocks the bowlers off their length*
> *Till New South expects*
> *In every game*
> *Young Don will get his century.*

Bradman had attracted publicity before, but now it became part of his daily life. Unfortunately, publicity is a two-edged sword. There are always those who want to wield it to 'cut down the tall poppies'. The headlines and articles about Bradman triggered a counter-current of rumour, gossip and detraction. He was not unique in suffering in this way. In 1950, writing about Ponsford, he said that Ponsford 'was the victim of much jealousy (until I began to take the load off his shoulders)'.

Bradman was able to survive the erosion of both praise and jealousy because he was so solidly based upon the enduring foundations of his upbringing. He never forgot them. When he was asked to select a gift for himself, to be presented during a dinner for the New South Wales cricketers, he chose a rose bowl so that he might give it to his mother. In his speech of thanks he said: 'There is someone who will treasure this rose bowl more than I do. I refer to my mother. The rose bowl is for her.'

The newspapers soon found a new Bradman sensation to fill their columns. During the Shield match against South Australia, in Sydney on 9–13 January, he was streaking down the pitch to avoid being run out when the returning ball, thrown by Clarrie Grimmett, hit him on the temple and he collapsed on the turf. He retired hurt, but batted again in the afternoon for eighty-one minutes before Vic Richardson caught him at slip. His score of 47 runs meant that he had scored 499 in his last two innings before being dismissed: the most ever scored in two consecutive innings for New South Wales.

The rest of the season, in both second-class and first-class cricket, was to some degree an anti-climax. Everyone was waiting for the announcement of the Australian touring team, and the list appeared at the end of January. The fifteen names, headed by Bill Woodfull as captain and Vic Richardson as vice-captain, inevitably included Don Bradman. After that, sportswriters and cricket lovers could talk only about Bradman's prospects in England.

The following series of photographs on pages 63–67 was taken in London in 1930 by the Sports & General photographic agency to illustrate Don Bradman's batsmanship. The photographs were reproduced in *Don Bradman's Book* (published late 1930) and some subsequently appeared in various English newspapers. The positions and strokes illustrated are:

Stance

Hook shot

Starting a drive

Off drive

Forward leg glance

SCOREBOARD: MARCH 1930

By the end of the 1929–30 cricket season, in March 1930, Bradman was aged twenty-one and seven months and he had been playing in first-class and Test cricket since 16 December 1927. He had played in 66 matches and established what were then a number of records. They include the following:

* Australia v. England, December 1928–January 1929, Melbourne: In this match he was the youngest player ever to make a Test century.

* New South Wales v. Victoria, January 1929, Sydney: His score of 340 was the highest by any New South Wales player in a Shield match; the highest against Victoria in any match; the highest by a New South Wales batsman against Victoria; the highest score on the Sydney Cricket Ground; the highest against Victoria in a Shield match. The innings, of eight and a half hours, was the longest for New South Wales in a Shield match and the longest that Bradman ever played. He was the youngest Australian batsman to play in an innings of 300 and over.

* Bradman's aggregate of 1690 for the 1928–29 season was the record for an Australian season. His aggregate of 468 was a record for a Test season for a batsman under twenty-one. His aggregate of 893 in Sheffield Shield matches was a record for New South Wales.

* By his twenty-first birthday, his record in first-class cricket was: 18 matches, 34 innings, seven not out, highest score 340, aggregate 2106, average 78.00, nine centuries. His aggregate was a record for batsmen under twenty-one for runs scored in Australia, and his average a record for batsmen under twenty-one who had played in more than 20 innings.

* New South Wales v. Queensland, January 1930, Sydney: His score of 452 was the highest ever made in a first-class match and is still the highest ever made in a first-class match in Australia. He was the youngest player ever to make 400, and he achieved it in the record time of six hours seventeen minutes.

Summaries

1927–28	Matches	Innings	NO	HS	Runs	Average	Centuries
First-class	5	10	1	134	416	46.22	2
1928–29							
All First-class	13	24	6	340	1690	93.88	7
Test matches	4	8	1	123	468	66.85	2
Matches v M.C.C.	7	13	3	132	778	77.80	3
Sheffield Shield	5	9	3	340	893	148.83	4
Matches for NSW	7	12	4	340	1127	140.87	5
1929–30							
All First-class	11	16	2	452	1586	113.28	5
Matches v M.C.C.	1	1	0	157	157	—	1
Sheffield Shield	6	10	2	452	894	111.75	1
Matches for NSW	7	11	2	452	1051	116.77	2

THE WORLD OF DON BRADMAN

Donald George Bradman was born into a world in which most things were harder, stronger, more natural and more enduring than those of today. Solid long-wearing sturdiness was the admired characteristic of the age, in people as well as their possessions. The ideal man was brave, honest, honourable and self-controlled. The ideal woman was virtuous, gentle, submissive and patient. The manners and morals of Australians had settled into the seemingly eternal pattern of Victorian England, composed of duty, honour, responsibility and patriotism. Of course there were flaws in the pattern and exceptions to the ideals, but they should not be scoffed at from our less confident age. They were supportive and reliable, and they held the British Empire together during the appalling trials of the first world war.

The world was in its usual condition of constant change, from the suffragette movement to the rise of the trade unions, and it was a time of huge technological advances, including aviation and radio. But a time-traveller from the 1980s would instantly notice the size, weight and solidity of almost everything in common use. They were made from heavy 'natural' materials because there was nothing else. The words 'synthetic' and 'plastic' were used only by scientists. The synthetic resins were only just

being manufactured by Dr Baekeland, in the United States, and the first plastics, bakelite and ebonite, would not come into general use until the 1920s. Artificial fibres, such as rayon, did not become popular until the 1930s. Nylon was not marketed until 1940.

Clothes were made of wool, cotton, linen or silk. Many men wore the same woollen suits summer and winter, often rather smelly because drycleaning was a mere novelty. Female garments covered the body from neck to ankle.

The phrase 'Made in England' was a guarantee of value for money and massive endurance, like the battleships of the Royal Navy that protected the peace of the world. 'Made in Japan' appeared only on such trifles as cheap tin toys. The power, trade and influence of Britain dominated the world, and most British subjects — including Australians — had a calm confidence in the glory and virtue of the Empire.

It was a world carried on the broad backs of draught horses. The sight of horses pulling ploughs and other implements was commonplace. In the cities, the dominant sound was the staccato of steel-

Piccadilly Circus, as Don Bradman first saw it in 1930, was then regarded as the hub of the British Empire

shod hooves and the grinding of steel-clad tyres, although the early motor vehicles wove their way among the horse-drawn traffic. They were almost as noisy. Their unsilenced engines hammered explosively, and emitted the stink of burning castor oil then used as a lubricant.

Only the wealthier folk owned private motorcars, solidly built from timber and leather, brass and copper, rubber and steel. Bicycles were the favourite form of private transport, even with shearers and other outback workers. Many people had no transport but their feet, and walked long distances to work, school or recreation.

A forty-eight-hour working week was standard, and plenty of people such as seamen, farmhands and domestic servants worked much longer hours. A great many women worked as domestic servants for minuscule wages, and boys received only a meagre wage during four-year apprenticeships. Unskilled labourers were lucky to receive thirty shillings a week (three dollars), including overtime. These long working hours were very productive. Houses and other buildings went up with remarkable speed. There were three postal deliveries a day in the cities, and the post office prided itself on the speed and infallibility of its services.

The coastal cities had close links with overseas nations and a continuous shuttle service of great overseas liners plied between them and Europe, America, Asia and Africa. London was only a month or so away through the Suez Canal, and the glamorous ships brought a constant flow of new settlers, new products, and new ideas. City folk prided themselves on keeping up with the times,

and in Sydney and Melbourne there was a feeling of urgent progress into the future.

In the country, life was slower, harder and more contemplative, and was still closely attached to the colonial past. When Don Bradman was a boy, there were plenty of elderly men who could still recall the days of gold-digging and bushranging.

Life was bound up with animals and the soil. Farmers spent at least two hours a day in harnessing and tending their horses, and many country children had to milk the cows before and after school. The qualities and traditions of the past, the mateship and mutual support of the pioneering days, provided a solid basis for society. People travelled long distances to attend church services, not only for spiritual refreshment but also to meet their neighbours.

Country amusements were simple and satisfying: reading, 'home-made' music, tennis and cricket in summer and football in winter. Every community that could muster a dozen able-bodied males had a cricket team and would take on all comers. In the little coastal townships they played against the crews of visiting ships.

Life was hard for countrymen and equally hard for women. Housekeeping was a continuous round of manual labour. Women did the washing by hand, cooked on wood-burning stoves, filled and cleaned the kerosene lamps that lit the rooms with a soft glow — and made them even hotter in summer — made many of their own clothes, swept, dusted, and scrubbed, separated the milk and churned the butter, looked after the hens and brought up the babies.

Back leg glance

Forward defence

Back defence

Childhood was often brief for a country boy or girl. A boy was expected to help with farm or household chores as soon as he was big enough to chop firewood, lead a horse or milk a cow. Girls learnt housekeeping and babycare by helping their mothers. By the time a country child reached adolescence, he or she was a responsible member of the family.

Luxuries were rare. Refrigeration was unknown and a country family was lucky if ice was available. A Coolgardie safe, to keep food reasonably cool, was a proud acquisition. Cool water came from the canvas waterbag under the verandah. The modern child's perpetual swilling of soft drinks lay half-a-century in the future, and instant coffee was unheard of. Tea, milk and water were the usual drinks, with an infrequent bottle of warmish lemonade as a treat. Fathers might drink beer, at threepence a pot, or mothers sip sherry on special occasions. The family fare was based on simple ingredients from the farm, garden or general store. The supermarket cornucopia lay in the future.

The first world war had the effect of dividing society into three distinct sections. One was the pre-war generation: men and women born as long ago as the goldrushes, and brought up in the 'horse and buggy' era with all its simple virtues and values. Another comprised men who had survived the horrors of Gallipoli and the Western Front, and seen all the old values torn apart in the savagery of that war. And the third consisted of young men and women growing into maturity during the 1920s, believing they would build a new world upon the ruins of the old.

It was a generation which used 'Victorian' as an epithet meaning everything dreary, cumbersome and slow. The favourite words were 'modern' and the strange new one 'sophisticated'. The sound of hoofbeats slowly faded into the past and the chugging of automobiles symbolised the beginning of the Jazz Age.

Young women bobbed or shingled their hair, discarded several layers of underclothing, and hiked their skirts above their knees. Young men serenaded them on ukuleles, wore 'Oxford bags' with twenty-four-inch cuffs, and yearned for two-seater autos. The boyish Prince of Wales, in his golf cap and Shetland jumper, epitomised the new wave of youth.

The young people jazzed their way into the future confident that everything was going to change for the better. The start of construction of the Sydney Harbour Bridge, in 1923, seemed to characterise all the great deeds that the new generation could perform. It was a time to turn away from the Old World and create a new society which lay somewhere between the solidity of Britain and the freewheeling glamour of America.

And yet a great deal of the past still remained. A 'flapper' might plaster herself with cosmetics and display silk-stockinged knees, but if she 'fell' then the consequences were as disastrous as they had been before 1914. 'Single parents' were unheard of, abortion was both a sin and a crime, and a divorced woman was likely to find her erstwhile friends turning aside.

Most young people still treated their elders with respect. They would not have dared to address

quare cut off back foot

Square cut off front foot

Late cut

them by their first names. A man did not really graduate into life until he was about thirty. Until then he was regarded as somewhat flighty and inconsequential unless he had proved himself otherwise. Society still retained a structure of formality, in which the correct dress for each occasion was of supreme importance. Clerical workers wore three-piece suits, hats, and collars and ties. There was no such thing as 'casual gear' apart from the correct garb for sports, weekends or the beach. A girl who appeared on the beach in a swimming costume without a skirt would have been warned off by the beach inspectors. The rigidities of the past had been shaken but not destroyed.

For the average person, life was markedly less secure than it is today. There was no health insurance and only a rudimentary type of unemployment relief. Once a man found a job he tended to stick to it for life, and the need to secure his position obliged him to behave circumspectly towards his seniors. Most of the jazzy youngsters and their girls soon settled snugly into the suburban groove.

Medicine, compared with that of the 1980s, was still in its infancy. Many thousands died during the influenza epidemic of 1919. There were no miracle drugs, no psychiatrists, no physiotherapists. Children and adults died of diseases which a medical student rarely even sees nowadays: typhoid, diphtheria, tuberculosis, scarlet fever, poliomyelitis. A heart attack usually crippled a man for life, because there was no such thing as a by-pass operation.

Don Bradman entered the life of the 1920s like a man stepping out of one world into another: out of the country background which still retained many of the traditions and ethics of the past, into the city life in which 'sophistication' was the new in-word. His appearance in first-class cricket, at a time when the media were avid for fresh examples of youth sweeping all before it, was exactly in tune with the times. The solid qualities bred into him by his country upbringing, the modesty and the unassuming acceptance of a fame which came almost overnight, perhaps saved him from the kind of sophistication which in fact means 'to be rendered worthless by adulteration'.

5

IMPACT ON ENGLAND

Journalists used the inclusion of Don Bradman in the touring team as a springboard for another series of stories about the 'Bowral colt', as they still insisted on calling the twenty-one-year-old batsman who had proved he was anything but a 'colt'. Some stories were inaccurate, some questionable, others ridiculous. One stated: 'Don Bradman when he first came to Sydney might have stepped out of one of Steele Rudd's books. Braces were essential to his cricket uniform, and even in his cricket he rested between overs in the bucolic method of sitting on the blade of the bat whilst holding the handle between his knees.'

Bradman himself was too busy to correct such journalistic fantasies. His instructions from the Board of Control for International Cricket, dated 31 January 1930, gave him a list of tasks to perform before the tour began at Melbourne on 7 March, and he was also committed to various first-grade and second-class matches. Two of the latter were as a member of a team formed by Bill Tidmarsh, a noted cricket supporter, to play Narooma and Bega on the south coast of New South Wales. He scored 107 not out and 127 not out in these contests with country teams.

He had to buy extra luggage for his tour, and have it painted with identification stripes in the Australian colours of green and gold; obtain his passport (from the Customs Department in those days) with visas for Italy, Switzerland and France, and an income tax clearance certificate; have himself measured for the Australian XI blazer and cap at Harding's Mercery in Hunter Street; have himself medically examined by Dr Minnett of Manly; assemble his own clothing and other essentials for the lengthy tour — including the dinner suit which every team member had to own — and visit William Hollins and Co., of York Street, to be measured for Viyella cricket flannels, shirts and pyjamas. The Viyella Company of England was presenting each team member with a complete outfit, to be delivered when the team arrived in London.

The team manager and treasurer were William Kelly and Thomas Howard respectively, both of them with a background in first-class cricket and lengthy experience in cricket administration. The rendezvous for the travellers was the Hotel Alexander in Melbourne, where they would lunch before boarding the Bass Strait steamer *Nirana* for Launceston. They were to spend eight days in Tasmania and play two three-day matches, return to Melbourne from Hobart in the Orient

Before the second world war, the State governments had a pleasant practice of issuing 'credentials' to respected citizens to smooth their way when travelling overseas. Don Bradman and the other members of the Australian Test team received these documents of accreditation in 1930

liner *Orford*, attend a Lord Mayor's reception, and then board the train for Perth.

They were to play Western Australia in Perth on 21–24 March, and immediately this match concluded they would board the *Orford* again for the voyage to Europe, with a one-day match at Colombo on the way. This tightly-scheduled opening to the tour was an introduction to a vigorous series of fixtures in England and Scotland. Between 30 April and 27 September, when they were to return to Australia aboard the *Oronsay*, they would play 109 days of cricket in five Tests and twenty-nine other first-class matches, plus 'other matches to be arranged at the discretion of the Executive Committee'. In the event, the committee did not squeeze any more games into the schedule.

In the last week of February, Don Bradman received his first touring contract: an eleven-page document which defined all the duties and responsibilities of the Australian Board of Control, the manager, treasurer, and players, with regard to the forthcoming tour. The players 'jointly and severally' covenanted that they would not 'commit any act or be guilty of any conduct which renders him or them incapable of playing in any of the aforesaid matches or renders him or them unfit to remain a member or members of the team and that they will at all times obey the directions of the Manager and/or the Executive Committee'.

The thirty-six clauses included one which forbade the players to be accompanied by any relations, or to have their wives and children in England during the tour. Another, clause 11, forbade them to 'accept employment as a newspaper correspondent or to do any work for or in connection with any newspaper or any Broadcasting'. Clause 11 was to get Don Bradman into trouble after the tour.

Bill Kelly was to receive £650 for the tour; Tom Howard and the players £600 apiece. The board paid them £50 apiece to equip themselves before the departure, £400 during the tour 'but not more than £80 per calendar month', and £150 on return to Australia 'provided that the last mentioned payment to players shall be dependent upon a satisfactory report being made as to the respective players by the Manager'. If a report was unsatisfactory the board could withhold all or a part of this final payment, 'and its decision shall be final as the Players doth hereby agree'. Apart from the principal payment, each player received thirty shillings a week for incidental expenses. The board paid all costs of travel and accommodation.

The remuneration of £600 was a substantial payment in that period when a family man thought himself quite comfortably off on £5 a week. In that Depression year of 1930 it would have represented a fortune to many people, and for young men like Bradman, McCabe and a'Beckett it was a magnificent sum. For Test matches in Australia they had received £30 a game, plus expenses, which is a sharp contrast to the amounts paid to players nowadays. Modern players also have the chance to participate in large incentive payments and, after a qualifying number of matches, in a provident fund. But a Test tour was a massive commercial operation for that period. The organisers could expect to recoup many thousands of pounds in gate money and various subsidiary rights, and the players were entitled to a fair compensation.

As usual, various self-appointed experts had their say about the composition of the Australian team. Many deplored the omission of

Bill Kelly, manager of the team, stands on the wet decks of the *Orford* as the Australians prepare to disembark in Naples for the overland journey to England. Stan McCabe stands next to him and Don Bradman looks over their shoulders

Jack Ryder; others said that the New South Wales wicket-keeper Davidson should have been sent instead of Walker of South Australia. Some shook their heads at the inclusion of so many young men, to act as Australia's giantkillers against veterans like Hobbs, Sutcliffe, Hendren, Hammond and Woolley. There were even those who growled that young Bradman was in for some nasty shocks. Look how he played on a sticky wicket at Brisbane, they said. He was all right in Australia, but those rainsoaked wickets of the English counties would soon show him up. And fancy including *eight* players who had never been overseas before!

But the die was cast, the farewells were said, and the fifteen Australians with the manager and treasurer boarded the *Nirana* for Tasmania. For a number of them, including Bradman, it was their first experience of such an unstable mode of travel, and it did not suit his metabolism at all. He says nowadays 'I never became used to sea travel. If the sea was rough on the last day of a voyage, I could be just as seasick as I was on the first.'

The pitching and rolling of the *Nirana* may account for his poor showing in the first match against Tasmania, at Launceston on 8–11 March. He went in at 163 for three on the second morning, made 20 runs, and was dismissed lbw after twenty-four minutes at the wicket.

The visitors won by ten wickets and drove south to Hobart, where Tasmanians were able to see the true potential of the much-vaunted mainlander. It was the first match in which he batted in partnership with Ponsford, and after eighty minutes' batting he was 70 not out at the close of the first day's play. On the following morning he batted for 152 minutes and brought his aggregate for the first-class season up to 1559, at an average of 119.9. He needed only 132 runs to break his previous season's Australian record of 1690, and everyone wondered whether the match in Perth would give him the opportunity to do so before leaving Australia. But it was not to be. He had only five minutes batting before bad light closed the first day's play, after he had gone in at 52 for one, and on the following morning Dick Bryant caught him at cover, off Evans, when he had made 27 runs.

The visitors won the match and piled into the cars which took them to Fremantle and the *Orford*. A few days at sea carried them across to Ceylon (now Sri Lanka) and their match against Colombo, which they do not seem to have taken very seriously. Arthur Mailey, travelling with the Australians as reporter for the Sydney *Sun*, cabled home that 'A record crowd of 10,000 people saw the Australian Eleven play a local team in intense heat today, and compile the very modest score of 213.

'The heat was so great that the Australians appeared in cork helmets. An Indian potentate said to the writer:

'"These fellows are making the sport look dam' silly. Who are they?"'

'Ninety per cent of the spectators were natives, who chanted songs. The score of 213 was disappointing, Ponsford making 62, Woodfull 52, Bradman 40, McCabe 20. The rest collapsed . . . a native, Kellard, took six wickets for 65. He is a splendid off-break bowler.'

'Kellard' was actually a local player named Ed Kelaart, who would not have been pleased at being called a 'native'.

Bradman had his first glimpse of Europe when the team left the

Orford in Naples, to make the fast overland trip across the continent instead of spending another week or so at sea. The 'boy from Bowral' delighted in the kaleidoscope of scenery and the stopover in Paris, where Kelly and Woodfull placed a wreath on the tomb of France's Unknown Warrior of the first world war.

The cross-Channel steamer to Dover landed them to a civic reception by the mayor and the first of a horde of autograph hunters; then at last they were in London to face a battery of newspaper and newsreel cameras in company with the English captain, the genial and debonair Percy Chapman, and such English cricketing tycoons as Lord Plumer and Lord Harris.

Soon after the arrival in London, a literary agent named David Cromb, of the firm of Cotterill & Cromb, approached Don Bradman with the suggestion that he should write a book. He said that the name of the young batsman was already so well known in England that it should not be difficult to find a publisher, especially if he gave a convincing performance during the 1930 tour. Mindful of Clause 11 in his contract, Bradman told Cromb that he could not write anything about the tour while it was going on, but agreed to start on the book with the idea that it should be published after his return to Australia. From

The Worcester cricket ground, with spectators well rugged-up against the cold winds and rain which swept the ground during Bradman's first appearance there. Bradman scored a double century in his first innings of his English tour — and repeated this achievement in 1934 and 1938, again playing against Worcestershire on the Worcester ground. In 1948 he scored a century in the opening match against Worcestershire

then onward he spent some of his spare time in writing reminiscences of his cricketing years before arriving in England.

On 30 April, he had his first experience of an English cricket ground and of English cricketing weather. The ground, at Worcester, was beautiful, in a setting of great elms and with the peal of Worcester Cathedral chimes marking the hours by playing the opening bars from such tunes as 'Home Sweet Home' and 'The Last Rose of Summer'. The weather would have been a fine winter day in Australia, with the sun appearing between racing clouds and a crisp cold wind blowing across the field. The Australians fielded in sweaters, and the bowlers huddled into them between overs.

Worcestershire batted first, and the English newspapers remarked that their modest score of 131 could hardly be ascribed to the prowess of the Australian bowlers. 'Steady rather than deadly' the *Daily Telegraph* commented, while the London *Times* sportswriter pontificated: 'I could not help thinking on Thursday that there is something lacking in the Australian out-cricket. It is absurd to imagine the Australian team of 1921, or even of 1926, spending over an hour and a half putting to death five Worcestershire men, and allowing Walters and Root to add 84 runs, as if they were doing no more than was expected.'

At last it was Bradman's time to play his first innings on an English wicket. The conditions could hardly have been more different from the concrete and matting wickets of his Bowral youth or the sweet-playing turf of the Sydney Cricket Ground. The lush, cushiony Worcester turf was dotted with worm casts, the deposits excreted by worms burrowing in the fertile soil; and even though the roller had broken these down, they left small slippery patches. The cool misty air and prevailing breeze favoured the bowlers, and caused unexpected variations in the flight of the ball.

The spectators, including the English selectors, watched intently as the young Australian paced deliberately out to the wicket, and played himself in under these unusual conditions. They soon realised he was calculating exactly how each ball would behave, and treating it accordingly. He judged every delivery with computer-like accuracy, and reacted with a stroke which seemed almost inevitable in its precision.

In partnership with Woodfull, he followed this technique for the first 115 minutes and completed his first century on English soil. Woodfull also scored a century, his second for a first match in England. After that, both batsmen opened their shoulders and flogged the English bowling all over the ground.

Woodfull 'threw his wicket away' with a careless stroke after he had reached 133, but 'the run-scoring machine' continued with his remorseless rhythm. His Sykes bat smacked each ball as though by some magical co-ordination, and while the cathedral bells chimed their serene punctuation he made a spectacular accumulation of runs. Men in the stands would later boast that they had seen young Bradman knock up his first double century on an English wicket.

During his 280 minutes at the crease they saw him total 236 before he skied a full-toss halfway down the pitch, and a fieldsman ran in and caught him. As he walked back to the pavilion, the English crowd cheered as ardently as though they had been his countrymen applauding 'Our Don' on the Sydney Cricket Ground.

Bradman's performance completely confounded his critics. On his

Don Bradman (left) with William Sykes of Wm. Sykes Ltd. Sykes was then one of the world's leading manufacturers of cricket bats. Bradman became very friendly with him and his wife during Australian tours of England. The 'Don Bradman Bat', first manufactured by Sykes, is still on the market, but the firm of Wm. Sykes Ltd was absorbed by another maker of sportsgoods

very first appearance on an English wicket he had set yet another series of records.

His 236 runs was the highest score ever made by an Australian batsman in his first match in England; the best by any batsman making his debut in a tour of any other country; and the highest score made by a visiting batsman in his first innings of a tour of England. These three records were to be the first of a long series marked up during his tour.

The Australians administered a resounding defeat to Worcestershire by an innings and 165 runs, and then hastened to catch the 3 p.m. train to Leicester.

Leicester gave them a gloomy welcome and a wicket much more difficult than Worcester's. The cold drizzle of an English spring drifted across the ground and the grass had not recovered from winter. Sawdust was spread to give the bowlers and batsmen a footing on the greasy soil, which made the ball so slippery that it was hard to handle. Nevertheless Grimmett showed his form by taking seven wickets for 46, while Walker, whose inclusion in the team had been criticised in Australia, stumped three of the Leicestershire men.

Bradman had forty minutes' batting at the end of the first day but was only nine not out at close of play. Next morning he faced very accurate bowling from Geary, Astill and others, and played a defensive game; but after lunch he opened out. He had compiled 185 not out when rain stopped play at 5.30 p.m.

The rain set in steadily on the following day and the match closed with a draw. The English sportswriters revised their opinions of Australian bowling and wrote generously about Bradman. The *Daily Chronicle* said: 'For fluency of stroke play Bradman is perfection, the beauty being that he uses his bat as a weapon of offence', and the *Morning Post* wrote: 'It is joyous to see Australia's second Trumper in his varying phases — particularly his favourite chop stroke.'

Invitations flowed in to Bill Kelly for the entertainment of the Australians, and some of them were the guests of the Leicestershire Aero Club at Desford airfield. But many people still regarded aircraft as chancy pieces of machinery, and the Australian Board of Control had specifically forbidden any of the players to fly anywhere during the tour. They had the frustrating experience of watching the flying without being able to leave the ground.

Woodfull rested Bradman during the Essex match, on 7–9 May. After that the team's next stop was at Sheffield, the steel town in the heart of what is appropriately known as the Black Country, to combat the dour and rugged Yorkshire team. The Bramall Lane ground had been used for football during the winter and was still showing the effects, with much of the outfields as bare — though not as dry — as an Australian country ground. The weather was warmer, but the sun shone only fitfully between clouds and industrial smog. Bramall Lane ground was almost surrounded by heavy industries, and the story ran that workers would tell each other 'The Aussies are batting, boys: stoke up the furnaces!'

The match opened on Saturday 10 May, with Yorkshire batting first. Their team included such Test players as Herbert Sutcliffe, Percy Holmes, Maurice Leyland and Wilfred Rhodes, and the spectators settled down to see them 'give the Aussies some stick'. They were appalled when the Yorkshire stars fell like ninepins before the deadly

Bradman the music-lover recorded that one of the most memorable experiences of his 1930 tour was a visit to the Royal Albert Hall, London, with others of the team, to hear the Australian singer Harold Williams in the title-role of 'Hiawatha'. In this photograph, Williams is seated between Bradman (left) and Grimmett. Other tour members include Vic Richardson, seated behind Bradman

During the 1930 tour, Don Bradman visited the factory of Wm. Sykes Ltd of Horbury, Yorkshire, and saw 'Don Bradman Bats' being made from 'the finest-grade close bark willow', with handles of Sarawak cane and a treble rubber shock-absorbing spring. He spent most of the visit signing a number of the bats to be sold under his name

combination of Grimmett and Walker. Grimmett took all ten wickets and dismissed Yorkshire for 155.

Bradman went in on the first evening, in bad light and increasing rain, so that he had only thirty-eight minutes of play. He made 24 not out, and continued his innings when the rain stopped early on the Monday afternoon. The wicket was damp and causing problems, and he faced a fierce combination of Yorkshire bowlers all bent on revenge. But he played them with supreme confidence and timing and made 50 in seventy minutes, until his first false stroke returned a ball from George Macaulay into the bowler's hands. In partnership with Woodfull, he made 78 out of 107 and brought his total for the tour so far up to 499.

The rain which had plagued the tour closed the match on the third day, for another draw. The Australians travelled on to Liverpool for their match against Lancashire on the Aigburth Cricket Ground. Grimmett's googlies hypnotised the Lancashire men and he was largely responsible for dismissing the north country team for 176; but when the Australians went in to bat they did not, at first, fare very much better. They faced a 'renegade' countryman in the form of 'Ted' McDonald from Tasmania, who had played Shield cricket for Victoria from 1918 and Test cricket for his country from 1920, but joined Lancashire in 1924. His fast bowling dismissed five Australians for 63 — including Don Bradman. He knocked Bradman's leg stump out of the ground after he had been in for nineteen minutes with a score of nine runs.

When the visitors began their second innings, on 16 May, they had to make 227 in 160 minutes if they were to win the game, but did not make a serious attempt to do so. English newspapers scoffed that the Australians were 'coddling themselves' in preparation for the Tests, and *The Times* huffed: 'For all the purpose they served the players might as well have spent three days at the nets.'

As soon as the Liverpool match ended the Australians were southward bound for London, to take on the M.C.C. at Lord's. The Marylebone Cricket Club had assembled a powerful side for the first 1930 confrontation with the Australians on the historic cricket ground. Their team included such crack bowlers as the fiery 'Gubby' Allen, the fast-mediums Allom and Alex Kennedy, the slow leg-spinner Ian Peebles, and the googly bowler Greville Stevens. They gave the visitors a hard time on the fastest wicket they had yet experienced in England, in bright sunshine before a crowd of 30 000.

An airship, possibly the ill-fated R101, sailed over Lord's Cricket Ground during Don Bradman's first appearance there in 1930

Jackson opened for Australia and was caught for a duck. Bradman followed him, in partnership with Woodfull, but played himself in very carefully. He scored slowly, taking eighty-five minutes to reach 50. After 110 minutes and 66 runs he seemed to be settling down when he pulled an attempted cover drive off Allom onto his stumps. He and Woodfull added 119 for the second wicket and it was about the best partnership in the first innings, which concluded with Australia out for 285.

Late on the second day, Bradman began his second innings at 14 for one and spent a very unhappy twenty minutes at the crease. The huge crowd which had heard so much about Don Bradman began to feel that England had not so much to fear from him after all. His first innings could be described as no better than acceptable, and now the bowlers appeared to baffle him. After his first run, he was very nearly caught in the slips off a ball from Allen. When he had made four cautious runs, Stevens trapped him lbw.

The match ended in another draw, but English cricket lovers took heart. Bradman's performance in his first English innings, the swift victory over Worcestershire, and Grimmett's massacre of Yorkshire had made them feel apprehension for the Ashes. After the M.C.C. match, however, they began to feel the Australians were not so frightening after all. The *Daily Telegraph* commented: 'They are capable, attractive players, but the idea which was getting abroad that England's task in the first Test is a desperate one no longer exists.'

The Times belaboured the Australians because Woodfull had taken them off the field after the seventh wicket fell, and many spectators thought they had declared. But they were only going into the pavilion to 'take tea', and *The Times* thundered: 'The tradition at Lord's says that the game shall always be played seriously, and the public have the right to demand they shall not be fobbed off with a farce . . . the tea-addicts put up a poor show after a bout of self-indulgence. The batsmen did not achieve anything stylish, and even the bowlers might be accused of dilatoriness.'

Unperturbed by such Blimpish comments, the Australians took the train for Chesterfield where they were to play Derbyshire on 21–23 May. Bradman's performance in this game made Englishmen feel that his early brilliance might have faded under the stress of the tour. The Australian bowlers were the stars of the match, which opened with Derbyshire batting in an 'icy blast' on one of the coldest days of that cold wet season. Percy Hornibrook's left-arm bowling accounted for six of the Derbyshire men, Tim Wall took three more, and Bradman dismissed Storer lbw. Hornibrook told Arthur Mailey he was 'disgusted with himself' for claiming only six wickets, and believed he would have taken all ten if the cold weather had not stiffened his fingers. Derbyshire's first innings score was 215.

When Derbyshire attacked the Australian batsmen, Ponsford and Jackson 'rattled up the runs in fine style' until Jackson was dismissed for 63. Bradman joined Ponsford at 127 for one, but he soon received two painful blows from the ball. As he wrote later, these cricketing wounds seemed to hurt much more in the cold English weather than in Australia. Perhaps they accounted for a lack of his usual high confidence, which made the spectators think that he batted more slowly and uncertainly than usual. In a 'patchy' exhibition of batting he knocked up 44 in eighty-five minutes before he was caught at the wicket.

Australia won by ten wickets, but the *Evening News* reported: 'Australia did not show to advantage in strategy in this game, nor was the batting, in most cases, impressive.'

The whole picture changed when the visitors returned to London, to meet Surrey on the Oval on 24 May. On yet another cold, damp and gloomy day, with the wicket soft but easy, Woodfull won the toss and sent Australia in to bat. The innings began badly when Archie Jackson was caught at the wicket for the third time in three matches, after he had 'waved a faltering bat at a rising off ball and the catch went straight to Brooks'. Bradman took his place, in partnership with Woodfull, and for a moment it seemed he would suffer the same fate.

He appeared to have some difficulty in playing Allom, until he settled down and played carefully until the lunch interval. After that he began to open out, and from then until 6.25 p.m., when rain stopped play, he gave a dazzling display of 'Bradmanesque' batsmanship. His best stroke was the cut, but he also scored many runs with forcing strokes on the leg side.

He took 145 minutes to reach his first century but after that he stepped up the pace and reached his double century in another eighty minutes. Woodfull was caught at first slip after their second wicket stand of 116, and Bradman played on in partnership with Richardson, Ponsford, McCabe and Fairfax. His performance developed into a characteristic Bradman combination of timing, footwork, accuracy and confidence: the despair of bowlers and the delight even of an English crowd.

Ironically, the captain of the Surrey side was Percy Fender, who had written derogatory and sarcastic criticism of Bradman after the 1928–29 Test season. He had plenty of time to reflect on his words as Bradman, on a rain affected pitch, belted Fender and his bowling colleagues to all parts of the Oval in a display that was a revelation to English spectators. Bradman thought it was one of the best innings of his career and did not conceal his delight in getting even with one of his detractors.

Don Bradman's famous innings of 334, scored against England on the Headingley Cricket Ground, Leeds, in July 1930, was played with this bat

THE DON BRADMAN BAT

The firm of Wm. Sykes Ltd, of Horbury (Yorkshire) and London, was a leading manufacturer of cricket equipment when Don Bradman first made his name as a batsman. They negotiated with him for the use of his name on their bats, and after his record-breaking performances in the 1929–30 season they used a photograph of his bat in their advertisements.

Part of the advertising copy read:

'For years past the majority of Test Match players on both sides have used Sykes' bats. Wm. Sykes Ltd., of Horbury, Yorks, and London, are makers of the world-famous "Roy Kilner," "Maurice Leyland," and the new "Don Bradman" autograph bats. The latter was named in honour of Australia's super batsman who, in 1928, showed his preference for Sykes-made bats. In January,

1930, this prolific run-getter, using a 4-crown test quality "Don Bradman" bat, made the world's highest score in first class cricket, 452 not out.

'"Don Bradman" bats are made from the finest grade close bark willow, cut from selected trees, matured in our scientifically built seasoning sheds. Each blade expertly hand-hammered and face-compressed. The handles are constructed by experienced craftsmen from finest Sarawak cane, including Sykes' well-known treble rubber shock-absorbing spring.

'Each bat packed for export is personally selected by one of our principals.'

The firm of Wm. Sykes Ltd was taken over by another manufacturer a good many years ago, but 'Don Bradman Bats' are still manufactured and still on the market.

At 207 he made a hard hook off Allom and might have been caught at short leg, but the fielder missed the chance and Bradman played vigorously on until stumps were drawn at 252. The crowd surged onto the ground as he returned to the pavilion and the police had difficulty in forcing a way through for him. Even after he had changed, a mob of men and boys joined him on the walk to the Underground station and some even sat with him on the trip to St Pancras where his hotel was situated.

It had been yet another record-breaking day: the highest score for any touring team against Surrey, or at the Oval. The *Observer* wrote: 'Bradman's innings was a marvellous display of clever, stylish, and almost faultless batting. The most ardent Surrey partisan could not grudge any of his runs. Recollection of the innings will always be happy to those privileged to witness it.'

Rain prevented Surrey from batting, the match was drawn, and the Australians had a brief break before travelling to Oxford to play the University on the Christ Church ground. Bradman had scored 922 runs for the season and spectators hoped to see him complete his 1000 during the game, but he made only 32 in sixty minutes before he was dismissed.

He was disappointed by this failure to notch up the 1000 at Oxford, but he hoped to succeed when the visitors played Hampshire at Southampton. The team drove down there from Oxford through the beautiful English countryside, including the New Forest, with Bradman enthralled by everything he saw. Every minute of the tour, since they left Australia, had been a wonderful new experience for him, and his mind was filled with pictures of the journey across Europe, the old towns of England, and such spectacles as the finals of the Inter-Collegiate Eights seen from the towpath at Oxford.

Southampton treated the visitors to another dull damp day, and they began to wonder whether they would ever see the sun shine over England. The game opened on Saturday 31 May. Lord Tennyson, captain of Hampshire, won the toss, and when the massive figure of George Brown opened the batting by flogging the Australian bowling all over the ground young Bradman wondered whether he would even have an opportunity to bat.

When Brown reached 56, he drove a ball towards Bradman between mid-off and extra cover. Immediately the stroke was made, Bradman was off and running towards the ball. He stopped it with his foot but over-ran it, and when Brown saw this he called for another run. But Bradman snatched up the ball, and in what he later described as 'the greatest fluke of his career' he threw it with deadly accuracy. He was almost broadside-on to the wickets but he knocked the middle stump out of the ground and ran Brown out.

After that, Hampshire soon collapsed. Grimmett took seven wickets for 56 and the county side totalled only 151. Woodfull was as keen for Bradman to make his 1000 runs as the young batsman was, and sent him in to open the batting with Archie Jackson. He had never been more anxious to make runs than he was on that day in Southampton. It was the last day of May, and this was his final opportunity to become the first touring batsman to total 1000 runs before the end of May.

He was surprised when Jackson was dismissed, in the first over, for a duck, to be replaced by Ponsford. Bradman had to make 46 runs

Clarrie Grimmett, a New Zealander who settled in Australia and played for Victoria and South Australia, was regarded by Bradman as the best slow leg spinner cricket has ever produced. In Tests he took 216 wickets and in first-class cricket 1424, including 10 for 37 v. Yorkshire in 1930

before the close of play to complete his 1000, and he accumulated them cautiously until he had scored 28 by the tea interval. As the players walked off the ground the rain-charged clouds which had been piling up during the afternoon began to deluge the pitch, and continued to do so without any sign of a break.

Don Bradman sat in the pavilion as the clock ticked steadily towards 6.30, scissoring away his chances of making the paltry 18 runs he still required. Just as he had given up hope, the rain stopped and the players hurried onto the sodden ground.

He made seven more runs before the rain began again, 'so heavily that I could not have complained if umpires and players had rushed pell-mell to the pavilion'. But Lord Tennyson, a true sportsman of the old school, did not wish to deprive the young Australian of his opportunity. He decided on one more over, and Bradman saw him say something to Newman, the bowler. The result was a comparatively easy full toss, and Bradman slogged it to the boundary. With only three to get, Bradman squinted at the bowler through the increasing rain and saw him run up but slip on the wet turf. The ball went clean over Bradman's head.

Newman picked himself up, accepted the slippery ball, faced Bradman again, and sent down a 'long hop' which Bradman sent flying to the boundary. It was the signal for all the rain-soaked cricketers to bolt for the pavilion.

Arthur Mailey wrote for the *Sun*: 'Some consider that the two balls Newman threw up, including the full toss, to deliberately allow Bradman to get the requisite runs owing to the downpour, somewhat marred the performance, but it was the only way possible.

'Lord Tennyson, the Hampshire captain, explained it . . . with a twinkle in his eye. ''The ball was so slippery the bowler couldn't grip it.'' Another Hampshire man said, ''We would have been annoyed if Newman hadn't done it.'' '

In the whole history of cricket only five Englishmen have scored 1000 runs before the end of May, and Bradman is the only Australian to have achieved this feat.

English Sunday newspapers gave generous acclaim to the new record, while the cricketers relaxed before continuing the game. Woodfull and Hornibrook tried their hands at trout-fishing, under the tutelage of two members of the M.C.C. committee. They caught nothing, but the owners of the trout-stream presented them with a parcel of fish for the Australians' breakfast. Others went to inspect the liner *Leviathan* in Southampton docks. In the afternoon a former Governor-General of Australia, Lord Forster, who had played for Hampshire in his day, entertained all the Australians. From his estate overlooking Southampton Water they could see Sir Thomas Lipton's yacht *Shamrock V* tuning up for another attempt on the America's Cup.

On the Monday, Bradman was able to notice a remarkable property of English wickets. Despite the heavy Saturday rain the Southampton wicket had dried out amazingly fast, although it was still somewhat damp and difficult. In Australia, a wicket similarly affected would have become sticky.

With the tension of that crucial opening behind him, he continued his innings and treated the spectators to 'a glorious display of hitting'.

The Hon. Lionel Hallam Tennyson, 3rd Baron Tennyson, was captain of Hampshire when Bradman played against that county at the end of May 1930 and became the first and only Australian to score 1000 runs in England by the end of May

In this action photograph taken during the 1930 tour, the great English wicket-keeper George Duckworth stands like Nemesis behind Don Bradman. But it is obvious that, on this occasion, Duckworth did not add Bradman to his total of 1150 dismissals in first-class cricket, of which 60 were in Test matches

On Don Bradman's first tour of England he became the first Australian ever to score 1000 runs before the end of May in England. This is the bat he used to accomplish this feat

He completed his century after 135 minutes, and in a sparkling partnership with Stan McCabe he brought Australia up to 200 in 145 minutes. He appeared to be set for another double century when he was caught after 191.

Two more matches lay ahead before the first Test of the season: Middlesex at Lord's, and Cambridge University at Cambridge: six days of cricket between 4–10 June.

Middlesex gave a dismal display of batting in their first innings, when Hornibrook and Grimmett knocked them out one after another for a total of 103. Their bowlers made up for it when they attacked the visiting batsmen. 'Gubby' Allen, Greville Stevens, Jack Hearne and Harry Lee gave the Australians a hard time. Allen dismissed Ponsford for five, McCabe for 31, Grimmett for 21, and Hornibrook for four. Kippax provided the bright spot of the innings, when he made his first century at Lord's before Allen dismissed him lbw. The wicket helped the bowlers and took a good deal of spin, but Bradman batted confidently for forty-five minutes and made 35 before Hearne dismissed him with a vicious spinner.

Australia ended their first innings with 270, and when the Middlesex men batted again they once more fell victims to Grimmett and Hornibrook, backed up by Fairfax and Hurwood. 'Patsy' Hendren was the only batsman to handle them with confidence, and his 138 accounted for much of the Middlesex score of 287.

Time was running out for the Australians and only seven men batted during the second innings. Middlesex brought up yet another of their dangerous bowlers, the medium-pace Nigel Haig, who sent Ponsford's middle stump flying after only ten runs. Bradman went in at 16 for one, and by the time he had made 18 in forty-five minutes he appeared to have settled down to unhurried run-making when he hit over a slow yorker from Stevens.

The Australians won by five wickets and entrained for Cambridge, to face the University side on the beautiful Fenner's Ground.

Cambridge batted first but did not stand up for long against the Australian bowling — including Bradman's. He dismissed three of the University men: two clean bowled, and one with a catch by Wall. He went in to bat after tea and scored 32 before he was caught in slips.

While Cambridge was batting he was much impressed by the graceful style of a bespectacled young theological student, Tom Killick. He wrote in *Don Bradman's Book* that Killick was 'surely a Test player in the making', and his instinct was correct. Killick did have a brief Test career before his premature death.

On the Sunday, the Australians enjoyed a rare experience. Viscount Downe, the son and nephew of M.C.C. Presidents and himself a potential President, had invited them to lunch at Hillinton Hall, King's Lynn, which bordered the Royal estate at Sandringham. After lunch, he was to introduce them to King George V and Queen Mary.

Most of them were surprised by the informality of the occasion. The King greeted Woodfull as an old acquaintance and chatted to him about Australia's chances in the Tests. The Royal couple made the visitors feel perfectly at home as they showed them around the estate, and were unperturbed by the constant clicking of cameras.

The Cambridge match continued on the Monday with a second innings for the University, and Bradman again showed unusual prowess as a bowler. He disposed of three of the batsmen and completed the best bowling analysis of his first-class career: 11-1-35-3 and 17-3-68-3.

Australia won by an innings and 134 runs, in a match which had been chiefly notable for a double century by Woodfull. So far, they had won or drawn every match of the tour. In a mood of cheerful confidence, they travelled to Bath for a couple of days' rest before they faced the challenge of the first Test.

Below: Cover of a brochure giving full details of the Australian touring team and their itinerary, distributed to fellow-passengers aboard the liner *Orford* en route to Europe in March–April 1930

BY SEA TO ENGLAND

AUSTRALIAN XI
ENGLISH TOUR
1930

With the compliments of the
ORIENT LINE

When Don Bradman made his first voyage to England, the passenger ships serving Australia had been in competition for about seventy years. The Peninsular and Orient Line had run regular services since 1859 and the Orient Line since 1871. Several other British and European companies, and Australia's own Commonwealth Government Line, operated 'liner' services at various periods.

Intense competition for passengers caused a building race in which each company tried to outdo its rivals by offering bigger, faster and more luxurious ships. Eventually this became a battle between the two giants, the P & O and Orient Lines, which ended when they amalgamated in 1965.

By that time, the day of the great ships had passed except for their holiday cruise services. They could not possibly compete with air travel.

They took twenty-eight days to cover a distance which a jumbo jet flies in as many hours. They consumed as much fuel in a day as a jetliner needs for the whole distance, and needed about one crew member for each two passengers.

But when Don Bradman climbed the gangway of the *Orford* in March 1930, the passenger liners were approaching the zenith of their glory. Each of them was a triumph of the marine architect's art, carrying up to 1000 passengers and crew in conditions ranging from very modest comfort for the crew members to extreme luxury for the first-class passengers.

The shipping companies prided themselves on the first-class public rooms aboard each ship: panelled in rare timbers, ornate with costly inlays and gilding, thickly carpeted, luxuriously furnished. The designers and decorators tried to make the passengers feel they were travelling in a palatial hotel.

Depending upon the ship and the class in which one travelled, from a six-berth cabin on a lower deck to a suite in the first class, return fares to England ranged from about £60 to around £200. Allowing for the devaluation of currency since those days, the fares compare with air fares to Britain nowadays, but passengers received very much more for their money. The shipping company fed them all the way, very well in second-class and sumptuously in first-class, and they enjoyed brief stopovers in such ports as Colombo, Port Said, Naples, Marseilles and Gibraltar.

Socially-inclined passengers could spend a good deal of money during the voyage, even though drinks and cigarettes were at duty-free prices. It was easy to spend a pound a day, and the shipping companies relied on bar profits to cover some of their overheads. Shore trips in the various ports, with visits to such places as the Mount Lavinia or Galle Face hotels in Colombo and purchases from Simon Arzt's store in Port Said, took even more out of the passenger's pocket.

The Orient Line had secured the contract to carry Test teams to and from England, on terms advantageous to the Australian Board of International Cricket Control because of the publicity value of the operation. Passengers planning a trip to England in a year when a Test series was to be played there would try to book on the Orient Liner carrying the team. Between 1930 and 1948, Don Bradman became familiar with several of the ships of the Orient Line.

The *Orford*, like all the other great liners, was constructed as a floating Grand Hotel. The service matched the magnificence of her public rooms. A host of stewards in crisply-starched white uniforms (and with an eye to the tips expected at the end of

The liner R.M.S. (Royal Mail Steamer) *Orford*, of 20 000 tons and steaming at better than 20 knots. The photograph of one of the first-class public rooms in the *Orford* shows how the marine architects and decorators of the 1920s strove to make the passenger accommodation of the great liners resemble that of a luxury hotel.

the voyage) attended to the passengers' every need. Cabin stewards, deck stewards, dining-room stewards, bar stewards, smokeroom stewards and bathroom stewards all strove for perfection under the eagle eyes of the purser and chief steward. The ship's master and her chief engineer, and their juniors, all displayed a placid joviality designed to keep the passengers calm and contented. Behind this façade, a complex organisation functioned as smoothly as the huge engines which kept the ship running to a rigorous schedule. Those were the days when most ships at sea flew the Red Ensign, and British seafarers prided themselves on their efficiency and expertise.

Don Bradman was impressed by the comfort of his cabin, the splendour of the public rooms, the spaciousness of the decks, and — when the sea was kind — the meals served in the first-class res-

taurant. They rivalled, if not surpassed, those of the finest Australian hotels of that period.

The atmosphere in first-class had some resemblance to that of a long party in a splendid English home. There was a certain rigid formality as to dress and behaviour: Flannels and blazers were acceptable dress for breakfast and luncheon, but evening dress was *de rigeur* for dinner. Public opinion discouraged such casual behaviour as wearing shorts in the restaurant or parading the decks in a swimsuit. There was an air of gaiety and relaxation within the bounds of convention.

The passengers made most of their own amusements, with the aid of stewards and crew-members whose duty was to keep them happy. The active young men of the Test teams enjoyed an almost continuous round of deck games: quoits, shuffleboard, deck tennis, swimming in the pool, and cricket matches against teams enlisted from the officers and crew. They played between nets with a rope ball and a bat smaller than standard size, watched by passengers who would later boast of this opportunity to see the Test cricketers at close quarters.

Many ships had small orchestras which played for dancing in the evening or accompanied impromptu concerts arranged by the passengers. When there was nobody else around, Don Bradman enjoyed the use of the piano in the music-room.

On the voyage to England, the Test teams often left their ship at a Mediterranean port and travelled across Europe to the cross-channel steamer from Calais to Dover, thus cutting about four days off total travelling time. On the way home they boarded the liner at Tilbury, the passenger ship terminal downriver from London.

The outward voyage was a time of active relaxation before the challenge of the county and Test matches in England; the homeward run was a time to wind down after four and a half months of continuous effort and tension. Nowadays, Sir Donald Bradman remembers those liner voyages to and from England as happy and refreshing intervals in a crowded life.

Don Bradman (in shorts) competing in one of the series of deck games during a voyage to England in the 1930s. Bradman was a frequent winner in the sports. These are two of the 1st prize certificates he won on one of his voyages to England

6

FIRST TESTS IN ENGLAND

Alf Stephens, ex-mayor of Bowral, had fulfilled a long-standing promise: that if Don Bradman ever played a Test Match in England he would be there to watch him. Bradman spent some of the time between the Cambridge match and the first Test in company with Mr and Mrs Stephens, and their homely company and conversation helped to ease some of the tension. When he and the others arrived in Nottingham for the match on the Trent Bridge ground, they felt keyed-up but full of confidence.

By that time, English cricket lovers did not quite know what to make of the Australians. They had won or drawn all their first-class matches in England, under conditions of weather and wicket totally unfamiliar to the younger members of the side, but their performances had been a trifle erratic. Archie Jackson, who had such a brilliant cricketing record in Australia, had proved disappointing in every English match. The mighty Ponsford had been dismissed with remarkable ease on several occasions. He had made only seven against Cambridge, five against Middlesex, one against Surrey, and six against Yorkshire. His score of 220 in the Oxford University match seemed only to demonstrate the wild swings of fortune in the Australian batting so far.

By the time Don Bradman began his first tour of England, he was already so well known that this letter from Australia addressed simply 'Bradman England' reached him safely. The postage cost was only three-halfpence, the equivalent of about two cents. The postmark 'Air Mail Saves Time' referred only to domestic airmail in Australia. There was no overseas airmail service in 1930

Bradman's playing had been equally unpredictable. A graph of his scores in his eleven matches since 30 April would have shown Himalayan peaks and valleys: from four in the second innings versus the M.C.C. to the magnificent 252 at the Oval.

English newspapers tended towards sarcasm in mentions of Woodfull's 'coddling' of the Australian team. He had kept them in 'secret' quarters near Bath, to spare them the attentions of autograph hunters and publicity hounds, and journalists made much of his issue of 'Do Not Disturb' signs to his players to be hung outside their hotel doors. When they moved to Nottingham he asked for the clock chimes in the Council House, opposite the hotel, to be silenced so that the bells would not disturb their sleep.

Mr Marshall, the Trent Bridge groundsman, put the finishing touches onto the Test pitch, which had not been played on since 1926, and told reporters it would stand up to a week's play if necessary. English sportswriters predicted that England would win. The *Daily Telegraph* wrote: 'England is not only the favourite, but a hot one. Her Eleven is comparably the stronger. Supposing the Australians were Englishmen, then only Bradman and Grimmett would be chosen for the English Eleven.' *The Times* said: 'Though Grimmett and Hornibrook have bowled well, the attack does not attain to previous standards. The prospects encourage England.'

Mr and Mrs Alf Stephens were among the 'full house' of spectators who crammed the Trent Bridge stands when the Test opened on Friday 13 June. England won the toss and batted first, and Grimmett quickly made nonsense of *The Times*' lofty comments about the 'Australian attack'. He took four wickets for 71. A gloomy day for England ended when they had lost eight wickets for 241.

Don Bradman went in to play his first innings before an English Test crowd on the Saturday afternoon; but 23 000 people, including many of his own countrymen, saw him fail dismally. Overnight rain had made the wicket wet, even greasy, and it created conditions relished by Maurice Tate and Dick Tyldesley. Neville Cardus wrote of Bradman: 'Tyldesley bothered him, Tate tormented him until mercifully bowling him with a breakback to which Bradman held out a bat as limp as it was crooked.' Alf Stephens must have wondered what had happened to the 'Bowral wonder', who appeared totally ill at ease during his brief spell at the crease.

Tate dismissed him for eight, in an Australian debacle in which Woodfull fell for two, Ponsford for three, and Oldfield for four, while Grimmett, Wall and Hornibrook saw the fatal zero go up on the board. At the end of the first innings, Australia lagged far behind England with 144 against 270.

But Bradman more than made up for his early performance when he went in at 12 for one towards the end of the third day. In thirty-five minutes batting he made 31, and when he continued his innings on the fourth day he came close to winning the match for Australia. He treated the bowling with extreme skill and care, never launching out into the whirlwind aggression which had delighted his fans in the past but nevertheless making every stroke count. He took a total of 100 minutes to complete 50 and was 88 not out at lunch, after a narrow escape when Tyldesley missed a catch. At 2.45 p.m. he reached his century, and raised his cap to the cheers which greeted a new record:

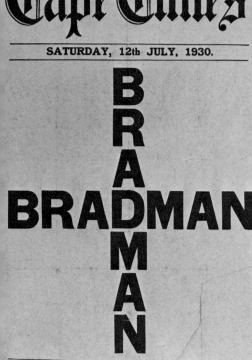

Cape Times

SATURDAY, 12th JULY, 1930.

BRADMAN

BRADMAN

A 'novelty poster' printed by the *Cape Times*, South Africa

the first Australian ever to score a Test century at Trent Bridge.

After that, in partnership with Stan McCabe, there was a strong possibility that he might save Australia from defeat. The visitors had seven wickets in hand, and 225 minutes to make 200 runs; then disaster struck Australia. It came suddenly and for a strange reason.

Larwood was suffering from gastritis and did not take the field. Normally, of course, he would have been replaced by the selected twelfth man (Duleepsinhji) but he had already replaced Sutcliffe whose thumb had been broken by a Tim Wall bouncer. The English captain sought Woodfull's permission to use one Copley, a member of the Notts ground staff.

Woodfull agreed. At mid-on, Copley took a fantastic diving catch low down to dismiss Stan McCabe. The Australian supporters caused a mild furore claiming Woodfull had been 'taken for a ride' — that he was unaware what a brilliant field Copley was. This catch might well have decided the match but, as the Australian captain had consented to the use of Copley, the matter was a *fait accompli.*

Soon after Copley's catch, Bradman got his feet a bit mixed up and failed to protect his off stump from a wrong 'un by Robins, at which he made no shot. Bradman had made 131, and his dismissal was the beginning of the end.

THE 'RIVALS' OF DON BRADMAN

Don Bradman always provided good 'copy' for journalists from the days of his first epic battle in the country against O'Reilly, and one of their favourite angles was to compare him with batsmen who might rival his performance.

Of the men close to his own age, the Indian batsman Kumar Shri Duleepsinhji seemed most likely to rival his aggregate in 1930. Duleepsinhji, then twenty-five, was a member of a noble Rajput family, princes of Nawanagar, and a nephew of the equally great batsman K. S. Ranjitsinhji. During the 1930 Tests, newspapers claimed that 'Ranji' gave his nephew £2 for each run up to 50 in each Test, and £4 for each run thereafter.

On 3 August 1930 the *Daily Mail* said: 'The chief feature in the season's first-class cricket averages is the race between Bradman and Duleepsinhji for the highest aggregate. Bradman at present has a total of 2156 runs and Duleepsinhji 2124. Nobody is within streets of them . . . as far as averages are concerned, Bradman stands alone with a terrific 102.66 against Duleepsinhji's 68.51.'

Duleepsinhji was a swift and confident batsman and a reliable fielder. His greatest innings was at Lord's during the 1930 series, when he hit 173 off 'the deadliest of Australia's bowlers'. Ill-health prevented the full flowering of his cricket career,

Kumar Shri Duleepsinhji (1905–59) played for Cambridge University, Sussex, and England. During the 1930 Test series the newspapers sometimes compared him with Bradman and on 3 August the *Daily Mail* pointed out that his season's aggregate to that date, 2124, ran close behind Bradman's 2156

which ended in 1932 after he had played in twelve Tests for 995 runs at 58.52, including three centuries.

Illness also destroyed the cricketing potential of Archie Jackson, who many people believed would surpass Bradman. Sir Donald Bradman wrote in 1981 that, when the 1930 tour was chosen, 'the majority of Australians (in my opinion) believed that the batting star of the team was likely to be Archie Jackson'.

Jackson's career in first-class cricket was as meteoric as Bradman's. He played his first Shield match, for New South Wales, when he was seventeen, in the 1926–27 season, and his first Test at Adelaide in 1929. His 164 in that match, followed by 182 in the 1930 Test Trial, assured him of a place in the tour. Unhappily, he was to disappoint himself and his supporters. Although nobody knew it at that time, he was already weakened by the onset of tuberculosis and he rarely showed his true cricketing brilliance during the tour. His death in 1933 robbed Australian cricket of a batsman who might indeed have rivalled Don Bradman.

At the time when sportswriters were discussing various 'rivals' for Don Bradman, they could not of course foresee the total magnitude of his achievement. The year 1930 was a vintage year for Australian batsmen and Bradman still had a long way to go. They ranged from men newly launched on Test careers, like twenty-year-old Stan McCabe, to veterans like Jack Ryder, and included Ponsford, Kippax, Fairfax, Richardson and Woodfull. In the chancy world of cricket, no-one could say what another decade would do to these 'rivals' of Don Bradman or whether 'the Don' himself would survive their competition.

In the end he outstripped all of them. None came anywhere near the Test aggregate and average he had recorded by the end of his career: 6996 runs at 99.94, including twenty-seven centuries, in fifty-two Tests.

Ponsford and McCabe ran almost neck-and-neck behind him, although it was still a very long gap. Both had careers in first-class cricket covering fourteen years. McCabe played in thirty-nine Test matches against Ponsford's twenty-nine, aggre-

gated 2748 at 48.21 against Ponsford's 2122 at 48.22, and six centuries against Ponsford's seven.

Similar comparisons apply against the great English batsmen of the period: such men as Jack Hobbs, Frank Woolley, Herbert Sutcliffe and Wally Hammond. Each had aggregates in first-class cricket which greatly exceeded Bradman's 28 067, from Sutcliffe's 50 138 to Hobbs' 61 237; but their careers were all longer than Bradman's and English county cricket provides many more batting opportunities than Australian interstate cricket. In Test cricket, he left them all far behind.

In 1930, it would have needed a bold prophet to suggest that there could ever be a serious rival to Jack Hobbs: the Grand Old Man of cricket who was then nearing the end of a first-class career which stretched from 1905 to 1934. He played in nine more Tests than did Bradman, but his aggregate of 5410 fell short of Bradman's eventual total by more than 1000 runs and his average, 56.94, was certainly not comparable.

Sutcliffe played in fifty-four Tests, for 4555 at 60.73, and sixteen centuries. Woolley, in sixty-four Tests, aggregated 3283 at 36.07, with five centuries.

In Wally Hammond's long career, 1920–51, and eighty-five Test Matches, his Test aggregate of 7249 runs outstripped both Hobbs and Bradman although his first-class total of 50 551 was well behind that of Hobbs. His Test average, 58.45, came nowhere near Bradman's. He scored twenty-two centuries, but it is perhaps not unkind to remark that he had thirty more Tests and sixty more innings than Bradman in which to make them.

Early in Don Bradman's career, sportswriters frequently canvassed the likelihood of his breaking the records set by Victor Trumper, who was the premier of Australian cricket before the advent of Bradman. He was a popular favourite, and cricket lovers lamented his death in 1915, at the age of thirty-seven. He played in forty-eight Tests, for an aggregate of 3163, including eight centuries, at 39.04. Sportswriters commonly suggest that his comparatively early death cut short a brilliant career; but since he had already played for nineteen years, it is probable that his best years were behind him when he died.

'Comparisons are odious', and there will of course always be those who argue that the innumerable subtle differences between batsmen prevent a computer-like assessment of their achievements. Bradman himself applauds the various merits of numerous other batsmen. But it is certain that the potential rivals of Don Bradman, in his own era, never came close to challenging his overall performance.

Left: Bill Ponsford, born 1900, had a career in first-class cricket from 1920 to 1934

Right: Stan McCabe (1910–58) was the 'baby' of the side when he toured England in 1930 at the age of eighteen. His Test career lasted only from 1930 to 1938

Arthur Mailey wrote: 'His innings was a great display. It was not spectacular at any time. The position of the game was too nearly hopeless to expect it; but cautious, solid, and purposeful, he fought his opponents grimly and unceasingly, never leaving an opening for his defence to be penetrated. It was a tiring effort, full of pluck, determination, and mental concentration, and will be remembered as one of the greatest of all individual fighting efforts in Test history.'

The English *Daily Mail* said: 'The youthful Bradman showed nerves of iron and the poise of a veteran. Cricketers will be proud of England's success and prouder still to think that it was accomplished against foemen such as these.'

Australia lost by 93 runs, but Bradman's magnificent stand made his countrymen feel that it had nevertheless been a kind of victory.

The Australians had to play two more county fixtures before the second Test at Lord's: against Surrey at the Oval and Lancashire at Old Trafford. After the close-fought struggle at Trent Bridge the spectators looked forward to some cricketing thrills, but they were sadly disappointed. Arthur Mailey wrote: 'One cannot account for Australia's immobility in the last two matches. On the last day at the Oval, against Surrey, they showed no more enterprise than Chelsea pensioners, while to-day ordinary bowling was treated as gently as Mills bombs.' *The Times* said scornfully of the Old Trafford match: 'The cricketers might as well have spent three days at the nets.' Bradman survived for only ten minutes at the Oval and was out for five. He made 38 in his first innings at Manchester and 23 in the second.

But figures published just before the start of the second Test showed him to be the dominant batsman of the Australian side. His total of 1435 runs in fifteen matches, at 95.66, far outstripped Woodfull's 836 (59.71), Kippax's 671 (55.91), and Ponsford's 668 (51.38). No wonder the Sydney *Sun* proclaimed him 'Bradman the Mighty' — and he was not yet twenty-two.

The travellers returned to London for the second Test, at Lord's. They were to be introduced to the Duke of York (later King George VI) before the game, and the team was assembling for this honour when, as the *Daily Pictorial* reported, 'Consternation, even dismay, was caused when the quiet Bowral boy was found to be missing . . . The position became serious when Don did not appear with the team to meet the Duke of York, but it became almost a national crisis when, a few minutes before the start of play, he had not turned up.

'The position grew desperate. Messages flew. Jackson was warned to be ready to play, and stripped ready to take the field. There was gloom in the Australian dressing room. Don arrived! Suddenly everyone burst out singing! He changed like lightning, and whipped on to the field.

'That's Don Bradman, nonchalant, delightful, quiet, undemonstrative run-getter.

'He had merely slept in.'

Woodfull lost the toss — as often happened on that tour — and England batted first. Even though Fairfax dismissed Jack Hobbs for one run, the English team gave a powerful performance and closed the first day's play with 405 for nine. The fielding of Bradman and McCabe was about the brightest spot of the day for Australia, with Bradman saving many runs on the boundary and catching Duleepsinhji when the great Indian batsman had reached 173.

Above: The London *Evening News* of 17 June 1930 had no doubts about the most important batsman in the Australian team

Below: Another English newspaper poster reporting Bradman's July 1930 innings at Leeds

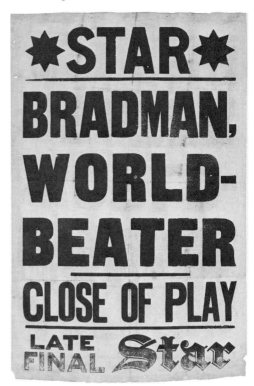

Duleepsinhji, nephew of the more illustrious Ranjitsinhji, had made a notable century in his first Test, much to the admiration of his adoring uncle who watched every stroke from the pavilion.

On the Saturday, Australia began rather slowly. Woodfull took twenty-five minutes to score his first run: a single which the crowd greeted with ironical cheers. But he and Ponsford wore down the English bowling in an opening stand of 162. Credit for breaking the great opening stand must go to King George V, because the first wicket fell just after an interruption in the match so that the players might be presented to the King. Bradman went in at 3.30 p.m.

Don Bradman (left) about to meet royalty for the second time, when he was presented to King George V during the second Test, at Lord's, in 1930. He and the other Australian cricketers had already met the King and members of the Royal Family during an invitation to afternoon tea at Sandringham

At last he treated an English Test crowd to a real display of the virtuoso batting which had made him famous in Australia. When Jack White bowled the first ball against him, he went yards down the wicket to meet it and drove it powerfully for a single. The first smack of willow against leather signalled the start of a new series of records. Allen, Tate, White, Robins and Hammond alternated in efforts to dismiss him, but his brilliant footwork and unerring eye defeated them every time. By the end of the day he was 155 not out.

On the Monday morning he opened a little more carefully, and took another eighty minutes to bring up his 200th run, but he was up to 231 by lunch. After that, cricket statisticians felt certain he was on his way to breaking 'Tip' Foster's 1903 record of 287, the highest score ever made in a Test between England and Australia.

The bowlers tried every trick in their repertoire to defeat him, but he batted steadily on until Chapman dismissed him with a wrong-handed catch, low down at extra cover, off a tremendous drive. Sir Donald Bradman still says that it was the greatest catch he has ever seen. He had brought his score up to 254, out of 423 scored while he was at the wicket. Sir Donald claims it was technically the most perfect innings he has ever played.

It was the highest score ever made in a Test Match in England, the highest by any Australian in any Test, and the highest against England in a Test Match. Bradman himself was to break all these new records, but his 254 remains the ground record for a Test at Lord's.

Bradman remains the youngest batsman to score a double century in a Test for Australia, and his time of 245 minutes for reaching 200 was faster than any previous Test record set in England.

A *Sun* headline said 'Many Records Topple Before Bradman's Flashing Bat', and Mailey confidently predicted defeat for England. He was right, and Australia won by seven wickets although Chapman caught Bradman for one, with yet another sensational catch, in his second innings.

One of the numerous cartoons which appeared in English journals during Bradman's first tour of England. Others showed him 'twisting the lion's tail' or otherwise humbling the English lion

The 1930 Tests were the first to be reported directly by radio in Australia from an overseas relay, with the Australian commentators picking up the British reports and repeating them for local listeners. The *Sun* reported: 'Local wireless fans are beginning to look very heavy under the eyelids. At the home of Mr W. McCabe, Stan's father, there is a nightly attendance of about 20, who stay till the final Test results are given at 3.30 a.m. Other homes have parties who listen all through the night.'

The listeners included Don Bradman's parents, who told the newspapers: 'It was a great performance, and naturally we are proud of him.' Mrs Bradman said: 'The excitement at times is nearly too much for me. I can assure you there is not much work done while the Test matches are on.'

The matches against Yorkshire, at Bradford, and against Nottinghamshire, preceded the third Test. The first was played between 2–4 July, and Bradman later wrote: 'Our score sheet made curious reading — Woodfull 3, Ponsford 143, Bradman 1, McCabe 40, Jackson 46, Richardson 3. Once again, Grimmett was too much for the Yorkshire batsmen, and our score of 302 enabled us to win by ten wickets.'

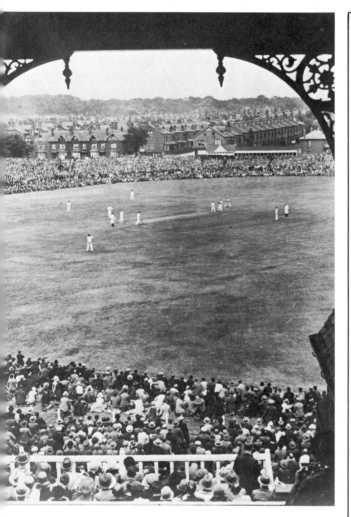

The Headingley ground, at Leeds, was the scene of some of Don Bradman's greatest cricketing triumphs. On his first appearance there, on 11 July 1930, he scored 309 in one day and then went on to his record-breaking 334

THE WONDERS OF SCIENCE

After the 1930 Test Ashes, newspapers commented that the Australian team members had established yet another new record, 'the most wonderful of them all', by talking to Australia through the new radiotelephone link.

The team was connected to Sydney at 3 a.m. Australian time, and the sponsoring radio station rebroadcast their messages and conversations for anyone who cared to 'listen-in'. Woodfull led the way by reading out King George V's telegram of congratulations to the Test team. Woodfull said: 'To me the victory came as a handsome present on my birthday.'

Oldfield, Grimmett, Fairfax 'who made no bones about being excited to flabbergasting point', manager Kelly, and Hornibrook also sent messages through this amazing new means of instant communication.

'Then came Don Bradman's boyish voice, first expressing the hope that his parents, and brother, and sisters were listening, because he wanted to tell them that he never forgot any of them ... he laughingly sidestepped Mr Williams' intimation that "all the girls of Australia were waiting to give him a welcome home."'

Williams, of the radio station, then had contact switched to Melbourne, where some of the 'cricket widows' were waiting to talk to their husbands. 'Woodfull, Ponsford, and Grimmett were able to chat with their wives ... it was a happy reunion by radio, and neither husbands nor wives seemed to care that half Australia was listening to their affectionate greetings.'

The *Daily Pictorial's* representative protested that Australia should have done even better. He wrote: 'Amazing decisions on the part of the umpires were responsible for the dismissals of Bradman, Jackson, and Richardson. Bradman hit a ball which struck his pad. Under the new rule which applies in County cricket, Bradman would have been out, but this rule does not apply to matches in which Australians are playing. Exactly the same thing happened to Jackson. Jackson, who is fighting hard for a place in the Test team, was crestfallen.'

But Bradman was unperturbed. He stood down from the match against Notts and enjoyed a holiday from cricket. He went back to London to watch the tennis finals at Wimbledon, and was delighted to see Australia win the mixed doubles. He took a trip up the Thames as far as Richmond, and 'had a look around London'. In the second week of July he set off for Leeds in a baby Singer car, 'which was something of an adventure, though a pleasant one'.

He found Leeds in turmoil, with every train pouring more cricket addicts into the city. Both teams were staying at the same hotel, which was besieged by admirers hoping to catch a glimpse of the stars. There was a tense and feverish atmosphere as the huge crowds poured into the Headingley ground, where Woodfull won the toss and Australia opened the batting on 11 July. The outfield was patchy and poorly grassed and the wicket also was rather patchy. A strong cool cross-breeze favoured Larwood when he opened the bowling.

Poor Archie Jackson failed once again when Larwood caught him off the fifth ball of Tate's first over, and Bradman went in to join Woodfull at one for two. He survived a close decision when a ball struck his pads, but after that 'he batted with the same delightful freedom as he displayed in the previous Test at Lord's'.

The fascinated spectators watched him stand up to Tate, Larwood, Geary, and Tyldesley, bowling in rapid alternation. He scored better than one a minute, completing his century in ninety-nine minutes when he hit Larwood to leg for four. Woodfull, playing as a cautious partner, was out when they had added 192. Kippax then joined Bradman in another long partnership.

By scoring 100 before lunch, Bradman had joined the immortal duo of Victor Trumper and Charles Macartney, who also scored centuries before lunch in Tests against England. No English cricketer has ever matched this feat in Tests against Australia.

By the tea interval, Bradman's score was 220. As the shadows lengthened he continued his remorseless treatment of the bowlers. After five hours and thirty-six minutes at the wicket he reached his third century; off the last ball of the day, a masterly off-drive brought his score up to 309 and his total for the tour up to 2000.

On the following morning he was about to leave the dressing room to continue his innings when someone handed him a telegram. He tore it open and read: 'Your house is on fire and your girl wants you.' He did not own a house and his 'girl' was far away in Australia, so he ignored the message as the work of a practical joker. He walked back to the wicket to find it was much faster than on the previous day, and Tate and Larwood in much better form. McCabe fell to Larwood and Richardson to Tate, and when Bradman had added another 25 to his score he snicked a ball from Tate into the hands of wicket-keeper Duckworth.

Above: An English newspaper poster reporting Bradman's historic innings at Leeds in 1930

Below: The London *Star* did not need to mention who 'he' was when an English bowler dismissed him

Above: Arthur Ernest Whitelaw, the Australian from Auburn, Victoria, who had settled in England and made a fortune as a soap manufacturer. He gave £1000 to Bradman 'as a token of my admiration of his wonderful performance' after Bradman's score of 334 at Leeds

Right: The telegram to Bill Kelly, manager of the Australian team, presenting Bradman with £1000 in recognition of his huge score at Leeds. When Kelly passed the telegram on to Don Bradman the young batsman thought at first that it was a practical joke

Later in the day, while Bradman was fielding on the leg boundary, Woodfull received a telegram which he passed on to Bradman. It said: 'Kindly convey my congratulations to Bradman. Tell him I wish him to accept £1000 as a token of my admiration of his wonderful performance. (Signed) Arthur Whitelaw, Australia House.'

Bradman thought it was another practical joke, but Woodfull and Kelly assured him it was genuine. A. E. Whitelaw, an Australian, had settled in England and become a wealthy soap manufacturer. He said later: 'I thought Bradman's performance merited such recognition . . . we must encourage our cricketers in every way possible, since cricket is the greatest of all games. This is not so much a gift as a mark of appreciation on behalf of all Australians.'

The munificent gift, equivalent to at least $50 000 in our debased modern currency, matched the grandeur of Don Bradman's achievements. Many other Australians, feeling themselves and their country immeasurably increased in stature by his innings in the third Test, wished themselves able to contribute an equal amount.

His immense score delighted cricket lovers in every corner of the Empire, and after cricket statisticians had worked on it during the next few days they realised he had broken even more records than they had thought at first. (*See insert 'Day of Splendour'*.)

Bradman rounded off his performance in the third Test with a spectacular piece of fielding when the master batsman Jack Hobbs was facing Grimmett. Arthur Mailey wrote: 'Sutcliffe played a ball to Bradman, who lazily threw it back to the bowler, giving Hobbs and Sutcliffe the impression that an easy run could be obtained.

'Next ball, Grimmett sent down a similar delivery, and Hobbs played it to Bradman who, unseen, had sneaked five yards closer. Picking it up like lightning, he threw Hobbs's wicket down.

'Hobbs never looked at the wicket, being yards out of his crease, but walked back to the pavilion with bowed head.'

Wisden records of this incident: 'Nothing during the whole tour could have been more dazzling than the manner in which he threw

Hobbs out.' English cricket lovers could hardly believe that the Australian youngster had trapped their cricketing hero, Hobbs, for a mere thirteen runs.

The weather had deteriorated steadily, and heavy rain kept the cricketers kicking their heels in the pavilion until the clouds began to clear. Woodfull asked the umpires to start play again on the Monday afternoon, but they waited until 5.30 before they allowed England to continue. The restless crowd hooted impatiently when the English batsmen appealed twice against the light.

English sportswriters said bluntly that England's delaying tactics had not been in the true spirit of the game. The long wait to recommence play, and the appeals against the light, caused the match to end in a draw; and all but the most one-eyed barrackers were convinced that Australia should have had a victory. The forthright Yorkshiremen in the Headingley stands had booed the English side, and cheered the Australians, during the delays.

Bradman could have been chaired through the streets of Leeds if he had chosen to expose himself to the tidal wave of publicity which broke after his Headingley innings. The modesty and privacy of his nature, however, made him prefer to remain in his hotel room, writing or listening to music, rather than expose himself to the roistering crowds or even join the other players in the lounge. One London newspaper, writing about the Australians, stated: 'Don Bradman is the most

The English cricketers applaud, and Don Bradman raises his bat to acknowledge the plaudits of the crowd, after he completed his third century in one day at Leeds in 1930

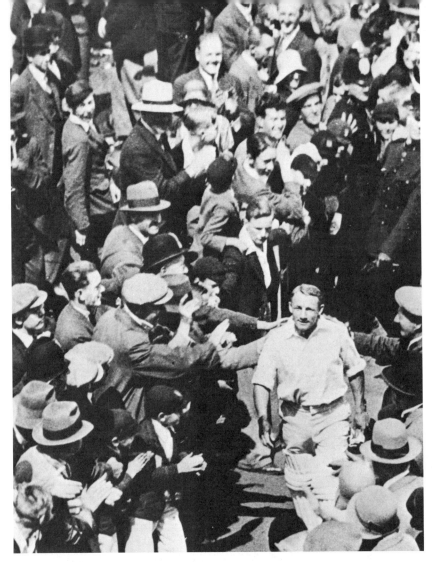

The crowd of admiring Yorkshiremen and women surges forward to acclaim Don Bradman as he leaves the ground after his triple century in the third Test, July 1930

This chart appeared in an Australian newspaper to illustrate the scoring-strokes of 46 fours, 6 threes, 26 twos, and 80 singles which comprised Bradman's historic 334 at Leeds. Probably it was based on a chart drawn up by the scorer W. H. Ferguson, who was one of the scorers in every one of Bradman's 52 Test matches

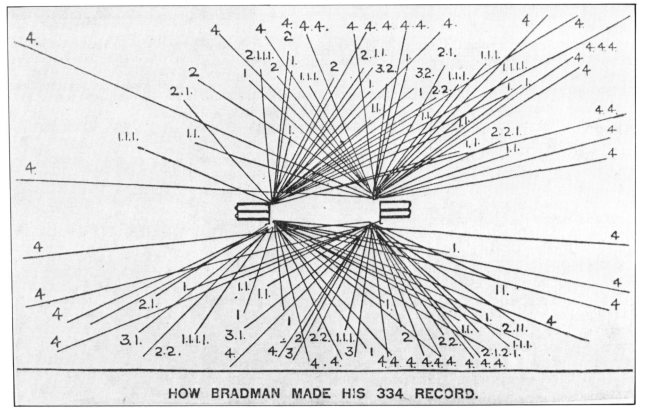

HOW BRADMAN MADE HIS 334 RECORD.

DAY OF SPLENDOUR

Don Bradman's performance in the third Test Match of the 1930 tour, which opened on 11 July, established another series of cricketing records. They include the following:

* He was the youngest batsman in history to aggregate 2000 in an English season.

* Highest number of runs (309) in a single day's play in any Test Match anywhere; most made in a day in any Test Match by an Australian; most in a day in any Test Match in England; most in one day in any England–Australia Test by any Australian.

* His time for reaching a century (99 minutes) is still the fastest on record for Tests between England and Australia. For reaching 200 (214 minutes) it is the fastest in any Test Match. For reaching 300 (336 minutes) it was the fastest for an Australian, best in an England–Australia Test, and best in a Test in England.

* His 334 for the innings was the highest-ever score for either side in a Test between England and Australia; highest in any Test anywhere; highest in any Test Match in England. It remains the highest score ever made by an Australian against England; in any Test for any country against England; by an Australian in any Test in England; and in any first-class match at Leeds.

* His match aggregate (also 334) was then the highest for any England–Australia Test.

* His single innings of 334 was then the greatest number of runs scored in succession in Test Matches by any batsman before being dismissed, and was then the greatest number scored in succession for any England–Australia Test.

* He was the first player to make two double centuries in two Tests in England and against England, and the first Australian to make

more than one Test Match double century.

* He is still the only batsman to have scored a treble century in a match both in England and in Australia.

* He is still the youngest, at twenty-one years 318 days, to have scored 300 in an England–Australia Test Match.

* In helping to increase the total by 506 while he was batting, he broke the record for any Test Match between England and Australia.

* His margin of 257 runs above the next highest score (Kippax with 77) was then a Test Match record and it remains a record for England–Australia Tests and for first-class matches by a touring batsman in England.

elusive man of all . . . preferring to write letters in his room or get away to a show. He also has a habit of going off sightseeing alone, or with only one companion. A more level-headed young man or one less likely to become spoiled by admiration never wore flannels.'

When the Australians were playing Somerset, another newspaper reported: 'Last night we arrived from Manchester and stayed at the historic Castle Hotel at Taunton.

'Someone suddenly discovered that Don was missing. Mr Kelly rushed round the hotel; page-boys darted here and there calling his name; someone suggested he had been kidnapped; others said he had missed the connection at Bristol.

'When the search was at its highest the soft sound of music was heard issuing from the music room, and there was Don quietly playing a little tune he had heard at a show a night or two previously.'

Some of his team-mates did not appreciate these retiring habits. They saw them as a kind of snobbery and they would have been more than human if they had not felt a twinge of envy at the interminable stream of Bradman-oriented reports, articles, cartoons, paragraphs and jokes which occupied the English newspapers. Unknown to them in those days before regular airmails, the Australian newspapers were

One of the newspaper reports acclaiming Bradman's 334, and comparing it with some of the records which Bradman had broken

BRADMAN V. ENGLAND:

Eclipses Record Test Score of 287
Made by R. E. Foster in 1903

WEAK ENGLISH BOWLING FLOGGED

W. G. GRACE.

Sparkling 100 Scored Before Lunch—Chapman Loses
Toss for First Time in Eight Tests

England's bowlers battered and exhausted; Don Bradman, aged twenty-one, the world's wonder batsman, triumphant and 309 not out after smashing still more records.

Such was the close of the first day of the Leeds Test match yesterday. "It was Bradman's day," says Mr. C. G. Macartney, the famous Australian cricketer, whose exclusive description of the match appears on page 6. Comments by Mr. P. J. Moss, the "Daily Mirror" ~ports Editor, are on page 18.

By an amazing display of hurricane hitting Bradman beat the previous highest Test score of 287 made by R. E. Foster for England at Sydney in 1903, and his own personal record of 254 made in the match at Lord's. He nearly doubled the highest score (170) made by Dr. W. G. Grace, the "father" of cricket, against the Australians in 1886.

R. E FOSTER

He is the only player to obtain a century in four successive Tests, and has equalled the feat of Trumper and Macartney in scoring a Test century before lunch. He has not yet made two separate centuries in a Test match. Bardsley did in 1909.

making equally free with Bradman's name. It was the beginning of a long process in which he would attract more and more publicity and retreat from it with an increasing resolution that it should not pervert his lifestyle.

The Australians travelled north from Leeds to play Scotland at Edinburgh and West of Scotland at Glasgow, but the bad weather which plagued the tour was in Scotland before them. Edinburgh was shrouded in a true Scots mist, and the visitors could hardly see Princes Street out of their hotel window. Bradman had looked forward to seeing 'Auld Reekie', as the Scots call Edinburgh, but he had to content himself with a visit to the imposing War Memorial and one or two other places of interest. The match opened during a break in the weather, but the Scotsmen had batted for only two hours when the rain poured down again and the match was abandoned.

The visitors made the short trip across to Glasgow, where they had three hours' play on the Saturday. The Scotsmen scored 140 for six wickets before their captain declared, in order to give the Australians a chance to bat. The Scottish fast bowler, A. D. Baxter, was in fine form. He dismissed Ponsford for six and McCabe for one, but Bradman gave the spectators their money's worth. In cold drizzly weather he scored 140, including nineteen fours and one mighty stroke which sent the ball out of the ground for six. The Australians scored 337 for six wickets.

Bradman was one of the Australians who carried a set of golf clubs around with him, and seized every opportunity to 'have a go' at the game. While he was in Scotland he enjoyed a day on the famous Gleneagles course. Mailey wrote a piece for the *Sun* in which he portrayed the cricketers as keen but inept golfers, and said: 'It is positively dangerous to be on a golf course on which the Australian cricketers are let loose. Members usually retreat to the comparative safety of the club house, and watch the game from the verandah.'

But he wrote of Bradman: 'He has the uncanny faculty of adapting himself to golf, just as he has with other games. He can drive a ball 260 yards without any trouble, and play approach shots like an expert, but he is not too sure on the green. I think he covets a secret hankering after golf honours and I would not be surprised if the Bowral lad made a name for himself at golf.' Bradman certainly became an excellent golfer, and at the end of his cricket career he maintained a golf handicap of scratch for years.

Only one match, at Durham, preceded the fourth Test, but Bradman was suffering from a stomach upset and did not take part in the game. News that he was 'indisposed' caused great alarm until reporters could say they had seen him 'wearing his usual cheery smile'.

The two Test teams assembled in Manchester in a mood of high resolution. The English sportswriters had descended from their high horses, and were admitting that Australia had a chance for the Ashes after all, while the English selectors had spent anxious hours in choosing the eleven for Old Trafford. The Australians found that the bowlers Larwood, Geary and Tyldesley had been replaced by a possibly more dangerous trio: the fast right-arm bowler Morris Nichols, the off-break bowler Tom Goddard of Gloucestershire, and the Scottish leg-spinner Ian Peebles.

Bradman felt an unusual foreboding about the fourth Test, and circumstances were to prove him right.

The match opened on Friday 23 July, in remarkably dry and sunny weather although the wicket was still wet enough to require liberal dressings of sawdust. A crowd of 20 000, including those in a special section booked by a number of Australians, watched silently as Chapman and Woodfull met for the toss. Chapman always used a 'lucky half-sovereign' salvaged from a Christmas pudding many years before, and Woodfull always called 'Heads'. On this occasion the luck favoured Woodfull, and he opened the batting with Ponsford.

They walked out to a generous burst of applause from the English spectators and 'cooees' from the Australians, and found a slow but dead wicket. When Nichols opened the bowling, followed by Tate, they seemed to have difficulty keeping their feet. The crowd saw Woodfull and Ponsford patting down pieces of turf cut up by the ball. They stayed together until Tate dismissed Woodfull for 54, with the score at 107.

The headline of an English newspaper had said 'Mr Bradman, meet Mr Peebles!' when Peebles was included in the English eleven, with the implication that the Scots bowler would be more than a match for the Australian record-breaker. These hopes came true when Bradman joined Ponsford. He seemed very uncomfortable on the soft wicket, and in half-an-hour he made only 14 before Duleepsinhji caught him off a ball from Peebles.

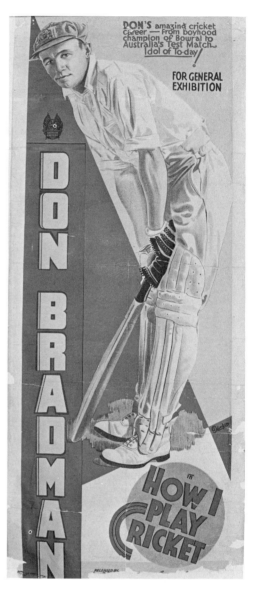

In the early 1930s Don Bradman 'starred' in an instructional documentary film entitled *How I Play Cricket*. This was one of the advertising posters

'THE DON' ON PUBLICITY

Don Bradman has broken many records, but there is one he would rather not possess. It is the fact that he has attracted more publicity, more consistently, and over a longer period of time, than any other Australian in history. No politician, entertainer, or other public figure has been the subject — or target — of so much sustained publicity for so long. In 1950, he described his attitude towards publicity in his book *Farewell to Cricket*, when he wrote:

'I was often accused of being unsociable, though I fear the charge was applied in a very loose sense. In substance it boiled down to my dislike of artificiality and publicity.

'There were those who thought I was unsociable because at the end of the day I did not think it my duty to breast the bar and engage in a beer-drinking contest. At least I made no attempt to interfere with the habits of others, and if I thought my most important need was a meal and a cup of tea, I had as much right to complain of their late entry into the dining room as they had to complain of my absence from the bar.

'I well remember being accused of snobbery because in the evening, following my world's record Test score, I stayed in my room listening to music. Was I expected to parade the streets of Leeds?

'Any exceptional performance makes great demands upon the physical and nervous resources of the performer. Some people try to overcome the resultant

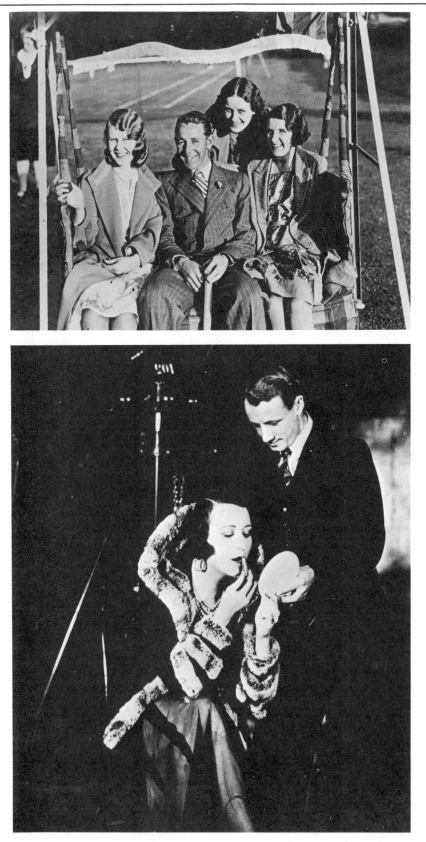

fatigue by the use of stimulants — others by seeking a counter-excitement. I always obtained best results by seeking quietness. Music is a tonic to jaded nerves. It may not be to a musician, but it is to me.

'In any case, my preference for the more homely and peaceful side of life was a perfectly simple explanation of my reticence to make public or semi-public appearances.

'Throughout my career I genuinely disliked the private lionising and fêting with which people are afflicted only because they are temporarily in the headlines.

'Public acclamation associated with one's performance is in another category. That is a natural and enjoyable manifestation of community interest and appreciation.

'The ordinary citizen has not the remotest idea what it feels like to be a public figure, recognisable at sight in the trains of Melbourne, the buses in the Strand, or even in the shops at Port Said.

'Another chap and I tried to go shopping one morning in Aberdeen. I had never been in Aberdeen before, yet I was stopped some twenty times in little more than half an hour by people of all ages, usually seeking autographs.

'On one occasion a woman wheeling a baby in a pram asked me to sign an autograph because *he* would like it when *he* grew up. *He* wasn't interested. She had neither pencil nor paper. The sentimental folk will say "What a compliment". That is probably so, but try it yourselves for twenty years and see what it does to your nervous system.

'Remember, you can't turn this thing on or off like a tap. It goes on perpetually in trains, trams, buses and ships all over the world. If I tried to walk anywhere in London I was often followed by a crowd of small boys.

'It is not much use trying to explain to people who crave publicity and can't get it, that one's greatest need may be quietness and privacy . . . Some have been positively rude to me because I dared to refuse their entry into my private home to take photos or into my room at an hotel.

'This matter of publicity automatically brings up the question of professional men in that walk of life.

'Some of my greatest friends are in the newspaper and radio field. I have the most profound admiration for the men themselves, their difficulties and problems . . . On the other hand I have no time for the type of journalism which lives by sensationalism. I deplore articles which by their innuendoes and half-truths can be most misleading.

'I believed in treating all journalists as trustworthy men until I found out anything to the contrary, but if ever I formed the opinion that a confidence had been betrayed I seldom risked a second opportunity.'

Above left: Archie Jackson relaxes with some female admirers during a garden party in England

Left: A publicity photographer posed this shot of Don Bradman holding a mirror for an actress during the Australian cricketers' visit to Elstree Studios, London, in 1930

Right: The cover of the menu of the Farewell Dinner for the Australian team in 1930. It was a stately occasion, at which Dame Clara Butt and other noted singers of the period entertained the diners

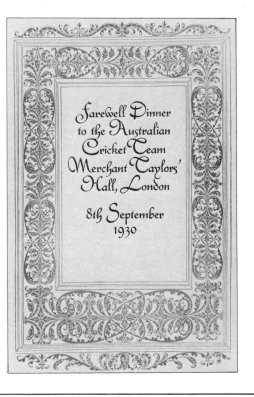

Farewell Dinner to the Australian Cricket Team Merchant Taylors' Hall, London 8th September 1930

After the game he told the *Evening News*: 'Peebles is a grand bowler. England is lucky to find him. I was beaten fairly and squarely.' In the true camaraderie of cricket, Peebles later became one of Bradman's most intimate and cherished friends and remained so until his death.

English relief that someone could deal with Bradman was almost palpable. The *Observer* wrote: 'Bradman, after all, is human. Cricket remains one of life's most glorious uncertainties.'

The Australians batted doggedly on against the powerful new combination of bowlers, and totalled 345. When England opened their innings, the weather once more took a hand in the game. Ominous banks of cloud piled up above the ground, and then opened and flooded the pitch. In occasional bright intervals, groundsmen ran out to scoop water from the wicket into buckets and even mop it up with wads of sacking, but repetitive torrents caused them to labour in vain. The huge crowd barracked impatiently and called out 'Play the game!'; 'Come on, Chapman!'; 'Come on, Woodfull!' although it was obvious that sheets of water were making the wicket unplayable.

At last the captains decided to try again, after the groundsmen had poured buckets of sawdust over the worst patches. England continued their innings at 5.30 p.m. on a very erratic wicket, and played for forty-seven minutes before the heavens opened again. The day ended with England eight wickets down for 251, and that was the end of the game. By the following morning the pitch was completely waterlogged and the match was abandoned, for another frustrating draw.

The visitors travelled south to Somerset to face the county side at Taunton. It was dull weather but at least it was not raining, and the wicket was easy. The match was noteworthy for a fine century by Archie Jackson, but his 118 and Bradman's 117 did not satisfy the critical sportswriters. They, and the crowd, had expected fireworks from Bradman and were not satisfied by cool and careful batting. Arthur Mailey wrote: 'The almost unheard of thing has happened. Don Bradman has been barracked for dreary batting. Today against Somerset he did not display his usual aggressive batting, and the disappointed crowd expressed its feelings.'

Australia won by an innings and 158 runs, and went on to play Glamorgan at Swansea in South Wales. Bradman the music lover was delighted by an invitation for the team to attend the National Eisteddfod at Llanelly, where he and the others were impressed by the choir of 800 white-clad children. They were also interested in the loud-speakers used to keep a cricket crowd informed of the progress of a match, the first time they had seen such an innovation. Bradman had the novel experience of hearing himself announced as 'Don Bradman next' when he walked out onto the St Helen's ground as third man, to join Archie Jackson after the dismissal of Ponsford.

The match developed into an unexpectedly close-run contest. A Welsh bowler, J. Mercer, delivered in-swingers that Bradman treated very carefully, and he took twenty minutes to reach eight. A crowd of 28 000, the largest so far at the county matches, was disappointed when Bradman was dismissed for 58. Richardson declared, leaving Glamorgan with 218 runs to get in 225 minutes, and they very nearly succeeded. When stumps were drawn they needed only 21, with three wickets to fall, and the match ended in another draw.

A portion of the huge crowd which saw Don Bradman score his 334 at Leeds

Before the Glamorgan match, Bradman had delivered the first portion of his book to his literary agent, who had succeeded in selling serial rights to the London *Star*. The first instalment appeared on 4 August and it was to have unexpected repercussions.

By that time, the tour was proceeding through one of the wettest seasons ever recorded in English cricket. Their next fixture, at Birmingham to play Warwickshire, was 'deluged out' after three hours' play, and continuous rain forced abandonment of the match. Gloomy officials told Arthur Mailey that the rain was a severe blow to the club's financial situation. The errant sun reappeared for long enough to allow the Northamptonshire match to open on Saturday 9 August at Northampton, but it soon vanished again and occasional showers interrupted the first innings by the local side. They batted well but ran poorly, and Bradman thought their total of 249 should have been at least 50 more.

Sunday was another day of downpours, and Australia floundered on a really sticky wicket. Vallance Jupp, the slow-medium off-break bowler who had played in several Tests, dismissed them with monotonous regularity. The day ended with Australia all out for 93, their worst innings of the tour.

The Northants captain gave them a chance to regain their tattered glory by deciding that they should follow on. The wicket had improved and they totalled 405, although Bradman was caught for 35. Sportswriters thought that Woodfull should have declared before the end of the innings, to give Northants a chance to bat again, but he decided to bat on until stumps were drawn. His decision aroused a good deal of criticism but it was the last chance for the Australians to gain some batting practice and rest their bowlers before the fifth Test.

They returned to London in an atmosphere of mounting excitement. On 14 August, with only two days to go before the Test opened at the Oval, the English selectors whipped up a storm by dropping Percy Chapman as captain and replacing him with Bob Wyatt. The newspapers lashed out at the selectors' 'play safe' attitude which resulted in a team averaging thirty-three years of age, against the Australian average of twenty-seven-and-a-half.

On Saturday 16 August, a remarkably fine day for that tour, Wyatt won the toss and Hobbs and Sutcliffe opened for England. The hopes of the English spectators slumped when Hobbs, at 47, tried to hook a ball off Tim Wall to the fence but mistimed his stroke and sent a simple catch into Kippax's waiting hands.

Sutcliffe 'plodded along drearily' and the crowd showed no excitement until he reached his century, after five hours at the wicket. The newspapers described the innings as 'very dull batting' and 'a war of attrition', although the *Daily Mail* still believed that England would win.

On the Monday, the tail-end of the English batting quickly collapsed. They had made 405, of which Sutcliffe accounted for 161.

Woodfull and Ponsford opened for Australia and immediately showed how the game should be played. They attacked the bowling with great élan, although Woodfull soon reverted to a defensive game. Ponsford continued 'a slashing innings', and Bradman joined him at 159 for one.

He had only an hour at the wicket, for 27, before rain stopped play. England's cantankerous weather continued on the Tuesday, with the

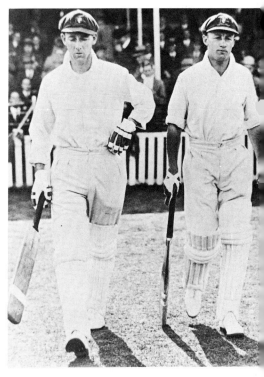

Don Bradman (right) and Archie Jackson leave the pavilion for their great stand in the fifth Test, at the Oval, in August 1930. It was during this Test that Larwood bowled short bumping balls which hit Jackson and Bradman many times, in a bowling performance later seen as a precursor of bodyline. Arthur Mailey wrote: 'Frequently the young men, after being hit, writhed in pain, but, bruised and battered from head to toe, they carried on.' He said that Bradman's innings under these conditions proved he was 'the greatest batsman of all time'

sun shining between showers, but Bradman settled in quickly and at 1.5 p.m. he completed his fourth Test century for the series.

Rain and bad light stopped play twice after lunch, and the second interruption led to one of the strangest incidents of the series. With Bradman's score at 129, Woodfull and Wyatt disagreed as to whether play should resume, and the umpires decided to continue the game with only five minutes to go. Most of the crowd had left because they thought play was over for the day, and those remaining booed vigorously. When Bradman and Jackson walked slowly back to the wicket it was 'to the accompaniment of rowdy abuse'.

Australia ended the day only two behind England's score, with seven wickets intact. The *Daily Mail* reversed its opinion and said: 'There is nothing to say about this match except that Bradman is a definite menace to English cricket . . . we shall have great difficulty in avoiding defeat.'

Defeat seemed even more certain when Bradman and Jackson continued their partnership on the Tuesday, although they had never played on such a dangerous and uncertain wicket. Larwood and the other bowlers took full advantage of it, in a kind of preview of the notorious bodyline Test. Larwood bowled short with bumpy balls which hit the two youngest again and again, and the spectators saw them wince with pain. The newspapers said that some spectators watched 'with tears in their eyes'. But despite this fierce attack they defended their wickets and hit back at the bowling with confident aggression. They knew that Australian hopes of a triumphant victory rested upon them, because their dismissal might be followed by a quick collapse.

Bradman reached 200, his third double century of the series, at 12.55 p.m., after six hours twenty-three minutes. He was 228 at lunch, and added four more in the following twenty minutes before he was caught at the wicket, having added 98 before lunch.

Unhappily the innings ended with an umpiring mistake. Umpire Hardstaff gave Bradman out caught behind, off a ball from which he withdrew his bat but which may have flicked his shirt. Evidence of this is clearly given in the photograph of the dismissal, which shows the appeal was at best half-hearted in contrast to the usual vocal unison.

When the 1932–33 bodyline furore erupted, Larwood tried to justify his method of attack by referring to the way in which Bradman had batted against him at the Oval in this 1930 innings.

Nothing could have been less justified than this excuse, which degraded one of Bradman's most determined innings. Throughout the whole of his 403 minutes at the wicket, the pitch was affected to some degree by rain. His 98 before lunch was probably his greatest-ever performance on a bad pitch.

He walked back to the pavilion after the most courageous and relentless performance of his cricketing career hitherto. Bruised and battered by the wounding deliveries, including a bad blow on the chest from Larwood, he had not faltered in his grim determination to make the biggest possible score for his side. He had guaranteed a triumphant victory.

Rain interrupted the second English innings, and on the final day Hornibrook played havoc with their batsmen. They were all out for 251.

Archie Jackson writhes in pain after being hit by a ball from Larwood in the fifth Test . . . a scene which foreshadowed bodyline

The Times made generous amends for its earlier attitude towards the Australians by writing 'Australia takes the Ashes, and Bradman, her bright particular star, most of the new records'.

The *Daily Express*, reviewing England's performance, said: 'The first to be sacked should be the selection committee . . . we should recognise that the day of our veterans is done.'

Bradman's 232 had set yet another record: the highest score in any Test Match at the Oval. He was to surpass it in 1934, when he made 244, to be followed by Ponsford's 266. Len Hutton far outstripped all these records when he made 364 at the Oval in 1938.

The rest of the tour, with four matches still to play, began to seem like something of an anti-climax. The Australians had stretched themselves to the limit to secure the Ashes and they were in a 'morning after' mood as they took the train to Bristol to play Gloucestershire. The match opened on 23 August and developed into a remarkably exciting contest. Their old antagonist Wally Hammond was playing for the county side, which seemed determined to compensate for the defeat at the Oval.

A scene at Canterbury, Kent, while the Australians were playing the county side after the conclusion of the 1930 Test series

They batted first, and Hornibrook, Hurwood and Grimmett disposed of them for only 72. The Australians did not do very much better in their first innings, with a score of 157, although Bradman's 42 carried his tour aggregate up to 2606 and broke Victor Trumper's long-standing 1902 record of 2570 for an Australian touring England.

Hammond batted supremely well in his second innings, far better than he had done at the Oval, and Gloucestershire ran up 202 before their last wicket fell. The Australians felt they had a reasonably easy victory ahead, needing only 118 to win, but Tom Goddard and Charlie Parker began to make hay of their wickets. The spectators sang, cheered and clapped with wild excitement as they dismissed Ponsford and Kippax for ducks, Richardson for three, Bradman for 14, and others for equally paltry scores. The prospect of Australia's first and only defeat seemed close at hand, and was evaded only when Walker and Hornibrook played on to a dramatic finish. The game ended in the only tie between an Australian touring team and a county team.

'The sun in splendour' at last appeared when the Australians arrived in Kent for a match which opened in weather conditions resembling those of Sydney rather than England's Canterbury. Perhaps for this reason it was rather a sleepy game, apart from the bowling of 'Tich' Freeman in the first innings. They kept the Australian score down to 181. Kent scored 227 in their first innings, and for the second time since the victorious Test the Australians faced a possible defeat.

Bradman more than saved the day in his second innings. In blazing sunshine, he treated the crowd to an enlivening display of Bradman footwork, reached his double century in five hours forty-three minutes, and finished with 205 not out. The game ended with another draw.

Bradman did not play in the next and last of the county matches, against Sussex at Hove. He took the field against a South of England Eleven at Folkestone, and during his score of 63 he brought his total for the tour up to 3000.

Two more matches lay ahead: against a Club Cricket Conference Eleven at Lord's, and against Mr Leveson-Gower's Eleven at Scarborough. The latter was known as the 'Festival' match.

The first of these games gave Australia some unpleasant shocks, with Ponsford, Hurwood, McCabe and Oldfield all dismissed for ducks; but they still won by an innings and 41 runs.

The last match of the historic tour in which Bradman consolidated his reputation was played against a side including Larwood, Tate, Parker and the legendary Test veteran Wilfred Rhodes. Despite the weather's reversion to cold winds and torrential showers, both sides pleased the spectators with a display of vigorous cricket. It ended with a drawn game, and Vic Richardson gathered all the stumps together and tossed them up into the air to signal the end of the tour.

DIVISION OF THE SPOILS

On 18 March 1931, the Sydney *Sun* published an article by Arthur Mailey in which he gave the financial figures for the 1930 tour.

He said the gross receipts from gate money for the five Test Matches amounted to £97 887, of which the Australians received a quarter.

Australia's share of all gate receipts, including the games in Hobart, Launceston, Perth and Colombo, was £38 180.

The net profit from the whole 1930 tour of Britain was £20 483 sterling, plus £1789 added by the favourable rate of exchange when the money was received in Australia. (£1 sterling = £1.5.0 Australian.) The addition of a share of sums from subsidiary rights increased the profit to £22 319.

Mailey wrote: 'When it is considered that only 50 per cent of the gross outer gates was given to the Australians, the credit balance of the tour was very satisfactory.'

'Outer gates' referred to the system in which spectators all paid the same entrance fee at the main gate of a cricket ground, and then paid extra premiums for different parts of the stands once they were inside the ground.

In London a spectator paid three shillings for admission and then paid from five to twelve shillings for a place in the stands.

Mailey deplored the inequitable division of receipts, and also the complex financial system of certain county cricket clubs which offered 'casual' membership for two guineas (£2.2.0) while the Australians were playing. Each 'casual' membership allowed entry for one male adult, all the women of his family, two boys under nineteen, and two friends from outside the county, plus parking space for his car . . . and Australia did not receive a share of the two guineas because it was a membership fee and not an entrance charge.

'LISTENING-IN' TO DON BRADMAN

'Listening-in' to the 'wireless' was a pastime less than seven years old in Australia when Don Bradman played his record-breaking Test series of 1930. Recreational radio broadcasting began in New South Wales on 13 November 1923 (three years after the USA and one year after the UK) with a concert broadcast by station 2SB. It was one of four stations to go on air in that month, including 2FC Sydney, 3AR Melbourne and 2FC Perth.

Most radio receivers were the simple 'crystal' sets, which gave good reception but would not power a loudspeaker. Families sat around the set in a tangle of earphone connections.

There were only about 14 000 licensed radio receivers in Australia in 1924, but the pastime quickly grew so popular that the number rose to about 350 000 by 1930. The sets became more complex as listeners proved willing to pay for valve radios, fitted with loudspeakers resembling old-fashioned gramophone horns. High aerials and cumbersome wet and dry batteries were essential components of home radios until the technology improved during the 1930s.

In 1930, all news and entertainment programmes originated 'live' in the city studios. 'Taping' of programmes was unheard of, and only a few enthusiastic radio hobbyists possessed equipment powerful enough to pick up overseas broadcasts. But the first radiotelephone link between London and Sydney opened in April 1930, and permitted the first 'direct' broadcast of Test Matches. In fact, the English

McMichael, an English firm which manufactured radio sets, presented Don Bradman (right) with one of their new portable receivers during the tour. The portable, which closed into the shape of a suitcase, contained a heavy dry battery and a wet-acid accumulator and was a weighty piece of apparatus

commentary was relayed by radiotelephone to the Sydney studios, where announcers wearing earphones listened to the English commentators. They repeated the story in their own words — often with some added zest and excitement.

For the listeners, it was a vivid new experience: the nearest possible thing to watching the Tests being played on the other side of the world. Owners of wireless sets invited friends to 'Test Parties', in which groups sat around the receivers for several hours in the middle of the night. Newspapers carried jokes and cartoons about bleary-eyed employees turning up late to work after listening to another Bradman stand at the wicket.

After the 1930 tour, radio stations featured increasingly sophisticated presentations of Tests played in England. They used recordings of crowd applause to point up some notable feat, and the commentators became adept at tapping the table with a pencil to simulate bat on ball. With the aid of charts on which they pencilled changes on the field, they 'acted out' the games so skilfully that many listeners believed the broadcasts came direct from England.

Vic Richardson, vice-captain of the Australians on the 1930 tour, later became one of the most popular of the ABC commentators on these 'live' broadcasts. His personal knowledge of the players on both sides, and of the famous English cricket grounds, helped him to fill in with vivid background detail which made his commentary even more convincing. In later years, when Arthur Gilligan accompanied English Test teams to Australia, he often partnered Richardson at the microphone and Vic would discuss the progress of the games with him. Vic's query 'What do you think, Arthur?' became a catchphrase.

Late in the 1930s, and during the war, the British Broadcasting Corporation installed powerful high-frequency transmitters capable of broadcasting to most parts of the world. When they transmitted the first post-war English Test commentaries, Australian owners of suitable receivers strained their ears to hear them through static and interference. Most people still relied on the quick-witted local 'interpreters', using the superior ABC receivers.

Radio technology developed rapidly after transistors came into general use during the 1950s, and eventually the ABC could relay the BBC broadcasts directly through their own transmitters without the intervention of local commentators.

'Listening-in' to overseas Test matches has been an Australian tradition for more than fifty years, although most people now enjoy the benefits of satellite television and watch the matches on their home television screens.

7

FAME AND A £50 FINE

The victorious Australians arrived in Fremantle, aboard the Orient liner *Oronsay*, on 28 October 1930, and Don Bradman was thrown immediately into the frenzied publicity which was to surround him from then onwards. Western Australians had not thronged the wharves in such numbers since their troops returned from the first world war, and in October 1930 the atmosphere was one of total acclaim without any of the wartime undertones of sadness. Australians badly needed a tonic for their spirits, because the Great Depression was biting home and unemployment was close to thirty per cent. They welcomed their cricketers with a rapture rarely seen nowadays and usually reserved for teenagers flinging themselves before the 'juggernaut' of some new pop star. The ships in harbour blew their sirens while police struggled to prevent the crowds from bursting through the barricades. When the cricketers walked down the gangway, excited groups broke through and tried to hoist Bradman onto their shoulders. He fought free of them and remonstrated: 'If you carry me, you have to carry all the team.'

Cars were waiting to carry the team to a civic reception in the Fremantle Town Hall, and the organisers made yet another attempt to single Bradman out from the others. They tried to urge him into a car by himself, but he insisted on travelling with some of his team-mates. At the reception, Woodfull thanked the Fremantle folk on behalf of the team, but the guests were more interested in hearing what Bradman had to say. They called 'Put Bradman in!' Eventually he stood up for a moment to let them see him.

After the reception the organisers again urged him into the 'special single-seater' set apart for him, to join the motorcade up to Perth. He could resist no longer, and waved to crowds of flag-waving school-children along the route.

The cars carried the cricketers to the Prince of Wales Theatre, where the Perth City Council welcomed them and General Motors representatives awarded them special medals. It was yet another in the series of receptions which the team had enjoyed — or endured — since their Ashes victory. There had been the great Farewell Ball in London, organised by the Australian community, where Arthur Whitelaw had presented Bradman with his cheque for £1000 — and the other players with ashtrays. The Merchant Taylors Company had given them a magnificent dinner, with Sir James Barrie among the speakers and Dame Clara Butt singing 'The Lost Chord' and 'Land of Hope and Glory'. There had been many other visits, entertainments and invitations. Bradman had visited the Wm. Sykes factory where he signed a number of bats, and the Columbia recording studios where he cut a record of himself at the piano. (An English journalist wrote: 'He plays cricket as he plays the piano. Syncopation and jazz, quick movements, and an occasional classic.') Walter Lindrum had given him lessons in billiards, and he watched Lindrum play in Thurston's Hall. He and other members of the team had been received in some of the 'stately homes of England', including Sir Phillip Sassoon's palatial residence, and they had been treated to a variety of send-off luncheons. They had been fêted and lionised, and even on the voyage home there had been crowds on the wharf at Colombo and a presentation to Don Bradman from the people of Ceylon. It was a splendid silver model of the Buddhist temple at Kandy.

Otherwise the voyage home had been uneventful, apart from the occasional rough day when Bradman noted in his diary: 'Stayed in bed all day. Not too good.'

But there were two clouds on the horizon of Bradman's homecoming. One was that William Kelly, the tour manager, had deplored the publication of *Don Bradman's Book*, claiming that it transgressed Clause 11 of the touring contract.

Bradman believed he had adhered strictly to the contract. As he understood it, Clause 11 precluded him from publishing anything about the tour while it was in progress, but placed no ban on references to his earlier life. He had told his literary agent specifically about his obligations, and the newspaper serialisation of the book did not include anything about the tour until it was concluded.

However, Kelly doggedly maintained that even if Bradman had abided by the spirit of the contract, there had been a technical breach. He had reported Bradman to the Australian Board of Control, which august body would have the final say.

Kelly's attitude might have been understandable if Bradman's 'off the field' activities had interfered with his team obligations or reduced his effectiveness. But clearly he was maintaining himself in a condition of extreme physical fitness and performing beyond anyone's wildest dreams. He wrote the book only at night, or during matches in which he was not engaged, so there was no interference with team responsibilities. It seems that Kelly felt the need to 'pull rank' on Bradman, or perhaps he felt more than a twinge of jealousy at his success.

Sir Donald Bradman smilingly recalls that 'Kelly was never noted for his diplomacy'. He retains vivid memories of an occasion when Kelly burst into his bedroom one morning while he was still in his pyjamas. Kelly brandished a London newspaper carrying a report that Bradman had accepted a contract to appear on the stages of a music-hall circuit, and demanded to know what the young batsman thought he was doing.

He simmered down when the astonished youngster replied that he had never even heard of such a contract. The story was yet another figment of some journalist's imagination.

The other matter looming ahead was Oscar Lawson's determination to cash in on the publicity value of Don Bradman's achievements. Bradman was under contract to Mick Simmons Ltd, and Lawson,

Early in the 1930s, a Sydney street photographer snapped this picture of the dapper young businessman Don Bradman

DON BRADMAN'S BOOK

Sir Donald Bradman recalls that although his father left school at eleven he developed an excellent practical command of English. Sir Donald himself left school at fourteen — and has sometimes regretted the brevity of his education — but his father's example, and the meticulous teaching of English in State schools earlier this century, gave him an advantage denied to many youngsters nowadays. He uses the English language with an enviable flair and accuracy. Those who have come in contact with him in the business world have noticed how carefully he weighs each word for its precise meaning, and how business letters and reports are models of 'logic and expression'.

Like many writers, he began as a diarist. Plenty of people keep diaries, but few continue them. Bradman was unusual in that he applied the same discipline to the keeping of his diary as he used on the cricket field, and he wrote it up each night regardless of how crowded his day had been. He also enjoyed writing letters, although the sheer bulk of his fan mail prevented him from answering all of them.

With this background in regular and disciplined writing, plus an excellent memory, he was fully prepared to accept the challenge offered by the London literary agent David Cromb in April 1930. It was a substantial challenge, because Bradman had to make time to write a book amidst all the other demands of the tour.

Soon after Bradman signed the contract, Cromb sold serial rights to the London *Star* and book rights to the publisher Hutchinson & Co. Ltd, of Paternoster Square. Bradman had to prepare sufficient material for the serialisation to begin on 4 August 1930. He applied himself to the task with the same kind of concentration which served him so well at the wicket; although his frequent self-imposed isolation, to work on the book, supported his team-mates' opinion that Don Bradman was a 'loner'.

The publishers arranged for an English sportswriter, Ben Bennison, to edit and polish Bradman's work, but Bennison soon found that Bradman rejected the insertion of any words or phrases which he would not normally use. And Bradman's handwriting, learned under the 'copybook' discipline of Bowral school, was so clear that it did not need a typist to prepare a copy for the typesetter.

The *Star*'s publicity for the serial announced that Bradman would describe how he progressed 'From pale, lonely beginnings, to amazing early triumphs, and helped by nerves such as few veterans acquire, on to the highest peak in cricket'. This portentous phrasing was totally unsuited to the style of the book.

The *Star* began publication of the serial on 4 August 1930, and Hutchinson published the book in November 1930. They issued a paperback edition, updated by the sportswriter Bruce Harris, during Bradman's third tour of England in 1938.

Many cricketers had published their reminiscences — Clarrie Grimmett's appeared during the 1930 tour and sold well while he was toppling the English wickets — but Bradman set yet another record by being the youngest player ever to publish a book. When it appeared, so soon after his spectacular achievements on his first Test tour, it was an instant success.

The great English cricketer P. F. 'Plum' Warner wrote an introduction to the book, concluding: 'Certainly he showed no signs in England that that fair and well-shaped head of his was in danger of requiring a larger-sized cricket cap. On the contrary, he took his long succession of triumphs with a becoming modesty, which is reflected in this interesting book of his.'

The text of the original book is quite brief: less than 50 000 words plus twelve pages of hints on batting, bowling and fielding. It is written in a pleasant, witty and good-humoured style, and it is certainly remarkable for the 'becoming modesty' which is so characteristic of Don Bradman. He says far more about the achievements of other players, on both sides, than he does about his own. He gives every credit to his team-mates, and shows a professional appreciation of their performances.

Don Bradman's pleasure in his first book was somewhat marred by the reactions of the Australian Board of Control *(see this chapter)* and it gave fresh ammunition to those critics who sneered enviously at the mushrooming Bradman legend with all its associated publicity and acclaim. But the critics have departed, and the book remains essential reading for those who seek further insight into the phenomenon of Donald Bradman.

quite naturally, wanted to make the most of it. The General Motors Corporation of the USA, which had been manufacturing cars in Australia since 1926, also wanted to get in on the act. They planned to present Bradman with a new car as a publicity gesture, and to combine with Mick Simmons Ltd in cashing in on his publicity value.

When the *Oronsay* reached Colombo, Bradman received Lawson's request for him to leave the tour at Fremantle and return to Sydney ahead of the others while they sailed on to their home ports aboard the *Oronsay*. The tour contract allowed this, provided the Board of Control did not have to pay the difference in fares, and General Motors intended to pay these. Not only would they pay his rail fare to Adelaide, but they would also charter an aircraft to fly him to Melbourne and then to Goulburn, where the famous racing driver 'Wizard' Smith would be waiting to speed him home to Bowral and then on to Sydney.

On the last leg of the voyage home, Bradman sent a radiogram to the Board of Control requesting permission to leave the tour in Fremantle. This was granted, and his team-mates were not very pleased to read a subsequent newspaper paragraph stating: 'The whole Australian team, whose cohesion has been its strongest point, is to be broken at Adelaide on November 1. From that moment it will become a comet with a long tail — Bradman being the head, and the rest of the team the tail.'

The reporter might have phrased it more felicitously. Even though Bradman told the newspapers, over and over again, 'If credit is due to any player more than another it should go to our captain, Billy Woodfull', the journalists and public persisted in behaving as though Bradman had won the Test single-handed. He was not responsible for what they said or wrote about him, but his team-mates felt an increasing resentment in their position in the 'tail' of Bradman's 'comet'.

After the ceremonies in the Prince of Wales Theatre the team lunched at the Palace Hotel with the Governor of the State and the Western Australian Cricket Association, then visited the Digger's Hospital where Bradman received a polished-wood cigarette box. Dinner at the Esplanade Hotel preceded a special appearance at the Theatre Royal, where a crowd of about 1000 waited outside and struggled to

Above: A packed house watched the presentation to Don Bradman on the stage of the Theatre Royal: one of the ceremonies to welcome him back to Australia after his first record-breaking overseas tour

Below: Don Bradman rewrote the record books on his first tour of England, with an aggregate of 2960 and an average of 98.66. Such achievements made the people of Australia welcome him home like a conquering hero. Perth newspapers said the city had not seen such scenes since the victorious troops returned from the first world war. In this photograph, Bradman is seen as the 'star of the show' as he accepts a presentation on the stage of the Theatre Royal, Perth

BRADMAN AND THE GIRLS

Journalists seeking a new 'angle' on the young batting star of 1930 soon sought the female viewpoint. One English writer quoted a 'well-known Society woman' as saying: 'He's as shy as a gazelle and as modest as a buttercup. I felt like taking him in my arms and kissing him, he's so nice!'

Another reporter claimed to have been at the Farewell Ball organised by the Australian community in London. He said that he suddenly saw about twenty 'flappers' rushing towards him, but just as he braced himself for the impact 'the shining-eyed, pretty creatures' all ran past him. He turned to see the attraction, and saw that it was Don Bradman.

The journalists did not take long to report — or create — a rumour that Bradman had fallen in love with an English girl. Reports that he was engaged to an unnamed young lady appeared in English newspapers and even reached Australia.

When he landed in Fremantle, the *West Australian* reported coyly: 'Don Bradman paid duty on a small parcel among his massive pile of luggage landed from the *Oronsay* yesterday.

'It contained two beautiful silk shawls.

'One was for his sister. The other? He didn't say.'

secure Bradman autographs. He estimated that he signed at least 500 during the day.

The immense publicity value of his name became apparent when the manager led him onto the stage of the theatre, to stand amidst the garishly-dressed cast of the variety show and various personages of the theatrical circuit. Every seat in the house was occupied from the front stalls to the upper circle, and when he stood smiling behind the footlights the audience exploded into the kind of applause which the actors seldom experienced.

They applauded again when he accepted a cheque for £100, and listened intently when he said a few words about the tour. He repeated his statement about Woodfull, and said: 'His opening partnerships with Ponsford made things much easier for those who followed him . . . and we must not forget that wonderful bowler Clarrie Grimmett, whose work throughout was phenomenal.'

But these obviously sincere acknowledgments did not soften the attitude of some of his team-mates. Human nature being what it is, they ignored the fact that his employers had virtually ordered him to make the priority trip to Sydney, and regarded it as an attempt to steal all the thunder. Some of the semi-professional cricketers among them, or those who owned their own businesses, were eager for just the kind of publicity which Bradman unwillingly attracted. Ironically, it deepened the rift between Bradman the publicity-hater — as he was soon to become — and those who sought publicity, just as his self-imposed isolation in England had separated him from those who enjoyed convivial leisure hours while he sought quieter pastimes.

When he left the Theatre Royal to catch the 9.30 p.m. Transcontinental Express to Adelaide, yet another crowd awaited him: gaping, giggling, touching him, thrusting autograph books and scraps of paper into his hands, trying to overhear everything he said. The adulation of English crowds had been only a foretaste of what his own country had in store. He began to feel he would never know privacy again — that the world was full of prosy old gentlemen who wanted to tell him how cricket used to be played, boys begging for his autograph, and chattering flappers and hungrily-staring men and women of all ages avid for some of his unsought glamour to illuminate their drab lives.

It could have been heady stuff for a young man of twenty-two, but Sir Donald Bradman says bluntly nowadays: 'I didn't like it.' He had savoured every moment of the tour (except when he was seasick), and his mind and diary were crammed with impressions of places, people and events; but he was far from certain about his future. He did not know whether he might be compelled to use his success as the foundation for a career as a professional cricketer, or whether he could continue to do what he always wanted, and enjoy cricket as a sport rather than a job. He loved to *play* cricket, but he doubted whether he wanted it to form the mainstream of his life. As a professional, his joy in the game might be eroded by the pressures and uncertainties of competition, and all this publicity might prove to be a Frankenstein monster. At present, it showered him with unsought gifts and acclaim. What would it do if he could not keep up the pace?

He soon discovered that the publicity was only just beginning. General Motors had arranged for a reception at Kalgoorlie, where 3000 people crammed the Town Hall to see and hear Bradman. When he rejoined the train, word had flashed along the line that 'Don Bradman is coming!' Whenever the train stopped at the tiny railway settlements a group waited to see him. He noted in his diary: 'Crowds of boys everywhere.' Oscar Lawson and the GM representatives travelling with him in the train were delighted. It was a euphoric journey and he was borne along on the tide of their pleasure.

Above: Don Bradman's employer, Mick Simmons Ltd, and General Motors, staged a triumphal progress for Don Bradman as he travelled across the continent from Perth to Bowral and then to Sydney. In this photograph, the motorcade lines up to take him from an Adelaide hotel to Parafield airfield, South Australia

Left: Don Bradman at the wheel of the car which headed the motorcade from Adelaide to the airfield. The man next to him is Oscar Lawson, who was in charge of publicity for Mick Simmons Ltd

A great crowd thronged the Adelaide railway station to welcome the slim youngster with his unaffected smile, and on the following morning he drove down to Port Adelaide at 7 a.m. to meet the rest of the team as they arrived aboard the *Oronsay*. This early start preceded a long day of speeches, presentations, receptions, radio talks, and photographs for the newspapers and the General Motors publicity men.

Lawson, W. H. Jeanes the secretary of the Board of Control, and the General Motors men all basked in his reflected glory as he set out for Parafield airfield on Sunday 2 November, to board the tri-motor Fokker airliner *Southern Cloud* chartered from Australian National Airways. The normally quiet Sunday streets of Adelaide were lined with well-wishers watching the General Motors motorcade, led by Don Bradman in a car decorated with streamers.

Pilot T. W. Shortridge of ANA welcomed them to the aircraft, but the farewells were so prolonged that he was well behind schedule when he took off. A few months later, Shortridge and the *Southern Cloud*, with a co-pilot and six passengers, were to vanish on a flight from Sydney to Melbourne. Flying was a hazardous business in those days, because pilots did not have electronic navigational instruments to help them keep on course. There was some anxiety during the flight as Shortridge was apparently off course, but he finally touched down at Essendon well behind schedule. Bradman had flown only once before, on a brief joy-ride in western New South Wales, and he found the flight to be cold, bumpy and noisy. But once he had recovered from a bout of airsickness he enjoyed sitting beside Shortridge in the co-pilot's seat and absorbing yet another new experience.

The scene at Parafield airfield shortly before Don Bradman boarded the tri-motor Fokker airliner *Southern Cloud* for the flight to Melbourne. A few months later, the airliner vanished with her passengers and crew. The sign 'Lord Mayor's Relief Fund' on the Chevrolet motor-car refers to the fact that General Motors donated a number of cars to the Lord Mayors of Australian capital cities, to be raffled to raise money for the unemployed of the Great Depression of the 1930s

One or two of the South Australian members of the team, now home in Adelaide, could hardly be said to wish him well on his journey. During the following week, Vic Richardson broadcast a talk on the tour and said: 'We could have played any team without Bradman, but we could not have played the blind school without Clarrie Grimmett.' It was an unkind remark, since Bradman repetitively gave full credit to Grimmett and all the other Test cricketers, and like some other comments made by the returning travellers it may smack of sour grapes. Richardson's batting average for the tour was 26.83, against Bradman's 98.66, and his aggregate 832 against 2960. His Test average was 19.60, compared with Bradman's 139.94, and he was in fact dropped from the side for the final Test of that tour.

In 1930 the Melbourne airfield of Essendon lay far out in the more scattered suburbs, but this did not prevent 5000 people from making the long trip to see Bradman arrive. When the *Southern Cloud* landed they broke through the barriers and surged onto the airfield. The press reported that 'Bradman hesitated in the doorway of the plane amazed, and for a few seconds it seemed he could not face the hero-worshipping crowd. Someone from behind pushed him forward. A smile flickered across his lips, and, waving his hand timidly, he stepped to the ground.' The picture was very different from that of the publicity-hungry star painted by those team members who were jealous of his rewards.

The ponderous form of Warwick Armstrong, 'The Big Ship', who had captained Australia in eight successive Test wins against England in 1920–21 and 1921, rolled forward to welcome Bradman with Jack Ryder behind him. Mounted police cleared a way for them to mount a truck tray, and Fox Movietone cameras whirred as Bradman spoke to the crowd. Once more he paid tribute to Woodfull and the whole team, which 'worked together like a machine without the slightest friction, and the Test matches were won by all hands'.

Parked cars lined the road into Melbourne, with occupants straining to catch a glimpse of Bradman as the welcoming committee drove him into the city. The newspapers sought every possible peg on which to hang a Bradman story, and the *Daily Pictorial* was delighted to discover that 'Granny' Scholtz of Cootamundra was visiting her daughter in the Sydney suburb of Petersham. 'Granny', then eighty-five, told the reporter: 'Bless my heart and soul, I brought the little chap into the world. It was at my hospital, Irena, in Adam Street, Cootamundra. Don was always a good boy, and a bonny baby. He was a sturdy little chap . . . His father was a great cricketer, too, but he never had a real big chance.'

Bradman's Monday in Melbourne passed in another whirl of receptions and cheering crowds. The 'Mothers of Melbourne' entrusted him with a bunch of roses for his mother, and Lord Beauchamp presented him with a cheque 'on behalf of a number of admirers'. In the evening, Bradman and the Victorian members of the Test team, who had just arrived in the *Oronsay*, attended an official welcome-home theatre party at the Theatre Royal, where they saw 'Mr Cinders'.

On the Tuesday morning he boarded the *Southern Cloud* for the flight to Goulburn: a gruelling experience in the face of gale-force head winds. The aircraft shuddered and bounced along like a boat in rough seas, but Pilot Shortridge followed his orders to fly a circuit around every large town on the route so that the earthlings might marvel at the thought of 'the Don' flying over their heads. Bradman, cold and nauseated in the aircraft cabin and deafened by the roar of the three seven-cylinder engines, was literally powerless in the grip of the publicity machine.

His father and brother awaited him with 'Wizard' Smith's roadster at Goulburn airfield, where he accepted the mayor's invitation to drink a cup of tea in the town 'provided there was no reception'. Bowral was only about an hour's drive away and he was in a hurry to get there.

Then at last he was at home again — back in Bowral where the

Home at last. Don Bradman's father (right) and his brother Vic welcome him as he lands at the Goulburn airfield en route to Bowral

Young Don Bradman, at twenty-one, was the hero of Australia in 1930, but when he stood on the Bowral bandstand to address his old friends and neighbours he said he found it harder to make a speech to them than to any other crowd which had welcomed him home

crowd was much smaller than the mobs which had besieged him but infinitely more satisfying to his eye. He knew most of them, if only by sight: he had been to school with the younger men and women, and they had all played some part in fashioning his life.

The town band played 'Our Don Bradman' as he stepped from the car into his mother's embrace and gave her the roses from the mothers of Melbourne. There are no words to describe the feelings between mother and son.

The town was gay with flags and bunting and the council had erected a dais in Corbett Park. The familiar faces of the mayor and aldermen beamed at him as he and his family mounted the dais, his generous former employer Percy Westbrook clasped his hand, and the crowd clustered closer to listen to the speeches.

People were not afraid of sentiment in those days, and the mayor and aldermen laid it on fairly heavily as one after another spoke of the young man who had brought glory to the name of Bowral. Percy Westbrook said: 'His success is largely due to his personal charm and ability, and he comes back to us the same carefree, clear-eyed, clean-limbed boy he was eight months ago.'

Bradman's response to the series of speeches was rather short because he was 'visibly affected'. But he was becoming used to public speaking, although he said 'it is more difficult to speak in my own town than anywhere else, because here you are all old friends while elsewhere they are strangers'.

At long last the ceremonies ended and the cheers died away, so that his family could have him to themselves. He was exhausted after the long day and slept so late on the following morning that 'Wizard' Smith had to make up the time on a dash to the outskirts of Sydney, sometimes driving at over eighty miles per hour.

He dropped Bradman at the Cross Roads Hotel, Liverpool, where

General Motors fitted out the 'Don Bradman Car' as a custom-built vehicle as their gift to the young batsman

a General Motors representative handed over his new car. It was a custom-built vehicle unlike any other GM product and they had christened it 'the Don Bradman Car'. The newspapers described it as 'a cheeky-looking sports roadster of de luxe type, upholstered in pigskin, maroon in colour, and a mass of silver plating'. The publicity campaign associated with the gift was related to the General Motors donation of a number of cars to the Lord Mayors of each capital, to be raffled at sixpence a ticket to help relief funds for the unemployed.

He drove his new car to Mick Simmons headquarters in Sydney for an enraptured welcome by the staff before he went on to the Royal Automobile Club for lunch with the Lord Mayor, the Chief Secretary and other dignitaries.

The official conclusion to the tour came when Bradman and others welcomed the New South Wales contingent of the team — except for Archie Jackson — when the *Oronsay* berthed at the Orient Line wharf, followed by an official welcome at the Town Hall. The newspapers made some play with the fact that Archie Jackson had slipped back into Sydney unwelcomed and unrecognised. He had left the ship in Melbourne; and although a crowd of admirers gathered to meet the train on which he was expected in Sydney, he evaded them by travelling by air. Even his family were surprised by his unheralded arrival.

Critics soon found an opportunity to contrast this modest return with Bradman's triumphal progress, and the newspapers took sides in explaining why Bradman had had to obey the orders of his employer or hinting that he should not have done so. The story soon spread overseas, where the London *Daily Express* said it was a pity 'to see Bradman treated and behaving as though he alone had won the Ashes'.

This was a totally unfair comment. Bradman had simply said all the right things and made all the right gestures. It was part of his job as an employee of Mick Simmons Ltd, who had invested in him for his publicity value and now saw their investment paying enormous dividends. It would have been wrong and ungracious for him to reject the tributes and turn away from the unsought publicity, which at times had almost frightened him. Rejection would have offended and disappointed the public and, in effect, broken his contract with his employers. He smiled, waved, and responded to speeches because it was expected of him, but he certainly never behaved 'as though he alone had won the Ashes'. He was always at pains to give credit to the rest of the team.

Partisans on both sides enjoyed the dissension while yet another public row simmered slowly in the background and then suddenly boiled over. It was the matter of *Don Bradman's Book*.

'The Mothers of Melbourne' contributed towards a magnificent bouquet for Don Bradman's mother, Emily Bradman. He carried it with him from Melbourne to Bowral and the publicity cameramen staged this rather formal presentation

This cartoon by Arthur Mailey in the Sydney *Sun* was one of the many ways in which the newspapers mocked at or abused the Australian Board of Control (for international cricket) when they fined Bradman fifty pounds for allegedly breaking his contract by publishing a book. Clarrie Grimmett also published a book during the 1930 tour but the Board took no action against him

At that time, nobody in Australia had seen the book. Copies did not reach Australia until late in 1930. But someone leaked the story of Kelly's disapproval of the *Star* serialisation, and the newspapers began to publish hints that the Board of Control planned to discipline Bradman for some misdemeanour committed overseas. They did not know the complete story, but they did not hesitate to start chipping away at the base of the pedestal on which they themselves had placed Bradman.

Aubrey Oxlade, acting chairman of the Board of Control, was a solicitor, and he was careful not to commit himself in one way or another. He told the press: 'The statements are thoroughly unfair and unjust. We will not know anything about the tour until December 29.

'Indeed, it looks very much as if some irresponsible persons were desirous of stirring up strife and discord in the cricketing world.'

He asked the public to believe that Kelly had not said anything to any member of the Board about events on the tour. Officially, they remained in total ignorance about the tour until they met on 29 December to discuss Kelly's report.

The editor of the Sydney sporting journal *The Referee*, who had always been a staunch supporter of Don Bradman, came out firmly on his side in a lengthy editorial. He opened with a reference to 'cryptic charges being laid against Bradman by other newspapers', and said: 'It looks as though there are some who would like to see humiliated the young batsman who has startled the world. Bradman is discovering that a man has only to win eminence in any sphere to invite and encounter blasts of criticism from men of smaller mould.'

That irreverent publication *Smith's Weekly* had earlier forecast: 'When Don Bradman comes back to Australia the Cricket Board of Control will yammer and squeal. There'll be a great clucking among the cricket-governing hens!

'This superb young cricketer, showing as much initiative and acumen in business as he does at the batting crease, has snapped like a lot of pack-thread the tangle of prohibitions and restrictions woven by the Board of Control to debar Australian cricketers from making any money from their cricketing fame . . . The young wonder batsman, on his first triumphant tour of England, is reported by ''Smith's'' London office to have probably accumulated enough capital to set himself up in business when he returns to Australia. Good luck to him!'

This was of course a gross exaggeration, but newspapers seldom miss a chance of good copy.

Smith's Weekly printed two racy and provocative articles on the subject, one headed 'Champion Is Reaping Handsome Fortune During Marvellous Tour in England: Manager Kelly Cannot Chain Young Napoleon', and the other, printed after Bradman's return to Australia, 'Will Don Bradman Be Bossed By The Board of Control?'

The newspaper's opinion was that a sportsman was perfectly entitled to cash in on his fame, and quoted a businessman, Sir Mark Sheldon, as saying: 'In the life of a young man there comes a time when he must decide between business and sport . . . he cannot do both.' *Smith's Weekly* said that Bradman was 'surely entitled to consolidate his position'.

While the journalists waited for the Board's decision they maintained a solemn discussion as to whether a cricketer should be allowed

A LETTER FROM A SUPPORTER

When the Board of Control passed a vote of censure against Don Bradman, and fined him £50, most cricket lovers in Australia and England rallied to his support. A letter from one of them, a Mr W. H. Hartley of Sydney, encapsulated their feelings. He wrote:

'As one who has played the good old game for over 50 years I hereby extend to you my sympathy, and also express my contempt for the miserable attempt on the part of the N.S.W. Board of Control to besmirch your reputation. Believe me the cricket loving public hold you in high esteem, and many to whom I have spoken express themselves in terms of disgust at the unwarranted and injudicious action of the Board. However don't let this scandalous treatment daunt your courage or in any way affect your career. Play the game as you have always done for the love of it.

'No doubt the action taken against you was the result of envy and jealousy which if looked at from a right angle is rather complimentary, for envy and jealousy are really admissions of inferiority.

'With kind regards and best wishes,

'I am yours faithfully,

'W. H. Hartley.'

to profit by his skill at the game. There were those who deplored the 'commercialisation of cricket' and supported the Board's attempt to restrain profitable activities. They said that if one cricketer could make more than another, it led to ill-feeling which eroded the team spirit. Those on the other side pointed out that a cricketer's professional career was liable to be short, and that he was entitled to make the most of it while he was in the public eye. They said that cricketers had frequently received payment for allowing their names to be used in advertising, and that Clarrie Grimmett had published a successful book during the tour without drawing any objections from Kelly.

The crux of the matter appeared to be the size and suddenness of Bradman's success, together with his reserved and frugal attitude during the tour. If, after the £1000 gift during the Leeds match, he had thrown a party for his team-mates, they might have been able to forgive him his good fortune. But it was not in his nature to roister with his companions. He had been strictly brought up in a family and community which did not encourage extravagance, and he was a sober, serious-minded young man far more interested in absorbing new experiences than in drinking in hotel lounges. And, above all, he was still overwhelmed by his sudden fame and fortune and he needed time to adjust himself. Numerous writers of the period referred to his 'business-like attitude to life', and this was based on an instinctive need to plan each step forward. It was no more possible for him to make a sudden change in his lifestyle than it was to change his style of batting.

Some of his team-mates told the newspapers 'He was not one of us during the tour', and they were quite right. He had shown that he would be greater than any of them, so they could hardly expect him to resemble them in other ways.

Bradman took no part in the dissension about his activities. He did not even contradict one of *Smith's Weekly*'s wilder implications: that Kelly had had almost physically to restrain 'Don Alexander Napoleon Bradman' from appearing on the stage of London music-halls.

Bradman had more urgent things on his mind, especially the first-ever series of Test Matches in which Australia would meet the West Indies, between 12 December 1930 and 4 March 1931. But the burden of good and bad publicity, added to the prolonged strain of the overseas tour, certainly affected his cricket. He played rather mediocre innings in three matches prior to the first Test against the 'Windies' at Adelaide, and in that match he gave a woeful exhibition. He went in at 55 for one on the second day, played insecurely for fifteen minutes and made four runs, then cut at a wide ball and delivered it into the hands of Grant at third slip.

The critics chuckled, but only two days later he played for New South Wales against South Australia and recaptured all his natural brilliance. In a thrilling partnership with Archie Jackson he attacked the bowling of the South Australians, including Clarrie Grimmett, with such verve and gusto that he reached the tenth double century of his career, more than any other Australian had made, in 234 minutes. His total of 258 helped New South Wales to win by an innings and 134 runs.

But on the way home to Sydney, in a Shield match at Victoria, the volatile young batsman failed again. He made only two runs in nine minutes before Hendry caught him in the slips off a'Beckett.

Back in Sydney, the Board of Control summoned him to hear their decision on Kelly's report — and kept him waiting outside the board-room for two hours. When he emerged, hovering reporters observed that he wore the usual Bradman smile.

The board had decided to cut his £150 'good conduct money', pay-able to each player on returning to Australia, to £100. Effectively, they were fining him £50 for the *Star* having serialised a portion of *Don Bradman's Book*.

Sportswriters did not smile when they heard about the verdict. The London *Sporting Life* wrote on 1 January 1931: 'Sporting writers in the Australian newspapers criticise the Cricket Board of Control's action in penalising Bradman to the extent of £50 because, after receiv-ing a lump sum from the publishers for his life story, his book ap-peared in serial form in an English newspaper . . . Others point out that when Grimmett applied to the chairman of the Board for per-mission to publish his book, the chairman replied that permission was not necessary, but permission was given.

'If permission was not necessary', says the writer, 'it is difficult to see in what way Bradman has offended.'

The verdict was a paltry victory for Bradman's enemies and it was scorned by his countless friends. There is certainly an enormous con-trast between that smug and narrow-minded decision and the situation today, in which current players write every day about their matches even to the extent of making what many believe to be very indiscreet comments about their colleagues.

The London *Daily Herald* wrote: 'Bradman is apparently suffering from a combination of hero worship and official irritation. The fact that one-half of Australia expects him to score centuries without effort, and the other half thinks that he is a bad boy, must have an adverse mental effect on one who, after all, is little more than a schoolboy.' *The Referee* commented: 'If he pleased he could snap his fingers in the face of officialdom, as he could command almost as much as he pleased if he consented to play in England', and demanded that the Board should either remit the penalty 'or make further enquiries into the activities of other players, who apparently have not been reported by the manager'.

The Bowral newspaper was furious and the editor wrote that the Board 'should now fine themselves fifty runs apiece, the said runs to be made barefooted over a specially prepared pitch of unblinded blue metal, or, preferably, Bowral chip, at the Sydney Cricket Ground on the next public holiday'.

Bradman gave his own opinion in a restrained and sincere statement published by *The Referee*. He said the Board had received him courteously and he appreciated the opportunity to put his case to them, but he had a 'firm and honest belief that I had not acted contrary to the agreement, for no sum of money, however large, would compen-sate me if my honor or character would be affected in the slightest degree'.

He explained that he had not played any part in the sale of serial rights to the *Star* and had not received any payment from the news-paper. His only part in the matter was to stipulate that the serialisation must cease at the point where the story reached the selection of the Australian touring team.

If Bradman required any compensation for the loss of the £50, *The*

Below: Don Bradman in the recording studio when he recorded a Lee Sims arrangement for the piano

The bat with which Bradman made 223 not out against the West Indies, Brisbane, January 1931

Referee provided it by commissioning him to write a series of eleven articles on his life and cricketing experiences. He opened the series with the words 'I am to write a series of articles on cricket for "The Referee." That sounds easy.

'Yet it is probably the most difficult task I have had to do. For with me, cricket success has followed my day dreams as a youngster so quickly that I don't really know where to begin.

'If I were a novelist, I might call my articles, "Day Dreams Come True." But I'm not; I'm a batsman and can't day-dream any more. So I'll get on with my job.'

He had to find time to write the articles amid all the other demands on his energy. In the first two months of 1931 he played in the remaining matches of the West Indies tour; a Shield match against Victoria in Sydney; for New South Wales against the West Indies in Sydney; and for St George whenever he could make the time. Oscar Lawson kept him busy with commitments for Mick Simmons Ltd; he received innumerable invitations to lunch and dinner; and various organisations were still anxious to honour him with receptions and presentations. The Menzies home in Burwood was a quiet haven from the hero-worshippers, and the Menzies family anticipated that he and Jessie would soon announce their engagement.

Sydney cricket lovers demonstrated their faith in him on New Year's Day, 1931, with a standing ovation when he walked out for his first innings in the second Test against the 'Windies'. He settled down confidently, but Barrow caught him at the wicket off a rising ball when he had made 25.

In the third Test he more than compensated for his variable performances in that season. In a classic display of batting he reached his double century in four hours eleven minutes and at the close of play, thirty-nine minutes later, he was 223 not out.

This score broke Trumper's 1910–11 record score for an Australian batsman in a home Test Match, when he made 214 against South Africa. Bradman had made the most runs ever scored in one day's play in a home Test Match.

In the Shield match against Victoria, on 24–28 January, he made only 33 in his first innings, but the second was a triumph. At 76, he completed his 1000 runs for the season and became the only batsman ever to have completed 1000 three times in Australian seasons. After four hours forty-two minutes at the wicket he completed yet another double century, and was 208 not out overnight. He finished the innings with 220.

In the fourth Test, enthralled spectators at the Melbourne Cricket Ground watched him make his third-fastest Test century. He attacked the bowling, including that of the famous Learie Constantine, immediately he went in after tea at 50 for one. In seventy-eight minutes he carried his bat for 92, and on a sticky wicket the following morning he reached 100 after 102 minutes. When Roach caught him off Martin, he had scored 152.

His first innings in the fifth Test enabled him to give a brief but brilliant display of batting on a spiteful pitch at the Sydney Cricket Ground, scoring 43 in fifty-one minutes before Francis caught him in the slips off a ball which kicked viciously. In his second innings, Griffith bowled him for the first duck in his Test career. He misjudged the flight of a ball, hit across a yorker, and thus lost his wicket after only ten minutes.

Australia won the Test series, although Bradman wrote later that 'my form was patchy, and I think the same may be said of practically the whole of the Australian team'. He believed that Australia was much too good for the West Indies but he praised some of their players, including George Headley and Derek Sealey and especially Learie Constantine: 'the greatest all-round fieldsman I have ever seen . . . the phenomenal agility and anticipation of Constantine made him a perpetual danger in any position'.

Constantine's cricket career was then nine years old and he was well on his way to becoming one of the greatest all-rounders of his generation.

Soon after the fifth Test, Bradman joined an eleven led by Alan Kippax on a kind of 'charity' tour of Queensland centres. It was a 'charity' because the cricketers received only ten shillings a day apart from their travel and accommodation expenses, and the object was to give isolated cricketers a chance to match themselves against some of Australia's best players. Kippax's eleven included Stan McCabe, Wendell Bill, and some other well-known names.

Early in 1931, Don Bradman accompanied a team of New South Wales cricketers on a tour of north Queensland to play against local sides. The visit aroused enormous interest in north Queensland and the Cricket Carnival was advertised by such means as these souvenir programmes. But the tour ended badly for Don Bradman, who broke his ankle in one of the earliest games and had to return to Sydney on crutches

Bradman 'aboard the rattler', looking out of a north Queensland railway carriage early in the tour

Mick Simmons Ltd, the Sydney sportsgoods distributors who employed Don Bradman from February 1929 to February 1932, naturally made the most of his name in their advertising. This advertisement, which appeared after his return from the 1930 tour, linked Mick Simmons Ltd with the Don Bradman Bat

The tour began at Cairns, and the easiest way to get there in those days was by sea. On 17 March they left Sydney aboard the coastal passenger liner *Ormiston* for an enjoyable cruise which showed Bradman the beauty of the Queensland coastline and the Barrier Reef islands. From Cairns, they went inland to play at Eacham and then made their way home through the principal coastal towns, playing fixtures in each town and taking side trips to places of interest.

The Queenslanders gave them an ebullient welcome and the trip became a pleasant holiday as well as a sporting tour. The Cairns newspaper wrote 'Never before has Cairns seen such cricket as was seen at Parramatta Park over the weekend', while local businessmen made free with Bradman's name in their advertisements. Buchanan's Hotel, Townsville, proclaimed: 'This will be the HOME of the VISITING SOUTHERN CRICKETERS including DON BRADMAN.' John M. Headrick advertised: 'Foster's is the Bradman of Lagers.' Emery & Connor Ltd, Gents' Outfitters of Rockhampton, said: 'We All Admire Don Bradman! Are We Admired? We will be if the cut and texture of the clothes we wear are right. Men's Suits from £6/6/-.' The children's page of the Rockhampton *Evening News* printed an article about Bradman, remarking: 'Don Bradman also plays tennis and golf, and can dance. He does not smoke, drink strong liquors, or swear. (At least I am sure he does not swear, as he looks much too sweet-tempered.) He does not undertake any special exercise for training or keeping fit, he is just naturally a born cricketer and a true "Aussie" sport.'

But the tour came to an abrupt and disastrous end for Don Bradman. At Rockhampton the visitors fielded first, and within minutes of the opening over Bradman stepped in a hole in the rough outfield when he was chasing a ball. He fell heavily and broke his right ankle.

He spent several days in Rockhampton hospital and convalesced at the home of a local benefactor before returning home, still on crutches. Luckily there was time for the injury to mend before the opening of the next cricket season.

'Don Bradman's here!' Sydney crowds flock towards Mick Simmons Ltd

8

ACCRINGTON AND THE SOUTH AFRICANS

It was all very well for *Smith's Weekly* to write boldly — and inaccurately — about Bradman returning from England with enough money to 'set himself up in business', but there had rarely been a less propitious time for any kind of commercial venture. The situation in Australia reflected that of the whole world, swamped by the black tide of the Great Depression. Then as now, the economic disaster hit hardest at school-leavers, semi-skilled workers, and elderly employees; but it struck also at all sections of the community. Those businesses which survived the Depression did so only by cutting staff and slashing wages. In numerous industries, such as building, one out of three men was unemployed. The prices for primary produce were the lowest on record and farmers with heavy mortgages had to abandon their properties and work for 'sustenance' in the cities. Overseas bankers were demanding that State governments should repay their huge loans, public service wages had been cut by twenty per cent, and the politics of New South Wales was in chaos.

For a young man of twenty-two, Don Bradman was unusually well-equipped to weather the storm. He still had his job at Mick Simmons Ltd, and it seemed likely that Oscar Lawson would renew his contract when it expired in February 1932. He had accumulated enough to give him a comfortable start in married life. He could hold his job, play as much cricket as he liked and benefit from such 'fringe benefits' as payments for the use of his name in advertising — although these were very small and restricted by comparison with those enjoyed by some modern cricketers.

The problem was that neither he nor Jessie Menzies wanted this kind of future. Everything in their solid colonial background resisted the notion of a life reliant on his performance at the wicket, at the mercy of a fickle public. Most of them loved him at the age of twenty-two, but how would they feel in twenty years' time? A couple of bad seasons, or an injury such as that which put Jack Gregory out of the game after only nine years, could relegate him to the pages of cricketing history. The broken ankle, which kept him on crutches for three months, was like a warning of the uncertainties of a life founded on cricket. He had sampled enough of its strains and tensions, as well as its pleasures and rewards, to know it was not for him. He regarded

The courting couple. A snapshot of Don Bradman and Jessie Menzies taken about 1931

cricket as a game, not a profession. As he says nowadays, 'I wanted something more permanent and tangible'.

He and Jessie Menzies discussed the problem during the winter of 1931, just as they discussed the appropriate moment to announce their engagement. He had proposed to her before he left on the English tour, but the level-headed young lady had asked him to wait until his return from the tour and see how they both felt then. Their feelings were unchanged and that part of their future, at least, was assured.

The prime difficulty was that Bradman was not qualified for anything except cricket. If he was as supremely skilled in any other occupation, there would have been no problem. He was not even sufficiently educated to begin studying for one of the professions. When the young couple balanced the bleak economic situation against his unwillingness to commit himself to a life in cricket, there was no easy answer.

Unknown to them, a gentleman whom the newspapers later called 'the mystery man' was working behind the scenes on Don Bradman's behalf, and his activities were to resolve the problem in a totally unexpected way.

He was Claude Spencer, a Sydney man well known to the local cricketing fraternity for his fanatical devotion to the sport. He had never made a name for himself as a cricketer but he would do almost anything for his heroes of the pitch. On some occasions he acted as a kind of unofficial manager for Sydney teams playing against country clubs, and packed his own car with cricketers to drive them on such tours.

He had a glass eye, and Sir Donald Bradman retains vivid memories of sitting in the passenger's seat beside Claude as he drove fast along a country road, talking enthusiastically about cricket while he literally spared no more than half an eye for what lay ahead.

Spencer's devotion to cricket, and his friendly acceptance by local cricketers, brought him into contact with Learie Constantine when the great West Indian was in Australia in 1930-31. At that time, Constantine was the professional cricketer attached to Nelson Cricket Club in the Lancashire League.

The position of 'professional cricketer' had no exact equivalent in Australia. In an English club, the professional was a full-time paid employee with a wide range of duties, especially that of helping to win matches and, by his skill and reputation, attracting more spectators and increasing the gate money. He coached the amateur players and worked with them as guide, tutor, example, and 'stiffener', like a veteran sergeant with a squad of volunteer recruits. He advised the captain and manager, helped to plan strategy, and in some cases looked after the equipment and supervised the groundsman.

A notable professional cricketer could command a healthy remuneration. The club paid him a substantial annual retainer, plus a 'talent fee' based on the number of runs made and wickets taken in each innings, and arranged a number of 'exhibition matches' for which he received separate payments. As an added inducement, the cricket-minded manager of some local business would arrange extra employment for him during the off-season, and he could engage in other money-making activities so long as they did not interfere with his cricket.

It appears that, in 1931, Accrington Cricket Club in the Lancashire League sought a top-notch professional to bring new life and lustre to their team, which had not won the league title since 1916. Sir Donald Bradman has no clear picture of the links between Accrington, Constantine and Spencer, but he agrees it is possible that the club asked Constantine to keep his eye open for a suitable Australian during his Test visit. Sir Learie Nicholas Constantine (Lord, Baron of

An advertisement inserted by Wm. Sykes Ltd in British sports magazines in 1931

Maraval and Nelson) died in 1971, so it is no longer possible to elicit the background story.

Probably Constantine discussed the matter with Spencer and canvassed various names. There can be no doubt that Spencer — with his consuming interest in everything to do with cricket and cricketers — offered to act as intermediary. Certainly he must have corresponded with Constantine, and perhaps with the Accrington club, during the Australian winter of 1931.

On 25 August, two days before Bradman's twenty-third birthday, Constantine sent Spencer a cable saying: 'Local club offers five hundred pounds per season for 3 seasons passage both ways cable reply.'

The fact that Constantine did not mention Bradman's name in the cable indicates that the two men had discussed the young batsman as a possibility. Constantine's use of the words 'local club', instead of naming Accrington, probably was to maintain confidentiality.

Spencer astonished Bradman with the news of the offer and gave him plenty of food for thought. An overriding problem was his touring contract with the Board of Control, which specifically forbade him to play for an English team before September 1932 — too late for the English season of that year. If he accepted the offer, he could be reasonably sure that the Board would never approve him for another Test eleven.

At the same time he knew that the opportunities for a cricketer were more extensive in England than in Australia, and that there was nothing unusual about Australians playing for English clubs. If he accepted the offer he would be following a well-trodden path. At least fourteen Australians had become professionals in England, including the great fast bowler Frederick Spofforth who played for Derbyshire. Blackpool had invited Ponsford to join them in 1927, and he would have done so but for the public outcry in Melbourne and the inducements which persuaded him to remain in Victoria.

Bradman found himself faced by a 'devil's alternative'. The offer was extremely tempting, because it would enable him to play cricket in the English summers and still have time to return home each September for the Australian seasons if he wished to do so. It would

The 'Snappy Fox Trot Song' entitled 'Our Don Bradman' was a popular piece of music in the early 1930s — except among English cricketers

A MUSICAL INTERLUDE

The countless stories, rumours and reports about Don Bradman included one which alleged that he intended to abandon cricket for a theatrical career. Another said that he had received an offer from Hollywood.

They were inspired by his interest in music, which included the composition of a piece for the piano and the making of a record when he was in London. He played the piano with a 'backing' group of musicians.

During the first visit of a West Indies team to Australia, a Sydney newspaper reported 'Mr Don Bradman, the famous cricketer, was present at the Grand Opera House last night to hear his song "Every Day is a Rainbow Day for Me" which is introduced in the pantomime "Beauty and the Beast". The song, composed by Mr Bradman to words by Mr Jack Lumsdaine, was sung by Miss Elsie Hosking, and proved pleasantly melodious and sentimental, with a refrain in which saxophones and brasses vigorously supported the vocal theme, ere it was taken up smartly by a well-trained ballet.

'After the song there was great applause for the composer as he walked on to the stage, accompanied by Mr George Marlow. Mr Bradman said he had enjoyed very much the experience of hearing his composition sung in public. "I hope," he added, amid renewed applause, "that we shall be able to apply the title of this song to our experiences in Australia in the year now opening, and that every day will be a rainbow day for us." On his own behalf and that of Mr Lumsdaine, he presented a box of chocolates to Miss Hosking, and complimented her and the orchestra and ballet upon the performance.'

enable him to increase his nest-egg, consolidate his reputation in both hemispheres, and secure a substantial future for at least the next three years.

On the other hand, it would be a final commitment to a life reliant on cricket; a self-inflicted wound in the sense that he would never again know the crowning challenge of participation in Test matches; and a kind of semi-exile in having to spend much of his time overseas. If he continued to work as a professional after the Accrington contract expired, it would inevitably be in England.

His instincts rejected the offer, but after consultation with Spencer he decided he might as well open negotiations to see how far the 'local club' would go. On his behalf, Spencer replied to Constantine: 'Offer disappointing prepared negotiate through Claude Spencer two years contract what is maximum.'

Constantine answered on 31 August: 'Final offer six hundred pounds cable immediately.'

All parties had intended to keep the matter confidential, but someone leaked it to the press and the London representative of the Sydney *Truth* picked up the story — with some embellishments. The newspaper printed an article with a sub-heading: 'If Bradman Decided to Play For a Living, He Could Start with an English Club at a Salary of about £1500 a Year. Not too Bad a Salary for a Young Man of 22.'

Truth had tripled the salary and taken a year off Bradman's age, and the article stated that the offer was for only one season. In its usual breezy style, the newspaper summarised the story with such comments as 'Australian cricket offers very little to a batsman of Bradman's brilliance. He . . . would be slipping up as a businessman if he didn't capitalise his cricket while he still owns a portmanteau name.

'. . . And what sort of attraction would Don be to the English fans? Eminent detective Ashton Wolfe would have difficulty in laying hands upon an English "pro" whose batting really stimulates an English crowd.

'The average professional batsman "digs in", scratches round like a Leghorn with lumbago, and is the surest cure in the world for insomnia.

'Bradman would provide the champagne of cricket on "the other side", and with millions of people to pay for it the St George batsman is in a position to almost command his price.'

Most of the metropolitan newspapers in England and Australia immediately picked up the story and printed their own comments. A. G. Moyes wrote in the *Sun*: 'Being young and ambitious, he will naturally seek the best market and it will be an extremely difficult task to keep him in this country.

'One would regret intensely to see other countries getting the benefit of skill which is Australian in birth and development, even though a cricketer is as much entitled to reward for skill as the singer or the actor.'

Most of the newspapers wrote as though Bradman had already signed the contract, and some of the English journalists wrote quite vehemently against this 'decision', whereas the Australians tended to support it. The editor of the *Manchester Chronicle* tried excitedly to persuade Bradman, by cable, to give him a scoop on this item of Lancashire news, but Bradman was playing his cards very close to his

SUNDAY, SEPTEMBER 6, 1931

BRADMAN IS GOING TO ENGLAND!

The Sydney *Truth* poster of 6 September 1931 proclaiming the erroneous news that Bradman had accepted a contract to play for an English cricket team

chest and replied only 'Offer still under consideration'. This did not prevent the newspaper from saying it 'understood' that 'Don Bradman, the famous Australian cricketer, today replied to the Accrington Cricket Club, saying that he is willing to sign a two-year contract instead of the three-year contract the club offered him . . . the contract figure is not stated, but it is believed to be £25 a week'.

The editor tried again to obtain an exclusive story, and the degree of Don Bradman's fame at that time is shown by the fact that the editor could send a cable addressed only to 'Don Bradman Cricketer Sydney' and be sure that it would be delivered. He said: 'Would appreciate further cable from you immediately you decide come to Accrington in view of that club's amended offer all Lancashire sportsmen eagerly awaiting good news.'

Bradman replied: 'Details receiving consideration. Information will not be withheld when decision arrived at.'

He gave an equally restrained answer to Australian journalists who besieged him for the story. Even Arthur Mailey, who knew him well, could not extract any details from 'the Sphinx'.

The London *Daily Express* cabled for the story; the editor of the *Manchester Sunday Chronicle* offered £150 for a series of weekly articles; the London *Evening Standard* 'revealed' that Bradman 'is definitely expected to turn out for the Accrington Club from the middle of April'.

Everyone — except Bradman — was prepared to offer an opinion on

Opposite: A piece of advertising material for the Don Bradman Cricket Boot, one of the few products to which Bradman lent his name in the early 1930s

THEY BOWLED BRADMAN FOR 0

The two men who dismissed Bradman for ducks at the beginning and end of the 1931–32 season, at Brisbane on 6 November 1931 and at Sydney on 22 March 1932, were totally different characters in every way.

The Queensland bowler was Eddie Gilbert, an Aboriginal from Barambah. The same age as Don Bradman, he was a wiry man of medium height: a right-arm bowler with exceptionally long arms. He was a modest, retiring personality except when he was bowling, when he took a few shuffling steps and then exploded into a blur of motion which propelled the ball at terrifying speed.

He began his cricketing life at Barambah and was picked for the Country Colts XI in 1930–31. His appearance against Bradman was in his second Shield match.

Batsmen, fieldsmen and managers all protested against his unusual style and often accused him of throwing. When he toured with the Queensland Shield eleven the southern umpires frequently 'no-balled' him, but he was extremely popular with Queenslanders.

Trouble with his shoulder ended his career in the 1935–36 season. He had taken 87 first-class wickets at 28.97.

Gilbert suffered a mental breakdown and entered Cherbourg Mental Hospital in 1949. He lost the power of speech and lingered on until 1978.

Thomas Welbourne 'Tim' Wall, who bowled Bradman for 0 in the Shield match at Sydney in March 1932, was a South Australian right-arm bowler of great speed and accuracy. Tall, slim, dark and good-natured, he was noted for his slow walk back to his bowl-

ing mark which was in great contrast to his vigorous run-up and kicking action as he delivered the ball.

In a career which ran from 1924 to 1936 he took 56 Test wickets at 35.89 and 328 first-class wickets at 29.83. He was one of only three bowlers to take all ten wickets in an innings in Shield matches.

Tim Wall, Don Bradman, and their wives and families became lifelong friends. Wall was originally a State school teacher, and with Bradman's encouragement and assistance he became a master at St Peter's College in South Australia.

Wall was very popular with his team-mates, spectators, and opponents on the pitch. He died in 1981 at the age of seventy-seven.

the subject. Mr Justice Draper, patron of the Western Australian Cricket Association, 'when informed today that Bradman had accepted the Lancashire offer, said that as one born in that county he deprecated the action of that club'. Dr C. E. Dolling, one of the Australian selectors, said that 'ideals in cricket would be better preserved if the respective countries produced and retained the services of their champions'. The London *Daily Sketch* published a cartoon of Bradman being chaired in honour of his record score of 452 against Queensland in January 1930, above the caption 'Well Paid, Sir!' Tom Webster of the *Daily Mail* drew a cartoon of a kangaroo telling a blushing Bradman: 'The story of Esau who sold his birthright for a mess of pottage.'

These hurtful and uninformed opinions spurred Bradman to his only definite reply to journalistic queries. He said 'I certainly do not appreciate some of the caustic comment which has been made in England about my accepting the Accrington contract, for I have not done so. Should I accept the contract, that will be the time for comment. They are pulling me to pieces before I have done anything.'

Few people outside Lancashire knew anything about Accrington, and an English journalist went to have a look at the town. He wrote: 'If Don Bradman comes to Accrington he will need to appreciate that kind hearts are more than boulevards. For whatever Accrington is, it certain is not beautiful.

'I asked a bus conductor if he could help me to find an official of the Accrington Cricket Club. "Are you Bradman?", he asked seriously. I believe he thought he had got a scoop!'

The writer said that club membership totalled only 475, including sixty women, and that its officials counted on Bradman's name to bring a substantial increase in their gate money which then averaged less than £1000 a season.

Gideon Holgate, the secretary of the Accrington club, tried to urge Bradman into a decision by taking the unusual step, for those days, of putting a telephone call through to Australia.

He clarified the Accrington offer by telling Bradman that in addition to the guaranteed £600 for each season he would receive twenty-one shillings 'talent money' for every completed innings of fifty runs or more. He would be expected to play in thirty matches per season, twenty of them on Saturdays, and Holgate said the club would arrange at least fifteen exhibition matches per season. Bradman could nominate his own fee for each of these but it would be at least £10 a match. The usual length of club matches was five hours.

Bradman would be expected to attend practice on Tuesday, Wednesday and Thursday evenings, but the club would not expect him to perform any of the groundsman's duties sometimes required from professionals.

The club had no objection to his writing newspaper articles, such as those requested by the *Manchester Sunday Chronicle*, and Holgate thought it would be possible to arrange extra employment for Bradman. The firm of E. J. Riley, a sporting outfitter and manufacturer of billiard tables, had its headquarters in Accrington, and the managing director's son played for the Accrington team. The club would pay Bradman's fare to England and back, and arrange his board and lodgings for about £2 a week.

A Melbourne *Herald* poster for its issue which reported English reactions to Bradman's possible move to England

Altogether, the offer could have brought Bradman something like £1000 a year, the equivalent of the salary of a top executive in those hard times. But Bradman refused to commit himself, and when Holgate sent him a cable confirming the telephone conversation, and asking for a decision within seven days, he answered on 10 September: 'Decision impossible prior receipt your letter. Commencing three weeks cricket tour today.'

The letter was to contain a contract for Bradman's signature, together with a full written explanation of the Accrington terms. Holgate prepared the contract and explanation for posting on 15 September and posted it by airmail, but in those days that only meant that it would go by air for a part of the distance and the rest by sea. It still took more than a month to reach Australia.

Sir Donald Bradman says nowadays that the offer was 'hard to resist'. He knew that a famous Lancashire League professional could make a great deal of money from various subsidiary activities, and there was no reason why he should not quickly consolidate his name in the United Kingdom. He recalled the crowds of cheering fans who had mobbed him in every city visited by the touring team, and could be fairly certain that manufacturers of sportsgoods, newspaper editors and others would be eager to pay for the use of his name.

But he still did not want to commit himself, and he was glad to be able to escape on the cricket tour he had mentioned to Holgate. He travelled with an eleven led by Alan Kippax, to play against country clubs in New South Wales. They played ten matches in a 1600-kilometre swing through central eastern townships, going as far west as Parkes, and thoroughly enjoyed themselves at the dances and other social occasions arranged by their hosts.

However, Kippax had the misfortune to have his nose broken by a ball which lifted sharply off a matting wicket. During the same season, in a Shield match against Queensland, he received a terrific blow on the head, and the two incidents following so closely upon one another sapped his future confidence against fast bowling.

If Accrington officials heard anything about the tour — which was unlikely in those days — they would have been even more anxious to

It was often said of Don Bradman that everyone expected him to make a century whenever he appeared at the wicket. This strip cartoon of the 1930s emphasises that popular feeling

obtain Don Bradman. He pleased the country crowds with some spectacular batting displays and scored centuries in four of the matches. One of his mighty strokes smashed a headlight of a car parked near the boundary at Forbes.

While he was away from Sydney, the controversy as to whether he should or should not leave Australia continued even more vigorously, with the partisans unhampered by their ignorance of the facts. Many people thought that he had already signed the contract with Accrington. A journalist named Campbell Dixon lamented: 'The disappointment with which I learned of Bradman's decision yesterday will be shared by every other Australian.' The English *News Chronicle* sneered: 'Accrington's acquisition of Bradman is a doubtful gain to English cricket . . . Lancashire already abounds in the uninspiring and ''efficient'' type of batting, in which Bradman is unrivalled. Moreover, his relatively poor performances recently argue the awful possibility that his astounding records here may have been more fortunate than was originally supposed.' Australian editors wrote lengthy editorials, phrased more in sorrow than in anger, to the effect that Bradman could not be blamed for responding to the lure of big money rather than the demands of patriotism.

Truth filled fifty column-inches with a lengthy article in support of Bradman, beginning: 'Why all this outcry about Don Bradman? One would think the young cricketing genius had violated one of the commandments simply because he has enough business ability to consider his own future.

'He has been offered a lucrative position in the English cricketing world. Why shouldn't he accept it?

'There is no excuse for the pitiful wails which are resounding throughout Australia. Bradman is a free agent. A marvellous gift has been bestowed on him. It is sheer stupidity to imagine that it is his duty to remain in the land of his birth if his gift is more valuable elsewhere.'

The article pointed out that every Australian of merit had had to go overseas to receive proper remuneration and recognition, and said that even Charles Kingsford Smith had said he would leave Australia 'if things don't look up at home'.

Some supporters wrote directly to Bradman. One was the Commonwealth parliamentarian W. Maloney, who wrote: 'I deeply resent the criticism that you have been subjected to. I resent strongly the contemptible fining of you after your return with your glorious record. I know in the past that snobs and cads on the Selecting Committee insulted our best cricketers . . . I know also that many international cricketers who helped to win glory for Australia suffered want in their old age, and some of these even had to pay admission to see cricket played. Under these circumstances and using all the wisdom I have garnered in seventy-seven years, I strongly advise you to accept the position that has been offered you, and when you have saved enough to ensure your middle and old-age from want, then act as you please.'

Dr H. V. Evatt wrote from the Judges' Chambers of the High Court of Australia, asking Bradman to 'balance against going at all, the hopes of so many of your personal admirers . . . If I can be of any assistance with the object of enabling you to remain permanently in Australia, I would like to be informed as there are many people enthusiastic and anxious about it all.'

The London *Evening Standard* poster reporting that Bradman had not accepted the contract to play for an English team

FROM SIR DONALD'S SCRAPBOOKS

Sir Donald Bradman's collection of cricketing memorabilia includes a number of scrapbooks and photograph albums which he, or his friends and relations, assembled during his active career. They provide countless fascinating insights into the way in which his contemporaries thought, felt, wrote and talked about him at various times. Here are some samples from the early 1930s:

An irreverent 'prayer' by an anonymous hand

Our Harbour which art in Sydney
Good-Oh be thy name
Thy Bridge be done
In 1930 or 1931
Forgive us this day our Pig-headedness
As we forgive those snobs in Melbourne
that trespass against us
And lead us not into Stagnation
But deliver us from Taxation
For ours is the Harbour
The Bridge and the Bradman
For ever and ever Amen

Neville Cardus' recollection of the third Test, at Leeds in 1930, written in 1941

On July 11 at Headingley, Leeds . . . Don Bradman played one of the most wonderful innings in recorded cricket history . . . Bradman began without delay to get the ball in the exact middle of the bat: he scored a century before lunch; he scored a century between lunch and tea. He was not out 309, all made in a single day, in a Test match; heavens, we said, 309 is not a bad rate of scoring for the first day of a Test match for the whole side, two men batting in form at both ends!

No shadow of fallibility fell for a moment on the gleaming surface of Bradman's batsmanship that day — it was streamlined efficiency and assurance . . . He ran to the pavilion, not out 309 — and there was not a trace in his face of weariness; his hair was beautifully parted; he looked as though fresh from a bandbox.

The Don Bradman Dahlia

An enthusiastic dahlia grower called one of his new hybrids the Don Bradman, 'because of its strength and vigorous growth. In colour it is toned from a deep orange to chrome yellow with a blush of pink.'

A Sydney newspaper ran a children's essay contest on the theme 'What famous Australian would you most like to be?' The prizewinners included T. W. Nathan of Darlinghurst, who said in his essay:

I would like to be our idol, our star of hope, Don Bradman! I would hit up wonderful scores for our team, and imagine, even while away on English ground, I could hear the encouraging cheers of Australia. And I would smile when sweet young things hunted me, requesting an autograph!

From the London 'Daily Mail'

Bradman is the boy wonder of cricket. His gigantic innings, following previous scores, shows his consistency and his genius. He was Macartney's confidence and perkiness. English crowds are yearning to see him in action.

From advertisements

Don Bradman, Super Batsman and Star Cricketer, is at your service at Mick Simmons!

Don Bradman made the World's Batting Record in a "Freesleeve" Shirt (patented).

Say Good-Bye to Don Bradman at Mick Simmons! Bring that boy of yours along . . . he'll remember it all the days of his life.

A professor's opinion, from a newspaper report of a lecture by Professor H. Tasman Lovell to the Musical Association of New South Wales

Bradman is making centuries in England because a part of his brain is highly developed. He was born with a highly developed muscle sense.

From an interview with the parents of Don Bradman

'You might just add that Don made his own way in the cricket world without any effort on my part,' Mr Bradman continued. 'His enthusiasm, grit, and determination, coupled with the right temperament, have carried him through. And now he is sure of a trip to England, where I hope he will be as successful as he has been in Australia.'

'Perhaps the gentleman would like to see some of Don's mementoes,' said Mrs Bradman, and the 'Sun' representative was led into another room, where were a silver tea and coffee service, presented by St George admirers; the gold-mounted ball secured at the end of the third Test in Melbourne, the honor cap and badge donated by Mr J. J. Giltinan to commemorate the 340 not out score against Victoria; and, among numerous smaller trophies, a beautiful cigarette case and matchbox.

'And he doesn't even smoke,' laughed his father.

Note: Giltinan was the man who, with Victor Trumper, played a leading part in the development of Rugby League football in New South Wales. The unofficial honour cap he gave to Bradman was similar to a Rugby player's cap.

True or false? By a gossip columnist

Before the team left for England I sat in a Sydney theatre next to Mr and Mrs Alan Kippax and a sweet young thing, scarcely more than a flapper, with whom Don was playing a perfect innings.

That evening the comedians made merry at the expense of married life. Alan and his wife laughed outright; but Don and the girl-friend smiled shyly.

I happened to be holidaying in the district whence came Bradman when that young man began to shine in Sydney grade cricket. "Well," I observed to a local chap, "you've lost Bradman for good."

"And good riddance," rejoined the native. "We could never get the cow out!"

A Bradman joke

1st Bowral man: 'There'll be a hot time in town when Don Bradman comes home.'
2nd Bowral man: 'But Don doesn't drink.'
1st Bowral man: 'No, but I do!'

In search of Bradman's secret, by Clyde Foster of the London 'Evening Standard'

Every newspaper and every Englishman who has an interest in cricket is discussing the secret of Bradman's wizardry. Opinions are divided between eagle-like vision, steel-like wrists, and fairy-like feet.

In the hope of settling the argument I crept, between the morning's showers, upstairs at the Queen's Hotel and found Bradman yarning with the Australian journalist, Geoffrey Tebbutt. Tests of wrist strength were immediately carried out, in which Tebbutt was first, I myself was second, and Bradman was third. When asked what was really his secret, Bradman said, 'There is none. It is simply this — I am trying all the time to find what is behind the bowler's mind. It is a constant battle, I have to hit him or he has to beat me.'

An opinion by Pelham 'Plum' Warner, the doyen of English cricketers and cricket writers and among the first men to be knighted (in 1937) for services to cricket. He wrote in 1930:

Facing Larwood, he adopted original methods and evolved a new idea to counter an attack to which he was unaccustomed. The reply to those who criticise him is clearly the number of runs he made. He is clearly a genius.

. . . and opinions by various sportswriters . . .

. . . Some people have criticised him, or his cricket, at times. But that is the fate of everyone who does anything. He is as utterly unspoiled by success as Victor Trumper was. He is only a little chap, but there has never been a stronger, nor do I think a finer personality among the exponents of cricket in this country than Don Bradman.

. . . He does not possess the refinement of Jackson. He is more enterprising, businesslike, and unorthodox; in fact, he is a little devil. He has the confidence and cheek of Macartney, and is a nasty fellow to bowl at.

If he scores a century he laughs, takes fresh block, and starts on his second century. If a good ball beats him he laughs. If he is bowled he laughs, and above all his laughs are sincere . . . He is Australia's best outfield, and bowls a handy leg break.

... As quick on his feet as a ballet dancer, his timing of the ball, his stroke play, his dash, his restraint at times, and his stamina were all remarkable. He appeared to hypnotise the bowlers and decree the length they should bowl to him.

His consistency and stamina are remarkable. I have no hesitation in placing him with such other giants of cricket as the famous 'Ranji', Grace, Maclaren, Hobbs, and Macartney.

... The only thing wrong with Don Bradman's cricket is that, in doing what he has done while still a youngster, he has made a few others envious, so that anything he may do is viewed through the microscope to minimise its value to the side or the game.

Don Bradman listens patiently as an 'old stager' tells him how they used to play cricket in his day

Extracts from some verses by an admirer

A sporting crowd in thousands came
To watch and cheer them through
The King and all his courtiers came
The Australian team to view

The day grew cold and Nobles sought
To take the King away
No, No, he cried, I shall not go — until
I've seen Don Bradman play

We can all imagine Woodfull
How he scored his half a hundred
And luckless Archie Jackson
Just what poor Archie wondered

But never mind young Jackson
And we trust that you won't fret
For one failure by a chap like you
Australia must forget

But for Bradman fair-haired Bradman
How the flappers' hearts must jump
As they watch him with the willow
Give every ball a thump

Aye now fair-haired Donald Bradman
In the waning years to come
When you're settled down and married
In Australia's sunny home

When the aged tears dim your eyes
When your race is nearly won
You'll look back to nineteen-thirty
To those wondrous deeds you've done

Now we're waiting for the finish
And now be it lost or won
We will not forget our Bradman
Our dashing fair-haired Don.

Another letter said: 'Dear little boy, take the advice of an old woman, hit while the iron is hot. Australia soon forgets, England never. You were not too well treated on your return with the greatest record in Cricket. Go & marry an Heiress, with your face and record you can. Good luck.'

Those who prayed that Bradman would stay in Australia were horrified by an irresponsible *Truth* report saying: 'We go one better this week and tell the world that Bradman will accept the offer.'

September and most of October ticked away with Australian cricket lovers still keeping their fingers crossed and English editors still writing pompous articles. The London *Daily Telegraph*, which had stated earlier that it knew, 'on good authority', that Bradman had accepted the offer, published a leading article headed 'The Bradman Case'. Its

One of the numerous letters written to Don Bradman by his supporters

writer said: 'No considerable number of people in England and Australia would wish to encourage the development of cricket as an entertainment industry, played by professionals, whose only interest in the game is commercial.'

Truth virtually camped on Claude Spencer's doorstep, and was probably the first Sydney newspaper to know when the contract at last arrived. The editor sent a reporter to waylay Bradman on his way home from playing against a ladies' cricket team in Newcastle, and the journalist wrote: 'He jumped out of his slick-looking roadster and said he had had a wonder trip "on the concrete" from Newcastle, where he had been playing the local ladies.'

He told the reporter that he had not seen or signed the contract, and then 'Still smiling, Don hopped off for Hurstville, en route for Parramatta to play for St George.'

Unabashed by its previous erroneous forecast, the newspaper went on to claim that a number of 'wealthy sportsmen' were clubbing together in an offer to keep Bradman in Australia. 'If Bradman accepts, he will be in clover.'

Rumours continued to fly and Bradman continued to tantalise the reporters. After he played in a charity match to aid St George Hospital, at the Hurstville Oval, a reporter tried to lead him into an admission by talking about his golf form and then asking 'I suppose you'll be playing a game at Gleneagles in a few months time?'' Bradman's smiling answer was "You never can tell".'

Bradman had already asked the Board of Control to define their attitude if he accepted the offer. Their reply was: '. . . the Board expects the Clause of the Agreement referred to to be observed by the members of the Team and if the Clause were broken by any member of such Team the Board would not approve of his selection for Australia.' *Truth* shrieked 'Board's Bluster Won't Bounce The Brilliant Bowral Boy'; but in fact the cool and unequivocal response made Bradman realise that acceptance of the offer would guillotine his Test career.

B. J. Kortlang, a Sydney journalist and former cricketer who had travelled with the 1930 tourists, said that if Australia lost Bradman 'she would have the jealousy of other cricketers to thank for it'. He said that during the tour he had often heard other members of the team say jealously of Bradman such things as 'Here comes the team', and the remarks were not made in a pleasant way.

Ernie Jones, then sixty-two, the ex-miner who had been Australia's fastest right-arm bowler during his 1892–1907 career, said he had always regretted his own refusal to play for an English county side and that 'Bradman would be foolish if he refuses a chance of earning £25 a week to play for Accrington. He is only young, and three years cricket in England should put him on his feet.'

Truth had been partly right in claiming that a group of Australians was working out some way to keep Bradman in his own country, but they were not 'wealthy sportsmen'. They were executives of organisations with a close interest in the commercial aspects of sport as a marketable commodity: Associated Newspapers Ltd, the Sydney radio station 2UE, and the Sydney outfitters F. J. Palmer and Son Ltd who had a sporting department.

Sir Donald Bradman does not know how or when these groups got

SCOREBOARD 1932

During the twenty weeks of the 1931–32 season in which Don Bradman played Test and other first-class matches, he outclassed every other Australian and South African batsman. The 'runners-up' were Stan McCabe with an average of 87.80, Jim Christy with an aggregate of 909 for South Africa, and Vic Richardson with 873.

Bradman established yet another series of records, of which some remain unbeaten until the present day. The list included:

* His average of 201.50 is still the highest on record for any Test Match rubber.
* His total of 1190 runs, scored in four Tests and two other matches against South Africa, remains the most ever made in one season in Australia off any touring team's bowling.
* His aggregate of 806 in his four Tests against South Africa was the highest by any Australian in any series against South Africa.
* In the Test series and in all first-class matches he achieved a century average, for the first time by any batsman in any country.
* He was, and still remains, the only batsman of any country to score more than one double century in all Tests against South Africa.
* The six centuries scored against South Africa were a record against any touring team.
* Bradman was the only batsman ever to have made more than one double century in a season off a touring team's bowling.
* For the fourth consecutive Australian season his aggregate exceeded 1000 runs, thus breaking Hendren's record.
* His average of 116.91 in all first-class matches was the highest on record by a New South Wales batsman.

Don Bradman (left) in the summer of 1931–32 with a team of the 'Sun-Palmer colts' whom he coached as a part of his contract arrangements with the Sydney *Sun*, Radio 2UE, and Palmer's department store

together, or whether Claude Spencer made a direct approach to any or all of them. Late in October 1931, Spencer arranged a meeting between Bradman and the executives of the three organisations, at which they presented a combined offer designed to keep him in Australia. If he accepted then he would write cricket articles for Associated Newspapers, give cricket talks over 2UE, and represent F. J. Palmer in much the same way as he had worked for Mick Simmons.

The combined offer was not as lucrative as the Accrington invitation and all its potential side benefits, but it had the great advantage of securing his future for at least two years without exiling himself from Australia and — so he thought — without affecting his Test career. He did not foresee that the Board of Control would object to his writing articles for Associated Newspapers.

He signed the three-part contract to remain in Australia and on 30 October he cabled Holgate: 'Regret decline your offer. Appreciate pleasant nature negotiations. Writing full details.'

His old friend A. G. 'Johnnie' Moyes broke the story in the Sydney *Sun*, a member of the Associated Newspapers group. He wrote: 'The great batsman will write constructive cricket articles for the Associated Newspapers. His wonderful cricket brain is well known to all who follow the game, and he wields the pen with the same facility as he does the bat . . . It was obvious that no single firm could hope to compete with the magnificent offer from England, but the three, working in conjunction, have been able to hold the champion.

'"I am delighted," said Don, with a happy smile, "that I am staying here. I did not want to go away or to lose touch with Australian cricket, nor become a professional cricketer if I could avoid it".'

Some of those who criticised him, including the English newspapers, now congratulated him on his decision. Those like Evatt, who had asked him to stay, wrote their thanks and appreciation. Others, including Lord Tennyson, reacted less graciously. Lord Tennyson said it was just as well that Bradman was not going to England 'because he still has a lot to learn, and the sooner he does not want to get his name into print the better'. As usual, Bradman's critics blamed him for the newspaper publicity which surrounded him whether he wanted it or not.

Station 2UE, Sydney, placed this advertisement in New South Wales newspapers as soon as Don Bradman signed the contract which committed him to nightly broadcasts on cricket over the radio station

TUNE IN TO
"OUR DON"
Who Broadcasts
EXCLUSIVELY
Every Night Commencing
To-night at 8 o'clock
From
STATION 2UE
Together With
UNCLE
LIONEL
AND THE
LISTERINE
SERENADERS

In March 1932, Station 2UE advertised: 'Tune in to "Our Don" who broadcasts EXCLUSIVELY every night commencing to-night at 8 o'clock from Station 2UE, together with Uncle Lionel and the Listerine Serenaders.' *Truth* responded with a satirical article about Bradman's 'Aero-Bat-Ics', describing an imaginary cricket match in which he made 1500 runs in a four-day stand at the wicket with intervals for commercials and then 'Left field to write account of happenings for evening press, using Invisible Ink Fountain Pen (17/- all ironmongers) . . . Uncle Liontamer and Don, with piano accompaniment, will be on the air to-night.'

By that time he had made further important steps forward in his life and his cricketing career. The first was his formal engagement to Jessie Menzies, announced in November 1931. The press swooped gleefully on this new morsel of news about Bradman and, as so often, embroidered it with tit-bits of their own. One story was that Bradman had bought her engagement ring in England, but its author confused the ring with a diamond and platinum wristwatch he brought back with him as her twenty-first birthday present. He had the ring made by a jeweller friend in Sydney, to match the wristwatch.

Jessie Menzies shortly before her marriage to Don Bradman

The press described Jessie Menzies as 'of medium height, with wide-apart hazel eyes and a brown wavy shingle', and said she was 'the least excited person over the romance'. It was reported throughout Australia and brought shoals of telegrams from all parts of the Commonwealth. She told one newspaper 'I am a calm sort of person' but 'confessed to just a little thrill' when her workmates in the Commonwealth Bank clustered around to admire her ring.

The other important aspects of Bradman's life were of course concerned with cricket. The South Africans toured Australia in the 1931–32 season for the first time for twenty-one years, and he was selected for the Australian and New South Wales teams which played against them. He still played for St George; he took part in various country matches such as a charity match against Bathurst, with an eleven assembled by R. L. Jones; and he batted for New South Wales in the Shield matches for that season.

His Shield scores show a peculiar sequence: 0, 23, 167, 23, 0. For the first and only time, he began and ended a first-class season with a duck. The first came in a match against Queensland in Brisbane, when the southern side faced the bowling of the Aboriginal cricketer Eddie Gilbert. They found that Gilbert had a remarkable bowling style, with a 'run-up' of a few shuffling steps prior to a rocket-like delivery. One of his balls smashed the bat clean out of Bradman's grasp, and he wrote later: 'I unhesitatingly class this short burst as faster than anything seen from Larwood or anyone else.'

Gilbert swung his right arm so fast that it was difficult to distinguish his action, but the New South Wales manager accused him of throwing. Bradman's later comment was that 'if he did not actually throw the ball then he certainly jerked it'.

Bert Ironmonger, who took 31 of the South African wickets at 9.67 in the 1931–32 Tests, also came under some suspicion of throwing, but Bradman explains his peculiar delivery by the fact that he had lost the first joint on the index finger of his left hand. This prevented him from spinning the ball in the orthodox manner, and probably caused his exclusion from touring Test teams in case he was 'no-balled' by English umpires.

Bradman compensated for his erratic performance in the season's Shield matches, which ended with a duck administered by Tim Wall of South Australia, with a magnificent batting display against the South Africans. He played in six matches against them — four Tests and two games for New South Wales — and scored four centuries and two double centuries. In the fourth Test, at Adelaide in January 1932, he came frustratingly close to a triple century. He carried his bat for 299, and after the fourth Test he did not have another opportunity to show what has been described as his 'overpowering mastery' of the

Jack Hobbs: '. . . no flaw in attack or defence'

South African bowling. In five Test innings his scores were 226, 112, 2, 167 and 299. The single failure came in the first innings of the third Test, when he was caught for two after only fourteen minutes. He did not bat in the fifth Test, which South Africa lost as it did all the others. He caught his boot sprigs in the coir matting of the dressing room just as the team was about to go on the field, and badly twisted his ankle.

In the New South Wales matches against the tourists, he scored 30, 135 and 219 in his three innings. For most of the season he was in superb form. He scored 246 for St George against Randwick, the record for the club, and in a match against Lithgow he scored 256 including 100 out of 102 added in only three overs.

He ended the season with a fresh batch of records, which relegated the comments made by Lord Tennyson and others to the region of wishful thinking. No doubt they would have enjoyed the report published in the *Cooktown Independent* in December 1931. It said: '*Don Bradman Dead* — Australia to-day mourns the loss of the greatest batsman the world has ever seen. During the progress of the Test Match in Brisbane (Australia v. South Africa) Don Bradman was attacked with dysentery, to which he succumbed on Saturday.'

Like Mark Twain, Bradman could have said 'Reports of my death have been greatly exaggerated'.

THROUGH DON BRADMAN'S EYES

Don Bradman played with, or against, all the classic cricketers of the period between the two world wars. In his book *Farewell to Cricket*, published in 1950, he recorded his impressions of some of these Australian and English cricketers.

Of Clarrie Grimmett, the great South Australian bowler born in 1891, Bradman wrote: 'He used variations in pace, cleverly exploited a breeze and was dynamite the way he could trap L.B.W. new players who attempted to play back to him . . . In later years he developed what came to be known among the players as his "flipper" — so-called because of the way he snapped his fingers as he let the ball go. It was delivered from the first and second fingers virtually squeezed out but a clever turn of the wrist made it appear to be a leg-break, whereas the ball went straight or turned very slightly from the off. He got many L.B.W.'s with this one.' Grimmett, who played for South Australia and Victoria, dismissed 216 Test batsmen and 1424 batsmen in all first-class matches during his long career.

Another bowler of that era was Bert Ironmonger (1882–1971) who was a big, slow and rather clumsy man with the incongruous nickname of 'Dainty'.

Bradman categorised him with Hedley Verity, Wilfred Rhodes and Jack White, saying: 'They depended almost entirely on accuracy. There is very little spin to be obtained when the wicket is firm, so this type of bowler must pit his wits against the batsman and force him into the mental state in which he commits errors.' As a left-arm medium bowler Ironmonger took 464 wickets in first-class cricket including 74 Test wickets, but he was no asset as a batsman. In 36 years of first-class cricket he totalled only 476 runs.

One of the English bowlers who gave Bradman the most trouble was Harold Larwood, born 1904: a rather small and wiry man who used a very long run-up to deliver balls of explosive force. Bradman recalls a moment during the 1928–29 Tests when Larwood was bowling to Ryder. The ball hit wicket-keeper Duckworth on the forehead, bounced off, and landed on the sight screen.

But Bradman thinks the fastest single delivery he ever saw was bowled to him by the Queensland Aborigine Eddie Gilbert. It knocked Don Bradman's bat clean out of his hands!

The Englishman Maurice 'Chub' Tate (1895–1956), the son of a well-known cricketer, began as a batsman but developed into a great bowler. His bowling in the 1924–25 Test season, in Australia, demonstrated his supreme skill when he captured 38 wickets. Bradman wrote of him: 'He had a glorious action — in fact his shoulder swing was so perfect that it should be used as the film example for all young bowlers to see. This beautiful shoulder swing, plus the combination of arm and wrist, enabled him to obtain tremendous speed off the pitch. In addition, he swung the ball well and varied his pace most intelligently.'

Wicket-keepers often tend to be dramatic and aggressive personalities, but there were great differences between the Australian Bert Oldfield and the Englishman George Duckworth. The latter, a Lancashire man (1901–66), was one of England's most aggressive 'keepers. Bradman remembers that his 'raucous "Howzat!" terrified many an unsuspecting victim. There is a story that after frightening the life out of some young player by his noisy appeal, Duckworth completed it by telling the quaking batsman he was out. At this the batsman, visibly relieved, replied, "Is that all? Thank God! I thought for a minute I'd been sandbagged!"

Bert Oldfield (1894–1976) was a very different character. Bradman's opinion is that he was 'for a few years indisputably the greatest wicket-keeper of his day. I played with Oldfield through a considerable portion of his career, and many times have marvelled at his skill . . . Never any suggestion of an ugly movement — feet always right — hands in perfect position, and remarkable speed when stumping — especially on the leg-side, off a medium-pace bowler . . . it was said of him that he never appealed unless certain in his own mind that the man was out. On occasions he adopted an air of apology. You could almost imagine him saying to the batsman, "Sorry, old chap — I stumped you and you're out. I didn't like doing it but it's in the rules you know." He recorded 661 dismissals in first-class cricket and 130 in 54 Tests.'

Jack Hobbs was nearing the end of his long career when the young Don Bradman first saw him at the wicket. Bradman commented: 'Of Jack Hobbs I write with some hesitancy, because I knew him only when past his prime, and from personal experience know such comparisons can be dangerous.

'He was the best-equipped batsman of all, in the technical sense — English or Australian.

'I could detect no flaw in attack or defence.

'His footwork was always correct, stroke production sound, and he seemed to get out simply because he was a fallible mortal and made errors of judgement . . . A movie film of Jack Hobbs as he was in 1912 should be the perfect batting example for coaching purposes.'

Writing in 1950, Bradman grouped Bill Ponsford and Arthur Morris (born 1922) as 'the finest of the period'. Ponsford (born 1900) retired from first-class cricket long before Morris appeared on the scene, but Bradman wrote of him: 'Bill Ponsford burst into cricket and instantly began to tear the record book to shreds with great rapidity and consistency. He carried all before him.

'He was the victim of much jealousy (until I began to take the load off his shoulders) and became a target for fast bowlers who would, in advance, organise an attack on him. I saw, and heard, it happen.

'The public had the impression in 1928 that there was some enmity between Ponsford and Larwood. Perhaps this view was coloured by an incident in the Sydney Test of that series when a ball from Larwood broke Ponsford's hand.

'From then on until the end of Ponsford's career in 1934 (a period which included body-line) he was always being "shot at". These tactics undoubtedly hastened his retirement. A pity, for Bill was still a magnificent player when he retired.

'There were innuendoes against Ponsford that he was afraid of fast bowling. Pure rubbish. I've seen him take tremendous thrashings — have seen his body black and blue — covered with bruises . . . He could play fast bowling splendidly. Many can testify to that fact. I still visualise the way he pasted Gubby Allen at Lord's in 1930.

'Against slow and medium pace bowlers his bat seemed exceptionally broad. Admittedly it did not always appear straight, but it was always in the same place as the ball.

'This bat, incidentally, was fondly termed "Big Bertha" because of its weight. Many people have wondered why Bill got such power into his shots with a short back lift. The secret was in strong wrists, good timing and this heavy bat . . . Some of his early figures were stupendous, and to this day I believe he remains the one player in history with 2 scores over 400 to his credit and with the record of scoring over 1000 runs in 4 consecutive innings.

'There were more beautiful players, but for absolute efficiency and results, where can one turn to equal him?'

Of the English batsmen whom Bradman encountered in the 1930s, he writes most glowingly of Wally Hammond (1903–65). Hammond was a 'natural' cricketer of enormous talent. Neville Cardus described his style as 'an almost statuesque nobility, easy and powerful of stroke-play but absolutely correct in its observance of first principles'. Bradman wrote of him: 'He was a batsman of the classical, majestic school. Of lovely athletic build, light as a ballet dancer on his feet, Hammond was the outstanding batsman between 1918 and 1938. His game was based on driving, and nobody was his peer when it came to the cover drive which he made with tremendous power and equal ease off either the front or back foot.'

Bradman was always generous with his praise of other great batsmen, and of Stan McCabe he wrote: 'Here was a lovely player. He, like myself, was a country lad but his style was all polish and grace, for he came to the city early and gained experience on turf before his style was set . . . his figures are better than those of Ponsford in Tests against England, and his style unquestionably more pleasing to the eye.'

Bradman wrote at length of McCabe's great in-

nings of 232 in the first Test at Nottingham in 1938, and said: 'Toward the end I could scarcely watch the play. My eyes were filled as I drank in the glory of his shots . . . such cricket I shall never see again, nor shall I ever feel competent adequately to describe this elegant display.'

When McCabe returned to the dressing room, Bradman gripped his hand. 'He was trembling like a thoroughbred racehorse. I can recall saying to him after expressing my congratulations, "I would give a great deal to be able to play an innings like that". No skipper was ever more sincere in his adulation of another's skill.'

Don Bradman's fan mail included a cheque payable to the great batsman Dr W. G. Grace on 1 May 1907. An English admirer of Bradman sent it to him as a souvenir of the tour

9

A CRICKETER'S HONEYMOON

For Australia's greatest century maker, it is appropriate that the most successful partnership of his life should already have endured for more than half a century. It is his marriage to Jessie Menzies, now Lady Bradman, which was solemnised on 30 April 1932.

The Bradman and Menzies families enjoyed the usual happy confusion of marriage arrangements during the early months of 1932, and the female population of Sydney was even more excited about the event. The marriage was scheduled for the early evening of 30 April, but a great crowd of girls and women thronged the street outside the church all through the afternoon. A good-natured squad of police tried to control them by erecting barriers to keep the approaches clear, but they pushed these aside and many of them joined the invited guests inside the church. The verger had to hurry from one group to another, begging them not to stand on the seats to obtain a grandstand view of the ceremony.

The press noted that 'hero worship seemed to develop into a positive frenzy'. By the time that Don Bradman arrived, with his brother Vic as best man and Roy Menzies as groomsman, the beautifully decorated church of St Paul's, in the Sydney suburb of Burwood, was crammed to the doors.

Canon E. S. Hughes of St Paul's Cathedral, Melbourne, the 'sporting parson' who officiated at the weddings of numerous well-known Australian cricketers, had accepted Bradman's request for him to perform the wedding ceremony. Canon Hughes was a significant figure in the Australian cricketing world, in the tradition of those English divines who played an important part in nurturing the great game. He played for East Melbourne before the first world war and was a president of that club, and he eventually became president of the Victorian Cricket Association.

Jessie Menzies' father led her up the aisle and the largely female congregation looked appreciatively at her wedding dress of white and silver brocaded satin, lace cap, and tulle veil. The bridesmaids, her sisters Jean and Lily, wore frocks of Nile-green georgette and orange velvet caps.

The newlyweds motored to Melbourne for their honeymoon and stayed at the home of a close friend in Toorak. Canon Hughes called one morning at about ten o'clock, and after enjoying his morning tea

Don Bradman with Canon E. S. Hughes, the 'cricketing clergyman' from Melbourne who solemnised Bradman's marriage to Jessie Menzies on 30 April 1932

GOOD LUCK, DON !

JUST HOPING THIS IS A RECORD PARTNERSHIP DON

FROM THE SPORTING PUBLIC

Don Bradman will be married at St. Paul's Church, Burwood, at 6.30 p.m. to-day.

The wish expressed by a Sydney newspaper cartoonist that the Bradman–Menzies marriage would be a 'record partnership' has certainly come true. Sir Donald and Lady Bradman celebrated their fiftieth wedding anniversary on 30 April 1982

he said 'Jessie, it's not too late if you want to change your mind. I was not used to the way they do things in New South Wales and I've made a slight error in the formalities!'

The most glamorous part of their honeymoon still lay ahead. It was to be an overseas trip, which was a rare boon for a young couple in that period, and they enjoyed it as the result of plans made by Bradman's old acquaintance Arthur Mailey.

Mailey, a man with a witty, irreverent and ebullient personality, probably derived more fun out of cricket than most other people connected with the game. Born in 1886 in humble circumstances, he became a plumber by trade and subsequently made a name for himself as a right-arm leg-break and googly bowler. The first world war delayed his appearance in Test cricket until he was thirty-five, during the Australian 1920–21 season. He took 36 English wickets in that Test series. In the following season he dismissed all ten Gloucestershire batsmen in one innings, an event which inspired the title of his most amusing book: *10 For 66 And All That.* He had a flair for writing and cartooning, which led to his employment as a sporting journalist on Sydney newspapers from the late 1920s onward.

Mailey loved to lead elevens on country tours played for enjoyment of the game, and at about the time of Bradman's engagement he dreamed up a more ambitious scheme. It was that of taking an Australian cricket team on a tour of North America, to play cricketers in

LETTERS FROM TWO FANS

Over the years since the 1920s, Don Bradman has received an enormous quantity of fan mail from people of all ages in all walks of life and of many nationalities — and it still continues. Two samples from 1931 are:

I ask you as a Seer and a Prophet as I am, to listen to me, your delightful simplicity, charm, and graceful manner is in itself a marvel of correctness, no living cricketer could possibly envy your exalted rank in that wonderful field of sport. It is gained by your hidden restless ambition to excel. I always say to our people in Victoria Mr Bradman must have a really wonderful eye. You do sir remind me of the Black Charlie Birds diving for fish high up over the Bay and Rivers. They can see the fish 300 yards from the water surface while flying in the air. I really believe you see in your creative vision the ball before it leaves the bowler's hands, and you may study ten times more alone over the game than your brother cricketers imagine.
— *from W. G. Ogden (aged 69) of East Melbourne.*

I thank you from the bottom of my heart for your kind reply dated 23-7-31.

Oh, How nice of you!

How my heart is leaping for joy! Words refuse to come and I needs must stop here.

I thank you once again — ay thanks. Truly thanks!
— *from M. S. Ranganathan of Bombay.*

Canada and the USA. Those two countries had adopted the old English game of baseball as their national summer sport, but many Canadians played cricket and there were also a few teams in the USA.

Mailey managed to sell his scheme to some North American promoters, especially the Canadian Pacific Railway, but they made one firm proviso: that Mailey should persuade Don Bradman to join the tourists. Canadian cricketers were well aware of his name and fame, and the promoters regarded him as the draw-card which would ensure the success of the tour.

Bradman was very uncertain whether he should surrender to Mailey's pleas. The idea of a visit to North America was a great temptation, especially since it could be combined with a honeymoon tour, but he was about to start work for his three new employers. Mailey sweetened the offer by agreeing to pay all expenses for Don and Jessie Bradman, and Bradman agreed to ask permission from the three contractors. Fortunately they took the attitude that the trip would be useful publicity during the Australian winter, when there was no local cricket to occupy Bradman as a writer or radio commentator, so he was able to go.

Mailey's next hurdle was that of the Australian Board of Control. Strictly speaking, the tour was none of their business because it was a private affair. But they were so conscious of their position as guardians of the ethics of Australian international cricket that they intervened with a set of special regulations.

They ordained that the touring team should not include more than six men with Test experience; that no player might receive more than £100 for the tour plus travel and accommodation expenses; and that the tourists' net profit from the tour should be distributed as the Board dictated.

Arthur Mailey's team to tour North America in the northern summer of 1932 pulls away from the Sydney wharf aboard the *Niagara*

Of course Mailey and some of the other cricketers could have ignored these regulations, but the displeasure of the Board was a powerful force that might have affected the futures of Test players. In the event, there was no profit to be distributed. Mailey had only a minor interest in profit-making activities and he was far more intent on giving everyone a good time and enjoying a lot of cricket. There was not even enough money available to pay the expenses of all the travellers, and several paid their own way. Dr Rowley Pope, a wealthy Sydney medico and cricket devotee, also paid his own way and accompanied the tour as its physician.

By the time of Bradman's wedding everything had been arranged. The twelve tourists included Mailey as manager, Vic Richardson as captain, Bradman, Kippax, Stan McCabe, and the promising young left-arm bowler 'Chuck' Fleetwood-Smith.

They sailed from Sydney in the Royal Mail Steamer *Niagara* on 26 May 1932, with journalists observing that 'Don's smile was not as wide as usual'. In fact he was Dr Pope's first patient on the tour and he had to spend the first two or three days in his bunk with a bout of influenza.

The tour was to be a strenuous exercise, travelling completely across the continent and back again with frequent stops for a series of local matches. The tourists played on a strange variety of wickets, ranging from perfectly-grassed cricket grounds to matting on grass and matting on antbed, against teams which included West Indians living in New York and Englishmen living in Hollywood. *Smith's Weekly* later condemned Mailey for persuading Bradman to join the tour and said he had 'brought him back a stale batsman to face the music of a fiercely-fought Test series'.

The team assembled by Arthur Mailey, with Vic Richardson as captain, to tour North America in 1932

Dr. R. Pope (Physician); Hanson ("Sep") Carter; Don Bradman; E. K. Tolhurst; Mrs. Don Bradman; L. O. Fleetwood-Smith; R. N. Nutt; Victor Y. Richardson (Captain); Arthur A. Mailey (Manager); Alan F. Kippax; Stan J. McCabe; W. F. Ives; E. R. Rofe; P. H. Carney

The honeymoon couple aboard the *Niagara*

Smith's Weekly did not like Mailey. It called him 'Captain of the "Sun-Telegraph" team, which plays cocksure cricket with pen and ink instead of bat and ball'. Mailey's close relationship with other Australian cricketers never softened his attitude towards them when he scented a controversial story, and *Smith's Weekly* was particularly annoyed when he claimed that Larwood had 'brought Bradman to the level of ordinary batsmen' during the bodyline Tests.

But all that lay in the future as the *Niagara* steamed across the Pacific, with the tourists enjoying pleasant visits to Auckland, Fiji and Hawaii. The relaxing days at sea ended when the liner berthed in the port of Victoria, Vancouver Island, on 16 June. The Australians shivered in a wind that seemed to blow straight down from Alaska, but they received a warm welcome from the Canadians, including 'Foxy' Dean whom the Canadian Pacific Railways had appointed to act as their guide and courier. Sir Donald Bradman recalls that Dean was an important asset, because Arthur Mailey was usually quite vague about such vital points as the times of trains and the names of hotels.

From the moment the tourists stepped ashore, the tour began to move at the pace which characterised it for the whole of their time in

North America. They scarcely had time to sort out their luggage before being whisked away to the small but beautiful cricket ground at Cowichan on Vancouver Island, where proceedings commenced against a local team.

In order to equalise the odds, the Canadians turned out eighteen men to face the visitors — and still received a merciless trouncing. They made 194 and the Australians replied with 503 for eight wickets. The visitors batted so hard and steadily that the bowlers had to keep four balls in play, to save time while fielders and spectators searched for lost balls in the dense trees and shrubberies surrounding the ground. Six separate balls were lost during the day. Stan McCabe hit one ball so hard, during a knock of 150, that it fractured a small bone in the leg of a woman spectator: the wife of one of the Canadian players. Richardson and Bradman added 50 runs in seven minutes during one stage of their partnership.

The following morning brought another match, against a team from the city of Victoria. Either the batsmen were the rankest of amateurs or Bradman was showing unusual prowess in bowling, because he dismissed six of the locals in one eight-ball over. Remarkably, it did not include a hat trick.

On the third day they moved across to the mainland to play three one-day matches on the Brockton Point Ground, Vancouver. Bradman later described this as 'without question the most beautiful ground in the world . . . I cannot imagine a more delightful place for cricket. The ground is on the edge of a beautiful wooded park. Sitting in a deck chair on the verandah of the rustic pavilion, one can look across the field towards the towering, snow-capped mountains, while in the foreground an arm of the harbour runs behind the sightboard, and lazy old ferries dawdle across the bowler's arm. To the right there are small clumps of ornamental trees. Then further to the right is the harbour where seaplanes come in to graceful foamy landings, and beyond is the city itself with its tall, stately buildings on the skyline.

'The fielding surface of the ground is a delight, but the wicket (when we were there) consisted of coconut matting on grass — the only blot on this perfect setting.'

The visitors were playing fifteen men of the Mainland All-Stars during the second match, and they lived up to their name. The local newspaper reported: 'Amid scenes of almost indescribable enthusiasm the Mainland All-Star cricket team turned the tables on the touring Australian eleven at Brockton Point on Wednesday, and when Bill Ivamy caught and bowled Rofe a few minutes after six o'clock the crowd of 1500 people cheered wildly, for the Vancouver players had inflicted the first defeat on the Cornstalks during their present tour by a margin of 28 runs. The Mainland side scored 147 and the visitors were dismissed for 129.'

Bradman wrote: 'It was in this game that I experienced for the first time the guile of Arthur Mailey. A batsman came in. Arthur sensed he might be a hitter, so offered him a cigar if he could hit a six. The batsman promptly hit a six, but without hesitation Mailey doubled the offer, and within a matter of seconds the scorer had recorded once more "caught outfield, bowled Mailey."'

The Australians were impressed by the beauty of Vancouver, but they soon had to leave it behind. With four victories out of five matches, they boarded the train for Toronto and enjoyed the splendours of the climb through the Rocky Mountains before the long haul across the prairies. The train trip was even longer than that from Perth to Adelaide, and they spent four nights and three and a half days in the Canadian Pacific coaches.

Toronto was the most 'English' of Canadian cities and the headquarters of North American cricket. Local cricketers gave the Australians an excited welcome and entertained them royally at the Armour Heights Cricket Club. Its tennis courts, dance floor, putting greens, locker rooms and other facilities were a sumptuous contrast to the spartan fittings of the average Australian cricket club, and the visitors realised that cricket was something of a social pastime in that part of the world.

They played one-day matches against the Toronto Cricket Council, Eastern Canada, and other teams, with overwhelming victories against the local sides whose standard of cricket, however, was 'quite good'. Toronto journalists did not quite know what to make of the young batsman whose fame had reached their city; and when the *Daily Star* printed a long interview with him, the writer treated it in jocular style. Somehow he had picked up the old story that 'when but a lad in Australia, he appeared, prepared to play, in black trousers and black boots, with no equipment at all, so destitute of it that the Sydney team even had to lend him a bat'.

A CANADIAN VIEW

One of the first newspaper reports of Don Bradman's tour of North America called him 'The World's Greatest Player' and went on to say:

Don Bradman, Australia's Babe Ruth of cricket, did his stuff with bat and ball for the edification of Vancouver fandom at the Brockton Point crease yesterday afternoon.

The master batsman of cricket, in scoring 110 runs before retiring undefeated at the wicket, gave a magnificent display of hitting. He showed in many ways that he is a cricket genius and his performance was a treat to watch.

Bradman was the man who the enthusiasts wanted to see. His name was on everybody's lips. He is a medium-sized youth with a stern countenance, and how he can whale a cricket ball.

It was interesting to listen to the various remarks, such as:—

'Isn't he just grand?'

'I don't know where he gets all that driving power.'

'He must have a wonderful pair of wrists and his timing must be perfect.'

'Just look how he stands. His footwork is about perfect and he seems to be always in position to hit any kind of ball.'

No matter what the Vancouver bowlers did, Bradman was their master all the way. Time and again the field was changed but the Aussie ace would look round and find an opening for a good clean hit or an out that would roll far from a fielder.

Bradman gave a finished exhibition of the art of handling a cricket bat. He only gave one chance and that was late after he had started to open up, when he sent a high catch to Pinkham in the long field and the fielder muffed the catch.

The interview concluded with a piece of colourful dialogue.

'"Any of the players' wives come along?" I enquired.

'"No, only mine," was the naive response.

'"Was that because of your imperative pre-eminence?" I asked, employing my best verbal strain for the tribute, which Mr Don quite failed to appreciate. He is a modest lad, and it was easy to see my superlatives were ignored if not resented.

'"No, nothing like that," he disavowed. "My wife only came because I've been married only two or three months and I wouldn't have come without her." (Which I hope the dear little bride will read in the *Daily Star* and account the same to me for righteousness, and buy 40 copies to send home to Australian friends.)'

After Toronto, the tourists had the unusual experience of playing cricket in the grounds of a prison. They travelled to Guelph to play Western Ontario, and it seems that the matting wicket, laid on grass inside Guelph Reformatory, was the only suitable arena. The surroundings must have unnerved the eighteen men of Western Ontario, who could muster only 88 runs against the Australians' 479 for seven wickets. Stan McCabe scored 119 and took eleven wickets for 33, while Bradman's score of 260 remained the highest made on Canadian soil until 1982.

Prison inmates served lunch and tea and the Guelph Country Club entertained the tourists to dinner before they drove to Ridley College for a match against Ridley students and old boys. The surroundings were very different from those of the prison and more like those of an English public school; but the Ridley eighteen made rather a poor showing except for one of them named 'Spark' Bell, who scored 109 not out. It was the only century against the Australians on the entire tour.

Above: The touring Australians played one of their matches in the somewhat unusual surroundings of a prison compound, at Guelph Reformatory, Ontario. Inmates of the reformatory served the cricketers at lunch and tea

Right: Part of the campus at Ridley College, Canada, where the touring Australians played a team of students and 'old boys'

After a side-trip to the scenic grandeur of Niagara Falls, the Australians travelled on to Montreal, the stately French-Canadian city on the banks of the St Lawrence. The vast majority of the inhabitants were totally uninterested in the English game of cricket, but Bradman

treated those who attended the three one-day matches to a vintage display of batting. The local newspaper wrote: 'The real Don Bradman was seen carrying his bat when the visiting Australian cricketers played the second of a three-day series of exhibitions against a hand-picked Montreal team yesterday at the Percival Molson Stadium.

'The Montreal side batted fifteen players and fourteen wickets were disposed of for the meagre total of 71 runs in a morning's innings. The Australians went in to bat after lunch and quickly accumulated runs with the great man Bradman lashing out for 200, not out, while his supporting cast gave him stonewall defence at the other end of the strip ... The local players were frantic in many of their efforts at quelling the master batsman as he kept his stance in the crease before all combinations of bowling. All styles, every bit of artistry in flinging that could possibly be employed was injected by the Montreal captain as he waved in one bowler and rapidly replaced him with another ... But the score was lost sight of in its unimportance to Montreal cricket lovers. They came to see the great Bradman. They saw him at his best. He was better than the day before when he was put out for a score of 97; a score for any outstanding cricketer, for Bradman but a practice innings.'

Don Bradman and other team members equipped themselves with fashionable summer attire for North America in that period: the straw hats which used to be called such names as 'boaters' or 'deckers'. The moustached man on Bradman's right is Hanson Carter, nicknamed 'Sep' or 'Sammy', the great Australian wicket-keeper of 1898–1921, who suffered a bad eye injury on the North America tour

The tourists played their last game in Canada on the eastbound journey when they took on sixteen men of the Ottawa Valley Cricket Council in the grounds of the Governor-General's residence, Rideau Hall. The wicket was matting on composition, an unusual combination but near enough to Bradman's earliest cricket experiences to make him feel quite at home. The match attracted an unusually large crowd, and the Ottawa press reported that he 'fulfilled all their expectations'. He 'proceeded at once to give a demonstration of how he became the greatest batsman in the cricketing world. He cut, sliced, and drove the ball in a manner that even one without the slightest knowledge of the game could see was most skilful. He played extremely carefully until after he had accounted for a century, something which nearly everybody present was there to see him score. After that he took liberties, and when his runs totalled 105 he knocked up a ball for what appeared to be rather an easy catch.'

Cricket in Canada retained much of the traditional dignity of the game, but when the tourists arrived in New York they found a very different style. The game was kept alive by West Indians living in New York and they tended to turn the matches played at Innisfail Park into somewhat casual and festive occasions. In Bradman's first innings he was caught for a duck, and the bowler immediately ran across to the fence and collected a hatful of dollars from jubilant spectators. The umpires took their job rather lightheartedly. One of them, while officiating at square leg, would stroll across to the boundary fence to chat with friends in the crowd.

But this happy atmosphere was clouded when a ball from McCabe flew sharply off the matting wicket, the batsman pulled his bat away at the last second, and the ball struck the Australian wicket-keeper 'Sammy' Carter in the eye. Carter had had an outstanding record in his long first-class career, and it was a sad irony that this ball in a minor match should rob him of the sight of one eye.

New York newspapers compared Bradman with Babe Ruth, the great baseball champion of the 1920s, and arranged for the visitors to watch a baseball game between the Yankees and the White Sox with Babe Ruth interpreting the match for them. According to the *New York World Telegram*, 'The Babe sat resplendent in brown sports coat, white striped trousers, buckskin shoes and a white cap — the true nabob', when the Australians were introduced to him. The journalist wrote: 'The Babe was surprised by Bradman's lack of size and weight. The greatest batsman cricket yet has boasted is no bigger than Joey Sewell. Don weighs 145 pounds, is 24 years of age, and according to

A meeting of champions. Don Bradman (left) shakes hands with George Herman 'Babe' Ruth, the great American baseballer of that period

the cricket experts ... is a scientist rather than a powerhouse. Bradman "hits them where they ain't," and has been known to score more than 1600 runs in little more than fourteen days of cricket.

'"From what they were telling me I thought you were a husky guy," remarked Ruth. "But us little fellows can hit 'em harder than the big ones!"'

The baseball game was one of various relaxations enjoyed by the visitors between their matches against the West Indians and at Staten Island against teams of local Englishmen, who put up a very poor display. They visited the new Empire State Building, heard Paul Robeson singing in *Show Boat*, and were guests of honour at a banquet given by Frank D. Waterman of fountain-pen fame.

They headed north again to play Illinois Cricket Association teams in Windsor and Chicago before returning to Canada. The strain of the tour was beginning to tell on Bradman, and he was tired and unwell when they arrived in Chicago, so that a local journalist could write: 'Australia's champions defeated the Illinois team yesterday at Grant Park, but there was nothing easy about the victory of the invaders ... Don Bradman, greatest of the Australian batsmen, was stopped for the second straight day, scoring only 10 runs before he was caught out ... The Chicagoans agree that this sort of thing can't go on forever, and expect Bradman, who has been ill for both games of the series, to break out in a rash of runs today or tomorrow that will send the Australian score up in the high hundreds.'

Bradman was not impressed with the local umpires. Kippax caught and bowled one of the batsmen, saw the non-striker out of his ground, and promptly threw down the wicket at the bowler's end. 'How's that?' he called, but the umpire answered 'Don't know. It was too quick for me.'

A twenty-hour train journey took the travellers back into Canada, where they went straight from the train to play Winnipeg in a one-day match, followed by a two-day match against Canada. The matches, in Assiniboin Park, were played in near-century heat on a ground infested with locusts, which swarmed over the pitch and gave the ball an action unexpected by bowler or batsman.

Australia won the match against Canada by an innings and 21 runs, but Winnipeg newspapers mourned: 'The fact that Canada's representative cricketers could muster only 88 runs in the first innings ... was not nearly so disappointing to the 4000 fans who sat out in the hot sun all day as the dismissal of Don Bradman for the paltry score of two runs.'

He compensated for this failure with a knock of 116 at Regina, and again with 110 at Moose Jaw. In *Farewell to Cricket*, he wrote: 'There was a lot of fun at Moose Jaw. One of the umpires was a traveller for the local chewing gum manufacturer. Copious supplies were handed round among the players, who promptly used some of it to stick the bails on (the day being rather windy).

'A liberal amount was attached to one bail which fell slowly towards the ground when one of our batsmen was stumped. On appeal, the umpire refused to give him out until the bail actually reached the ground.'

The strenuous pace of the tour continued unabated. The tourists drove from Moose Jaw to Yorkton, arriving at three a.m. but still

Australian kangaroo and American eagle front up to each other on the cover of this programme published in Chicago, for the tourists' match against the Illinois Cricket Association in July 1932

managing to trounce the local side on a matting wicket laid on dirt. With barely a pause for breath they pressed on to Saskatoon, Edmonton and Calgary, on their way back to Vancouver. They travelled, played cricket, and attended lunches and dinners arranged by local enthusiasts, almost without relief except for a side-trip to see the dramatic beauty of Banff and Lake Louise in the Rocky Mountains. Nevertheless, Bradman had returned to form and in four matches he scored as many runs as the total gained by all seventy-two batsmen in the eighteen-man opposing teams.

By 15 August the tourists were back in Vancouver, where they played two 'experimental' matches against Vancouver and British Columbia colts. The experiment was that Arthur Mailey should captain the opposition on one day, and Alan Kippax on the next, but all of Mailey's guile could not save the colts from defeat. In the match against the nineteen-man side, Bradman scored 125 not out and brought his total for the tour to more than 3000 runs.

The Australians played their last match in Canada on Vancouver Island, and then boarded the ferry *Princess Marguerite* for the scenic trip through Puget Sound to Seattle. Another long rail journey — two nights and a day by the Southern Pacific Railroad — carried them to San Francisco for matches against the Northern California All-Stars.

The first match was played in the Kezar Stadium, which was a strange and melancholy sight with only a few hundred cricket fans scattered among the seats built for 70 000 baseball addicts.

Bradman's opinion was that the Californians had little notion of cricket, but the match was an amusing experience. He wrote later: 'There were some West Indians in the team, and one of them came in for some barracking because, having played a ball to third man for a possible two runs, he refused to budge from his crease. Calling out "No" in determined tones to his partner, he shouted "Never mind them — let them do the hollerin' out there, we'll do the judgin' right here."'

Frank Percy, a former captain of an English college team, reported the game for local newspapers. Of the first match he wrote: 'California's aggregation of all-star cricketers can congratulate themselves on at least one feat yesterday. They got out "Dynamite Don" Bradman, the Bambino of cricket, for the ordinary score of 29 runs.'

In the second match Bradman made 122 and Tolhurst 117, adding 168 in thirty-four minutes. Percy wrote: 'Dapper Don Bradman, the Babe Ruth of Australian cricket, had only to unlimber his shoulders four times at Kezar Stadium to convince devotees of the game, as well as amaze first-timers at watching the pastime, that he came by his cognomen meritoriously. The four mighty heaves — all in succession — landed a ball high in the grandstand and aided a victory for the Australian tourists by an innings of 215 runs.'

On the following day the Australians travelled on to Santa Barbara, to stay at the Biltmore Hotel 'where the smart world of society and sport meet to play'. They gained a swift victory in a one-day match against Montecito Cricket Club and boarded a Greyhound bus next morning, bound for Hollywood and their last match in North America.

The film colony gave them a heroes' welcome in what was then the most glamorous show-business location in the world. Cricket in

Jessie Bradman in Hollywood with a group of polo players including 'Snowy' Baker (left)', the Australian film star of that period. Baker made his name in Australian films produced during the 1920s, but his move to Hollywood did not bring him the international fame expected by his fans

Jessie Bradman, a keen and skilful horsewoman, enjoyed the opportunity to ride local horses during the Australian visit to Hollywood in 1932

Hollywood revolved around the stately figure of Sir Charles Aubrey Smith, who had revitalised the game in that part of the United States. Sir Charles had played for Cambridge University, Sussex and the Transvaal before he went on the London stage and subsequently Hollywood, where he gained international fame for his portrayals of English officers and aristocrats in such films as *Little Lord Fauntleroy*, *The Four Feathers*, and *Lives of a Bengal Lancer*. He was captain of an English Test team, the first to tour South Africa, in 1888–89: twenty years before Bradman was born.

He led an eighteen-man Hollywood team which included Boris

Karloff, who created the part of Frankenstein, and other members of the English film colony, but they were not equal to the Australians. In the four innings, the visitors declared after the loss of only two wickets in each of the first three and five in the last, and still administered resounding defeats.

The Australians were perhaps less interested in the cricketing potential of Hollywood stars than in the opportunity to meet such leading ladies of the 1930s as Mary Astor, Jean Harlow, Myrna Loy, Maureen O'Sullivan and Norma Shearer. They visited the Metro Goldwyn Mayer studios and went to a party hosted by Leslie Howard, who was beloved for his representations of the perfect English gentleman although he was, in fact, of European birth and descent.

Hollywood, Santa Barbara and San Francisco had given the travellers some of their most pleasant memories of the North American tour, which came to an end when they returned to San Francisco and boarded the *Monowai* for the voyage home. They had played fifty-one matches in seventy-five days: a far more strenuous campaign than any Test tour, especially since it had involved almost 10 000 kilometres of travel by road and rail, with many nights spent in the train and never more than five or six nights in the same hotel. Of course the opposition was not as skilful as a player would experience in first-class cricket, but the tourists still had to treat it seriously. The tour had not been without its casualties, including Carter's damaged eye and a leg injury which still troubled Bradman when he boarded the *Monowai*.

He had played in every match and totalled 3779 runs: the equivalent of a lifetime's total for many a first-class player. His average was 102.1. He had also had to do a lot of bowling. McCabe was the next best in the batting totals, with 2361 at 54.9. He also took 189 wickets, at six, against Fleetwood-Smith's 238 at 7.5 and Mailey's 203 at 8.6.

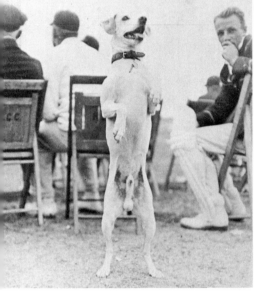

Don Bradman (right) upstaged by this performing dog 'stunting' while Bradman waits his turn to bat against the Hollywood cricketers in 1932

The Australians photographed with some of the famous Hollywood stars of the early 1930s. C. Aubrey Smith, the English star who revived cricket in that part of California, sits at lower right. Myrna Loy is in the centre of the front row, and Boris Karloff in the centre of the back row between Ronald Colman and the Australian captain, Vic Richardson

A newspaper in Wellington, New Zealand, published this cartoon when Bradman and the other Australians arrived in New Zealand in September 1932, aboard the *Monowai* on their way home to Australia. The newspaper noted that Bradman received far greater acclaim than New Zealand politicians returning from a conference in Ottawa and New Zealand sportsmen returning from the 1932 Olympics in Los Angeles

Bradman was in the headlines again when the *Monowai* touched at Wellington on the voyage back to Sydney. It was a cold, wet Sunday morning but New Zealand cricket fans thronged the wharf in the hope of catching a glimpse of him. The Wellington *Evening Post* reported: 'Although he had never set foot in Wellington before, this young man was no stranger; he was known by the deeds which have made him the most talked-of man in the world of cricket. Mr and Mrs Bradman were escorted with difficulty through the waiting crowds . . . For the small boys it was a memorable occasion — the nearer they could get to Bradman the more lasting, no doubt, the impression upon their minds. The crowd surged around the motor-car, and lustily cheered the Bradmans ere they broke clear of this remarkable demonstration.'

On 23 September 1932 the *Monowai* steamed into Sydney Harbour and brought Bradman home into a new storm of controversy. It had been grumbling on the horizon for several months and it broke on the very day of his return.

Early in February the Melbourne *Globe* had printed a story headed 'Bradman's Future in Cricket is Obscure', with the lead-in 'Don Bradman may not after all be playing for Australia against the

Englishmen next season'. The story went on to say that Bradman's contract with Associated Newspapers had raised the eyebrows of the Board of Control.

As the result of controversies earlier in the century, when Australian cricketers had written press copy critical of fellow players in Test teams, the Board's regulations included a strict ban against Test players writing for newspapers. They made only one exception to this rule, in cases when journalism was a cricketer's sole means of livelihood, but player-writers still had to apply to the Board for permission which might be withdrawn at any time.

Bradman was aware of this ukase when he signed the three-party contract in October 1931, but he had not thought that the Board would take such a narrow view of the 'sole means of livelihood' clause. As he saw it, all three parts of the contract depended upon each other. If Associated Newspapers had not participated in the offer which persuaded him to remain in Australia, then the other two parties could not have made it sufficiently attractive. Therefore, his obligation to write for the press — specifically the Sydney *Sun* — was an integral part of his 'sole means of livelihood'. It was in fact his living, not a mere sideline as it was for some other players.

He was astonished to find that the Board took a different attitude. They claimed that journalism represented only one-third of the ways in which he made his living, and therefore he could not be exempted from the ban.

This gave him the option either of accepting the Board's viewpoint, and thus breaking his contract with Associated Newspapers and reducing his income by one-third, or of sticking to his contract and giving up any hope of inclusion in the Test eleven to face the Englishmen in their 1932–33 tour of Australia.

He had no doubt about the correct decision. He told the *Globe*: 'I have entered into this contract, and I intend to stick to it. If the Board will not allow me to carry out my contract, then I will not be available for Test cricket. It is just as well that my position should be made clear.'

When he had sailed for North America, the position was still uncertain. The Board still had the opportunity to make a reasonable exception in his case, and thus retain an invaluable player for the forthcoming Tests, and the matter faded out of the public mind until the very day of Bradman's return.

But the press did not forget the issue, and pressed the Board for a statement to appear on the day of his return. They said that unless he could prove that journalism was his sole means of livelihood, they would not approve his selection for the Test eleven.

Bradman replied in equally forthright terms. He stated bluntly: 'I have signed a contract to write articles, and I must keep it. I cannot let cricket interfere with my work.'

However, he then made a formal application to the Board to be permitted to write for the *Sun*, pointing out that although journalism was not his sole means of livelihood it was an essential part of it.

This new clash between Bradman and the Board triggered another whirlwind of press and public speculation and argument, from *Smith's Weekly*'s larrikin jeers at the Board to the *Sydney Morning Herald*'s more reasoned arguments. Almost unanimously, Australians sup-

THE CONTROVERSIAL CLAUSE

Bradman was not the only Australian cricketer to be affected by the Board of Control resolution against player-writers, which read as follows:

'The Board will not approve of the selection for the Australian team to oppose England during season 1932-3 of any cricketer who, during the season, writes or contributes any articles for the Press, which, in the opinion of the Board, comment upon the play in any first-class match, or upon the prospects of selection of a cricketer or cricketers who may possibly be a member or members of such team; provided that any cricketer whose sole occupation is journalism may, upon first obtaining the written permission of the chairman of the Board, and until such permission is withdrawn by the chairman of the Board, write or contribute articles commenting upon the play in any such match.'

Woodfull, Ponsford, Grimmett and Oldfield had all written for various newspapers over the years. Clarrie Grimmett had also written a book, published during the 1930 tour of England, which aroused the wrath of the Board although they did not fine him in the same way that they fined Bradman.

The only 'full-time' journalist in the Australian Test team during the 1932-33 season was the right-hand opening batsman Jack Fingleton, whose first-class career ran from 1930 to 1940. He played in eighteen Test matches for a total of 1189 runs at 42.46. A professional journalist, who worked for Australian newspapers and for the Commonwealth Government, he published nine books on cricket including *The Immortal Victor Trumper*.

ported Bradman and decried the fuddy-duddy attitude of the Board. Many people saw it as yet another attempt to punish him for having written *Don Bradman's Book*, or as an oblique move on the part of Don Bradman's critics to 'put him down' for his enormous popularity.

English newspapers soon picked up the story but almost refused to believe that Australia could be so shortsighted as to prevent Bradman from playing in a Test series. Some of them dismissed it as little more than a publicity stunt, and said that Bradman was certain to play. But Alan Fairfax, who had accepted the Accrington offer which Bradman refused, wrote unkindly in the *Evening News* that Australia could win without Bradman. He said that the bowlers Grimmett and Ironmonger were more important to the Test eleven.

The Board quickly found themselves in the difficult position of men who have taken a stance on a matter of principle: unable to back down without weakening their future authority. But Bradman was equally determined not to abandon his principles. He had signed a contract, and he could not see any honourable way to release himself from its obligations.

An ironical aspect of the conflict was that Bradman's appearance in the Tests would attract many more spectators and thus swell the Board's share of the profits, but they wanted Bradman to abandon the arrangement which earned his living.

The prolonged argument kept everyone on tenterhooks even after the English tourists arrived in Australia, and Bradman went to Perth to play against the M.C.C. Twelve months earlier, the Accrington offer had made every Australian cricket lover fearful of the future. Now they dreaded a Test disaster if Don Bradman did not play.

Rumours abounded, including one that a large Australian corporation had offered to buy out Bradman's contract and pay him the same

Jessie Bradman in the garden of the first Bradman home, at McMahons Point, Sydney, late in 1932, with the recently-opened Sydney Harbour Bridge in the background

fee — if only he would play for his country. Sir Donald Bradman says that he never received such an approach at the time.

However, there was one very tempting offer from overseas. An English newspaper group cabled him an offer of £3000, a huge sum for those days, if he would abandon any hopes of playing in the Tests and cover the series for them.

By that time Associated Newspapers were under fire for 'holding Bradman to this contract', and some members of the Board had begun to flinch under the steady bombardment of abuse and criticism. They asked A. G. Moyes, then the sports editor of the *Sun*, to introduce them to R. C. Packer, the editorial head of the newspaper group, so that they might ask him to release Bradman from the contract.

Packer agreed to do so, but Bradman steadily insisted that he was under a moral obligation to fulfil the contract. His only offer of concession was to accept the English bid, drop out of the Tests and write for the overseas newspapers, and pay the huge fee over to Associated Newspapers.

Packer rejected this and said: 'You must play, Don.'

He answered: 'You can force me to write, but there's nothing in the contract which allows you to force me to play.'

Packer replied that Associated Newspapers only wanted him to forget about writing, and play for Australia. He spoke so persuasively that Bradman at last agreed to break his own inflexible rule.

Strangely, the Board consented to his talking about the Tests in his broadcasts over 2UE, but they would not allow him to write about them. To many people, it was a 'distinction without a difference'.

Only a few hundred cricket fans occupied the enormous Kezar Stadium, San Francisco, built to accommodate 70 000 baseball addicts, when the Australians played local cricketers there in 1932

10

THE BODYLINE ATTACK

In October 1932 Bradman had never been in worse condition to face the rigours of a first-class season. The preceding twelve months had been immensely demanding: physically, mentally and emotionally. When he and Jessie Bradman returned to Sydney they had been looking forward, like any other young couple, to establishing their first home together; but although they took a house on McMahons Point, it soon became a refuge against the clamouring world outside instead of a peaceful haven. He was even obliged to apply for an unlisted telephone number, which was a very rare thing in those days. And, on top of everything else, he was suffering from a long siege of dental trouble.

Despite all these problems he turned out for St George and revelled in the pleasure of playing cricket for its own sake, free from the pressures of inter-State or international competition. If any critics thought that he might be stale after his enormous compilation of runs in North America they were quickly disappointed. In his first grade match of the season, against Gordon, he scored a century in sixty-four minutes. He chalked up another century in the next match, against Mosman, and 145 in one of the trial matches at the Sydney Cricket Ground watched by the New South Wales selectors.

The English visitors for the 1932–33 Test season were already *en route* to Australia aboard the *Orontes*, and Bradman's effortless brilliance in his opening matches of the season added yet more fuel to the fire of the player-writer controversy. The English team was heavily weighted with speed bowlers, and Australians told each other that Bradman *must* play. They could not believe that the Board of Control would stick so stubbornly to their guns as to rob Australia of the surest hope of success.

When Bradman himself scanned the list of English players, he told a friend that a 'bumper' attack looked imminent, although he certainly did not visualise the strategy which Douglas Jardine, captain of the English eleven, had planned before leaving England.

With his immediate Test future still in doubt, he made the long trip across the continent to play in a Combined Australia side against the M.C.C. in Perth. In those days of slow travel the encounter was to be a gourmet feast of cricket for the Western Australians, and they mobbed the train almost as soon as it entered the State. Bradman had to lock himself in his sleeping compartment to avoid the throngs of backslappers and autograph hunters. When the easterners arrived in Perth it seemed that the whole population of the State had crammed the capital to watch the match, many of them wearing lapel buttons inscribed 'Bradman Must Play' to signify their support in his battle against the Board.

Most of them hoped for a first sight of Bradman at his best, but they were sadly disappointed. For Bradman, the three-day match from 27–29 October was a disaster. Vic Richardson lost the toss and the Australians had to spend two whole days in the field. The English batting kept Bradman on the move and he had to bowl nineteen overs, the longest bowling spell in his career; but at least he had the satisfaction of dismissing Jardine and Gubby Allen. After the second day's play, overnight rain saturated the pitch, and when Bradman went in to play it was a real 'gluepot'. Jardine was still keeping Larwood, Voce and Bowes under wraps, so there was no hint of what was to come; but Allen and Hedley Verity were in great form. Verity took seven for 37 off eighteen overs, and Bradman was among his victims. He was caught after only seven minutes, off a ball which jumped viciously. In his second innings, Allen dismissed him after only twenty-two minutes. It was a drawn game, but the Western Australians felt they had not had their money's worth.

A Shield match early in November seemed to reassure Bradman's supporters that he could be the backbone of the Test team if only he were allowed to play. In two magnificent innings against Victoria he totalled 290. In the first innings he reached his century in seventy-three minutes and his double century in 172 minutes. The Sydney *Referee* rated it the equal of any innings ever seen on the Sydney Cricket Ground. In the second innings he carried his bat for 52.

Ten days later, on 18 November, he appeared in Melbourne for an Australian eleven against the M.C.C. On this occasion the curtain rose on the greatest controversy in Test cricket — and perhaps the greatest controversy ever recorded between Britain and Australia. Probably more words have been written and spoken about 'bodyline' than about any other wrangle between the two nations.

It all began during the English summer, when Douglas Jardine knew he was likely to lead the twenty-fourth English team to tour Australia. Jardine, a lawyer, was a man with a cold and calculating personality, and he set himself to long-range planning on the best way to defeat the Australian batsmen — primarily Bradman, but also such men as Richardson, McCabe, Woodfull, Ponsford and Fingleton.

Apparently he discussed his strategy with a number of men who had played against Australia, including Frank Foster, of Warwickshire, who had a tremendous bowling success in 1911-12. Together with Sydney Barnes, he was largely instrumental in wresting the Ashes from Australia. He took thirty-two wickets at 21.62, and Barnes took thirty-four at 22.88. Foster gave his leg-side placings to Jardine but later said he would not have done so if he had realised how Jardine would use them.

Early in that tour, Foster found that his left-arm bowling did not worry the Australians and he developed what became known as 'fast leg-theory'. After the tour, Warner wrote: 'Foster is the best bowler of his type I have ever seen. Bowling round the wicket with a high

The manager and captain of the controversial 1932–33 English 'bodyline' team. P. F. 'Plum' Warner, later Sir Pelham Francis Warner, on the left, was one of the most notable English cricket personalities. As manager of the 'bodyline' team he maintained an urbane attitude towards the controversy. Douglas Jardine the captain (right), was described as 'the best-hated man in Australia' during the 1932–33 Test series

delivery his action was the personification of ease. A few short steps, an apparently medium-paced ball through the air, but doubling its speed as it touched the ground, he kept an exceptional length on the leg stump. The angle of delivery made the ball swing into the batsman.'

This was *genuine* leg-theory: an attack on the leg stump which could trap the striker into turning the ball into the hands of the leg field. But in Harold Larwood's book *Bodyline?* published in 1933, he claimed that 'Fast leg theory was born in the Test Match at Kennington Oval in August 1930, unknown to anybody but myself.' He went on to say that 'It is claimed that Gregory and Macdonald bowled it in 1919 and 1921, but neither of them bowled true fast leg-theory. Neither had any setting of the leg-side field, and without that there can be no genuine fast leg-theory. Everything else is a kind of imitation.'

It is true that Gregory and Macdonald never bowled leg-theory. Both men were extremely fast and they bowled a fair ration of bumpers, but neither ever resorted to using a leg-side field.

One of Foster's comments about leg-theory is interesting. He said that no fast left-hand bowler should ever bowl to the leg-theory field over the wicket because it is too dangerous to the batsman, and no fast right-hand bowler should ever bowl leg-theory, for the same reason.

Harold Larwood and Bill Bowes, who were right-arm bowlers, and Bill Voce who bowled left-arm, either did not know of these warnings or did not heed them.

Larwood's comment about the 1930 'birth' of leg-theory refers, of course, to the innings in which he tried to dismiss Bradman and Jackson with bullet-fast deliveries which injured both batsmen. (See Chapter 6.) Larwood wrote: 'My great friend Archie Jackson stood up

ENGLISH BOMBSHELL

F. R. FOSTER TELLS
England Is Shamed By The Victory

WOODFULL WAS CLEAN

(RADIO FROM "SMITH'S" LONDON OFFICE. COPYRIGHT.)

"JARDINE IS WELCOME TO THE ASHES, AT THE PRICE ENGLAND PAID FOR THEM."

Thus Frank R. Foster, the famous English bowler, opened his statement in London to "Smith's Weekly." And he went on:—

"Say this from me to the captain of the English Eleven in Australia :—

"DOUGLAS JARDINE. I AM ASHAMED OF ENGLAND'S WIN. I WILL FACE YOU ON YOUR RETURN WITH THESE WORDS ON MY LIPS.

"You allowed Woodfull to beat you in every sense of the word Cricket.

"Woodfull won the Second Test by clean methods. We won our four matches by other methods.

"I take my hat right off to Woodfull, for resisting the temptation to retaliate in body-line bowling. Cricket history has no finer example of sportsmanship.

"My name has been used in the body-line controversy, in connection with Warner's tour of 1911-1912. I indignantly repudiate the suggestion that I ever used body-line bowling.

"I may have struck men by accident. What fast bowler hasn't? But I never deliberately sent the ball at a batsman's head or body. I aimed always for good length balls. Batsmen like Hobbs or Macartney were never struck by me, because they knew how to use their feet.

Allen Should Lead England

"Being a left-handed bowler, I never once in my whole cricket career bowled over the wicket. A left-arm bowler, bowling over the wicket, immediately becomes a body-liner, for he cannot possibly see the three stumps.

"Body-line bowling is quite different from the leg-theory, which I understand and which I bowled.

"I am sorry that Nottingham, through Larwood and Voce, figures so conspicuously in the cloud surrounding England's victory.

"ALLEN HAS PROVED HIMSELF A PERFECT GENTLEMAN, AND ON HIS ABILITY AND SPORTSMANSHIP HE SHOULD BE ENGLAND'S CAPTAIN.

"Allen displayed strength of character in resisting Jardine's 'body-line' influence.

"I greatly regret Larwood's actions. As the finest fast bowler that England has seen for thirty years, he is too good to resort to any kind of leg theory.

"Unless the Marylebone Cricket Club does uphold the protest from the Australian Board of Control, the game will be ruined in the coming season. Even schoolboy fast bowlers, encountering difficult wickets and expert batsmen, will bowl bumpers deliberately at the man instead of the wicket.

"Body-line bowling must be abolished. The only solution is to give the umpire power to no-ball.

"AND IT MUST BE DONE BEFORE THE 1934 SEASON, AS JARDINE MAY STILL BE CAPTAIN WHEN THE AUSTRALIANS VISIT US."

Foster then concluded his statement to "Smith's Weekly" with a comment on Warner's presence in the visiting party, and a revelation regarding the body-line plan. Both were highly significant. Regarding Warner, he said:—

"In the whole history of cricket, there have never previously

(NOW READ ON TO COLUMNS 5 AND 6)

A portion of one of the *Smith's Weekly* articles in which the English bowler F. R. Foster, who initiated leg-theory bowling, assailed Douglas Jardine and the English bowlers of the 1932–33 Test series for their use of bodyline against the Australians

THE BODYLINE CONTRADICTIONS

One of the strangest aspects of the bodyline controversy is the number of contradictory statements — or excuses — made by some of those involved.

In a subsequent book, Douglas Jardine wrote: 'Though I did not take part in the Test Match against Australia at the Oval in 1930, I have been told on all sides that Bradman's innings was far from convincing on the leg stump while there was any life in the wicket. I am sorry to disappoint anyone who has imagined that the leg theory was evolved with the help of midnight oil and iced towels solely for the purpose of combating Bradman's effectiveness as a scoring machine. It did, however, seem a reasonable assumption that a weakness in one of Australia's premier batsmen might find more than a replica in the play of a good many of his contemporaries.'

But he later attributed bodyline to a sudden inspiration during the first M.C.C. match in Australia during the 1932–33 tour, in Perth on 27–29 October, when they played a Combined Australia eleven. He wrote: 'To our surprise we found an almost totally unexpected weakness on the leg stump in the play of several leading players. This had been particularly apparent in the case of Bradman . . . when he came to Perth to play against us.'

As Sir Donald Bradman points out, 'He must have been amazingly observant', because Bradman batted only twice, on a pitch badly affected by rain, and was dismissed after only a few minutes in each innings.

Jardine did not employ leg-side tactics in Perth, nor did any of his three bodyline bowlers, Larwood, Voce and Bowes play in the match.

But his implication in the first statement is that bodyline evolved almost naturally, and in the second that it was invented after he reached Australia.

However, the English bowler Frank Foster, who played so successfully against Australia in 1911–12, showed conclusively that Jardine's attempts to deny a 'bodyline plot' were disingenuous.

After the 'Bodyline Tests' he told *Smith's Weekly*: 'Before Jardine left England he came frequently to my flat in the St. James and secured from me my leg-theory field placings. I had no hint that these would be used for bodyline bowling. I would like all my old friends in Australian cricket to know that I am sorry that my experience and my advice were put to such unworthy uses.'

Walter Hammond also alleged that Jardine spent many days in planning his bodyline tactics. He wrote that the English cricketer and sportswriter Percy Fender, whose 1928 predictions about Bradman turned out to be so inaccurate, suggested the idea to Jardine, who then carefully analysed all the scoring diagrams of the Australian batsmen's 1930 innings and subsequently visited Foster.

The position of the Marylebone Cricket Club in the dispute, and that of the English manager Pelham Warner, appear to be anomalous. Warner, later Sir Pelham Warner, was the manager of the English team and one of the most respected personalities in international cricket, but his character may be one of the greatest contradictions in the bodyline dispute. In *The Larwood Story*, published in 1965, Larwood wrote of him: 'He always gave the impression to outsiders that he was compelled to walk a diplomatic tightrope and exercised no influence over the captain. But he never spoke against bodyline on that tour as far as I was concerned. Behind the dignified and affable English exterior there was a shrewd brain and dominating personality that would not hesitate to drive home any advantage.'

Larwood himself, the great exponent of bodyline, made a variety of contradictory or provocative statements in his 1965 book, in press articles or interviews, and in his book *Bodyline?* published in 1933.

In May 1933 he wrote in the *Sunday Express*: 'Woodfull was too slow and Bradman was too frightened. Yes, frightened is the word . . . he was scared of my bowling.'

But in January 1975 the London *Observer* quoted him as saying: 'Bradman . . . used to back away, not because he was scared, but to try to make room to hit me through the off side.'

And in 1965 he wrote: 'I believe that no criticism of Bradman can be valid because above all he did try to score runs.'

In 1933 he wrote: 'I have never bowled at any batsman.'

In 1965: 'One Australian batsman claimed publicly that when he took block a yard outside his leg stump, my body-line balls still came straight at him. He was right. They did.'

On page 214 of *The Larwood Story* he wrote that 'any attacking batsman who could hook, and had a bit of luck, could have handled body-line', but on the same page he remarked: 'Body-line gave the crowd their money's worth. But it left a mark. For one thing it killed off the hook shot.'

The comment about hook shots may give a clue to the whole affair. Bradman was universally recognised as the greatest player of the hook shot and

pull shot that cricket has ever known. Bodyline prevented these shots from being played, but that applied to everyone. It would seem likely that the Englishmen wanted to cancel out two of Bradman's most effective shots, although they gave Jardine's unjust and hypocritical excuse that Bradman's batsmanship was 'far from convincing on the leg side'.

Undoubtedly bodyline was conceived in order to check Bradman's success. In a relative manner, it did so; but at the same time it effectively ruined the art of batting for everyone else and almost ruined the game itself.

A particularly cruel aspect of bodyline was that it became a splendid weapon for Bradman's enemies and critics, who used it in attempts to degrade him.

Warwick Armstrong, one of Australia's most successful Test captains, reported the 1932–33 tour for the London *Evening News* and made such cutting comments as 'There was no doubt whatever in my mind that Bradman was scared of Larwood . . . The rubber hinged largely on Bradman and Larwood, and Larwood conquered him . . . On the form shown in this series of Tests Bradman is nothing but a cricket cocktail.'

Armstrong made this unworthy comment despite the fact that Bradman's batting average in Tests facing bodyline was higher than the averages of *every* English batsman on that tour except Paynter, and they were never exposed to bodyline.

In *The Larwood Story*, Larwood quotes a 1938 article by Clarrie Grimmett in the Perth *Sunday Times*, in which Grimmett is alleged to have said that bodyline was not unfair and that batsmen must blame themselves for the slow footwork which made them helpless against Voce and Larwood.

But Bradman was to surpass Armstrong as a batsman by enormous margins, both in totals and averages, and Grimmett never faced bodyline. He was a great bowler, but in thirty-seven Tests his batting average was only 13.92 and he did not show up well against fast bowlers. He can hardly be regarded as an effective judge of fast bowling from the batsman's point of view, and Bradman's average of 56 in his four bodyline Tests would hardly support an allegation of 'helplessness'.

Larwood wrote that the 1932–33 season 'provided the only real test on hard wickets of Fast Leg Theory [as he called bodyline] in cricket's history', but he ignored the fact that Frank Foster used leg theory with enormous success against the Australians on the 1911–12 tour, without a word of complaint from Australia. Pelham Warner wrote of that tour: 'I am certain that they left a great name behind them in Australia for their conduct and bearing both on and off the field.'

Larwood decried the change in the rules which effectively ended bodyline, by restricting the number of fieldsmen on the leg side to five, and wrote: 'Why? A few drops of rain fall and the batsmen of today are convinced that the wicket is bad. Trumper in the 1902 Test scored 11 centuries in one of the wettest seasons in memory.'

The inference, perhaps, is that Bradman could not measure up to Trumper, and that if Trumper had faced bodyline there would have been no complaints. Other writers, especially Jack Fingleton, also have tried to suggest that Trumper had it all over Bradman on wet wickets.

In fact, United Kingdom rainfall statistics show that Bradman's summer season in England in 1930 was wetter than Trumper's in 1902. Trumper made 247 at 30, and Bradman 974 at 139.

In four tours of England, Trumper had 34 Test innings and totalled 863 at 27.8. In Bradman's four tours of England, he had 30 Test innings and totalled 2674 at an average of 102.84. Such figures speak for themselves.

In a 1982 edition of *The Larwood Story*, there is an addition headed 'Fifty Years After'. In this, it would almost seem that Larwood wishes to make amends for some of his comments of the past. He wrote: 'You hear talk that modern day batsmen like Greg Chappell are as good as Bradman . . . Chappell would not be in the same street, nor would any other Australian or batsman from any other country since the war.'

In Larwood's accounts of the bodyline Tests he is understandably loyal to his team mates, and he often refers to the loyalty and support of his touring companions. It is understandable that team members would find great difficulty in publicly dissociating themselves from the tactics and policy of their captain.

But at least two Englishmen on the 1932–33 tour, G. O. 'Gubby' Allen and Bob Wyatt, were against bodyline and not afraid to say so. It now seems clear that Allen had bitter arguments with Jardine on the subject, and that he courageously defied Jardine's request to bowl to the leg-side field. Apparently Bob Wyatt supported Allen. If other English bowlers had shown the same kind of moral courage — or had not been so eager to dismiss Bradman at any cost — the bodyline scandal would not have erupted.

to me, getting pinked once or twice in the process, and he never flinched.

'With Bradman it was different . . . I determined then and there that if I was again honoured with an invitation to go to Australia, I would not forget that difference.'

Larwood's implication seems to be that Bradman was afraid of his bowling, but press comments on that 1930 innings paint a very different picture. One journalist wrote: 'This Bradman is lion-hearted, physically and figuratively. He made a double-century despite the whirlwind rib-breaking shock tactics of Larwood.'

Another said: 'Despite the most difficult wicket, Bradman and Jackson gave the English people an exhibition of versatility, pluck, and determination rarely seen on a cricket field.'

And another wrote: 'The dangerous wicket helped the bowlers who made the ball fly, Larwood being particularly vicious. Frequently the lads, after being hit, writhed in pain but, bruised and battered from head to toe, they carried on.'

Percy Chapman, the deposed English captain, wrote of Bradman in the *Daily Mail*: 'This brilliant batsman is too good for us. He has never looked like getting out.'

These words do not add up to a description of a man who flinched from Larwood's 'whirlwind rib-breaking shock tactics', or of one who was likely to be defeated by them if they were repeated. But Larwood's remark about the 'difference' between Bradman and Jackson may have been no more than self-justification written in hindsight, after the tidal wave of protest aroused by bodyline in 1932–33.

Probably the truth about the planning of the bodyline assault will now never be known. On 11 January 1975 Jardine's daughter wrote a letter to the London *Times* in which she said that bodyline was 'discussed with and fully approved of by the M.C.C. as the one way to beat Bradman, before Jardine's team left England in 1932', but that the M.C.C. threw her father to the wolves during the subsequent uproar. It is possible that Percy Fender, who wrote sarcastically about Bradman during the 1928–29 Test season and was later forced to eat his words when Bradman gave his Surrey team an unmerciful hiding at The Oval in May 1930, suggested the idea to Jardine. Arthur Carr, captain of Nottinghamshire, who had played against Australia and who later became an uncompromising supporter of Larwood and Voce in the bodyline controversy, was certainly implicated. In his book *Cricket With the Lid Off*, he wrote: 'I may here say that I discussed that new form of bowling technique — leg theory, or whatever you like to call it — before Larwood went to Australia with Douglas Jardine's team.'

In Larwood's book *The Larwood Story*, published in 1965, the bowler mentions a dinner in the grill-room of the Piccadilly Hotel, London, with Carr as the host and Larwood, Voce and Jardine as the guests. Larwood wrote: 'Jardine and Carr were doing most of the talking. I didn't contribute much to the conversation . . . Bradman was the big problem. He was the key man in Australia and Jardine wanted to curb his run-getting.'

A little later in the book, Larwood admits that Bradman had 'pasted him' two years earlier and says that he had 'a score to settle'. The important words are: 'Any scheme that would keep him in check appealed to me . . . that's where it all started as far as I was concerned.'

The position of Pelham Warner in the dispute appears to be equivocal. Probably the most respected man in English cricket at that time, he travelled as manager of Jardine's team although he had already declared himself against the technique which later became known as bodyline. On 22 August 1932 he wrote in the London *Morning Post* of a match between Yorkshire and Surrey that 'Bowes must alter his tactics. Bowes bowled with five men on the on-side and sent down several very short-pitched balls which repeatedly bounced head-high and more. Now that is not bowling; indeed it is not cricket; and if all the fast bowlers were to adopt his methods M.C.C. would be compelled to step in and penalise the bowler who bowled the ball less than half-way up the pitch.'

Bowes, Voce and Larwood were to adapt this technique to the Test battle against the Australians, and yet Warner does not seem to have protested — or at least not in public. It is possible that Jardine's more dominating personality made him keep his thoughts to himself.

There is an old saying that 'Success has many fathers, but failure is an orphan'. It is possible that bodyline has 'many fathers' and that they would all have proudly claimed parenthood if it had not aroused such an uproar. Probably the truth is that the whole English cricketing world was so desperate to beat Bradman that they would accept any tactics to do so, right up to the shadow line of 'Fair and Unfair Play'. In a 1977 television interview, Larwood described it as a 'plot', and in 1965 he wrote '. . . *bodyline was devised to stifle Bradman's batting genius* . . . They said I was a killer with the ball without taking into account that Bradman with the bat was the greatest killer of all.'

Douglas Jardine, captain of England, appears to face the camera with calm confidence. The bespectacled cricketer directly behind him is Bill Bowes the tall rawboned Yorkshireman who was one of the leading practitioners of bodyline bowling

In a veritable blur of speed, Harold Larwood sends down one of the bodyline deliveries which aroused such an enormous controversy in the early 1930s

Prior to 1932 the word 'bodyline' had never been used in cricket. The English players doggedly persisted in calling it 'fast leg-theory' because it had some slight resemblance to Foster's inspiration. The origin of the word remains as obscure as the origin of the tactics. Possibly the trusted and revered Australian cricket writer Ray Robinson coined the word, although various cricket historians give credit to Claude Corbett, Arthur Mailey and others. The word annoyed Larwood, who called it 'detestable, unfair, and inaccurate'; but Australians claimed that 'leg-theory' was a misnomer because Larwood and Voce aimed many deliveries towards the striker's body. Vic Richardson, a fearless player and one of the best hookers in the

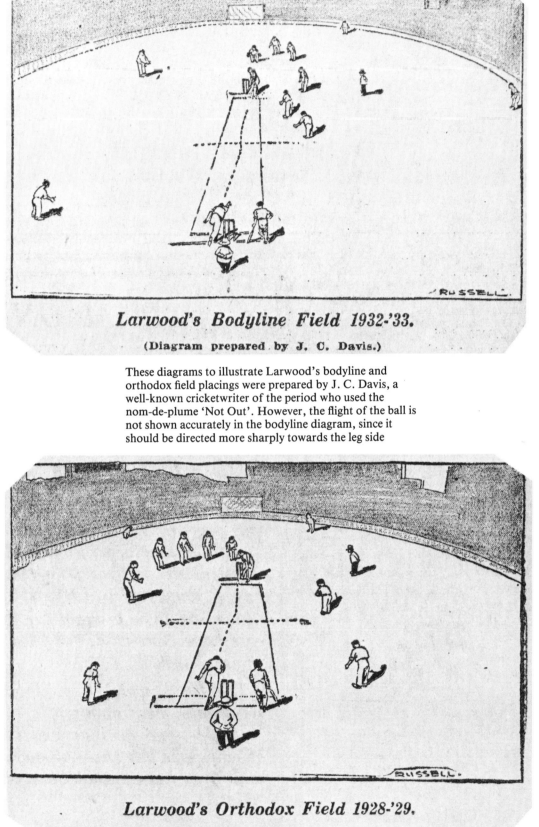

Larwood's Bodyline Field 1932-'33.

(Diagram prepared by J. C. Davis.)

These diagrams to illustrate Larwood's bodyline and
orthodox field placings were prepared by J. C. Davis, a
well-known cricketwriter of the period who used the
nom-de-plume 'Not Out'. However, the flight of the ball is
not shown accurately in the bodyline diagram, since it
should be directed more sharply towards the leg side

Larwood's Orthodox Field 1928-'29.

(Diagram prepared by J. C. Davis.)

game, was one who said this. In 1965 Larwood wrote: 'One Australian Test batsman claimed publicly that when he took block a yard outside his leg stump, my body-line balls still came straight at him. He was right. They did.' Obviously he referred to Richardson, but he painted a different picture in his 1933 book when he wrote: 'I have never bowled at any batsman.'

In *The Larwood Story* he maintained that he had never in his life bowled to injure a batsman, although he aimed to frighten and intimidate him. If a batsman were hit on the thigh, then 'I didn't shed any crocodile tears'.

But there is ample evidence that bodyline bowling hit batsmen in many places apart from the thigh. In those days before batsmen used helmets to protect their heads and faces they were seriously worried about dangerous injuries from such bowling.

It may well be that the 'fathers' of bodyline did not expect it to develop so dangerously. Nobody could accuse Larwood of trying deliberately to injure a batsman, and it would seem that the new method of attack had a two-pronged intention: to destroy the batsman's morale and shock him into a self-defeating stroke, and to place him in a position in which he would almost inevitably make such a stroke.

Larwood would bowl two or three overs with a conventional field until 'the shine was off the ball'. Then he switched his slips and other off-side fieldsmen to the leg-side, with the short legs in a rough semicircle between the batsman and the umpire and two men out deep. He left the off-side almost bare of fieldsmen.

So far these tactics had some resemblance to Foster's genuine leg theory, in which the intent was to attack the leg stump and trap the striker into turning balls into the hands of leg field. But Larwood was a very different type of bowler from Foster. Christopher Martin-Jenkins writes of him: 'With a run of about eighteen yards and with accelerating yet controlled rhythmical strides, his action built up like a long-jumper's to the explosive moment of delivery . . . He was exceptionally fast — his contemporaries believe the fastest of all.' Bradman wrote in 1950: 'Over a full season, under all sorts of conditions, I rank Larwood as the fastest bowler of all. At times he attained exceptional speed.'

Bradman made this remark before the advent of Frank Tyson. Sir Donald now believes that Tyson generated even more pace than Larwood — but he never employed a leg field.

In his bodyline action, the ball left Larwood's hand in a blur of speed, pitched short so that it ricocheted high towards the batsman. Sometimes it flew over the striker's head; sometimes at chest, shoulder or head height. The batsman had only two choices. He could use the bat as a shield for his body, with the strong chance that the ball would fly off it into the hands of one of the close-packed leg field. Or he could risk playing the ball uppishly towards fine-leg or square-leg, either short or deep. Whatever he did, he was dangerously liable to be hit by the ball or to be trapped by a fieldsman.

Voce bowled in a style similar to that of Larwood, except that he bowled over the wicket to the bodyline field, pitching balls well on his own side of half-way and straight at the batsman. Bowes' style was much like Larwood's, except that he was not so fast.

The immense force and effort that Larwood put into his attack was demonstrated by the fact that he injured his left foot so badly during the Test series, by its continuous pounding on the hard Australian pitches, that he never recaptured his 1932–33 speed. And Jardine's ruthless determination to win is demonstrated by the fact that he ordered Larwood out onto the field even when he could hardly squeeze his swollen foot into his cricket boot.

Jack Hobbs, who observed the Test series as a reporter for the *Star*, summarised bodyline when he wrote: 'If this sort of attack is persisted in, somebody will be killed sooner or later . . . If I had to play this type of bowling, I would get out of cricket.'

Jardine revealed his 'secret weapon' against Bradman on 18–22 November 1932, when an Australian eleven played the M.C.C. at Melbourne. The spectators, especially those in the press box, saw that Larwood's shock attack unsettled Bradman. Hobbs wrote: 'It gives a certain satisfaction to know that Don is only human after all, having the same dislike for lightning bumpers as all other batsmen.' Larwood dismissed Bradman for 36 in the first innings and 13 in the second, but the massively-built Lisle Nagel of Victoria avenged Australia when he scattered the English team in ten overs, taking eight wickets for 32. The match ended in a draw.

Nobody except the cricketers seemed to appreciate the menace of what was happening. The Australian press and public dismissed the event as unfortunate, but after all it had not been a Test match and one could not expect 'The Don' to score centuries in every innings. Nobody objected openly to the new English tactics except Bradman, who spoke to the Victorian cricket officials about them and predicted trouble for the future. However, the officials felt that Larwood's 'bumpers' were quite acceptable.

Larwood was jubilant. As he wrote later, 'Leg theory had succeeded far better than I expected. Don, caught in two minds by the leg trap, had jumped out of the way to avoid rising balls over the leg stump.'

When Bradman returned to Sydney a journalist cornered him as he stepped off the train, but the resultant interview owed more to imagination than to accurate reporting. It said that Bradman remarked: 'Don't worry about the shock bowlers. We shall be as right as pie.'

Sir Donald Bradman says that the comment, like many others attributed to him, was pure invention. It was to be quoted sarcastically during the coming weeks.

The apparently unquenchable flame of Don Bradman's stamina and spirit was now wavering under the effects of the past twelve months. When he appeared once more against the M.C.C., for his home State on the Sydney Cricket Ground, he was obviously unwell. Maurice Tate, who had himself been ill when the English team left London, and had followed them in a later ship, dismissed him for 18 in the first innings without recourse to bodyline tactics. (In fact Tate was never to use them.) Bradman spent the third day of the match in bed with a throat infection, but batted again early on the fourth day. He faced Bill Voce, and seemed to be settling down when Voce bowled him a very short ball. Bradman expected it to be one of the many 'bumpers' and went over to the off to let it fly past, but it stayed unusually low and broke his wicket. With a score of only 23 he went back home to bed.

Maurice 'Chub' Tate one of England's greatest bowlers (he took 2938 wickets during his 1912–37 career) was one of the bowlers who did not use bodyline tactics

An incident during the 1932–33 Test series. Herbert Sutcliffe plays a ball from O'Reilly onto his wicket but looks down in astonishment when he sees that it did not dislodge the bails

Every first-class batsman in the preceding history of cricket, including such giants as Hobbs, Ponsford and Sutcliffe, had had their down spells in which they disappointed their fans. Bradman himself had often shown that he was not infallible. But his second poor showing against the M.C.C. was a heaven-sent opportunity for his critics in both hemispheres to claim that he was 'finished'. They believed the new English tactics had opened a chink in the Bradman armour and he would 'never be the same man again'.

The player-writer controversy with the Board of Control had not yet been resolved, and it was still uncertain whether Bradman would be available for the Test series. Enemies sneered that Bradman's commercial contract would now provide a handy escape hatch, enabling him to avoid a Test confrontation with Larwood. This discordant melody lingered on as late as 1965, when Larwood wrote: 'Don's batting colleagues received a shock a week or so before the First Test when he asked to be dropped in the batting order.' This is an obvious canard. At no time, then or later, did Bradman ever ask his captain to put him lower in the batting order, and — as will be seen later — he was not in the first Test side, on doctor's orders.

Bradman's greatest triumphs, both before and after bodyline, were achieved when he went in first wicket down. It is worth recalling that his world record Test score of 334, made at Leeds against Larwood in 1930, was made when he went in to bat first wicket down, when the score was only 2, after Tate caught Jackson off Larwood. Larwood's comment gives a picture of a man trying to delay a confrontation if only by a few minutes, but later events were to demonstrate the truth.

Despite Bradman's erratic performance since the opening of the season, his countless supporters retained their faith in him. They believed firmly that the two M.C.C. matches had been a mere swing of the pendulum. It would swing back again, and 'Our Don' would punish the 'Pommie' bowling as he had done in 1930. They listened eagerly to his 2UE cricket commentaries; bought 'Don Bradman Shirts' from Palmer's; surrounded him in the street; flooded him with fan mail.

Bradman, as usual, did not reveal his innermost feelings to anyone except those closest to him. Jessie Bradman could observe the rapid deterioration in his health and it became so marked that he reported it to the Board of Control. Perhaps with some relief, because it gave them a little more time to think about the player-writer impasse, they decided he must have a medical examination.

Two doctors appointed by the Board declared him unfit to play, but said he was constitutionally A-1 and that a spell of complete rest should restore him to normal good health. The Board made a clumsy announcement of the doctors' prognosis on the day before the first Test and sparked off a bushfire of new Bradman rumours. The headlines blared 'Bradman Unfit to Play', and everyone 'had it on good authority' that he was suffering from some fatal disease; that he was suffering from a nervous breakdown like that which had delayed Tate's arrival in Australia; that his cricket career was finished; that he was 'burnt out'; and, most maliciously of all, that he was suffering from a 'diplomatic illness' which would save him from Larwood's assault.

Bradman delayed his rest period in order to watch the first Test and broadcast his evening commentary on the play. Jack Hobbs met him in the pavilion and reported sympathetically to the *Star*: 'I talked to Don for a few minutes. He does not look well, and has a drawn look . . . Somehow I felt he has not had a square deal.'

Despite Bradman's absence from the field, England used bodyline against some of the Australian batsmen — with notable success. A ball from Larwood injured Ponsford, and Australia lost by ten wickets. Stan McCabe, who made his first Test century during the match, put up the best performance for the Australians. It was a daring and brilliant innings, although the gods favoured him on several occasions.

The defeat rubbed home the truth about England's new tactics, and the spectators and reporters began to realise that they were more than 'lightning bumpers'. The first issue of the Sydney *Referee* to be published after the match spearheaded the angry Australian reactions. The journal deplored 'the pernicious body battering attack by England's fast bowlers', and said it was 'not only ruinous to cricket but . . . a direct and emphatic negation of the principles and traditions of the game'.

By that time Don and Jessie were staying at a shack owned by Tom Langridge, masseur of the New South Wales Cricket Association, at a quiet spot on the coast south of Sydney. It was hardly a conventional rest cure, because Bradman had to contend with a number of snakes infesting the bush around the shack and turn out to help local firefighters combat a bushfire; but at least he was secluded from the clamouring public and free of the usual daily demands.

The holiday gave him a chance to work out tactics to counter Jardine's new method of attack, and when he returned to Sydney he discussed them with 'Johnnie' Moyes. He asked Moyes to act as 'devil's advocate': to listen to his ideas and raise possible objections.

Now that Bradman knew what to expect, he could rely on his lightning reactions and quicksilver footwork to keep him out of trouble. But keeping out of trouble was not sufficient. A batsman dodging and weaving like a flyweight boxer would not please the crowd — or help to win the match — unless he could also accumulate runs.

He had decided that he could not play the conventional hook shot which a batsman would use against a conventional 'bumper', nor his own style of pull shot, past mid-on, like the drive off a high-bouncing ball in tennis. He usually employed this stroke with the ball coming towards the right shoulder, and it worked well enough with a normal bowler but would not do with Larwood. Larwood's deliveries came in to the body, and if Bradman missed his pull shot then he might stop the ball with his head. And the conventional hook stroke would not work because the ball flew at least head-high, and he was not tall enough to 'get on top of it' and keep it down.

Instead, he had determined to walk away from the wicket and try to hit the ball through the off-side field, left almost naked by the concentration of fieldsmen on the leg-side. If this worked, then a few successful strokes would outwit Larwood and force him to move

This newspaper photograph taken during the bodyline series bore the caption 'D. G. Bradman drives H. Verity through the covers for four. Sparkling cricket yielded the Australian batsman 71 runs'

fieldsmen from leg to off, thus restoring the game to more normal circumstances.

Moyes argued that if Larwood countered with occasional yorkers, it would leave Bradman as straddle-legged as the veriest amateur. But Bradman was confident that he could judge Larwood's length almost in the instant that the ball left his hand, and adjust his response accordingly.

He was well aware that however he tackled the new attack he was taking a tremendous gamble. If he failed, then plenty of people were willing to kick him when he was down. The remaining four Test matches could well be the turning point in his career, and he could go only up or down.

All those fans who relied on him to foil Jardine were delighted when he turned out for New South Wales in a Shield match against Victoria, in Melbourne. Rain washed out the first two days' play and on 26 December the visitors batted first, with Bradman going in immediately after lunch. He played carefully for ninety minutes, in which he compiled 50, and he reached his century after tea. After that he lashed out in an attempt to throw his wicket away, but he was still too good for the bowlers and he made his last 50 in thirty minutes before Bromley caught him off Ironmonger. He had made 157 in 199 minutes.

When he reached 130 runs, he had completed 10 000 runs in all first-class cricket, in his 126th innings. Ponsford, the previous record-holder, took 161 innings to reach 10 000.

Despite all the problems, all the criticisms, all the strains and worries of the previous couple of years, he had shown once more that he was the world's greatest batsman. At the age of twenty-four years and 121 days, with a comparatively brief first-class career behind him, he had reached the landmark score earlier than any other batsman including Trumper, Grace, Clem Hill, Woodfull, Ponsford and Hammond.

It seemed that he impressed everyone except the Board of Control. They were not prepared to make an exception from their regulations for the sake of the world's greatest batsman. On 29 December, the day before the opening of the second Test, they gave him an ultimatum. If he insisted on writing about the Test, then he could not play in it.

They won the battle because he accepted Packer's request that he should play, but on the day of the Test he issued a defiant press release about his decision. It concluded: 'Only through the generosity of my employers am I enabled to play to-day. While doing so, I most emphatically protest against the Board's being allowed to interfere with the permanent occupation of any player. To my mind the Board was never meant to have powers directing the business activities of players.

'It is certainly no encouragement to any player to remain in Australia when such restrictions are brought in.'

No cricketer in history had ever given the Board such a public rap over the knuckles, and the final sentence triggered a fresh explosion of speculation about Bradman's future. In fact, he had already received enquiries from Lancashire clubs about his availability as a professional. They had heard about his problems in Australia and thought he might be ripe to make a move.

If any Board members smarted under his public rebuke, they would no doubt have felt a cold pleasure at his performance during the first innings of the second Test, on Melbourne Cricket Ground. It was his worst Test failure on record. When he went out to bat, at 12.45 p.m. on the second morning with the score at 27 for two, a gigantic crowd roared their adulation. He passed Sutcliffe on his way to the wicket, and the Englishman made some friendly comment about the ovation. But Bradman had no illusions about the fickleness of fame, and he answered: 'Yes, but will it be so good when I'm coming back?'

In a matter of seconds he *was* on his way back, with the crowd watching in stunned silence. The first ball from the bespectacled Yorkshire bowler Bill Bowes pitched well outside his off-stump, and Bradman made a faulty pull shot which dragged it down onto his leg stump.

In the second Test of the 1932–33 series, Bradman walked to the wicket to the prolonged acclaim of a crowd of 63 993. A few moments later, they saw him bowled, first ball, by Bill Bowes. It was the first ball that Bowes had ever bowled to Bradman in a Test, and the only Test wicket that Bowes took on Australian soil

He met this disaster before a world record crowd of 63 993, but Australians still retained their faith in him. On the third day a crowd of 68 188 created a new world record. Many had camped all night in the gardens outside the cricket ground to be sure of admission, and a couple even tried to break in during the night to secure seats for themselves.

The tension was almost palpable as Bradman walked slowly to the wicket to open his second innings, with Australia only 86 ahead and two wickets down.

Now he had to withstand the full fury of England's bowling, both bodyline and orthodox, in an all-out attempt to sweep the Australians from the field. Larwood, Voce, Hammond, Allen and Bowes all had their turn at him, although Larwood and Voce were the principal antagonists. He rose to supreme heights in showing that he could handle anything they sent whistling down the pitch. The crowd gasped at the savagery of some of the balls which Larwood sent hurtling down to him — and roared like Romans applauding a courageous gladiator when Bradman slammed the balls into the empty off-side field. If Jardine and his shadowy advisers had hoped to frighten Bradman with bodyline, they had chosen the wrong man. All they had done was to introduce a disgraceful new element into cricket, which might frighten and puzzle lesser men but served only to inspire Bradman to new heights of skill, courage and endurance.

Each of Bradman's partners fell under the assault until there was no-one remaining but Bert Ironmonger. It was said of Ironmonger that his wife once telephoned the pavilion and asked to speak to him, and on being told that he was batting said: 'Oh, that's all right then. I'll hold on.' But even Ironmonger was inspired by Bradman's brilliance on that crucial day. Bradman walked to meet him as he came out to bat, to utter some word of reassurance, but Ironmonger got in first with 'Don't worry, son. I won't let you down.'

And he did not. He survived the last two balls of Hammond's over, and Bradman completed his century with a hit off Voce for three. Three minutes later, at 5 p.m., Ironmonger was run out in an attempt to give Bradman the bowling, but Bradman's 103 was the vital factor in giving Australia the victory by 111 runs.

When he returned to the pavilion the crowd burst into a frenzy of acclamation. Nothing in all his previous experience, not even the return to Perth after the 1930 tour, had equalled the uproarious welcome.

Immediately after the match, Bradman made another vigorous protest against bodyline. He argued with certain Board of Control members that the moment was exactly right to lodge an emphatic protest with the Marylebone Cricket Club. The Test series stood at one-all, and he had shown that bodyline could be handled by an Australian. Stan McCabe, in the first Test, had given a similar demonstration. Australia would be arguing from a position of strength. If they waited any longer, perhaps until someone had been badly hurt or until Australia was failing in the series, a protest would simply seem like that of a 'poor sport'.

Bradman's intense love for the game, his deeply ingrained sporting instincts, everything in the integrity of his character and background, made him argue vehemently that the time to protest was *now*, before bodyline had consolidated a precedent that would degrade cricket forever.

But the complacent members of the Board of Control, who had been prepared to sacrifice Bradman on the altar of their own mini-bureaucracy, would not heed his pleas and warnings.

As a cricketing personality, Bradman could have been the most influential man in either hemisphere. Newspapers would pick up and report his slightest comments on the game. He could easily have stepped outside the bounds of formality and made himself the stormy petrel of the controversy, and perhaps created such a difficult situation that the Board would have been forced to act. But his reticent and strongly disciplined nature restricted him to a fairly restrained press statement.

He said: 'On account of his great speed Larwood is able to pitch the ball short and make it fly rather dangerously. With a packed leg field the batsman is unable to protect himself with the bat defensively or he will fall victim to the close-in fieldsmen. A similar fate awaits the batsman who dares to attempt a leg-glance. Should he swing the ball into the outfield, men are waiting there expressly for a catch, and I have yet to find any batsman who can, with certainty, hit a ball of the 'bumper' variety (which rises head high) along the ground.

'At the same time, no batsman can be expected to stand at the wicket without attempting to use his bat, for self-preservation is the first law of nature.

'Only those who have played against bodyline bowling are capable of understanding its dangers. I do not know of one batsman who has played against fast bodyline bowling who is not of the opinion that it will kill cricket if allowed to continue. The objections to bodyline bowling are many, but principally they lie in the fact that it exposes the batsman to the danger of serious physical injury — not from an occasional erratic ball, but from the very nature of the bowling.'

The word 'bodyline' entered the language overnight and it was on everyone's lips, just as the bruises inflicted by bodyline were on the bodies of many Australian players. Some of them had adopted an armour like that of baseball players, with pads to protect the thighs and body. But the English attempt to erode the morale of the Australians had had the opposite effect. They were more angry than afraid, and McCabe and Richardson had also begun to hit out strongly at Larwood's bullet-like deliveries.

In the ten days between the Australian victory in the second Test and the opening of the third Test in Adelaide on 13 January, the atmosphere resembled that of a nation waiting for the declaration of war. Every day brought some new bodyline story, prediction or warning. The story went round that 'Gubby' Allen, who was born in Australia, had refused point-blank to bowl bodyline, and that he had defied Jardine to send him home to England.

The bodyline affair soon became infected with chauvinism and nationalism. Australia's economy was suffering, more than that of any other 'Western' country except Germany, from the effects of the Depression, and many people blamed this on the Bank of England's insistence on prompt repayment of the 1920s loans. They contrasted this attitude with Australia's unstinting sacrifice during the first world war, when so many young Australians suffered in 'England's war'. England was not popular, and the English cricketers became the target for venomous criticism.

In Adelaide they seemed likely to be the target for more than criticism. Almost exactly a year earlier, on 9 January 1931, unemployed men had fought a pitched battle with police in a protest against cuts in the dole rations, and the arrival of Jardine's men seemed likely to provide another escape valve for their seething anger and frustrations. The authorities believed that the sight of Australian cricketers battered by bodyline would incite the spectators to riot, and they behaved as though the populace were on the verge of revolution. On the opening day, mounted troopers of the Police Greys trotted into position around No. 2 ground and squads of foot police stood ready for action.

But the first day and the following morning passed quietly. England batted first, for a score of 341, and the crowd watched tensely as Woodfull and Fingleton opened for Australia. Allen dismissed Fingleton for only one run, and Bradman walked out to replace him. The English fieldsmen were still in the orthodox positions.

Bradman had barely had time to settle in when a ball from Larwood hit Woodfull a terrific blow on the chest. Ironically, it did not happen while Jardine was using the leg-side field. There was an instant's silence as he staggered away from the wicket, clutching his chest as though he had been shot, and then the crowd erupted in screaming abuse. Bradman thought they might invade the ground, but they quietened down again as Woodfull, ashen and groggy, returned to his crease.

Larwood poised himself for his run-up, and had actually begun to propel himself down the pitch when Jardine showed the astounding contempt for public opinion which characterised him. He clapped his hands to stop Larwood dead in his tracks, and signalled the off-side fieldsmen to move into bodyline positions.

Obviously this meant that Woodfull, already injured, would have to face the assault of bodyline. The crowd exploded for the second time, and they did not quieten down. Every man and woman behind the boundary fences roared and shrieked their fury at the Englishmen. Each time Larwood bowled, they counted him out. The ball left his hand to a terrifying crescendo of sound. The Australians played the rest of the innings in a continuous fusillade of barracking.

Jardine ignored the crowd and did not even seem to hear the threats and insults. He was interested only in winning, and bodyline was assuring victory for England. Woodfull struggled gamely on to make 22. Bradman was out for eight, after eighteen minutes, when he tried to defend his head against a rising ball from Larwood and give a simple catch to Allen. The other Australian wickets fell fast. Bert Oldfield, the great wicket-keeper, was the worst casualty of the match. A ball from Larwood hit him on the forehead and he received a linear fracture of the right frontal bone. Again, it was not bowled with a 'bodyline' field, and Oldfield later admitted that it hit him when he misjudged the ball while trying to hook. But the crowd was in no mood for such fine distinctions. Both press and public firmly believed that Jardine's men were trying to batter Australia into submission.

Despite the threatening fury of the crowd, only one man actually jumped the fence — and all he wanted was a photograph of Bradman. He managed to click his camera before the police brought him down. They hauled him off to court, where the magistrate fined him £2 with fifteen shillings costs, but he refused to pay and became a guest of the government.

Spectators at the Adelaide Oval erupted in fury when a ball from Larwood hit Bill Woodfull a terrific blow on the chest during the third Test, in January 1933. The incident led to Woodfull's comment to Plum Warner that 'There are two teams out there. One is trying to play cricket and the other is not'

Bradman attempts to glance a ball from Larwood, which takes his wicket

Jardine remained unperturbed by the hatred of the colonial 'hoi polloi'. At the end of the afternoon he could have left the ground by a side exit, but he insisted on leaving with the rest of his men, with his aquiline features unmoved by the distorted faces surrounding him and the continuous barrage of threats and insults.

Immediately after the first Australian innings, another furore erupted. It arose out of Woodfull's injuries. When he returned to the dressing room, he showered and then stretched out on the massage table for treatment of his bruises, one of them a large discolouration under the heart. Several men, including Jack Fingleton, were nearby when the English manager, Pelham Warner, entered the dressing room with his colleague R. C. N. Palairet. Warner went up to Woodfull and said 'We have come to say how sorry we are and to offer our sympathies.'

Woodfull answered curtly in some such words as 'I don't want to see you, Mr Warner. There are two teams out there. One is trying to play cricket and the other is not. The game is too good to be spoilt. It is time some people got out of it. Good afternoon.'

Someone in the dressing room leaked this story to the newspapers and it flashed around the entire cricketing world. It seems certain that

Jack Fingleton, the professional journalist, was the man who snapped up this tit-bit. Warner apparently thought so. Furious at the snub, he told Larwood 'I'll give you a pound if you can get Fingleton out quickly', when Australia opened their second innings. Larwood wrote: 'I think he wanted to see Jack Fingleton disposed of because he blamed him for leaking the story.'

Fingleton soon realised he had stirred up a whirlwind and he always denied responsibility for this breach of confidence. In later years he attempted to shift the blame onto Bradman, against whom he carried a grudge for an incident that had nothing to do with bodyline. Shortly before he died, he circulated an absurd fabrication about Bradman having a clandestine night-time meeting with the sportswriter Claude Corbett, and leaking Woodfull's words to him. However, he did not make this allegation until Corbett was dead and unable to deny it.

Bradman has always resented this slur on his reputation and integrity. He stoutly maintains that he did not hear Woodfull's remark, that Fingleton's story was a lie, and that he had no part in leaking the incident to the press. No-one who knows him would ever believe him capable of such an underhand action, and his entire life and career demonstrate that he has always placed honour and integrity above material gain. Fingleton's story was yet another of the smears invented by lesser men.

The Englishmen were still smarting over the comment 'One is trying to play cricket and the other is not', which Australians felt was a perfect summary of bodyline, when the Australian Board of Control at last decided to take action. They informed Pelham Warner that they intended to cable a protest to the M.C.C., but did not allow him to read the wording. When they released it to a press conference, the phraseology added yet more fuel to the flames of bodyline. The cable said:

'Bodyline bowling has assumed such proportions as to menace the best interests of the game, making protection of the body by the batsman the main consideration. This is causing intensely bitter feelings between the players, as well as injury. In our opinion it is unsportsmanlike. Unless stopped at once it is likely to upset the friendly relations existing between Britain and Australia.'

The M.C.C. took five days to reply to this cable, and by that time the third Test was over with England victorious by 338 runs. In the second innings, Australia had had to make 532 to win, on a worn wicket. It was obviously a hopeless task but the batsmen made a gallant attempt. Bradman went in at 12 for two, on the fifth evening, and played an astounding innings. He sometimes retreated to square leg in order to hit balls from Voce or Larwood to the vacant off-side, and he snapped up runs from the other bowlers whenever he could. He made 66 in seventy-three minutes, in partnership with Woodfull, before he was caught and bowled by Verity. Just before the close of the fourth day he had the distinction of bowling Hammond for 85; the only wicket he ever took in a Test against England.

Woodfull was the hero of the match. Despite his injury, and the tremendous pressures of leading his side throughout the bodyline controversy, he carried his bat through the second innings for the second time in his career.

These performances, in the most acrimonious of the bodyline

THE AFTERMATH OF BODYLINE

An outbreak of bodyline violence followed the bodyline Tests, when bowlers in various minor Australian matches attempted the technique and the matches ended in brawls. Bradman's belief that bodyline might gain a victory for England, but degrade the game of cricket forever, was coming true.

When the West Indians toured England in 1933, the Englishmen received a taste of their own medicine. The fast bowlers Leary Constantine and Manny Martindale used Jardine's theory in the second Test, at Manchester. According to *Wisden*, Wally Hammond 'had his chin laid open by one of the many short-pitched rising balls'. Hammond is reported to have said he would retire from cricket if that type of bowling was not abolished.

The famous wicket-keeper George Duckworth thought the use of bodyline against the Australians was quite permissible. When he returned to England, and he and all the other tourists were received like conquering heroes, he said so loud and clear. But when he turned out for his home side of Lancashire, and Nottinghamshire bowlers used bodyline tactics against him, he changed his tune. Lancashire threatened to refuse to play Notts in the county championships, and used photographs of Duckworth's bruises as evidence of unfair play. Bodyline had become a cancer upon the good humour and good sportsmanship which are the lifeblood of cricket.

The Australian Board of Control had appointed Woodfull, Vic Richardson, M. A. Noble and Roger Hartigan as a committee to report on the action necessary to eliminate bodyline. They framed a suggested new rule and the Board submitted it to the M.C.C. for approval, but that august body still insisted that bodyline did not exist. They maintained this stance until the Windies and Nottinghamshire used it on the fair fields of England.

Peter Deeley, the author of a biography of Jardine, published an article in the Sydney *Bulletin* of 14 December 1982 in which he described the attitude of the M.C.C. towards bodyline. Deeley says that Viscount Hailsham, president of the M.C.C. in 1933, was a supporter of Jardine. He also established a committee of enquiry, including four other lords and two knights. 'Gubby' Allen told Deeley that he and Bob Wyatt were scheduled to give evidence to this committee, and they had determined to lay the facts on the line. But someone, perhaps Jardine, had their names removed from the list of witnesses.

In June 1933 this committee solemnly decided that the colonials were still confusing 'fast leg theory' with what they called 'bodyline'. The latter, claimed the noble lords, did not exist.

They changed their minds after Constantine and Martindale battered the English batsmen, and after Duckworth's complaints. Pelham Warner, who had never protested against the use of bodyline when he was on the winning side, told the *Daily Telegraph* that it was breeding 'anger, hatred, and malice'.

In Australia, cricketers and public still simmered with rage against the perfidious English. There was a strong chance that Australia would refuse to tour England in 1934 — and an equally strong chance that England would refuse to receive them.

Again, Bradman had been proved right in his predictions that bodyline would kill cricket. It came close to disrupting the fifty-six-year-old Test pattern.

The Australian protests had made no impact upon the M.C.C., but bodyline's appearance in England obliged them to call a joint meeting of the Advisory County Cricket Committee and the English Board of Control of Test matches. In November 1933 this meeting decided that 'any form of bowling which is obviously a direct attack by the bowler upon the batsman' should be an offence against the spirit of the game.

Having established this principle, the M.C.C. cabled an invitation for Australia to tour England in 1934 — although five committee members voted against the invitation.

The failure to outlaw bodyline by a change to the rules of cricket meant that it still persisted, and in November 1934 the M.C.C. proclaimed that 'as a result of their own observations and from reports received, the M.C.C. Committee consider that there is evidence that cases of the bowler making a direct attack upon the batsman have on occasions taken place during the last cricket season'.

The committee ruled: 'That the type of bowling regarded as a direct attack by the bowler upon the batsman, and therefore unfair, consists in persistent and systematic bowling of fast short-pitched balls at the batsman standing clear of the wicket.'

The committee outlawed bodyline, and thus in a sense admitted that the Australians had been right. King George V helped to heal the wound when he conferred upon Aubrey Oxlade, of the Australian Board of Control, the honour of Companion of the Most Excellent Order of the British Empire.

Wally Hammond, one of the most popular men in international cricket and several times captain of England, wrote after his retirement: 'I believe that only good luck was responsible for the fact that no one was killed by body-line. I have had to face it, and I would have got out of the game if it had been allowed to persist.

'I doubt if there was any answer to such bowling unless grave risks of injury were courted.'

matches, make nonsense of such Larwood comments as 'Woodfull and Bradman were failures against fast leg theory. Richardson and McCabe played me all right. Woodfull and Bradman could not.'

Bradman played in only four of the five Tests. In those four matches he totalled 396 at 56, Woodfull 298 at 42, Richardson 230 at 28, and McCabe 166 at 20. These figures make a mockery of Larwood's claim.

By the time the M.C.C. replied to the Board's cable, all Bradman's predictions had been proved correct. English newspapers, cockahoop at Australia's defeat in the third Test, were sneering that the Australians protested against bodyline only because it might rob them of the Ashes. The M.C.C. made a bland and discursive reply, in which they 'deplored' the Board's cable and said they had every confidence in Jardine and his men. They said that if the Board wanted to propose a new law or rule, it would receive 'careful consideration in due course'. Obviously they had no intention of taking any action.

However, their cable had a sting in its tail. It said 'if . . . you consider it desirable to cancel remainder of programme, we would consent but with great reluctance.'

This offer placed the Board in an impossible position. If they accepted, they would expose Australia to further jeers and sneers from England and claims that their cricketers 'couldn't take it'. Also, they would lose their share of the enormous gate receipts which the last two Tests were certain to accumulate. But, if they did not cancel, then they tacitly accepted bodyline for the rest of the series.

Eventually Jardine and his players forced a decision on them. The English cricketers were furious at the clumsy wording of the Board's cable, and they refused to play in the fourth Test unless it was withdrawn. The Board backed down and the series continued.

Before the fourth Test, in Brisbane on 10–18 January, Bradman had a taste of more enjoyable cricket by playing for his State against South Australia. The match was notable for a sensational bowling performance by Tim Wall. He took all ten wickets for 36 runs, a feat never before achieved by any other Shield player.

Bradman also played for New South Wales against the M.C.C., in a much friendlier atmosphere than that of the Tests. He made useful scores in both these interim matches although he did not come anywhere near any new records.

Jack Hobbs said that if he had to play bodyline he would get out of the game, but after the Test in Adelaide he wrote: 'I am satisfied that only leg theory can stop Bradman. The power he gets in his strokes, and their very wide range alike, are wonderful. He hits freely where others just defend.' Hobbs persisted in giving the name of 'leg theory' to bodyline; but, coupled with the words of his 'ghost writer', this was probably a form of loyalty to his countrymen rather than his own convictions. He admitted that he would not want to play bodyline, but he seemed to approve of it against Bradman.

The fourth Test opened in Brisbane in searing tropical heat and high humidity, with the tension between cricketers and spectators as great as it had been in Adelaide. Bradman had to withstand another siege of bodyline, but he countered it with his own new tactics and scored 76 before Larwood bowled him in the first innings. However, he had helped Australia off to a good start with 251 for three, and the match seemed fairly safe. But the rest of the batsmen collapsed one after another and the innings ended with a total of 340.

The Englishmen did not do much better, and they had lost six for 216 when the huge crowd witnessed the most moving event of the entire series. Eddie Paynter, the left-handed Lancastrian batsman, was sick in a Brisbane hospital when he heard about the likelihood of a first innings deficit for England, and he insisted on leaving his bed and taking his place at the wicket. He scored a valuable 83.

In the second innings Bradman again faced Larwood, but his new tactics did not save him from dismissal after only twenty minutes, with a score of 24, when Mitchell caught him off Larwood. Australia collapsed again, with a second innings total of only 175, and England won by six wickets.

Bodyline had won the Ashes for England, but the last act of the drama was yet to be played — in the fifth Test at Sydney on 23 February. By that time bodyline had moved into the political arena, with cables passing between the Governor of South Australia and Whitehall as well as between the M.C.C. and the Board. Whoever conceived the idea of bodyline, he or they could never have guessed that it would polarise relations between Australia and Britain. Many Britons still regarded Australia as a colonial outpost whose principal function was to provide cheap food for the homeland, and they were surprised and annoyed by the 'squealing' of Australians over a Test defeat. Many Australians, demoralised by the long grinding disaster of the Depression, believed 'the bloodsuckers of the Bank of England' to be responsible for their plight, and they resented British ownership of substantial shares of Australian land and commerce. They saw Jardine as a personification of British greed and arrogance, and bodyline as a symptom of Britain's determination to keep Australia inferior to the homeland. In some ways, bodyline accelerated the glacier-slow drift of Australia away from British influence — a drift which has continued ever since.

On 23 February 1932 a huge crowd packed the Sydney Cricket Ground. They buzzed like wasps with excitement and speculation as the cricketers walked onto the field, with 'The Hill' volleying barbed witticisms towards the impassive figure of Jardine, but most of the players were heartily sick of the tense and unhappy atmosphere of the series.

Jardine could have allowed that final Test to be played in orthodox style and let the better team win. If he had done so, and especially if Australia had won the match with the aid of a characteristic Bradman innings, then he would have healed many of the wounds. But it was not in his nature to show magnanimity towards a defeated enemy.

He insisted that Larwood should play, even though the bowler was having trouble with his foot and was tired and dispirited by his long effort and the unhappy mood of the series. He forced 'Gubby' Allen to play although Allen had strained his bowling arm.

Until then, Bradman's miraculous footwork and computer-fast re-actions had saved him from injury, despite his daring tactics. They confused many critics who thought he was dodging away from balls rather than placing himself to play them. They claimed he was not standing up to bodyline in the manner of some less successful batsmen such as Fingleton, who totalled almost as many bruises as runs. But Bradman's counter-attack actually exposed him to a far greater risk of injury than if he had merely moved inside the line of the flyers and let them pass harmlessly down the leg side. He was determined to do better than that, and Larwood was one of the few men who understood what was happening. In his somewhat contradictory accounts of the controversy, he wrote: 'I believe that no criticisms of Bradman can be valid because above all he did try to score runs.'

Jardine lost the toss and Bradman went in early on the first morning with the score at 0 for one. Once more he counter-attacked Larwood's

THE ARCHITECT OF BODYLINE

Everything about Douglas Robert Jardine annoyed the Australian public. To them, he was the personification of the 'toffee-nosed Englishman': arrogant, aloof, almost incapable of expressing himself to anyone outside his own strata of English society. Sir Donald Bradman, with a wry twist of the lips, describes Jardine as 'Taciturn . . . you couldn't talk to him'. He seemed devoid of what Sir Robert Menzies called 'the juicy humanity of cricketers'.

Even his appearance suited the Australian notion of the type of upper-class Englishman who looked condescendingly upon 'colonials'. He was very tall and slender, with a narrow beaky face topped with a gaily-coloured Harlequin cap. He spoke in what was then known as the 'Oxford accent': the clipped drawl which seemed to give every word a touch of sarcasm.

His nickname, 'The Iron Duke', seemed exactly right for his cold and authoritarian character. He was the product of Winchester College, the oldest, most elite and most exclusive of the great English public schools, and of Oxford University. He was captain of cricket at Winchester, and like his father he won his cricket blue at Oxford. He was a strong right-handed batsman and a fine player of fast bowling, with a Test record of 1296 runs at 48 and a total of 14 821 runs at 46.90, including thirty-five centuries, all in first-class cricket. In 1932 he was captain of Surrey as well as of England.

He seemed in every respect to be that mythical creature the 'typical Englishman': reserved, determined, haughty, precise. He read law at Oxford, and the stuffy exactitudes of that profession completed the picture.

But this 'typical Englishman' was actually of Scots descent. The name 'Jardine' is of Scottish origin. He was born in India, a child of the ruling class, and from his earliest days he absorbed the principle that society is divided into the leaders and the led. He, of course, belonged to the leaders, and he accepted the responsibility as well as the privilege of leadership — including the ethic of 'Never ask a man to do anything that you wouldn't do yourself'. When he himself had to face bodyline bowling, against the West Indies in 1933, he scored 127 off the bowling of Constantine and Martindale.

In a way, he was the victim of his own character and background. Himself physically brave — he had an excellent record in the second world war — he could not understand that other men might be of lesser stature. His upper-class background made him despise the mob, and so he was unmoved by the uproar against bodyline. He was born and trained to lead, and he insisted that his team should persist with bodyline tactics even after they had created bitterness and antagonisms among the English cricketers.

The mystery — and perhaps the tragedy — of this English gentleman is that he should have adopted tactics which could draw the accusation of 'unfair play'. A clue is given by 'Gubby' Allen, quoted by Peter Deeley in a Sydney *Bulletin* article about Jardine on 14 December 1982. According to Allen, Jardine told him that the only way to beat the Australians was by 'hating them'.

If so, then Jardine's hatred of Australians was self-defeating. He so besmeared his own reputation that his cricket career virtually ended in 1934. He died in 1958, aged fifty-seven.

bowling, with almost reckless brilliance. When he reached 28, he had accumulated 3000 runs in his Test matches since 1928. He batted on against Larwood and others with a blend of cool calculation and daring footwork, with the crowd roaring abuse at each of Larwood's deliveries and roaring acclaim as they saw 'The Don' handle them triumphantly. But just before lunch he moved over to the off to glance a well-pitched straight ball, and Larwood took his wicket for 48.

Australia totalled 435 in the first innings and it seemed for a while that they might salvage the final Test. But England fought back doggedly, and Larwood was among those who steadily piled up the runs. In a display of aggressive batting he totalled 98 before Ironmonger caught him, and the Sydney crowd showed their good sportsmanship when they cheered him as heartily for his batting as they had abused him for his bowling.

In Bradman's second innings, on the fourth day, the score was again 0 for one when he went in for his final duel against Larwood. Larwood seemed to be bowling at his usual express speed, and had already dismissed Richardson for a duck — his second for the match. Bradman gave a spectacular performance despite a painful blow on the arm as he cut at a rising ball: the only time he was struck by bodyline bowling.

He reached 50 in seventy-six minutes against Larwood and others, and the spectators relished his apparent mastery of bodyline bowling. They felt that if he could only protect his wicket for long enough he would kill the bodyline bogey forever.

Then, at last, Larwood broke down. The incessant pounding on the hard grounds had fractured two small bones beneath the toes on his left foot. He could hardly walk and he certainly could not propel himself with normal power. But Jardine insisted that he should bowl the last five balls of the over, so he simply stood at the crease and swung them to Woodfull, who patted them back to him.

Even after that, Jardine would not let him go to the dressing room. He had to stay on the field as though his mere presence would put Bradman off his game, and he stayed until Verity yorked Bradman as he jumped in to drive.

With Bradman out for 71, Jardine clapped his hands and said 'Right, Harold, you can go now.'

Australia lost the fifth Test by eight wickets, and Bradman wrote in 1950: 'It was a relief to all concerned when, with a dramatic off-drive right over the Sydney Cricket Ground fence for six, Hammond brought the series to an end.'

11

TRIUMPH AND DISASTER

Bradman emerged from the bodyline controversy with untarnished laurels. A. G. Moyes, in an article referring to Bradman's tactics against Larwood, wrote: 'At the start he was howled down in every city. He was accused of flinching from the fast bowlers and the charge must have been like iron entering into his soul . . . And in face of it all he carried on and he triumphed. At the end of the season one great player said to me, "When he started I thought he was wrong. I am satisfied now that he was right, but no one else in the game could have done it." '

Years later, Neville Cardus wrote in *Playfair Cricket Monthly*: 'Larwood himself told me that Bradman's shots to the off from his fastest balls, aimed on or outside the leg-stump, were "simply marvellous — unbelievable!" '

For Donald Bradman, the bodyline affair had been yet another lesson in the fickleness of public opinion. But he was unable to escape his public. If he travelled by tram, some well-meaning citizen would sit next to him and insist on discussing cricket. If he lunched in a restaurant, autograph hunters continuously interrupted his meal. When he played suburban matches, crowds of youngsters besieged him for autographs and some even scratched their names on his car.

The winter of 1933 was a welcome break from cricket, especially since he rarely felt totally well. He suffered from vague generalised abdominal pains and from days of dispiriting languor, but his doctor had no answer for his fluctuations in health. The only diagnosis was that of overwork and overstrain.

But when spring came again he looked cheerfully forward to another season of cricket. He felt he should have a deeper knowledge of the Laws of Cricket and all their subtleties, and studied for the examination of the New South Wales Cricket Umpires Association. He passed on 1 August 1933, with flying colours.

When he took a house at McMahons Point, on the northern side of Sydney Harbour, he lost the residential qualifications which enabled him to play for St George on the southern side. He played for North Sydney instead; and by an odd coincidence his old friend Bill O'Reilly, who had played for North Sydney, moved across the harbour and joined St George.

Bradman's season included another country tour for the New South

Wales Cricket Association; two testimonial matches — regarded also as trials for the Test eleven — for Don Blackie and Bert Ironmonger and for Collins, Andrews and Kellaway; the Sheffield Shield series; and several matches with the 'Sun-Palmer' team. This comprised a team of boys selected from various Sydney schools, coached by Bradman as a part of his contract activities. They profited by his coaching to such a degree that almost all of them went on to play first-grade cricket and many were to play for their State.

The Shield season ran only from 3 November 1933 to 30 January 1934, because of the need to get the Australian team away to England, but two of Bradman's most spectacular performances to date were included in that season. Both were in matches against Queensland.

Of the first match, one journalist wrote: 'Queensland cricket was dangerously near being held up to ridicule on Saturday afternoon . . . at one stage of the run-getting orgy there was a suggestion of the ludicrous in the complete mastery which the bat had established over the ball.'

Another enthused: 'Those who attended the Cricket Ground on Saturday went away with memories of a master innings by a master batsman. For sheer audacity it excelled everything we have seen in Sheffield Shield cricket for many a long day; for brilliance of execution it must have equalled the brightest efforts of any previous genius of the willow; for effective run-getting it could have been surpassed by nothing that any batsman ever devised. Twenty-six fours in a total of 200 was the result of uncanny placement, and of making openings where, if one relied on orthodox stroking, none really existed!'

Bradman took only ninety-two minutes to reach his century, and then went from 150 to 200 in a mere twenty-four minutes. In one over he took 23 runs off E. R. Wyeth's bowling. His partnership of 294, with Bill Brown, was a second-wicket record for matches between New South Wales and Queensland.

He deliberately skied a catch, to be caught on the boundary, after scoring a round 200: his seventeenth double century. One sportswriter observed: 'Australia has seen more artistic batsmen than Bradman, but the vital difference between the present-day wonder and the giants of the past is that Bradman goes from strength to strength in a manner which leaves the records of Trumper and others completely eclipsed.'

In the second match against Queensland he was again in devastating form. He scored 253, including four sixes and twenty-nine fours, in 204 minutes, before he threw his wicket away just before lunch.

On that day, 2 January 1934, he chalked up yet another trio of records. His 131 before lunch was a record for that time; at 189, he completed his 1000 runs for the season — the sixth in succession — earlier than any previous batsman of his home State; and his partnership of 363 with Kippax was then the highest for the third wicket by any Australians anywhere.

His only failure in that season was his first-innings dismissal in three minutes, having broken his duck, in the Shield match at Adelaide. He made seven centuries in first-class cricket and his aggregate of 922 was then the highest for New South Wales in any Shield season. His average of 132.44 for all matches in the season is still the highest by any New South Wales batsman.

These scores meant that he was able to end his career with New

Some of Don Bradman's most spectacular successes were gained in Sheffield Shield matches against Queensland. Two of them were in the 1933–34 season, when this photograph of him was taken

South Wales on a high note. Early in 1934 the people of that State were dismayed by the news that he was about to leave them.

His three-sided contract with Associated Newspapers, 2UE and Palmer's was due to expire in February 1934. He looked forward to its termination with some relief. The demands of working for three masters imposed a perpetual strain, relieved only by the devoted assistance of Jessie Bradman. She helped him to sketch out his newspaper articles and evening broadcasts, and of course looked after him in every other way; nevertheless, he had to devote most of his waking hours to thinking, talking, writing about, or playing cricket — to say nothing of the wearying spells of travel connected with the game. If he had been in his normal good health, he might have felt better equipped for this endless depletion of his strength and spirit. But he was heartily tired of it and longed for some occupation in which he could forget about cricket at the end of the working day.

The *Sun* made him an attractive offer of a permanent post on the

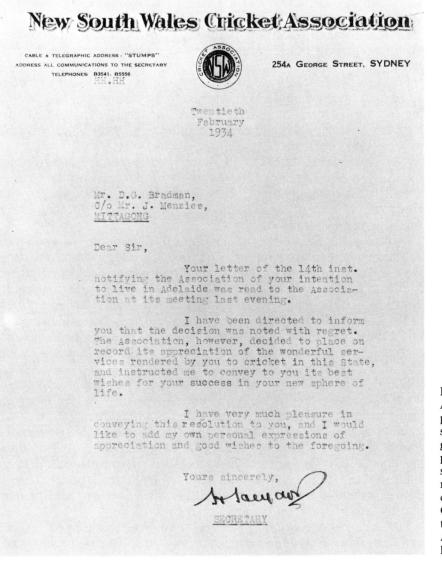

Bradman's decision to move to Adelaide from Sydney, to accept a position in H. W. Hodgetts' firm of stock and share brokers, caused great perturbation among the people of New South Wales and soon led to a steep drop in the number of spectators attending cricket matches at the Sydney Cricket Ground. The letter from the New South Wales Cricket Association expresses their regret at his departure

editorial staff when his three-cornered contract expired, and he received approaches from other directions. But they would all make cricket into a business, rather than pleasure, and he wanted to break that life-restricting bond.

The turning point came with an offer from an unexpected quarter. Henry Warburton (Harry) Hodgetts junior, a South Australian member of the Board of Control and a leading Adelaide sharebroker, offered Bradman a position in his firm and a place in the Kensington District Cricket Club, with which he was associated.

Bradman had met Hodgetts, and he liked him for his jovial extrovert nature. But acceptance would mean a tremendous upheaval for the young Bradmans — virtually a severance from all the associations of their youth. In those days of comparatively slow and difficult travel and communications, a move to another State seemed almost like exile to another country. And a transfer from sophisticated Sydney to sleepy Adelaide was rather like a step back in time.

Don and Jessie Bradman spent hours of anxious discussion on the pros and cons of the offer. Acceptance meant a venture into the unknown and — hardest of all for a young wife — separation from close friends and immediate family. But refusal meant a continuation of the present hectic and uncertain existence, made even more uncertain by his puzzling spells of ill-health. The move would at least permit a more settled and normal life, free from the eternal domination of cricket.

So, with considerable misgivings, they accepted, and on 14 February he advised the New South Wales Cricket Association that he was moving to South Australia. There was need for haste, because he had to establish a residential qualification in order to play for South Australia in the 1934–35 season.

They took a brief holiday in Bowral and entrained for Adelaide, travelling as 'Mr and Mrs Lindsay' to avoid publicity on the journey. They left the train at Mount Lofty in the Adelaide Hills and drove to Hodgetts' home in Kensington to evade possible crowds at the Adelaide railway station.

Naturally the South Australians were thrilled by the move, and an Adelaide newspaper triumphed: 'Don is Now Our Don.' It attracted the usual crop of rumours, including a totally false English report that Bradman had refused to sail on the Test tour of England unless the Board allowed his wife to accompany him. The cricket writer T. Clarke of the London *Daily Express* published a long article in which he attributed the move almost entirely to the influence of Jessie Bradman, and ascribed Don Bradman's natural courtesy and friendliness — which had always been notable — to the 'sophistication' of married life.

Shortly after Bradman's arrival in Adelaide he signed a six-year contract with Harry Hodgetts. It committed him to work for Hodgetts' firm and to play cricket in any matches for which he might be chosen by Kensington, the South Australian Cricket Association, or the Australian selectors. Hodgetts' side of the bargain was to give Bradman the time to play in such matches; to pay him at what was then the comfortable rate of £700 a year, reduced to the rate of £500 a year during the months when he might be playing overseas; and to teach him the art of stock and share broking.

For Bradman, security of tenure for six years, combined with the opportunity to learn a business not connected with cricket, was a great relief.

Hodgetts had brought off a cricket coup for South Australia and made a beneficial addition to his own business, because the name of Don Bradman would inevitably attract new clients. Journalists asked Bradman how he would adapt to his new profession, and he replied that seven years in real estate had given him a pretty good background in financial affairs. In fact the profession was ideal for a man of his quick, shrewd insights and he was to become a prominent figure in the commercial world of South Australia.

In March 1934 he would have been glad to settle down to learning his new business instead of joining the eighteenth Australian team to tour England. The Board of Control doctors passed him as fit to play, but he felt he was not. The mysterious ailment which plagued him, both physically and mentally, made him so unsure of himself that he sought an independent opinion from an Adelaide specialist at his own expense. The diagnosis was simply that he was 'extremely run down', and the specialist advised him to rest as much as possible and not to play any cricket until he arrived in England. The sea voyage should provide an adequate rest cure.

He was also suffering from another health problem, easier to describe than the more generalised malaise but equally hard to cure. Spectators often admired his seemingly effortless skill and confidence, but in fact a Bradman innings was often a gruelling test of physical and mental stamina. Earlier in that season he had begun to feel some of the effects of the previous few years in the form of back pains. In common parlance, 'he had done his back in', but the medical professional still knew very little about the muscular and skeletal problems of back injuries. Physiotherapy was still a minor branch of medicine and there was no easy relief for back problems, usually described simply as 'fibrositis'.

The Board of Control accepted his specialist's recommendations, which meant he would not participate in any of the usual matches played en route to England. The Test team entrained for Perth without him, and Jessie Bradman saw him off in the *Orford* at Outer Harbour before she returned to New South Wales to spend the time of waiting with her parents at Mittagong. The rest of the team joined the *Orford* in Fremantle.

Despite Bradman's dissensions with the Board of Control, they had appointed him vice-captain, under Woodfull, with the obvious implication that he was being groomed to be the captain of Australia. This was perhaps a blow to Alan Kippax, Bradman's captain in the New South Wales eleven, and the media later inferred that there was tension between the two men. In fact the appointment did not affect their friendship, and under Woodfull's wise leadership the Australian team was extremely well integrated. He advised them not to be drawn into controversial statements which might exacerbate the bodyline issue, and the English press called them 'the silent sixteen'.

The voyage was a pleasant period of relaxation. The Australian Davis Cup players were also aboard the *Orford*, and the presence of so many Australian athletes kept life interesting aboard ship. On one occasion they 'fixed' a deck tennis match between Clarrie Grimmett and the Davis Cup player Vivian McGrath so that Grimmett would win. Bradman wrote later: 'You would have thought Grimmett had taken 10 wickets in a Test Match. I still do not know whether he saw through the joke.'

Harry Warburton Hodgetts, Don Bradman's employer in Adelaide. Hodgetts was also a member of the South Australian Cricket Association and a keen supporter of Australian inter-State and international cricket — hence his eagerness to attract Don Bradman to South Australia

The cover of a brochure distributed
to passengers aboard the R.M.S.
Orford on her voyage which carried
the Australian cricketers to
England in 1934

The tourists were a little apprehensive about the effect of bodyline
on their reception, although there were signs that the English were
anxious to make a fresh start. In a January speech to the Millions
Club, in Sydney, the Earl of Wemyss said he had travelled home with
Jardine's men from New Zealand in May 1933 and had been 'surprised
to gather from them how much justification there was for the Australian protests. Let me say that you need not be nervous about the
treatment your team may get in England. It will get a heartier welcome
than any team ever received, and need have no fear of a smashing
bodyline bowling.'

Woodfull and his men soon found this to be true. Everyone, including Lord Hailsham of the M.C.C. and Prime Minister Ramsay

LONDON'S WELCOME TO THE AUSTRALIANS

BRADMAN ON LARWOOD

"Not Worrying About Him"

WOODFULL'S HOPE

Win the Ashes and Retire

LONDON accorded a great welcome to the Australian Test cricketers yesterday.

Immediately after their arrival at Waterloo from Southampton, W. M. Woodfull, the captain, and Don Bradman, vice-captain, drove with other members of the party to Whitehall to lay a wreath on the Cenotaph, and were greeted by great crowds with ringing cheers and shrill "coo-ees."

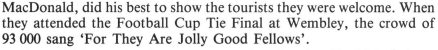

A *Daily Mail* "close-up" of Don Bradman's smiling response to the enthusiastic reception at Waterloo. He looks fit enough !

A portion of a *Daily Mail* article published when the Australian tourists arrived in London in April 1934

A map prepared by the State Library of South Australia to show the locations of county and Test matches played by Australian teams in Britain. The map is included in the series of albums compiled by the State Library to cover Don Bradman's career in cricket (*see Chapter 16*)

MacDonald, did his best to show the tourists they were welcome. When they attended the Football Cup Tie Final at Wembley, the crowd of 93 000 sang 'For They Are Jolly Good Fellows'.

The usual heavy touring programme lay ahead, with thirty fixtures to be played between May and September, and the usual crop of Bradman rumours had reached England. Their principal theme was that he was not well enough to play, and they seemed to be confirmed by press reports such as that by the sportswriter Trevor Wignall, who said: 'Many people noticed that he looked pale and drawn . . . 20 years older than his real age.'

Bradman himself still felt doubtful about his cricketing potential. The long rest had not effected the desired improvement in his health, and he asked Woodfull to omit him from the first match, against Worcestershire. Woodfull persuaded him that if he did not bat he would only confirm the rumours, and thus give a psychological advantage to England.

Reluctantly he agreed, and a local newspaper wrote: 'When Bradman emerged from the pavilion the excitement was terrific; he might have been the Loch Ness monster. Even the refreshment bars

In May 1934, Don Bradman scored his second double century at Worcester and his second on the first match of a tour of England. This photograph shows him foiling the expectant wicket-keeper with a square-cut off the back foot

were temporarily deserted. Men gulped down their drinks and fled to the scene of action. Bradman opened shakily; he looked curiously slender and somehow wistful. A cricketer is in no enviable state when he knows he will be counted as having failed if he scores less than fifty.'

The 'shaky opening' reflected his state of mind and body, but he made a supreme effort and repeated his 1930 feat of scoring a double century in the first match of the tour. His 206 runs seemed proof that all the rumours about him were only wishful thinking; but his performances in the next five matches, before the first Australian appearance in London on that tour, were erratic and disappointing. His best score was 65 against Leicestershire. At Southampton, scene of one of his 1930 triumphs, one of Lord Tennyson's men dismissed him for a duck.

When he appeared at Lord's, to play Middlesex on 26–28 May, the newspapers were asking 'What's the matter with Bradman?' He soon gave them a convincing answer. Australia opened badly, with both Woodfull and Ponsford dismissed for ducks, but Bradman stepped into the breach with every ounce of his old fire and confidence. He began scoring runs at the rate of more than one a minute, and when stumps were drawn he had reached his century in little more than an hour. The police had to clear a way for him through the cheering crowd which surged onto the field.

One newspaper described his innings as 'The Champagne of Cricket'. Others reported it in such glowing terms as 'He set about the bowling so furiously that he lashed the ball to the boundary nineteen times in 1¼ hours', and 'He adopted a do-or-die attitude at once. And there emerged, not the stolid impenetrable Don, with flashes of brilliance, that we have come to expect, but genius with the strength of Hercules. It was an amazing batting display.'

Next morning he continued in fine style, and in another forty-seven minutes he brought his total up to 160 before Hulme caught him inches from the boundary fence at long-on.

His performance seemed suddenly to impart new life to the tour. The sportswriters had been treating it rather dispassionately, but at last they had seen Bradman at his brilliant best. They called him 'forked lightning in pads', 'the laughing cavalier of cricket', and 'the Giant-Killer' for the way in which he had stood up to the deliveries of the massive Middlesex fast bowler J. Smith. The Middlesex captain said in a newspaper interview: 'Set a field for Bradman? Twenty-two men would not have been enough to plug all the holes he found in our run-saving barbed-wire entanglements during his masterpiece.'

William Pollock wrote: 'His timing was marvellous, the power he got into his strokes extraordinary, through the covers, straight past the

In the match versus Middlesex, Bradman delivers a powerful drive to the boundary off Enthoven

Above: Good news for English cricket lovers in May 1934, when Bradman was dismissed for a duck for the first time in England

Below: This poster appeared on the London streets during Don Bradman's triple-century innings at Leeds in July 1934

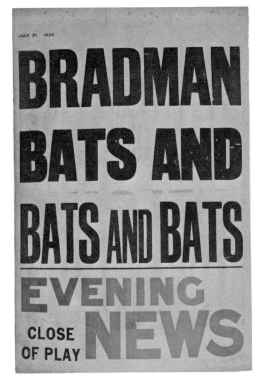

bowlers, round to leg, down through the slips the ball raced from his almost magic bat. All the shots were his, the whole field his kingdom . . . He danced down the pitch and hit. He flung out his left leg and drove. He lay back and pulled. I do not believe that any bowling in the world could have stopped the torrent of his run-making . . . Le Don has played the great innings of the season. If there is anything better to come from him or anyone else, may I be there to see and share.'

After this epic innings the cricketing world waited excitedly for the first Test match, at Nottingham on 8–12 June. The Australians avoided defeat in the eight matches before then, but on the whole their performance was not exceptional and Woodfull was sadly out of form.

The Nottingham Test provided plenty of excitement for the spectators, and Bradman played two brief but spectacular innings. His stroke play was risky and uncharacteristic and he managed only 29 runs in the first and 25 in the second. It was an unusual match in that no player on either side scored a century, although Arthur Chipperfield came frustratingly close with 99 and just missed his first century on his first Test tour.

Australia won by 238 runs — and almost lost Don Bradman for the next match. As stumps were drawn the crowd burst through the flimsy rope cordon around the ground, and as Bradman sprinted off the field he tripped on the loose rope. He strained his thigh so badly that he batted at number six and had to use a runner, in the match against Northamptonshire.

In the second Test, at Lord's on 22–25 June, the first two days provided a perfect wicket. England amassed the handy total of 440. Australia began the chase in good style and had reached 141 for one when disaster struck in a peculiar guise.

Bradman, going in at the fall of the first wicket, opened in the most devastating form. He appeared to be set for another historic score when he was dismissed in what Neville Cardus described as 'the crest of an innings of terrible power and splendour'.

Bradman had first to face the fast bowler Ken Farnes, who had taken five wickets in the first Test, but the six-feet-five-inches giant could make no impression. Geary followed, and Bradman crashed him through the covers with such velocity that the fieldsmen seemed paralysed. Cardus wrote: 'I could not take my eyes off Bradman for a second. My heart was beating as I saw his bat go back so masterfully, so grandly.' It seemed that Bradman was about to repeat his performance against Middlesex.

But then a strange thing happened. Woodfull, watching from the pavilion, became so worried by the audacity of Bradman's stroke play that he sent out a message begging him to restrain himself.

Bradman, against his better judgment, heeded his captain's request. When he jumped into a drive against Verity he held the shot back, and to his dismay gave an easy catch to the bowler.

Sir Donald Bradman still feels that Woodfull's request was the prime cause of his dismissal, which in turn meant that Australia's scoring on the Saturday was heavily retarded. Woodfull had not reckoned on the capricious English weather. Heavy rain over the weekend meant that Australia was caught on a sticky wicket on the Monday, failed to avert the follow-on by a mere seven runs, and lost the match outright thanks

to some wonderful bowling by Verity. If Woodfull had allowed Bradman to follow his own instincts he would almost certainly have mustered those extra seven runs — or more — on the Saturday. England, not Australia, would have had to bat on the wet pitch, and the historic result might well have been different.

Don Bradman square-cutting Farnes for four in the second Test, 1934

As it was, the Australians in their second innings could manage only 118 against the superb bowling of Verity, who took eight for 43 off 22.3 overs, and actually took fourteen wickets in the one day. Bradman was one of his victims on the Monday when he attempted a lofted shot into the unguarded outfield, only to sky a catch to the wicket-keeper. So Australia lost the Test by an innings and 38 runs.

Critics shook their heads at what they termed Bradman's 'flamboyant' performances in some matches, contrasted with his comparative failures in others. It seemed impossible to please them. Sports writers speculated as to whether the responsibilities of the vice-captaincy were affecting his form, or whether he was not really well enough to play. A mere 17 against Somerset, and a sound but unspectacular 27 and 61 (not out) against Surrey, disappointed those who had hoped to see the flashing Bradman brilliance.

By comparison with the venomous bodyline series, the 1934 tour seemed to be developing into a rather low-key affair. When a throat

Local businessmen frequently 'cashed in' on the visits of Australians and used much ingenuity to incorporate their names in advertising. This example appeared during the 1934 match against Somersetshire — but Don Bradman did not take advantage of Edward Stone's offer. (The Austin Seven, or 'Baby Austin', was a 1934 predecessor of the post-war Mini)

BATH AND WILTS CHRONICLE AND HERALD, SATURDAY, IUNE 23, 1934.

AUSTRALIANS
v.
SOMERSET

If D. Bradman comes to Stone's Garage he can have a second-hand Austin Seven for a present. (One Dozen still in stock.)

EDWARD W. STONE
Station Garage : Bradford-on-Avon

Don Bradman square-cutting Hammond

infection of some kind swept through the Australian team, it seemed almost to guarantee defeat in the third Test. Kippax, Chipperfield and Bradman were among the worst affected, and the doctors even thought they might have diphtheria. Kippax could not play; and both Chipperfield and Bradman, feeling wretchedly off-colour, were uncertain whether they could force themselves out to the wicket. But they both batted in astonishingly hot weather for Manchester, and then returned to their sickbeds.

Bill O'Reilly was the hero of the tourists, with a dogged attack on the English wickets which culminated in the few fateful minutes when in four successive balls he dismissed Walters, Wyatt and Hammond. But England made the huge first innings total of 627, and the match resolved itself into an Australian struggle to avert the follow-on. Bradman could contribute only 30 runs, but his team-mates saved the day and the match was drawn.

By 14 July, Bradman had played almost two months without scoring a century. Critics asked whether the 'run-scoring machine' was beginning to run down. But in the match against Yorkshire on 14–17 July he redeemed himself in a splendid partnership with Woodfull. They had to face the pride of Yorkshire in the form of Bowes, Leyland, Verity, Smailes, Macaulay and Turner; and to begin with, Bradman treated them with the respect they deserved. He took seventy-four minutes to reach 50, but after that he leapt into gear and hammered almost every ball whether it was a left-handed 'chinaman' from Leyland or an express delivery from Bowes. He completed his century in another twenty-six minutes, and added another 40 in twenty minutes before

Test scene, 1934: Bowes bowling to Bradman, Ames at the wicket, Hammond first slip, Hendren second slip, Verity point, and Ponsford the non-striker

Leyland dismissed him. His 140 was the highest score recorded for Australia at Sheffield.

One newspaper stated that 'Don Gladman' had 'staged such a comeback that there hasn't been so much excitement in Yorkshire since the Wars of the Roses', and that 'Don's press critics are babbling and eating their words'. Britons who had been rather relieved by Bradman's paradoxical fluctuations in form now began to regard him as a renewed menace to their Test hopes.

The fourth Test opened at Headingley, the scene of Bradman's great treble century in 1930, on 21 July. With three Tests gone and honours easy, it was of crucial importance. Bradman was anxious to make amends for his failures in the earlier Tests, but he refused to speculate to pressmen who asked him about his chances.

England batted first, and their wickets fell like ninepins before the fearsome spin attack of Clarrie Grimmett, Bill O'Reilly and 'Chipper' Chipperfield, with Oldfield deadly behind the wickets. Neville Cardus wrote that the Englishmen 'exhibited contemporary defensive technique at its comical worst . . . and turned their bats into crutches of senility. They pushed, groped, and stumbled with ludicrous feebleness'.

The signatures of all the Australian cricketers on the cover of a menu especially printed by the hotel in Grindleford, when they were playing Derbyshire

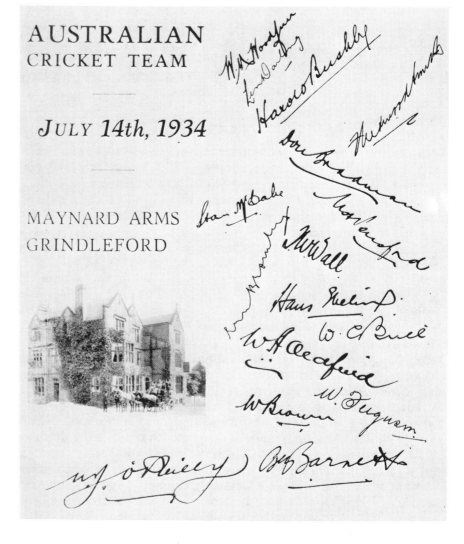

They ended their first innings with a modest 200, but it seemed at first that Bill Bowes would secure a quick revenge for England. He dismissed Bill Brown for 15 and Oldfield and Woodfull for 'blobs'. When Bradman joined Ponsford at the start of the second day, Bowes still had two balls to bowl of an incomplete over. The spectators held their breath, wondering whether he would find Bradman off-form and send him back to the pavilion.

Bradman's great friend (and critic) Neville Cardus had been so disturbed by his unpredictable play in the first three Tests, and was so anxious for him to settle down, that he made a special point of telling Bradman: 'If you make a four in the first half-hour at Leeds, I'll kick your bum!' How little did he realise what would happen.

Bradman treated those first two balls from Bowes with almost contemptuous ease. As though to signal his intentions for the day, he on-drove them both off the back foot for four apiece.

After that, he and Ponsford spent almost the entire day in a historic partnership, which ended only when Ponsford had the misfortune to dislodge one of his own bails at 5.57 p.m. Until then they had seemed unbeatable, in a performance which spurred the sportswriters to a contest of superlatives. They praised Ponsford for a magnificent 181, in 'a double concerto of classical cricket . . . woven like a superb counter-

Ponsford and Bradman joined in historic partnerships during the 1934 tour of England. This photograph shows Ponsford cutting one past Hammond, with Ames at the wicket

point in the texture of Australia's innings', and they filled column after column with praise for Bradman. They compared his display with the splendour of his 1930 innings, and found it even better. One wrote that in 1930 he had seemed to bat mechanically, but 'To-day's wonderful innings had the vitality of brain, blood, and nerve; every part of it throbbed with a consciousness that was of the spirit; it was a creative innings which took its shape hour by hour according to the will of a cricketer playing for Australia.'

At stumps he was not out for 271, made in six hours twenty minutes, and on the Monday morning he continued a partnership with Stan McCabe. The crowd hoped to see him surpass his 334 of 1930, but he seemed to be tiring and to lack the power and certainty of the Saturday. Nevertheless he reached his treble century before Bowes took his leg stump at 304.

The tremendous effort took its physical toll, and when he returned to the dressing-room after the first day he was so exhausted that his team mates had to undress him and carry him to the massage table.

Later in the match, when he was fielding in England's second innings, he chased a ball and stopped it with his foot. As he turned sharply he tore a muscle in the right thigh, and McCabe helped him to limp off the field with his face drawn with pain.

Soon after that a thunderstorm washed out the Headingley ground and saved England from almost inevitable defeat. With 200 in the first innings and 229 for six in the second, they had little hope of overtaking Australia's first-innings 584, to which Bradman and Ponsford had contributed so substantially. The downpour ended the match with a draw, followed by anguished post-mortems in the English press. In some quarters there was a dismal clamor to 'bring back Larwood' as the only man who could conquer Bradman in the fifth Test.

Bradman had an enforced rest in the private hospital of Sir Douglas Shields, an Australian who had made his name as a London surgeon, at 17 Park Lane. Sir Douglas kept Bradman's leg immobilised in plaster for a few days and then took him as a guest into his own spacious home, set in five acres of woodland at Slough, in order to keep an eye on him until the fifth Test.

Bradman's spell in hospital, and his omission from the matches between the fourth and fifth Tests, triggered a new campaign of newspaper speculation. One columnist wrote: 'I have heard all sorts of alarming stories during my cricket travels, but I am inclined to believe only the one, which came from a responsible source and which was to the effect that Bradman is a sufferer from anaemia. The symptoms are sudden spells of lassitude and loss of energy . . . I do not believe we shall see the Don taking part in the last Test match.'

This story from 'a responsible source', like so many newspaper stories about Bradman, was so much rubbish. His triumph in the fourth Test enabled him to rest contentedly, feeling that he had done something to conquer the mysterious force which had affected him for so long. He spoke to Jessie Bradman on the radiotelephone, listened to music, and looked forward to the final great contest of the tour.

The fifth Test opened at the Oval on 18 August. The English team included three of England's fastest bowlers — Bowes, Allen and Clark. 'Nobby' Clark was a left-hander of the Voce type, who often used a leg-side field similar to that employed by Larwood in the bodyline Tests.

An aerial view of the Oval, London, the scene of some of Don Bradman's triumphs and disasters on his tours of England

Australia won the toss, and Bradman went in at 21 for one at noon on the first day, again in partnership with Ponsford. England's hopes sagged as the two batsmen began to repeat their Leeds performance, although Bradman started more cautiously. After lunch he began to attack the bowling with increasing vigour, and he showed himself at his very best against the full armoury of the English bowlers. He batted with such overwhelming superiority that even Ponsford's splendid efforts paled by comparison. Clark resorted to his leg-side tactics, and Bradman's reply was to hook a vicious bumper high over square leg into the crowd for six. In five hours and sixteen minutes at the wicket he never made a false stroke until he tried to hook one of Bowes' high bumpers, and snicked it to wicket-keeper Les Ames. His total of 244, off 272 balls, rewarded an innings of classic grandeur. It contained one six and thirty-two fours, and *Wisden* described it as 'flawless'.

He and Ponsford had added 451 runs for the second wicket, and on the Monday morning Ponsford carried on to a total of 266 — then the highest Test score by any Australian except Bradman.

Australia was 380 ahead on the first innings but did not enforce the follow on. Bradman batted again after tea on the third day and carried his bat for 76, but on the following morning Bowes dismissed him after he had scored one run off Verity.

Australia won a resounding victory, by 562 runs, and recaptured the Ashes. Bradman had set a new record, with 765 in his last four first-class innings — the most ever made by any overseas batsman in England. The two Bradman-Ponsford partnerships made cricketing history, and at last eased the sting of Australia's defeat in the bodyline Tests.

Bradman had done everything his supporters had hoped of him, and had overcome the self-doubts inflicted by his lingering malaise. Even

Don Bradman starts a run after turning a ball from Bill Bowes to leg past Wyatt, during the fifth Test at the Oval in 1934

the most niggling critic could no longer deny his domination of the Test arena. More cheerfully than for many months, he set out on the final stages of the tour, extending from Folkestone on the Channel coast to Forres in northern Scotland.

The last two first-class matches were against An England Eleven at Folkestone and against H. D. G. Leveson-Gower's Eleven at Scarborough. The English labelled them 'Festival' matches but took them very seriously, and the Australians responded accordingly. The matches provided Bradman with some of his most thrilling cricket of the season.

At Folkestone he made his first century in ninety minutes and then proceeded to hit 'Tich' Freeman for 30 in a six-ball over. The ball from one of those sixes is probably still in the gutter of the pavilion roof, where it landed. His final score of 149 not out was made in 104 minutes, with four sixes and seventeen fours.

His innings created four new records. His 30 off Freeman is still the most ever scored by an Australian off one over (4,6,6,4,6,4). His 149 is the highest score by an Australian on the Folkestone ground. He had reached the fiftieth century of his career in 175 innings, against W. G. Grace's previous record of 282 innings for fifty centuries. At twenty-six years eight days he was (and is) the youngest batsman ever to reach fifty centuries; and he completed them in the shortest time, six years 262 days, from his debut in first-class cricket.

Before the Australians met the eleven assembled by Henry Dudley Gresham Leveson-Gower (known as 'Shrimp'), they tried to persuade this well-known cricketing personality that he should not try to turn the Festival match into a sixth Test match. Their entreaties fell on deaf ears. 'Shrimp' chose the fast bowlers Farnes, Bowes and Nichols as his main strike force, with Verity to back them up.

This rather obvious attempt to humiliate the tourists did not please the Australians one little bit. They won the toss and batted first, but Farnes bowled Brown for 3. Bradman took his place, and he probably never displayed his superiority over everything more than he did in that match.

He was out before lunch, but in ninety hectic minutes he hit one six and twenty-four fours, in an unforgettable display of power, to compile 132 runs. He had set yet another record — the highest score for any touring batsman before lunch on the first day of a match in England. The Australians won by an innings and 48 runs.

In Bradman's last eight first-class innings on that tour he compiled no less than 1144 runs at the astounding average of 163. At long last he seemed to have conquered the malady which had repetitively affected his form.

In the third week of September the Australians returned to London to prepare for the homeward voyage and attend a round of farewell entertainments. Bradman, staying with the others at the Langham Hotel, could look back on a season which had been a triumph of will-power. On so many occasions it would have been easy to throw in the towel and surrender to the illness no doctor could diagnose. But he had fought his way through and he looked forward to the peaceful voyage home.

On Saturday 22 September he entertained an old Bowral school friend, Elsie Corry, who had become a well-known concert singer in

MEN AND WOMEN OFFER BLOOD

PROGRESS MUST BE SLOW | NATION IS WATCHING HIS FIGHT

(SPECIAL BEAM SERVICE)

LONDON, Thursday.

BRADMAN'S physician, Sir Douglas Shields, told the special representative of "The Telegraph" at 2 p.m. to-day (11 p.m. Sydney time) that the great cricketer's condition had slightly improved.

At 4.30 p.m. (1.30 a.m. Sydney) this improvement was maintained, and his temperature had fallen.

His progress, said Sir Douglas, must necessarily be slow for the next day or two, but in the circumstances it was satisfactory.

The whole nation is watching the progress of Bradman in his fight aga'nst the complications that followed his operation for appendicitis.

KING'S PERSONAL INTEREST

Sir Douglas Shields told "The Telegraph" that between 20 and 30 people had called or telephoned the hospital yesterday and to-day offering their blood.

Royal Sympathy

They included a member of the House of Commons, a prominent footballer, women, newspaper-men, ex-officers who had served with the Australians during the war, Diggers, and others in all walks of life.

Both friends of Bradman and people of whom he had never heard, hope that the transfusion will be unnecessary, but, in any case, it would be done through the normal hospital services, said Sir Douglas.

Following the inquiry by the King and Queen before the launching of

the new Cunarder, the King asked that regular bulletins be sent to Balmoral. Sir Douglas added that Bradman was delighted to hear his wife had

telephoned, but he was not well enough to send a reply.

He appreciates the New South Wales Government's cable offering the use of its services.

"A Lancashire sportsman friend of mine," said Sir Douglas, "also offered to pay Mrs. Bradman's passage.

"The telephone is ringing day and night. A constant stream of callers, and innumerable flowers are arriving."

The inquirers included Lord Hailsham, Sir Herbert Austin, Mr. J. H. Thomas (Dominions Secretary), Mr. S. M. Bruce, and Lady Darnley, who sent flowers.

ANXIOUS MOTHER

RAY OF THANKFULNESS THAT HELPS HER

BOWRAL, Thursday.—"I am very anxious about Don, particularly as he is so far away," Mrs Bradman, senior, said to-day.

"The only thing that is helping me to bear up is thankfulness that he became ill before he boarded the boat for Australia, and the knowledge that he is being given the best possible attention," she added.

"On Monday I received a letter from Don, in which he said that it wouldn't be long before he was home."

H.M. THE KING, who has asked for regular bulletins

LORD HAILSHAM, who called to see Bradman yesterday

A Sydney *Daily Telegraph* report, compiled by 'Special Beam Service' (radio) from London, on Don Bradman's near-fatal illness at the end of the 1934 tour of England

England, to afternoon tea at the hotel. While they were yarning about old times he felt the slow onset of abdominal pain, steadily growing more intense. Eventually he told Woodfull he could not attend the dinner arranged for that evening, and went to his bedroom to endure this new affliction.

Mr John R. Lee, a Harley Street surgeon, was dining with the Australians that night, and Woodfull asked him to have a look at Bradman. Lee could not reach a diagnosis that night or on the following morning. To clear his mind, he went for a long drive through the quiet Sunday streets and into the country. When he returned, he had decided that the symptoms which Bradman had described to him were those of a long-standing appendicitis. He sought a second opinion from Sir Douglas Shields, who agreed with his recommendation for an operation. On the Monday afternoon, with most of the other cricketers away in the country, Chipperfield and Wall carried Bradman downstairs to an ambulance. Sir Douglas's younger brother, Clive, opened the abdomen at 4 p.m.

He found the appendix was not in the normal position but situated deep in the viscera: difficult to extract and so badly infected that the peritoneum also showed signs of infection. The secret of Bradman's long puzzling illness was at last revealed.

At first the operation seemed successful, until continued pain and a rising temperature showed the presence of peritonitis, an infection of the abdominal lining. At 8 p.m. on the Tuesday night the hospital issued a bulletin which revealed the gravity of Bradman's condition.

Rumour-mongers instantly turned this into a story that he was dead. A journalist actually telephoned Alan Fairfax, then living in London, at 4 a.m., to tell him about Bradman's 'death'.

When the news of the crisis reached Australia, the editor of the Sydney *Sun* contacted Jessie Bradman and offered to help her to leave for London immediately. She accepted, and he quickly made the arrangements. The fastest way for her to travel was by rail across the continent to catch the P & O liner *Maloja* in Fremantle, sail in her to a Mediterranean port, and then go across Europe to London. She would still take about four weeks but there was no other way — although the great aviator Charles Kingsford Smith offered, a few days later, to fly her to London. He was preparing to fly his new aircraft *Lady Southern Cross* to England to take part in the London–Australia air race, and he offered to take off earlier than planned in order to speed Jessie Bradman to her husband's bedside. He did in fact compete in the air race, but he and his aircraft disappeared over the Bay of Bengal.

The *Sun* forced all the formalities for Jessie Bradman through at frantic speed and she was soon on her way. In London, the hospital had been forced to close its switchboard to the flood of callers who wanted minute-by-minute news of Don Bradman's progress, and to turn away countless wellwishers who brought flowers, presents and messages.

When the hospital issued the first bulletin, King George V was in Glasgow for the launching of the new Cunard liner *Queen Mary*, then the largest in the world; and when he went on to Balmoral he telephoned London with instructions that he should be kept advised about the course of Bradman's illness. This was a probably unique display of interest by the monarch in the welfare of a subject.

Newspapers in Britain and Australia published daily reports, together with lengthy articles in florid prose. One reviewed his career and then said he was 'To-day in the cool shadows of a sickroom. Lying in white sheets with a mind irked and dulled with the torture of pain and sickness. Wrists so fluent, so strong, so full of magic so short a time ago, lie pallid and listless and ordinary on the bed coverings. That such genius could be reduced to impotence seems incredible. The tragedy of it is that we know it is true.'

Neville Cardus, on a sea voyage, received a cable from his editor asking him to prepare Bradman's obituary. He did so, but later refused to show it to his old friend.

Penicillin and the sulphonamides were still in the experimental stage, and doctors could do little but rely on Bradman's own spirit and stamina to pull him through the crisis. He fought the infection for three days of high temperatures, nausea and pain. When word went round that he had lost a lot of blood during the operation and that the hospital was planning a transfusion — a rare and drastic technique in the 1930s — a number of men immediately offered to act as donors. The newspapers devoted more space to Bradman's illness than to that of any other person before or since except reigning monarchs, and the British public read the reports with an interest as anxious as if Bradman had been one of their own people.

When Jessie Bradman reached Melbourne on her way to Fremantle, to be met by Canon Hughes, a sudden rumour flashed around Sydney and Melbourne to the effect that Bradman was dead. Fortunately, Hughes was able to allay her fears with a cable asking her to telephone London for the latest news, and she spoke to an associate of Sir Douglas Shields who told her that Bradman was still holding his own. She travelled on to Perth, and while she was still *en route* she received a message saying that the crisis was over. Representatives of the Western Australian Cricket Association met her at the Perth railway station and rushed her to Fremantle, where the captain of the *Maloja* had delayed his sailing so that she might hurry aboard. The ship's rails were crammed with passengers watching this act of the drama.

With unfortunate timing, Douglas Jardine's book in which he criticised Bradman's batting during the bodyline Tests appeared during the crisis. It was indignantly received, and the *Star* said the criticisms might not have been made 'if Jardine had realised how pluckily Don was carrying on under a handicap he was too proud to broadcast. The wonder is that Don rose to such heights and fielded so magnificently. Everybody hopes that more humanity will be shown on the next tour.'

In a strange way, Bradman's illness showed conclusively that he had become an athlete of international stature, whose genius belonged to the whole of mankind rather than to one nation alone. Regardless of how much longer his career was to endure, he had joined the immortals of the ancient game.

The fever burning through his tissues gradually cooled down, his pulse and temperature became almost normal, and on 29 September the hospital bulletin struck a hopeful note. Don Bradman wrote later: 'There can be no doubt that for some time I hovered on the brink of eternity.' However, the immediate danger was past.

The illness which had lasted for nearly two years, and its near-fatal

Happy reunion. Don and Jessie Bradman in London after her hurried trip from Australia during his illness

A fashionable lady of 1934. Jessie Bradman just before disembarking from the liner in which she and Don Bradman returned from England after his convalescence

Above right: Safely returned to Australia after his illness in England, Don Bradman poses for press photographers before landing on home soil

culmination, left Bradman totally exhausted. Sir Douglas Shields kept him in hospital until the day before Jessie Bradman arrived, and told him he must spend six months in recuperation. There would be no more cricket for twelve months, and even then his doctor said he was not sufficiently recovered to go to South Africa with the 1935–36 Australian team. He thus missed the only opportunity in his career to play cricket in that country.

After a joyous reunion the Bradmans spent a few weeks' holiday in Britain and Christmas in the south of France, then boarded an Orient liner for Sydney. They passed the remainder of the Australian summer with their families and friends at Bowral, and on 25 April 1935 began their new life in Adelaide.

Opposite: In a match against Leicestershire, a leg cutter from George Geary penetrates Bradman's defences after he had scored 65

SCOREBOARD 1934

Even though Bradman was in poor health during the 1933–34 season in Australia and the 1934 tour of England, he was still successful in a number of new achievements and new records. They include the following:

* In Sheffield Shield matches, his average of 184.40 is the highest ever achieved by any batsman for any State.

* In four successive innings for New South Wales he scored a total of 645 runs, a four-innings record for that State.

* In the match against Worcestershire in May 1934 he became the first English or Australian batsman to make more than 200 in his first innings of two English seasons. (The previous double century was also against Worcestershire, in May 1930.)

*When he scored 65 against Leicestershire, in May 1934, he had made more than 50 runs in each of seven successive innings, then an Australian record.

* His score of 304 in the fourth Test made him the only batsman to score two treble centuries in Test matches. (The previous treble-century was at Leeds in 1930.)

* In the fifth Test, the Bradman-Ponsford partnership of 451 was then a world record for the second wicket. It remains the Test record for Australia for that or any other wicket.

* At Folkestone, against An English Eleven, he became the youngest batsman ever to score fifty centuries in first-class cricket. He made his fiftieth century in his 175th innings, six years 262 days after his first-class debut, and bettered the previous record-holder, Herbert Sutcliffe, by almost two years.

* In the match against Mr Leveson-Gower's Eleven, at Scarborough, his 132 before lunch was the highest ever scored before lunch by any tourist on the first day of a match in England. When he reached 112 in that match, he became the first Australian to complete 2000 runs for the season.

* His Test match aggregate of 758 was much the highest for either side. Ponsford, with 569, was next best.

FROM SIR DONALD'S SCRAPBOOKS

Sir Donald Bradman's collection of scrapbooks includes one assembled by his literary agent, David Cromb, from British newspapers published during the 1934 tour. It contains many sidelights upon the Australian tourists and especially on Don Bradman, such as:

O'Reilly and Ponsford are the pipe smokers of the sixteen. Bradman has an occasional cigarette. The rest seem rather abstemious. Ebeling likes a mug of beer. — *Daily Mail*

I hear that before he left Australia Bradman's health was not quite normal . . . He was violently sick all the way from Adelaide to Fremantle — the best batsman in the side is the worst sailor . . . but recovered on the delightful run to Colombo, and is now in the best of health and spirits. — *Daily Telegraph*

They all look very fit. Bradman has less colour than any of them. Wall, who wears glasses, is a dour sort of fellow, but Ponsford is all smiles. — *The Star*

He has an eye like a hawk, capable of discerning a ball's direction and flight half-a-second before ordinary cricketers; he has a lovely wrist and great strength of forearm; he has the quickness of foot of Anton Dolin . . . He has quick wit. His mental reactions are as speedy as his physical ones. Next to watching Bradman bat, one likes to watch him fielding. Amazing anticipation in running for a catch, quickness in gathering the ball, lightning low-trajectory returns seeking Oldfield's gloves — all these are part of a combination sometimes criticised for being over-spectacular. But showmanship is part of Bradman's nature; why not add a touch of it in the cricket field? — *Evening Standard*

Congratulations to J. G. W. Davies, the Cambridge University cricketer, who bowled Bradman for a duck, must be tempered with a word of warning. The crowd came to see Bradman bat, and, for preference, to knock up a hundred or so. Will bowlers please note that getting Bradman out for a duck should be reserved for Test matches only? — *Daily Express*

Don Bradman, you must not disappoint all the girls like you did at Lord's yesterday. It's just too bad, that when they all turn up specially to see you bat, out you go for a mere five. A girl sitting next to me was almost tearful about it. — *Daily Herald*

Ever since Don Bradman arrived in this country, he has been literally bombarded with insulting, abusive, and threatening letters. None of the writers has signed his or her name. The letters bear such pen names as 'Britisher,' 'Fairplay,' 'Cricket Lover,' and so on. The letters threaten personal violence, and question Bradman's sportsmanship . . . it surely is absolutely foreign to English sportsmanship that this barracking by mail should be directed at a famous visiting cricketer. — *Northern Dispatch.*

In Nottingham, the story went round that the local miners planned to invade the pitch in protest against Australian barracking against the bodyline bowling of Larwood, who was a local man. The *Nottingham Guardian* quoted the secretary of the Miners' Association as replying 'The mere suggestion I consider a reflection on the good sportsmanship of Nottingham miners. Time will show that the miners know how to play the game.'

A good many late arrivals in City offices today could have been truthfully explained by the following conversation I overheard between a would-be spectator and a policeman.
  'Is Bradman still batting?'
  'Yes, and he looks like batting until Tuesday evening.'
  'Right. If he had been out I should not have come in.' — *Nottingham Journal*

The trouble with Don Bradman, of course, is that unless he scores a century in every innings the newspapers print sensational bills about him. When he struck that bad patch shortly after the tour began, 'Bradman's Duck' was placarded up and down London in bigger type than if another war had been declared. — *Sussex Daily News*

Bradman's innings had to be seen to be believed. If a boy had played like that at school he would have got into very hot water, but Bradman is now a law unto himself. Whereas in 1930 he was a run-maker, he is now a fun-maker . . . Macartney, in all conscience, was an impudent striker of the ball, but he was a cautious miser compared with this young man. — *The Bystander*

What has happened to Don Bradman? Has he lost his nerve as a result of Larwood's terrific bowling on the last Australian tour, and the consequent adverse publicity? . . . I cannot believe Bradman is just another infant prodigy who has burnt out. — *The Star*

One of Don's friends, realising he was depressed and worried, rang up Australia and said 'Find Mrs Don Bradman! Search Australia for her! And when you have found her connect her to the Midland Hotel, Manchester!' Ten hours later Mrs Bradman was located in a place called Mittagong, more than 100 miles from Sydney, and from there she talked to Don, putting new life into him. — *Daily Mail*

Bradman is the particular idol of the crowd. No sooner do they settle in their seats than they ask 'Which is Don Bradman? Where is he fielding?' The astonishment when he missed a catch in the deep was profound. — *Daily Telegraph*

When he came in there was a rush, especially of women, to pat him on the back. Although women are great cricket fans in Australia, I have never seen so many at a cricket match in England. — *Daily Mail*

He was marvellous in 1930, but assuredly he is still more remarkable now. — *The Times*

The hotel where the Australians are staying has become one of the show places of the city. As soon as the day's play has ended, the crowds converge on the hotel, most of them armed with autograph books and pens, and generally it is Bradman they want. — *Daily Herald*

Bradman is now the world's greatest batsman, though Hammond is a rival. Except to very fast leg theory, he is a complete master, his stroke play being magnificent and brilliant in the extreme . . . Short in height, Bradman has long arms, wrists of steel, a very strong forearm, and a wonderful eye. He seldom plays forward. He is either right back or feet out of his ground attacking the bowler — indeed, he is always attacking. — *Everyman*, quoting from P. F. Warner's *Book of Cricket*

The newspapers discovered that two of Bradman's great-aunts were still alive, one in London and the other in Northumberland. They used the name of Bradnam, and the press immediately claimed that his correct name was *Bradnam*, not *Bradman*. The *Shields Gazette* said he was 'very annoyed' by such statements.

The agile movement of Bradman's feet was worthy of a Pavlova. One shot, among many, lingers in the memory most bewitchingly. One ball looked like hitting his boot — a 'Yorker' from the Yorkshire son of Anak, Bowes; then, hey presto! the feet twinkled, stepped a pace back; bat and ball were in perfectly timed contact, and lo! the ball was in the crowd in the twinkling of an eye! All kinds of bowling came alike to the silvery willow he wielded . . . What power there is in Bradman's forearm! Again and again balls pitched close up were forced away to the boundary, where first-class batsmen would have been satisfied to have simply defended their wicket. And so hour after hour went by and one wondered if that lissom figure could ever get out.

— The *British Weekly*

Bradman and Ponsford Show Us How To Do It. Record Breaking Partnership. Bowes Clouted All Over The Ground. — *Sporting Life*

I can only describe Bradman as a freak batsman. I have already written that where an ordinary Test batsman gets a hundred Bradman gets two hundred. And so it proved in Leeds. — Jack Hobbs in *The Star*

One of the fifty-one large albums covering Sir Donald Bradman's cricketing career compiled by the State Library of South Australia

12

CAPTAIN OF AUSTRALIA

South Australians were enraptured by the knowledge that the great Don Bradman was to settle in and play for their State. This 'unofficial impression of Bradman's arrival in Adelaide for keeps', published in an Adelaide newspaper when he arrived there in April 1935, reflects the feelings of South Australians

In 1935, the notion of a world-famous Sydney personality moving westwards, into what seemed like obscurity on the edge of the outback, was almost revolutionary. The people of Sydney and Melbourne felt the world revolved around them, and that the capitals of other States were little more than large country towns.

In some ways they were right. The 1935 population of Adelaide was only about 315 000, living in leafy suburbs widely scattered around the city centre and merging into farms, vineyards and orchards. The great amphitheatre of hills across the eastern skyline was still almost unscarred by 'development'. The atmosphere was one of complacent

isolation, self-sufficient and conservative. The industries were comparatively small and progress had slowed almost to a standstill during the Depression.

But Bradman had a small-town background, and the placid new environment suited him very well. He found all the excitement he needed in the intricacies of his new profession. After the initial strangeness had worn off, he and Jessie Bradman soon found themselves at home. They rented a colonial villa on Holden Street, in the pleasant suburb of Kensington Park, bought a block of land in the same street, and began to plan the house that they would build.

The operation in London had removed the focus of infection which had troubled him for so long. After his convalescence he felt the need for physical activity and he joined the Mount Osmond Golf Club. Tramping over its rolling course, with its panoramic views over Adelaide, improved his golf and put him in better trim for the opening of the new cricket season.

The leading South Australian cricketers such as Vic Richardson were off to tour South Africa, and the South Australian Cricket Association asked Bradman to act as one of the Interstate Selection Committee, together with H. H. Bridgman and Dr C. E. Dolling, with the responsibility of building up a team to contest the Sheffield Shield matches. And, with Richardson absent, he was the natural appointment for State captain.

Other South Australian cricketers, especially the young men of Kensington, were somewhat dazzled by the brilliance of the international star who had suddenly appeared in their midst. They soon found that he exhibited all the natural qualities of a leader: fair, patient, friendly, approachable, determined, and ready to impart the knowledge he had learned the hard way on Shield and Test battlefields. He spent many hours of arduous practice with the State colts and the district club, coaching and advising the players.

On 28 September 1935 he captained his first South Australian team, Kensington A, against Kensington B. He played his first district match in South Australia, Kensington v. Adelaide, on 5 and 12 October. Local newspapers said 'Bradman in Form at Kensington. Scores 60 Runs in Hour'. After subsequent matches they wrote of his 'reassuring brilliance'; his 'quickness in getting into position to punish the fast bowlers'; and his 'crisp drives and cannon-like square cuts'. South Australians were delighted by their new acquisition and they looked forward to seeing him face sterner challenges.

The first came with a four-day match when South Australia encountered a 'goodwill' team of M.C.C. players, led by the Surrey captain Errol Holmes, which toured the antipodes in 1935–36. Understandably, Bradman played like a man out of touch with the rigours of first-class cricket. He made only 15 in his first innings, but showed better form with 50 in the second.

In South Australia's first Shield match of the season, against New South Wales, he showed something of his old brilliance — and his eleven showed the benefit of his coaching. Clem Hill wrote in the *Sporting Globe*: 'With his wonderful cricket brain he has imparted a tremendous amount of confidence to the players . . . His personality is such that the younger players, in whom he has taken an unusually deep interest, regard him as a great leader.'

Apart from playing for Australia and South Australia, Don Bradman also played first-grade cricket for Kensington, a club in the eastern suburbs of Adelaide. This photograph shows him hitting out in a Kensington match against Glenelg, a club in the western suburbs

Bradman was content to take runs as they came rather than try to dominate the bowlers, but he still compiled his first century as captain and made 117 in 158 minutes.

South Australia won by an innings and 5 runs and Clem Hill predicted that Bradman would lead the State to victory in the Sheffield Shield series. The next match, against Queensland, seemed to prove him right. The first matches of the season had been something of an endurance test for Bradman after his long spell out of the game, but now he slipped smoothly back into his most brilliant form and attacked the Queensland bowling with the same flair that brought his record-breaking 452 in a match against that State. He scored 233 in 191 minutes and set two more records: the highest score ever made in matches between South Australia and Queensland, and double centuries in three successive innings against the bowling of one State.

Any Australian who feared that Bradman's illness, his long absence from the cricketing scene, and his 'retreat' to South Australia might affect his Test potential, was instantly reassured when he encountered Victoria on 1 January 1936. He went to the wicket early on the first day, in his fifty-fifth Shield innings, and at 17 completed 5000 runs in Shield matches. He spent 157 minutes in compiling his first century, and then, in grilling heat, he speeded up a little and at stumps was 229. Next morning, he began to hit out ferociously. He was 338 at lunch. In the afternoon, when he had accumulated 357 in seven hours one minute, wicket-keeper Quin caught him off a skier.

Sportswriters acclaimed the emergence of a 'new' Bradman: no longer the 'impish carefree batsman' of New South Wales days or the 'impetuous' Test player who lost his wicket when he lashed out at Bowes. One saw him as 'a more sober, more mellowed, more restrained, and a more sinister Bradman, from the bowler's viewpoint, than ever before'.

It was as though the responsibilities of leadership had acted as a catalysis, blending all the influences on his life until that date into one dominant whole. Until then, writers had still tended to play upon Bradman's youth. After that Melbourne innings there could be no doubt that he was a formidable and authoritative man.

E. H. M. Baillie wrote in the *Globe*: 'It was a new Bradman — a Bradman on whom had been cast a tremendous responsibility, which he shouldered like the champion he is. And what a masterly display of batting he gave! . . . he never flattered the bowlers with the faintest suggestion that they would ever get him out.'

The Victoria match was drawn, but Bradman again led South Australia to victory against Queensland. For himself, it was one of his less impressive performances. He had to face Eddie Gilbert's shotgun deliveries and never showed himself comfortable against them.

The Shield match against New South Wales had a slow beginning and a sad conclusion. Rain washed out the first day's play, and the game was abandoned when news of the death of King George V reached Sydney on 20 January 1936.

When South Australia faced Victoria at Adelaide, on 21–25 February, Bradman had only just broken his duck when he was caught at second slip. But the team he had coached rewarded him with a convincing victory, consolidated by 'Jack' Badcock's 325. South Australia won the Shield for the first time in nine years. It was yet another

Bradman accomplishment, wholeheartedly applauded by the people of his new home State.

He ended the season with a stunning exposition of batsmanship in a match against Tasmania on the Adelaide Oval. He scored 369, the highest score ever made on that oval and a record for South Australia, in four hours thirteen minutes. Clem Hill, the great South Australian batsman of 1892–1923, held the previous record with a score of 360. With characteristic humour he telegraphed from Melbourne: 'Congratulations you little devil for breaking my record.'

The news that 'Bradman was back', in ferocious form and with yet another string of cricketing records to his credit, cast some gloom over English selectors ruminating over a choice of players for the 1936–37 Test series. In London, A. G. Gardiner wrote an article on the subject, headed 'Who Is To Get Bradman Out?' He reviewed the bowlers available to England, the possible choice of captain, and the accomplishments of English batsmen, concluding 'There is plenty of material here for a great team, and in normal times a winning team. But there floats before the mental vision a slight athletic figure at the wicket that seems not a man but a whirlwind, a natural element that is more than human, and I am left wondering "Who is to get Bradman out?"'

For Don and Jessie Bradman, the winter of 1936 was a time of great contentment. Don had settled firmly into his new profession, and he knew the satisfaction of having justified South Australia's faith in his cricket. Jessie was expecting her first baby, which they anticipated with the deep reverent pleasure of young parents. They had built their dream home: the fine two-storey house, with its beautifully matured garden, in which they still reside. Bradman, like any other young husband, had scratched his head over the cost, and at first rejected the highflown idea of including a billiard room. But the architect persuaded him that he would never be able to add such a facility so cheaply in the future, and that billiard room has since entertained many famous visiting cricketers.

Dr Dolling died in 1936, and Bradman received the not altogether welcome honour of appointment as a selector of Test players. In future, when he watched or played in first-class matches, he would carry some of the burden of assessing the players' potential for the Test arena.

He opened the 1936–37 season with district cricket performances that showed him to be in excellent form, and followed up with a grand display in the Testimonial Match for Warren Bardsley and Jack Gregory, in Sydney on 9–11 October. He captained The Rest of Australia v. Australia, the latter comprising Vic Richardson's team which had defeated the South Africans. In Bradman's first innings he made hay of Bill O'Reilly and the other bowlers and his 212 runs contributed to victory for his eleven. A. G. Moyes wrote 'Test Hopes Soar as Bradman Triumphs Again. Amazing Riot of Runs in Trial Cricket.' Arthur Mailey, en route to Australia with the English team, radioed that 'Bradman's score, published in this morning's wireless news, was a terrific shock to the English cricketers ... They are usually hearty breakfast eaters, but most of them turned away from their customary kippers when they heard the dread tidings.'

In that match, Bradman drew level with Bardsley as the leading Australian century-maker in first-class cricket. The 212 completed his

AUSTRALIA'S GREATEST BATSMAN

Don Bradman's old friend Arthur Mailey, the cricketer, journalist, and cartoonist, drew this cartoon of 'The Don' in the 1930s. The original, which is shaded in watercolours, hangs in Sir Donald Bradman's study

fifty-sixth century in less than nine years, including nine against England, two against the West Indies and four against South Africa.

The English tourists, led by the popular G. O. B. Allen, arrived in Fremantle on 13 October. Allen's team included Leyland, Voce and Hammond, and Wendell Bill wrote in the *Sydney Mail*: 'I have no doubt at all that the team will mould into a powerful combination and be a tough proposition for Australia to combat in the Test matches.'

Allen, nicknamed 'Gubby' from his initials, was the ideal captain for the first English Test team to visit Australia after the bodyline controversy. His opposition to Jardine's tactics was well known, and he had the distinction of having been born in Australia. His uncle Reginald appeared for Australia in the second match of the 1886–87 Test series. 'Gubby' was a tremendous right-arm fast bowler, a strong and determined batsman, and a splendid fieldsman: probably the best all-rounder among the English amateurs. He and Bradman knew and respected each other, and looked forward to the first conflict as captains of their respective sides. It was scheduled for 29 October, when South Australia was to meet the M.C.C. on the Adelaide Oval.

Bradman awaited another event with much more eager expectancy. His first-born was due to arrive at any moment, and on 28 October Jessie Bradman gave birth to a son.

But the prognosis was not good. That evening, Bradman called on Neville Cardus at the latter's Adelaide hotel and asked the famous writer and music critic, an old friend of the Bradmans, if he would care to spend the evening with him. He drove Cardus to his home and they enjoyed a discussion of the forthcoming Tests, with Bradman saying that he thought Hammond could be controlled by O'Reilly's leg-stump attack, pitched a good length. On the way back to Cardus' hotel he stopped briefly at the hospital to say good-night to his wife, and when he returned to the car he said 'I'm afraid the poor little chap will not pull through.'

Bradman had kept the unhappy news to himself all day, and he had received countless congratulations with the knowledge heavy on his heart.

The baby boy died on the day the match opened, and the groundsmen lowered the Adelaide Oval flags to half-mast. As a cricketer's gesture of condolence, Allen allowed South Australia to hold Bradman's place open until lunch, in case he should decide to play, but of course he could not leave his wife at such a time.

Jessie Bradman watches one of the Tests in the 1936–37 series, the first in which Don Bradman captained Australia

He did not play again until 14 November, in the Shield match at Melbourne. An attack of gastro-enteritis kept him off the field for the first day, and when he went to the wicket on the second afternoon he looked far from well. Victoria had assembled a formidable battery of bowlers, including the fierce pace bowler Ernie McCormick, to keep Bradman under control, and they had already given South Australia a hard time. But Bradman soon tamed McCormick. As soon as he had the measure of the Victorian bowler he countered hurricane bowling with hurricane batting. Some of McCormick's deliveries made him duck and twist as though he were facing a bodyline attack, but he survived them gallantly. A change in bowling pace, when other Victorians tackled him, made no difference. One sportswriter said '. . . After he had reached his century a perfect tornado of runs came from his bat, with the poor bowlers absolutely helpless . . . in the last 46 minutes he added 89 in a frenzy of hitting, the last 42 runs in 16 minutes. In the end he lost his wicket in what looked like attempts to drive the slow bowlers out of the ground.'

He made 192 in 180 minutes, and limped off the field exhausted. The Australian newspapers revelled in his 'orgy of batting', which held little comfort for the tourists. But when he faced the M.C.C. for the first time that season, with a bitterly cold wind flailing the Sydney Cricket Ground, Worthington dismissed him at 63 when he appeared to be well set. Journalists saw his performance as the high spot in a slow match, with players on both sides showing a puzzling lack of form. 'Stork' Hendry wrote in *Truth* that the English batsmen were 'lamentable', with little chance of Test victory.

On 4 December 1936, Bradman made his first appearance as captain of Australia. The newspapers had had plenty to say about his team, which included five men making their Test debut ('Jack' Badcock, Ernie McCormick, Ray Robinson, Maurie Sievers, and Frank Ward), and some criticisms about the omission of Clarrie Grimmett, then aged forty-five. However, C. G. Macartney wrote that in the 1933–34 season he seemed to have lost the 'devil' which had made him so dangerous. The selectors, including Bradman, had replaced him with Frank Ward, the South Australian right-arm leg-break bowler.

The 1936–37 Test series attracted an unusual number of women spectators — especially when Don Bradman was batting. This photograph shows a portion of the crowd in Sydney. The cricketwriter Neville Cardus commented on the 'hideous new fashion' of sunglasses for women

The first Test of the 1936–37 series was only the third against England to be played in Brisbane, and the sportswriters noted that a Test in that city had ominous portents for Australia. The two previous matches against England had both ended in defeat.

The match opened on a dark and threatening day, with the forecast predicting thunderstorms, but the 'Gabba wicket was 'in perfect order, and the playing area looked fine'.

England batted first, and opened disastrously. McCormick's first ball of his first Test dismissed Worthington, and he swiftly disposed of two more batsmen. Leyland and Barnett retrieved the situation, watched by a huge crowd, 'coatless but perspiring'.

England's first innings ended with 358 and Fingleton and Badcock opened for Australia. Badcock made a good start but lost his wicket for eight, and then the crowd bellowed acclaim as Bradman paced out to the wicket. It roared again when he cut Allen for four and 'pulled him gigantically' for another four. He seemed to be set for another of his great scores but defeat came swiftly. Worthington caught him off Allen when he had made 38.

It was the beginning of the end. Fingleton, with 100, and McCabe with 51, were the only Australians to distinguish themselves. The other batsmen all fell for 10 or less and the innings ended with 234.

The first Test, Brisbane, 4–9 December 1936. L. E. G. Ames, the wicket-keeper, ducks as Bradman pulls to leg over Ames' head and scores yet another four

England could muster only 256 on her second attempt, leaving Australia with 381 to win. On a dry pitch, this was a forbidding but not impossible target. But heavy rain overnight left Australia to face the task on a sticky wicket, and disaster struck. Voce and Allen massacred the batsmen. They dismissed five, including Bradman, for ducks. Oldfield, with 10, and Chipperfield, 26, were the only men to reach double figures. They were all out for 58, with a casualty list comprising Ward with a broken nose, Bill Brown with a thumb injury, and McCormick with a strained back.

Bradman, going in at 7 for three, had survived only two balls from Allen. The second pitched on a length, lifted sharply, and hit the shoulder of his bat before he could withdraw it. Fagg caught him at third slip.

Australia's defeat by 322 runs caused the newspapers to snort such comments as 'Sheer Bad Batting' and condemn the 'dreary play' on both sides. But several made kindly remarks on Bradman's captaincy. One wrote '. . . the general verdict was that he had done an excellent job. His moves were not made spectacularly, but he carried out his duties with a quiet watchfulness and judgment that were generally approved. He handled his bowlers capably, except, perhaps, in one instance, placed his field skilfully, and made several tactical moves that brought good results.' Nevertheless his first appearance as a Test captain had been humiliating. His duck, when so much rested upon him, had been particularly depressing, even though it was only his ninth 'blob' in first-class cricket.

The tourists' victory made little impact in England, where the newspapers were full of the Wally Simpson affair. However the

Schoolboys swarm around Don Bradman in the eternal quest for his autograph as he walks off the pitch after stumps

sportswriters commented that England's chances were good. *The Times* commented that Australia relied overwhelmingly on Bradman, and that 'If he fails, Australia crashes'.

The weather, and the luck of the toss, seemed to favour England to begin with. When the second Test opened at Sydney on 18 December, Allen's men played a slow but profitable two-day innings and scored 426 for six before Allen declared. Then the heavens opened and drenched the pitch, presenting Australia with the second sticky wicket in succession. Badcock was sick, and the Australian batsmen collapsed again. O'Brien, McCabe and Ward did not break their ducks. Bradman, going in at 1 for one, played an indeterminate stroke to a good-length ball from Voce, which reared up towards his face, and Allen snapped him up at short leg.

In the follow-on, it seemed that two successive ducks caused him to play very cautiously on the improving wicket. On reaching 27 he passed Clem Hill's previous record aggregate of 2660 for an Australian in Tests against England. Hill made his aggregate in seventy-six innings; Bradman in thirty-four.

Bradman was 57 not out overnight, and next morning Verity dismissed him for 82 after 212 minutes at the wicket.

Apart from McCabe's 93, Bradman's score was the best for his eleven. They totalled 324 and lost by an innings and 22 runs, amid journalistic plaints that Australia was short of effective bowlers. Bill Woodfull wrote in the *News Of The World* that 'Bradman made use of his bowlers, ringing the changes with commendable judgment, but nothing would go right for him. If he had had one more fast bowler, he might have been able to turn the first day's play on Friday to account.' Moyes wrote that Bradman was 'making a good fist of an awkward job', but that some people felt he should give up the captaincy and concentrate on batting.

Two successive defeats, and a barrage of criticism including allegations that his team were not co-operating with him, did not affect Bradman's confidence. Armchair cricketers told each other that he should recall Grimmett, that the selectors should not have discarded Vic Richardson, that they should drop Bradman as captain, and so on, but he ignored them apart from a press statement in which he refuted the rumours about his team not backing him up. He said: 'My teammates have, in many cases, gone out of their way to help me and made my job as captain easier.' He displayed one of the prime qualities of a true leader: refusal to be swayed by the mob when things were not going well.

For the crucial third Test, O'Brien, Badcock and McCormick were omitted while Chipperfield, with a jaw injury, was ruled unfit. Their places were filled by Brown, Darling, Fleetwood-Smith and Rigg, Fleetwood-Smith having missed the first two Tests with a leg injury. Ward, who still had some difficulty breathing through his nose, was passed fit by the board's doctor.

The third Test opened on New Year's Day 1937 at Melbourne, with the English sportwriters predicting victory for Allen's men. But Bradman won the toss for the first time in that series, and put his men in to bat on a splendid wicket. Neither he nor the others used it to full advantage and he continued his low-key performance with a mere 13 before Robins caught him off Verity.

Opposite: A point-of-sale card for the Don Bradman Bat in the 1930s

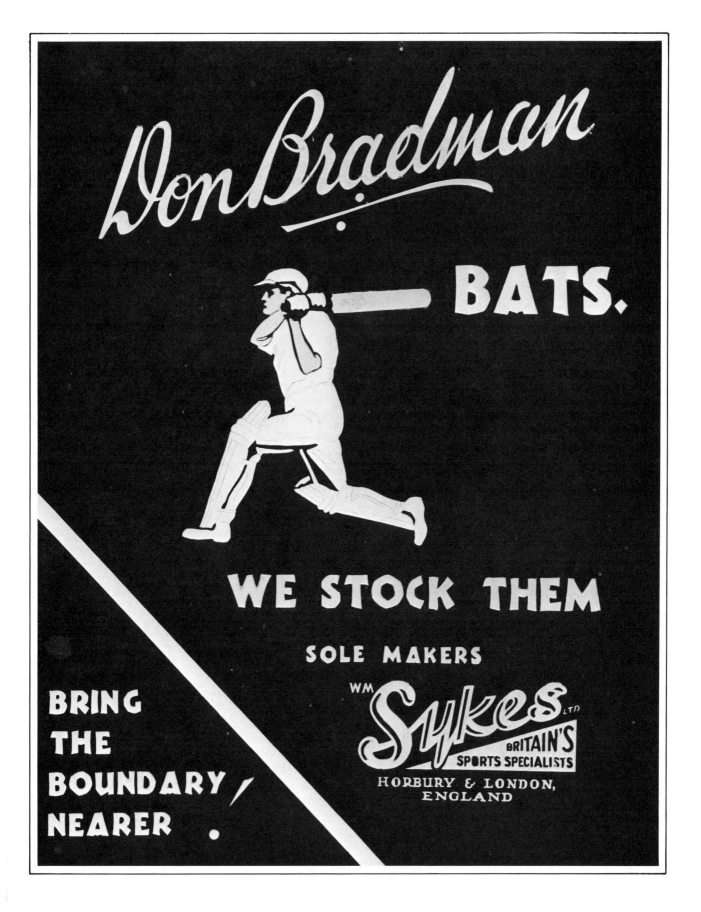

The weather was changing again and he took the gamble of declaring at 200 for nine. It paid off when a summer storm forced England to open on a gluepot wicket, which he later described as 'the worst I ever saw in my life', but initially it seemed that the Englishmen would outwit him with their stubborn batting. Len Darling saved the day, with three spectacular catches that dismissed Hammond, Leyland and Barnett.

For a little while, Bradman thought his tactics might work against him. If England collapsed too soon, Australia would have to take over the atrocious wicket before it recovered. He told his bowlers to nurse England along, and when they obeyed him he feared that Allen would see through his tactics. The sportswriters certainly did not, and they wrote later about 'Puerile Play' because English wickets fell so slowly. When Allen at last realised what was happening he declared at 76 for nine and Australia was required to spend the rest of the day on the gluepot.

Bradman countered by sending two of his poorest batsmen, the bowlers O'Reilly and Fleetwood-Smith, out to the wicket as openers. He wrote in *Farewell to Cricket*: 'I can still picture the look of incredulity on Fleetwood's face when I told him to put the pads on. He said, "Why do you want me to open up?" and at the risk of offending his dignity I told him the truth. "Chuck," I said, "The only way you can get out on this wicket is to hit the ball. You can't hit it on a good one, so you have no chance on this one."'

O'Reilly was immediately caught and bowled by Voce, but Ward and Fleetwood-Smith managed to hang on until an appeal against the light was upheld. The weather rewarded Bradman with a cool, dry, sunny day when Fleetwood-Smith returned to the wicket on the Monday morning. Bradman's theory about him had been so correct that he lost his wicket to the first ball that touched his bat.

Now the fate of Australia rested on the remainder of the innings. Bradman's staunch journalistic supporter, A. G. Moyes, had written 'Black Outlook for Ashes', after Bradman declared, but the English declaration had allowed a ray of hope. The enormous excitement was reflected by the new world records for the crowds cramming into Melbourne Cricket Ground, rising from 78 630 on Friday to 87 798 on the Monday. In Bowral, groups of men stood outside Vic Bradman's menswear store to listen to broadcasts of the play.

Neville Cardus described the Monday wicket as 'as easy as middle age, old slippers, and vintage port. You could scarcely make the new ball rise knee-high'. The enormous crowd was in two minds as Bradman joined Fingleton at 97 for five. Would he be on form, or would he continue the lamentable run of luck which had marred his Test batting that season?

He quickly set their minds at rest as he launched into an innings which displayed all his old familiar power and majesty. He opened at 2.50 p.m. on Monday, batted for the whole of Tuesday, and ended only after he had batted for fifty-nine minutes of the Wednesday. His time of seven hours thirty-eight minutes was then the longest played by an Australian in Australia.

Jack Fingleton partnered him for six hours four minutes of this time and between them they added 346: still the sixth-wicket record for Australian Test cricket. When Ames caught Fingleton he had scored

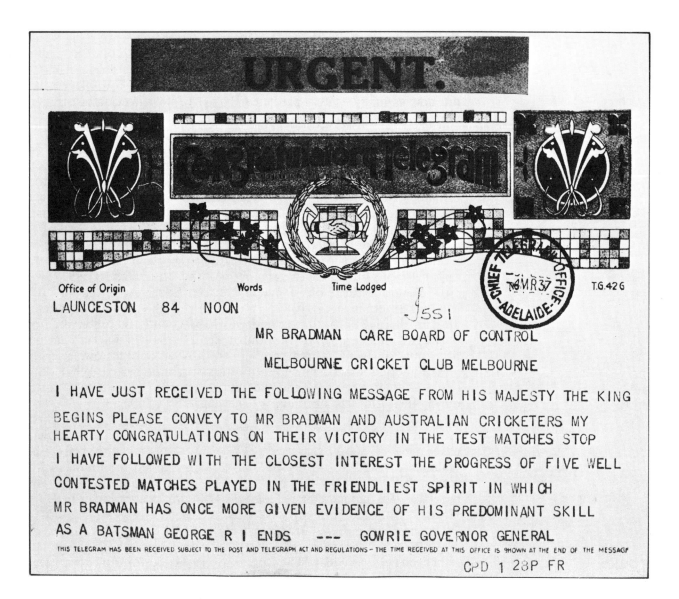

The 1936–37 Test series, with Don Bradman as captain of Australia and 'Gubby' Allen as captain of England, did much to eliminate the ill-feeling between the two nations which had resulted from the 'bodyline' tour of 1932–33. This message from King George VI shows the importance placed upon cricket as a link between Commonwealth countries

136, while Bradman went on to total 270 before Allen caught him off Verity. Cardus described the Bradman-Fingleton partnership as 'a nightmare to England'. The crowd roared like spectators at a bullfight, greeting Fingleton's century, and Bradman's first and second centuries, with cheering so prolonged that it held up play.

Australia's 'tail' soon collapsed after Bradman's dismissal, but the mighty partnership had sealed England's doom. Australia won by 365 runs. Instead of the easy Test triumph that so many writers had predicted for England, they still had to battle for the Ashes.

Immediately after the third Test, the Board of Control took the shine off Australia's success. Without reference to Bradman, they summoned McCabe, O'Reilly, Fleetwood-Smith and O'Brien before a 'tribunal' of Board members. The Board and the four players refused to disclose the reason for this 'carpeting', so the press naturally enjoyed an orgy of speculation. The *Daily Mail* suggested that the incident concerned an alleged wish on the part of the Australian team for McCabe to replace Bradman as captain. Other newspapers attributed the physical unfitness of the four men, or dissension among the team, or 'advice from another State that the four men would not be available for the fourth Test'. Sir Donald Bradman says he still does not know the reason for the ill-timed incident, which angered the four players but did not, as many writers predicted, have 'a fatal effect on Australian morale'.

Bradman's success in the third Test did not stifle his critics, who seemed always able to find some new quibble with his performance on or off the field. Alan Fairfax told the London *Daily Express*: 'You must mother a cricket team, and Don Bradman is no mother. He is too brilliantly individual.' And the usual crop of wild-eyed rumours went the rounds. Many people believed one which said that Bradman had lost a leg in a motor accident.

The eccentric summer weather continued when the tourists went to South Australia for the fourth Test. Adelaide folk often do not see a millimetre of rain during the summer months, but in January 1937 two days of rain washed out a match between South Australia and the M.C.C. Bradman strained a leg muscle during the match, made only 38 with the aid of a runner, and was subsequently in subdued form during his first innings of the fourth Test. He had made only 26 off fifty-four balls when he played a ball from Allen onto his own wicket.

Exasperated journalists and supporters once more asked 'What's the matter with Bradman — and the rest of his men?' Bradman's scores during the series had been like a fever chart: 38-0-0-82-13-270-26. The Australians totalled only 288, on a perfect wicket, in their first Adelaide innings. Fortunately Allen's men did little better. Barnett gave them a good start, with 129, but after his dismissal even Hammond could do no better than 45. They ended the innings with 330, a shaky enough lead but sufficient for London newspapers to proclaim 'England's Great Test Start'. *Truth* headed an article by Hendry 'Only Houdini can save Australia'.

On the third evening Bradman went in at 21 for one, with one of Australia's best batsmen, Jack Fingleton, dismissed for 12. Allen had set a deep field, to check 'The Don's' propensity for rattling off a series of boundaries, and he had to piece together a score by ones and twos.

He was 26 not out overnight, and returned to the wicket next morning determined to do or die. Allen, equally determined, manoeuvred his fielders like chessmen to suit the needs of the moment. When McCabe joined Bradman, Allen had silly point and silly mid-on crouching almost at McCabe's feet. When McCabe settled down, Allen set an unorthodox field to take advantage of Hedley Verity's left-arm spin bowling. Verity bowled with no slip field, and two men stationed side by side at silly point. The sportswriter Denzil Batchelor said this novel placement should earn one of the fielders the title 'lunatic point'.

None of these manoeuvres made any difference to Bradman. He batted implacably throughout the day: calmly, shrewdly, cunningly, carefully; treating venomous deliveries from Voce with the same apparent disdain as he did the leg-breaks and googlies of Walter Robins. His razor-edged bat cut all the Englishmen down to size. Allen, streaming with perspiration and with his hair hanging over his forehead, seemed close to exhaustion when Bradman was still there at stumps with 174 against his name.

Bradman's indomitable performance magnetised the people of

'The Don' in the late 1930s

Adelaide and attracted one out of every eight of the population to swell the record crowd. London editors, reading the reports cabled from their representatives, wrote such comments as 'It was England v. Bradman to-day, and Bradman won.'

On the third morning, with fingers and thumbs swollen from continuous pressure on the bat, Bradman resumed a partnership with Gregory. He survived an over of leg theory from Verity and played steadily on, with the same calm deliberation, to a total of 212 before he was caught and bowled by Hammond. The innings, of seven hours twenty-one minutes, had been one of the longest and slowest in his career, but it was monolithic in its sheer dedication and concentration.

The remaining Australian batsmen lost their wickets cheaply and the second innings ended with 443. England still had an excellent chance,

Twelve years before Donald
Bradman received his knighthood,
an English supporter suggested to
Prime Minister Joseph Lyons of
Australia that Lyons should
recommend Bradman's inclusion in
the Honours List

PRIME MINISTER,
CANBERRA.

CONFIDENTIAL.

6th March, 1937.

Dear Sir:

I desire to acknowledge the receipt of your
letter of 10th February, in which you suggest that the
bestowal of a Knighthood upon Mr. Don Bradman, whose pre-
eminence in the world of cricket is so widely acknowledged,
should be recommended to His Majesty the King

Your friendly interest in this matter is
appreciated and the representations you have forwarded
will be given careful consideration.

Yours faithfully,

Prime Minister.

Stephen St. John Martin, Esq.,
Grosvenor House,
Grosvenor Jardens,
St. Leonards-on-Sea,
ENGLAND.

Don Bradman with his fellow-
selectors for Australia: Bill
Johnson (left) and 'Chappie'
Dwyer. Bradman once remarked
that the difference between a player
and a selector was that a player
could sometimes be right

especially when Hammond played a backs-to-the-wall game and was
still at the wicket on the morning of the sixth day.

Fleetwood-Smith had taken the first two English wickets, and
Bradman suddenly remembered a remark made by the old wicket-
keeper Sammy Carter during the North American tour. He said of
Fleetwood-Smith: 'That lad might win a Test for Australia one day.'

Bradman handed the ball to the bowler whom he later termed 'this
erratic genius', and told him that the match — and the Ashes —
depended upon him. Fleetwood-Smith responded magnificently, with
'a glorious sinuous ball which swerved away from the bat but then
viciously spun back between bat and pad as the flight drew Hammond
forward'.

It was the end of Hammond and the end of England, who lost by
148 runs.

With Test honours even, the entire nation awaited the fifth Test in
an atmosphere of seething excitement and a blizzard of advice and
criticism from the sportswriters. Strangely, they took the attitude that

it was not good enough for Bradman to win Test matches literally off his own bat. They insisted that Australia should be able to conquer England without the 'abnormal assistance' of Bradman.

Before the fifth Test, Bradman led South Australia to a second victory over Queensland. He compiled 123 in his first and only innings. On their way home the 'Croweaters' played Bradman's home State in a match at Sydney, where his old mate Bill O'Reilly dismissed him for 24 in the first innings. Rain stopped play after he reached 38 in the second. South Australia needed an outright win to retain the Shield, but lost by nine wickets to Victoria in the last match of the season.

Early on 26 February 1937, queues up to a kilometre long radiated from the Melbourne Cricket Ground like the spokes of a giant wheel. The first arrivals turned up at dawn and waited almost five hours for the gates to open. Bradman won the toss and Fingleton and Rigg opened for Australia, in a staunch partnership against the English attack. But they were both out before lunch and Bradman went in at 42 for one.

He immediately launched into an exhibition of dynamic batting which brought him 169 runs in 223 minutes. McCabe, with 112 in 163 minutes, and Badcock with 118 in 205, proved ideal partners. In scorching weather, Allen launched all his own fire and impetuosity at Bradman, backed up by Voce and Farnes, but Bradman repeatedly played 'that conjuring trick of a stroke, a straight drive past a fast bowler off his right foot with his body curved back over the wicket'.

The English bowling slowly lost its zest against the aggressive Australian batting, and even though the tail-enders fell fast the Australians made a first innings total of 604. When England batted the right-arm fast bowler Laurie Nash, appearing in his first Test against England, together with O'Reilly and Fleetwood-Smith, handled them with diabolical efficiency. In five hours twenty-four minutes they were out for 239.

Bradman enforced the follow-on, and the Englishmen batted again on a wicket soaked by overnight rain. The trio of Australian bowlers dealt with them even more efficiently than before. With a second innings total of 165, England lost by an innings and 200 runs.

Luck was equally distributed in the Test series. Australia was caught on wet wickets in the first and second Tests, England was similarly disadvantaged in the third and fifth, and the fourth was played in fine weather throughout.

Post-mortems on the series continued for some time after the fifth Test, with sportswriters taking full advantage of hindsight to explain that Bradman's men had retained the Ashes more by good luck than good judgment, that Allen would have won if only he had declared earlier in the third Test, and so ad infinitum. They seemed almost aggrieved that Australia's victory had depended so largely upon Bradman's two great scores, but all agreed that the good sportsmanship of the Test series had erased the bitter memories of bodyline. Allen and Bradman had been the ideal captains to heal the breach.

Allen, en route to New Zealand with his team, wrote a letter to Bradman saying 'Just a line to bid you a final good-bye and to tell you once again how much I have enjoyed my cricket with you . . . I have been in bed ever since the boat passed the Sydney Heads and I am so damned tired that I don't intend to get up until we reach Wellington.'

A photograph taken during the late 1930s of Don Bradman's stance at the wicket

THE WORLD OF DON BRADMAN
1929–1939

The opening of Sydney Harbour Bridge in 1932, and the consecration of the Australian War Memorial at Villers Bretonneux in 1938, might be seen as benchmarks of Australia in the 1930s. The bridge, nine years in the building, arose in harmony with Australian aspirations during the 'Roaring Twenties'. The memorial commemorated 10 680 Australians, killed in the first world war, who have no known graves. In 1932, Francis de Groot's action in galloping ahead of Labor Premier Jack Lang, to forestall his ceremonial opening of the bridge, symbolised a society which had become deeply divided. By 1938, Australians were half-sadly, half-cynically aware that the glories of the Great War enshrined by Villers Bretonneux had been tarnished by the Great Depression, when many returned soldiers had literally to beg their bread, and that another world war loomed over the horizon.

The first tremors of that depression had been felt for some time, in declining prices for primary produce. When Wall Street collapsed with seismic suddenness, the impact hit Australia harder than any other 'Western' nation except Germany. British financiers recalled the loans which had fuelled Australian progress, and sent Sir Otto Niemeyer to demand repayment at the cost of cuts in the Australian standard of living. Many hard-won social advances quickly evaporated. The working week, cut to forty-four hours, was restored to forty-eight. The male basic wage, averaging about £4.10.6d a week, dropped to little more than £3.

By 1932, many thousands of Australians did not even have the basic wage, and there was no Social Security as we know it today. The 'dole' was a ration of basic foodstuffs. Many people relied on charity for the rent, clothing, and other necessities.

One survivor of those days, Mr Bruce Bowley of South Australia, recalls: 'I was lucky because my dad had work and so I had lunch to take to school. But it was hard to eat because so many kids had nothing and they'd stand around and watch every bite.'

There was an enormous gulf, even wider than today's, between the employed and the unemployed. Those who did have work, about seventy per cent of the workforce, were reasonably prosperous because prices were low and stable. A pocket watch advertised for ten shillings (one dollar) in 1930 was still ten shillings in 1939.

In decimal currency equivalents, a man felt reasonably secure on ten to twelve dollars a week, very comfortable on twenty, wealthy on fifty. He could dress himself presentably, including shoes, hat, underclothes, shirt, socks, suit, and tie, for $12. He could buy a good home for less than $1000, on 3½% interest, and furnish it completely for about $400. He fed his family on such prices as a loaf for five cents, milk for three cents a pint, sugar for three cents a pound and butter for ten cents.

A clerk or shop assistant still living in the parental home — as the vast majority of unmarried young men and women still did in those days — could maintain himself or herself very adequately on four to six dollars a week and even afford an annual holiday. (Hotel rooms were forty to seventy-five cents a night: a twelve-day cruise to Fiji cost $26.) A young man could give his girl an enjoyable night out for a dollar.

Despite the number of 'down-and-outs', and the bands of men roaming the country in search of work, it was a very orderly society. Public violence was rare, and even the infuriated spectators at the bodyline Tests restricted themselves to verbal abuse. The parents and teachers of children drilled them in a social code based on respect for women and obedience to the law. The casual bashing, raping, vandalism, and mindless brutality of modern society were virtually unknown. Petty crime was minimal, and many people hardly bothered to lock up their cars and homes. Of course there were crime and violence but on a smaller scale than today — perhaps because the punishments were much more severe.

It was not only a more stable but also a more static society. Less than one person in ten owned a private motor car, and few travelled very far. The summer holiday to a beach resort was an annual adventure.

Australian sporting achievements were a kind of antidote to economic gloom. Don Bradman the cricketer topped a long list of 1930s sporting heroes: Hubert Opperman in cycling; Norman von Nida and Jim Ferrier in golf; Walter Lindrum in billiards; Jack Crawford and Harry Hopman in tennis; Bobby Pearce in sculling; Claire Dennis in swimming. They all helped to reassure Australians as to their basic national virtues, and set healthy examples for the young.

Culturally, Australia made slower but significant progress. Charles Chauvel headed a flourishing movie industry. The Australian Broadcasting Commission, founded in 1932, provided high-quality music and entertainment for all who cared to listen. Australian publishing produced many excellent journals and magazines, far more than today, at prices from two to ten cents a copy. Australian writers, artists, and performers made names for themselves — even if, like Eileen Joyce and Robert Helpmann, they had to go overseas to do so.

Entertainment was cheap and plentiful. Live entertainment, in the form of plays, musical comedies, vaudeville, and light orchestras, was still in full swing. Countless young couples spent 'Saturday night at the Palais' to dance to the bands of Jim Davidson and other band leaders. Commercial radio took music, comedy, and romantic or dramatic plays and serials into suburban homes. And the 1930s comprised the great glamour era of Hollywood. Every suburb had its movie theatre: every city had a number of splendid 'picture palaces' such as the State in Sydney and Hoyts in Melbourne. 'Going to the pictures' was part of the pattern of life, with some families booking the same seats in the same theatres every Saturday night.

The strictly moral heroes and heroines of Hollywood epics confirmed that all would come right in the end. The talkies Americanised the language with such phrases as 'Oh yeah? Sez you? Okay, chief', and set a standard of sophistication and worldliness to be emulated by a million dreamers in the dark theatres. Young men modelled themselves on the ruggedness of Brian Donlevy, the romantic flair of Clark Gable, the suavity of Frederick March, the manly sincerity of Gary Cooper and Cary Grant. Young women glimpsed a new world of romance through the screen affairs of Kay Francis, Katherine Hepburn and Irene Dunne. Most people loved the songs of Nelson Eddy and Jeanette MacDonald, the crooning of Bing Crosby, the dancing of Fred Astaire and Ginger Rogers, the great singing and dancing spectaculars of Hollywood. The 1930s products of the 'dream factory' have been criticised as being artificial, but they opened new horizons for countless restricted lives and buttressed the old beliefs that faith, honour, courage, morality are the proper attributes of men and women.

The depression slowly faded into history — but not out of the minds of those scarred by its experiences. The price of wool rose (with Japan becoming a steady customer) and trade in strategic metals flourished. Brewery profits rose steeply as men returned to work.

There was a sudden new wave of technological progress. The British Broadcasting Corporation began TV broadcasts in 1936. British railway trains surpassed 100 mph. Cars took on a new look with the fashionable 'streamlining' that appeared on many artefacts from ashtrays to suburban homes. Aviation took giant steps as flyers like Amy Johnson, Jim Mollison, Jean Batten and Nancy Bird set new records. A flying-boat service from Southampton to Sydney opened in 1937 and took only ten days for the trip, reducing to five in 1939. Commercial aviation became a viable proposition and several airlines flew scheduled services within Australia.

Fashions in clothes, art, architecture, furniture, and general design continued the steady trend away from the solid and traditional. Women's underclothes were described as 'mere scraps of elegance'. Men began to wear shirts that opened down the front instead of being pulled over the head, with collars attached instead of having to be fastened on with collar studs, and single instead of double cuffs. Beach pyjamas were modish for women, some wore slacks, and a daring few donned swimsuits without skirts or even two-piece costumes. Men took to swimming trunks instead of full-length swimsuits. New artificial fabrics such as rayon made their appearance. The artistic trends of surrealism and cubism were reflected in fabric designs, furniture, and architecture. One had to be 'modern' to be fashionable, but the old traditions still underpinned society. Divorce was still an expensive and complex procedure, most women expected to become housewives, and such words as pornography, abortion, and homosexuality rarely entered conversations between the sexes.

The affair of Mrs Wally Simpson and King Edward VIII seemed to deal a shocking blow to the traditions, but they quickly recovered. Edward, who had been so enormously popular as Prince of Wales, seemed unable to shed his 'playboy' image when he succeeded his father on the throne, and rumours of his association with an American divorcee began to spread during the summer of 1936. By autumn they were being openly discussed. The Archbishop of Canterbury and Prime Minister Stanley Baldwin told Edward that the idea of a twice-divorced woman reigning as Queen of England was unthinkable, and Edward replied that he could not bear the weight of the crown without the help of 'the woman I love'. He abdicated in favour of his brother, who as King George VI was to become one of the best-loved sovereigns of the United Kingdom.

The last four years of the 1930s were a kind of pale preview of the affluent society of the 1960s. Employment opportunities increased every year. Goods and services were cheaper, more profuse, and more widely distributed than ever before. The inventiveness and industrial might of the Western world seemed to offer new horizons for the ordinary man.

True, there was a civil war in Spain, Japan had invaded China, Italy had annexed Ethiopia and the Jews and Arabs were fighting it out in Palestine, but the British Empire held firm and the politicians made reassuring noises. David Lloyd George of Britain said in 1936 'Germany has no desire to invade her neighbours.' S. H. Challis, professor of history in Sydney University, interviewed Hitler in the same year and compared him with Savonarola, 'but with much more humanity and infinitely more compassion for the mortals around him'. And in 1938 Neville Chamberlain proclaimed 'Peace in our time'.

By 1939, everyone knew that the return to world prosperity was destined for an inevitable end. Nobody could guess how cataclysmic that end would be.

A Don Bradman innings always had enormous drawing power, as demonstrated by this photograph taken during the 1930s. When he left New South Wales for South Australia, gate receipts at the Sydney Cricket Ground fell away disastrously

SCOREBOARD 1937

The 1935-36 and 1936-37 seasons in Australia enabled Don Bradman to accumulate another series of records. They included:

* The highest score ever made in matches between South Australia and Queensland: his 233 in December 1935.
* The highest score ever made against Victoria: his 357 in January 1936.
* The highest score ever made for South Australia and the highest on the Adelaide Oval: his 369 against Tasmania. In the same match he reached 300 in the record time for Australian batsmen in Australia: three hours thirty-three minutes.
* In the second Test of the 1936-37 series, he passed Clem Hill's record aggregate of 2660 in Australia v. England Tests, in his thirty-fourth Test innings against Hill's seventy-sixth.
* His score of 270 in the third Test is still the highest 'captain's innings' by any Australian captain against England in Australia.
* In the fourth Test, he completed his season's 1000 runs on 2 February 1937: nineteen days earlier than the previous best, by Clem Hill. In the same match, he exceeded by 82 the previous highest total of runs ever scored in Australia: Clem Hill's 11 129. Hill scored this aggregate in 233 innings: Bradman in 135.
* Also in the fourth Test, his 212 was the highest yet made in a Test v. England at Adelaide. His score included the seventeenth Test century in his career, one more than the previous best.
* His two double centuries in the Test series made him the only batsman to make more than one double century in Tests against England in Australia.
* His aggregate of 1552 for the 1936-37 season is a record for any Australian season by a South Australian batsman; his average of 90.00 was a record for Australia-England Tests played in Australia; and his Test aggregate of 810 was the highest by any Australian in any Test series in Australia.

13

A CASUALTY OF CRICKET

The twelve months from March 1937 to March 1938 were among the busiest and happiest of Bradman's life. The economy was more buoyant than it had been since 1929; Harry Hodgetts' business was booming; and Bradman was becoming adept in the fast-moving complexities of his new profession. He whittled steadily away at his golf handicap in the winter and he became interested in a new game, squash, which was not widely played in Australia in those days. He found its 'concentrated exercise' to be a good way in which to keep in trim for cricket and an antidote for the tensions of office life. The tennis star Harry Hopman advised him not to play squash for more than thirty minutes at a time, but he took to the game so enthusiastically that in the winter of 1939 he beat the Davis Cup player Don Turnbull in the final of the South Australian championship. He found the hour-long tussle to be more exhausting than a full day's cricket, and he never played competitive squash again.

At his home in Kensington Park he enjoyed the domesticity which has been the sheet anchor of his life: gardening; playing the piano and listening to music; entertaining friends; keeping dogs, cats and canaries; playing billiards; going to concerts and the theatre; tackling household jobs and chores like any other city businessman with a home in the suburbs.

However, unlike other businessmen, he was not allowed to live in contented obscurity for very long. The outside world intruded when the London *News of the World* made him a tempting offer to write his life story for serialisation during the 1938 Australian tour of England. Bradman's literary agent worked out a contract for serialisation and book publication — with a strict proviso that he should not write anything about the 1938 Tests while they were being played — and the newspaper sent the journalist William Pollock to Australia to help him with the book.

But Bradman has never needed much help in writing clearly and cogently. His journalistic and radio experience with the *Sun* and 2UE had taught him to assemble his thoughts quickly and concisely, and he had written an instructional book, *How To Play Cricket*, in 1935. When Pollock arrived, Bradman had already written most of the new book. It was a great success in serial form, and a bestseller when it was published as *My Cricketing Life* in July 1938.

The 1937–38 cricket season in Australia was free from the hectic conflicts of a Test series, and Bradman could enjoy cricket which did not attract the same kind of fierce publicity. He played a number of first-grade matches and twelve first-class matches. The first of these, South Australia v. New Zealanders at Adelaide, found him far from his best form. He was caught for a mere eleven.

In the next first-class match he led an eleven against V. Y. Richardson's Eleven, in a Testimonial Match for Vic Richardson and Clarrie Grimmett. The two South Australian cricketers shared the gate money and donations. Grimmett, perhaps in somewhat unforgiving mood after his omission from the previous season's Tests, was in top form.

Bradman, having been pegged down for a while, jumped out to drive a well-flighted ball but hit over the top of it and was bowled.

The elated Grimmett rushed over to Richardson in the expectation of compliments, but Richardson replied in some such words as 'You bloody fool — by bowling Bradman you've probably cost us a thousand quid in gate money!'

Apart from this minor disaster, the match was badly interrupted by rain. Nevertheless, Bradman's boss Harry Hodgetts, who was chairman of the organising committee, produced a final balance sheet which enabled each player to receive a cheque for some £1028.

A comparison with the retail index shows that this sum would be worth the equivalent of more than $27 000 apiece in 1983 currency, so Richardson and Grimmett were handsomely rewarded for their contribution to cricket.

In Shield cricket, Queensland must have dreaded the leisurely stroll of Don Bradman out to the wicket, presaging yet another disaster for the Sunshine State. When Queensland met South Australia at Adelaide in December 1937, Bradman made yet another huge score off Queensland's bowlers. In six hours four minutes he totalled 246 in his first innings: the highest ever made in matches between the two States. South Australia won by eight wickets, and in the next encounter, at Brisbane in January, Bradman compiled two more centuries (107 and 113). But rain saved Queensland and the match was drawn.

South Australia drew one more match in the Shield contests, lost two, and won another. New South Wales won the Shield, but Bradman had set three more records. His aggregate of 983, and four centuries in a season, were records for South Australia. With another century, his 101 against Western Australia (which did not play in the Sheffield Shield series in those days) he broke Clem Hill's 1897–98 record of four centuries in a season for South Australia.

Bradman had had a double responsibility during the season: those of captain of South Australia and selector for Australia. The latter was perhaps the most arduous, and it certainly attracted the most publicity. Bradman and his fellow selectors, 'Chappie' Dwyer and Bill Johnson, could agree without difficulty on some of the sixteen players to go to England in 1938, but others caused much anxious thought.

It was a particularly difficult side to pick. Australia was almost devoid of fast bowlers except Ernie McCormick of Victoria, who had extreme pace but lacked stamina and a robust physique. Harold Cotton of South Australia was second to him in speed; but Cotton's action had caused some eyebrows to be raised, so he could hardly be considered.

BRADMAN THE GOLFER

Sir Donald Bradman began playing golf in the 1920s when he was living and working in Sydney, and he gradually became more and more interested in the game. Lady Bradman took up the game before her marriage, and they often played together until recent years, when open heart surgery ended Lady Bradman's golfing days. Sir Donald still enjoys his golf on South Australian courses.

One of Sir Donald's scrapbooks contains a cutting from an unnamed Australian newspaper, probably printed in 1936. The journalist wrote: 'Don Bradman's rapid rise as a golfer in South Australia demonstrates that natural ability is worth years of practice. In a few months Don has accomplished what would-be golfers have been striving after

Bradman's 'eagle eyes' follow a golf ball with the same intense concentration that he devoted to cricket

for years. He has won his club championship and has reduced his handicap from 14 to 5 in a few weeks. South Australian admirers think they have a future golf champion in Bradman. He began to take the game seriously only this season, when he joined the Mount Osmond country club. In the final of the club championship a few weeks ago, he went round the somewhat tricky course in 75 . . . the match was followed by a gallery of 250. It was flattering but rather staggering to Jones, Bradman's opponent, to receive so much public attention, and under the nervous strain his game suffered. Bradman, however, accustomed as he is to huge cricket crowds, was not affected in the slightest degree. He walked jauntily down the fair-

ways, carrying his tee between his teeth, never played better, and returned his best card for the season.

'. . . Bradman has no regard for the theory of orthodox golf style. He makes use of cricketing positions. He plays some of his golf shots with his left foot well forward, as if shaping up for a powerful drive to the boundary.

'His putts, which are one of the strongest features of his game, are played from a cricketing stance.'

Sir Donald probably played his best golf in about 1960–62, when he reduced his handicap to scratch and became a pennant player. He still retains the cards of four creditable club sub-par rounds, which read as follows:

CLUB	THE THEN PAR	SIR DONALD'S SCORE
KOOYUNGA (S.A.)	73	69
PENINSULA (Vic.)	73	69
VICTORIA (Vic.)	73	71
KINGSTON HEATH (Vic.)	74	70

Conversely, the country was overloaded with wrist spinners, who are usually more effective in Australia than in England. Of these, O'Reilly was without peer and had to be the spearhead. Next in line were Fleetwood-Smith, then twenty-seven, the young left-hand googly sensation from Victoria whose bowling of Hammond at Adelaide in 1937 had almost certainly decided the fate of that test; and Frank Ward, twenty-nine, a splendid orthodox leg-spinner who had moved from New South Wales to South Australia to further his cricket career and had forced his way into the Tests in 1936–37.

And then there was Clarrie Grimmett, who had possibly been Australia's greatest leg-spinner apart from O'Reilly. But he was forty-five, a poor batsman, and a liability in the field.

Six years earlier, he had been a complete failure against the M.C.C. side in Australia. For his State, seven wickets cost 55 runs apiece. In the first three Tests, his miserable bag of five wickets cost 65 runs apiece and demanded the unacceptable total of twenty-nine overs per wicket. His Test batting average was only 7, so it is no wonder that the Test selectors dropped him.

Because of unwarranted criticism of Bradman in later years over his omission of Grimmett in 1938, it is important to make the point that Bradman was not a member of the selection committee which dropped Grimmett from the 1932–33 Test team. Bradman played no part in those selections.

He was, of course, on the committee in 1936–37, when Grimmett was not considered to be good enough for any of the Tests. Grimmett did bowl against the M.C.C. in Adelaide, but his two wickets cost 44 runs apiece. Moreover, the erratic young genius Fleetwood-Smith had already established himself as second only to O'Reilly among Australian spinners.

'Chuck' Fleetwood-Smith burst into the limelight in the 1934–35 season, by taking a record 60 Sheffield Shield wickets for Victoria at the astounding strike rate of one wicket every four-and-a-half overs, and he was confounding the batsmen with his prodigious spin and often unpredictable bosey.

In addition to O'Reilly and Fleetwood-Smith, the selectors had to consider Ross Gregory of Victoria and Chipperfield of New South Wales, both fine all-rounders, and Sid Barnes, who had to be chosen for his batting ability. All three bowled useful leg breaks, and Chipperfield was then Australia's finest slip fieldsman.

White of New South Wales and Christ of Queensland were orthodox left-hand first-finger spinners, of the type usually successful in England.

Clearly there was a plethora of spin available but a lack of speed. Despite the gap left by the retirements of Woodfull and Ponsford, a normal array of competent batsmen could be sorted out.

The final knotty problem was whether Bert Oldfield, historically perhaps Australia's finest wicket-keeper up to that time, should be retained at the age of forty in preference to the young bloods Walker, Barnett, or Tallon. Youth prevailed, but in retrospect it was a mistake to have excluded Tallon.

An English listing of the sixteen Australians selected to tour England in 1938 — with the optimistic comment 'We have the men'

AUSTRALIA'S 16 YOUNG MEN

Here are the 16 Australians. Eight are paying their first visit to England for Tests. They are:

C. L. Badcock. Aged 23. They call him Bradman No. 2.

S. Barnes. Aged 21. Useful slow bowler; capable wicket-keeper.

F. Ward. Aged 29. Good bowler; can be very expensive.

A. L. Hassett. Aged 24. Good fieldsman; useful slow bowler; capable wicketkeeper.

J. H. Fingleton. Aged 29. If he survives the opening overs he wants a lot of getting out.

E. S. White. Aged 24. He is over 6ft. in height. Left-hand bowler.

E. L. McCormick. Aged 31. Probably Australia's fastest bowler; not much good with the bat.

M. G. Waite. Aged 27. A very good all-rounder; the sort of man any side likes to have.

Here are the other eight who have been here before:

Don Bradman. Aged 29. Captain. Still holds run-getting record.

S. J. McCabe. Aged 28. Vice-captain. His average in 20 Tests is 49.03.

B. A. Barnett. Aged 29. Left-handed bat; first choice as wicketkeeper.

L. O'B. Fleetwood-Smith. Aged 29. Good left-hand slow bowler when in form. If he isn't, he is very expensive.

W. A. Brown. Aged 27. Graceful, straight-bladed, right-handed opening bat.

A. G. Chipperfield. Aged 32. Magnificent first slip; a fighting bat; slow leg-break bowler.

C. W. Walker. Aged 29. Wicketkeeper; useful defensive bat. Here in 1930.

W. J. O'Reilly. Aged 32. One of the best of the Australian bowlers; robs batsmen of all initiative; right-hand spinner.

But, as " Plum " Warner said recently, we have the men to beat them.

The unlucky ones were probably Keith Rigg, a splendid opening bat from Victoria, and Ross Gregory. Rigg may have lost out to Fingleton because of the latter's value to O'Reilly as a close-in fieldsman, while Chipperfield's specialist slip fielding probably gave him a hair's-breadth decision over Gregory.

Regrettably, neither Rigg nor Gregory ever made an Australian side to England. The latter would almost certainly have done so if he had not lost his life in the second world war.

In the end the selectors chose a team of comparatively young men, with an average age of twenty-eight. O'Reilly and Chipperfield, both thirty-two, were the oldest. Bradman was then twenty-nine. Eight had never been overseas, and four of these were new recruits to the Test arena.

The expected storm broke with such comments as Ponsford's 'sheer lunacy' over the dropping of Grimmett, and Joe Darling's blast against the selectors Dwyer and Johnson. He said they had 'never played first class cricket and did not understand English conditions', and that it was time for the public to 'force the Board to do things in the best interests of cricket'.

Many of those who disapproved of the final selection, including some newspapers, blamed Bradman for what they thought was wrong. They called it 'Bradman's Team', although A. G. Moyes protested in print that Dwyer and Johnson had 'been in the game too long for anyone to think, with justice, that they would be content to see any side announced, unless, in their opinion, it could not be improved . . . We may not agree with the chosen. I, for one, do not; but after all it is more than likely that the selectors are right, and we wrong.'

This controversial start made it inevitable that, if Bradman's men failed to retain the Ashes, he would be the target for most of the blame. He did not allow this knowledge to affect his style as captain of Australia's nineteenth touring team.

They assembled at Melbourne on 25 February 1938 for the start of a particularly busy tour. They would be away from home for eight-and-a-half months, play forty fixtures, and travel a total of 44 319 kilometres including 9280 kilometres in Britain and Ireland. They would make six sea passages, including the crossing to Ireland and back, and forty-five railway journeys of lengths varying from two hours to three days. One compensation was that the new Imperial Airways flying-boat service from Sydney to Southampton would deliver their home mail much faster than ever before. They would receive it in a mere twelve days.

The tourists played the customary preliminary matches in Tasmania and Western Australia, providing Bradman with two more centuries, and boarded the *Orontes* at Fremantle. The manager was W. H. (Bill) Jeanes, the Adelaide-based secretary of the Board of Control, making his first managerial tour in order to gain first-hand knowledge of the triumphs, trials and tribulations of a touring team. The camp followers included Bradman's old friends 'Johnnie' Moyes as the *Sun* representative, and Dr Roland Pope, the wealthy self-appointed medical officer and generous benefactor of Australian cricket teams.

Pope is a remarkable but now almost forgotten figure in Australian cricket. He sailed with a number of touring teams, with a complete medical kit plus many other useful or comforting items for the benefit

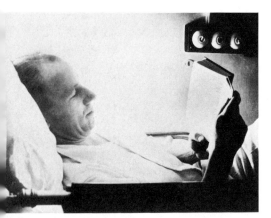

Don Bradman resting in his bunk aboard the liner taking him to England in March 1938

of the cricketers. In Sydney he used to send boxes of fruit to the dressing room for the players' refreshment, and whether at home or abroad he was always ready to aid cricketers who sought his help or advice.

Sir Donald Bradman recalls that Dr Pope gave him his first taste of alcohol. When the ship reached Colombo en route to England on the 1934 tour, Bradman felt so depressed and languid that he did not want to go ashore, but Pope felt he should do so. In a kindly-meant gesture he insisted: 'Come along ashore with me — I'm going to give you a drink.' Bradman was willing to try anything by that time, but Dr Pope's prescription made no difference to his condition.

The mental and physical exertions of preparing for his first tour as captain left Bradman very tired when the ship sailed, and he was suffering from 'a dose of 'flu'. He was glad to rest and recuperate and ponder his strategy for England, and he did not play in the usual one-day match at Colombo.

He and all the others were in good form when the ship touched at Naples, where they seized the opportunity to visit the ruins of Pompeii. Jeanes, suffering from lumbago, had to limp along with a walking stick, and McCormick raised a laugh by exclaiming 'Bill, old boy, I can hardly tell you from the ruins!'

The sights of Naples struck a grimmer note. The tourists counted 116 warships of various classes at anchor in the bay, and saw Italian marines drilling on the waterfront. In a private letter to his mentor Harry Hodgetts, Bradman commented on the warships and remarked prophetically: 'I guess they were not built to rust.' A deadlier conflict than Test cricket lay just over the horizon.

At Gibraltar, the team suffered their first casualty. Sid Barnes, hurrying onto the wet deck to see the sights as the *Orontes* made an early-morning landfall, slipped and hurt his wrist. Pope and the ship's surgeon thought it was a bad sprain, but X-rays in England revealed a nasty scaphoid fracture. Jeanes cabled the Board of Control for a replacement to be flown to England but his request was refused, and Barnes could not play until after the second Test. It was a bad blow to lose such a valuable player so early in the tour.

Bradman had an unusual new experience in Gibraltar. The Governor, General Sir Charles Harington, arranged a reception ceremony for the Australians and they attended a march-past of the King's Liverpool Regiment, then in garrison at the Rock. Sir Charles asked Bradman to take the salute with him at the march-past. Bradman, whose sole knowledge of military etiquette had been gained in the Bowral School Cadet Corps, stood beside the Governor and saluted bareheaded. Sir Charles said: 'Although I was taking the salute, not one man looked at me', and the newspapers later gave Bradman a gentle reprimand for saluting bareheaded.

The English press and public gave the tourists a great welcome. The arrival of Don Bradman in his first overseas Test captaincy intensified the usual interest, and the newspapers complimented him on his 'debonair courtesy' which they said was very different from the attitude of some previous captains. They published potted biographies of Bradman, predictions as to how he would or would not succeed in his captaincy, and various fanciful tales. A large crowd, admitted for a shilling a head, watched the Australians practising at Lord's, and the

Don Bradman Takes The Salute

AUSTRALIA'S CRICKET CAPTAIN shared in the salute taken by General Sir Charles Harington when troops marched past after a church parade at Gibraltar.

English newspapers commented that Bradman should not have saluted hatless when he stood with the military commander of Gibraltar at a march-past of the garrison

Part of a page of the 1938 touring contract signed by the Australian cricketers, showing clauses 7 and 8 which obliged them to prevent their wives, children, or any members of their families from accompanying the tour. The cricketers had to sign the contract or they would not go on the tour, but newspapers and others criticised these clauses as being legally unenforceable

newspapers were delighted when a bowler took Bradman's wicket with his first ball.

During the first week in London, Bradman called a meeting of his team to discuss clauses 7 and 8 in their seven-page touring contract. The players had to sign this document or they did not go. Under these clauses, the players had covenanted not to be accompanied by their wives, any members of their families, or any children under their legal control, and not to allow their wives or children 'to be in England or elsewhere outside Australia where the team may be from time to time touring'.

7.   The Players do and each of them doth hereby jointly and severally covenant with the Chairman and the Board that he will not be accompanied on the said tour or any part thereof by his wife or any member of his family or any relative.

8.   The Players do and each of them doth hereby jointly and severally covenant with theChairman and the Board that during the period of the said Tour of the Team heither his wife nor any of his children under his legal control will be inEngland or elsewhere outside Austrralia where the Team from time to time may be touring.

Many newspapers in Britain and Australia likened the Board of Control to Hitler and Mussolini for their strict contract clauses limiting many of the activities of the Australian players

HITLER NEVER THOUGHT OF THAT

CONSCIENCE-STRICKEN TEST-PLAYER WRITES HOME TO HIS WIFE AND CHILDREN AND FEELS SURE HE HAS TRANSGRESSED

THE THIRTY-THREE COMMANDMENTS
THOU SHALT NOT —
THOU SHALT NOT —
THOU SHALT NOT —
THOU SHALT NOT —
THOU SHALT NOT —
THOU SHALT NOT —

BOARD CONTROL
I CAUGHT YER!

AS ONE WHO ON A LONELY ROAD DOTH WALK IN FEAR & DREAD FOR WELL HE KNOWS A FRIGHTFUL FIEND DOTH CLOSE BEHIND HIM TREAD

They were peculiar clauses and perhaps not legally enforceable, because they implied that a player could force his wife and all his relations to stay out of the British Isles for six months. But Bradman had no intention of transgressing these clauses. He simply wanted to ask the Board whether they would make the same concession for him as they had done for Woodfull in 1934, and allow his wife to join him in London at the end of the tour and sail home with him.

Bill Jeanes and the players had no objection to the idea. The married ones did not ask for the same privilege, but they did ask that their wives be allowed to meet them in Colombo on the voyage home. Any such travel, including that of Mrs Bradman, would be at the players' own expense.

Jeanes set out these requests in a letter to the Board, and the team began the English tour in the hope that the privilege would be granted.

For the third time in succession, Bradman opened a tour of England with a double century at Worcester. He started very carefully when he went in at 9 for one, and took 105 minutes to score 37 before lunch, but after that he was in dynamic form and he totalled 258 in four hours fifty-three minutes.

Ernie McCormick made a strange start to his first tour. The umpire

no-balled him nineteen times in his first three overs for 'jumping over the line'. He tried again and again to correct himself but seemed unable to rectify the trouble. Bradman wrote in *Farewell to Cricket*: 'At one stage he was marking out his run afresh, and I might add that he ran about 25 yards. By the time he got to the 19th step, a spectator near the sight board called out: "Quick, shut the gate — he'll be out on the road."' McCormick never really recovered from this poor start, and his touring performance was disappointing.

With occasional lapses, Bradman continued on a steady course of run-scoring which boded ill for England's Test chances but delighted every cricket lover of both nations. He attracted such huge crowds that William Pollock wrote in the *Daily Express*: 'Lord's is too small for a Bradman Day. London needs a new cricket ground. Lord's wasn't big enough on Saturday for all those who wanted to see the Australians play the M.C.C. . . . it is a fair thing to say that, what with members and whatnot, 30 000 were there.'

In the matches preceding the first Test he played one innings in each match and scored 58 against Oxford University, 137 against Cambridge University, 278 against the M.C.C., 143 against Surrey and 145 against Hampshire. His failures were 2 against Northamptonshire and 35 in two innings against Middlesex, on a wet wicket. But by the end of May his tally of runs exceeded 1000 (1056 to be exact), this being the second time he had achieved the feat in three tours. It is a notable landmark, featured in Wisden. No other player has done it

Stan McCabe (left) and Don Bradman lay a wreath on the Cenotaph, the London memorial to British troops who fell in the first world war, soon after their arrival in London in April 1938

more than once, even though thousands of English batsmen have had perhaps twenty or more seasons in which to attempt it.

The tour, which was of course to be the last before the second world war, developed into a triumphal progress for Bradman and his men. One newspaper acclaimed them as 'The Happiest Team That Ever Toured'. In Northampton, the Dagenham Girl Pipers met them at the railway station and piped them to their hotel to the tune of 'The Bluebells of Scotland'. The newspapers filled their pages with cartoons and jocular articles on the impossibility of 'Getting Don Out'. It was all a pleasant contrast to the grimmer events shaping up in Europe.

Bradman himself proved the perfect ambassador for Australian cricket. In ten years he had developed from 'the country colt' into a man who could mingle confidently in any company, reply to public

Whenever Don Bradman walked along the streets of an English city, he was likely to attract a retinue of small boys seeking his autograph or basking in his reflected glory

speeches at glittering receptions, and show the same courtesy to crowds of urchins seeking his autograph as he did to the cricketing aristocracy at Lord's. The 'bronzed little Aussie' who once shrank from an adoring crowd had learned how to handle massive publicity with grace and good humour.

The newspapers sought vainly for any hint of controversy but they seemed to find it during the match against Surrey, when he did not enforce the follow-on; and in that against Middlesex when he declared twenty-one minutes before the close. But in the Surrey match he was trying to ease the pressure on some of his best players, who were suffering from various minor ailments and injuries, and in the Middlesex affair he wanted to give the English batsman Bill Edrich a chance to complete his 1000 runs before the end of May: a magnanimous gesture on Bradman's part. The crowd booed Bradman when he declared, but applauded when they understood the reason and then cheered each of Edrich's ten runs as he completed his thousand.

Some of the tourists were feeling the strain. One sportswriter said: 'These Australians may look tough, but they are not used to daily cricket.' Bradman's back was troubling him; O'Reilly also had a strained back; McCabe had endured bouts of neuritis; Fleetwood-Smith, McCormick and Waite had minor injuries.

The strain was heaviest on Bradman and it bore down from many directions. He could 'rest' one of his players, but county secretaries often sought an advance assurance that he would play because, if he did not, the gate receipts would shrink alarmingly. As captain, he had to maintain an attitude of cheerful confidence towards press, public and players. He received an enormous stack of mail, and he answered most of the letters personally. His typewriter clattered late at night in his hotel room. At every reception, luncheon or dinner he had to make a speech, which he always prepared with meticulous care. He was besieged with requests to write articles, judge beauty contests, open fetes and dog shows, and appear at every imaginable kind of public function. In the midst of all these requests, most of which he had of course to decline diplomatically, he had to keep his mind clear for the supreme demand of the Tests.

The first Test, at Nottingham, opened on 10 June. Obviously it could not be revealed at the time, but it can now, that the selection of Australia's team for the Nottingham Test did not meet with Bradman's approval. He wanted to use only one slow spinner apart from O'Reilly, on the grounds that if the English batsmen got set he would have a badly balanced attack and be unable to contain them. Bradman's choice was O'Reilly and Fleetwood-Smith, but his colleagues insisted on adding Ward because, in the match against Essex, he had taken seven for 51 and four for 26. Their insistence had the disastrous result which Bradman had feared.

Predictably, one journalist wrote after the match that Bradman must accept the blame for Australia's bad selection because, as captain, his views would certainly have prevailed. This is the type of uninformed accusation that a captain-selector has to live with.

Wally Hammond won the toss and led his team to a magnificent first innings score of 658 before he declared at eight. It was the biggest score ever made in a Test by England against Australia up to that time. When the tourists batted, Brown, Fingleton and Bradman fell for a

Above: Don Bradman's expression seems to show that he's thinking 'What — another photographer!' as he strides along a street in London

Right: Where did that one go? Answer: To the boundary. Bradman pulls a ball from G. Evans to the leg boundary in the Oxford University match, 3–6 May 1938

collective 138, and one newspaper used 'Second Coming' type to blare 'AUSTRALIA CRASHING!' The Kentish bowler Doug Wright had puzzled Bradman with his fast leg spinners, and Ames eventually caught him, at 51, off a ball from Reg Sinfield.

Stan McCabe saved Australia from disaster with an innings which Cardus described as 'One of the greatest innings ever seen anywhere in any period of the game's history'. Bradman wrote later: 'McCabe scored 232 out of 300. Towards the end I could scarcely watch the play. My eyes were filled as I drank in the glory of his shots.'

He called out to some players at the rear of the dressing room: 'Come and watch this. You'll never see anything like it again.'

McCabe and Fleetwood-Smith added 77 runs in twenty-eight minutes for the last wicket, and McCabe scored 72 of them. Sir Donald Bradman still says it was the finest batting he has ever seen. When he congratulated McCabe after the innings he paid him the supreme compliment of saying: 'I wish I could play as well as that.'

Australia ended the innings with 411, and had nothing left to play for except a draw. With two-and-a-half days to go, Bradman showed a remarkable new facet of his batting expertise. Those who had come to see his 'whirlwind batting' and 'flashing blade' looked for them in vain. Sportswriters called him 'Bradman the Snail' and 'Bradman the Bore' as he refused to be drawn into any daring strokes which might lose him his wicket. The crowd barracked his slow batting — and that of Fingleton, Brown and McCabe — but he knew exactly what he was doing. McCabe's glorious first innings had given him an opportunity which, as captain, he was not going to miss.

His century, the slowest of his career, took four hours thirteen minutes without ever giving a chance to the bowlers or fieldsmen. After that he played steadily on for a total of six hours fifteen minutes and 144 not out, when he declared fifteen minutes before the scheduled end of play. He limped from the field with his mission completed.

Moyes cabled the *Sun* that it had been a 'magnificent example of leadership', in which Bradman had subdued his natural propensity to strike out at the bowling for the sake of Australia. Moyes wrote: 'The tenseness of the occasion was reflected in Bradman's grimness and pallor. Usually he is capable of laughter, even in a Test, but . . . his whole attitude was a challenge to England to get him out.' Jack Hobbs wrote that Bradman's careful play had been 'a compliment to English bowlers'.

The match had seen the introduction to Test cricket on the English side of Len Hutton, Bill Edrich and Denis Compton: three batsmen who were destined to play an enormous part in future Test history. For the first time in a Test match, four individual hundreds were registered in one innings.

Bradman's forecast about his unbalanced bowling attack was all too starkly revealed by the massacre handed out to his slow spinners who, under the circumstances, he could not protect. It was only Bradman and Brown's superb defensive play, on the final day, which saved his team from defeat.

Only a day later, he relaxed with a 'gay innings' against The Gentlemen of England at Lord's, and scored 104 in 114 minutes. Against Lancashire, on 18–21 June, he made only 12 in his first innings but 101, his first century at Old Trafford, in the second. He had been very concerned by an unnecessarily slow and negative partnership between Fingleton and Brown, which caused the spectators much displeasure. Determined to make his feelings known to the players, he made his 101 not out in seventy-three minutes, the fastest hundred of the season up to that date.

The second Test opened at Lord's on 24 June, with London crammed with sports fans who had come to see either the Test or the tennis at Wimbledon. The Australians were able to sample both, because an English firm had placed a television set in the dressing room. They could use the new electronic marvel to see something of one of the world's first telecasts of a tennis match.

Just before the second Test, at Lord's, there was another minor selection drama. On the day before the match, Fleetwood-Smith had to undergo an operation for an impacted wisdom tooth. Although not a terribly serious matter, it meant that the bowler was not really fit to take his place in the side. With this in mind, and having regard to what happened at Nottingham, Bradman pressed for his slow spinner at Lord's to be Frank Ward. However, his colleagues wanted Fleetwood-Smith to play and Bradman had to submit to their decision. The left-hander could only show two wickets for 169 runs in the Lord's match, and Bradman, as captain, once more had to take the blame on his own shoulders and without comment.

To begin with, the second Test seemed almost a duplicate of the first. Hammond won the toss, England made a first innings total of 494 — based largely on a magnificent 240 by Hammond — and Verity dismissed Bradman for 18. He attempted to cut a ball outside the off stump, but it kept low and he dragged it onto his wicket.

The *Daily Sketch* triumphed: 'WE CAN'T LOSE NOW!' But Bill Brown held the fort by defending his wicket from the first to the last ball of the innings and carrying his bat for 206. Australia totalled 422.

England's second innings opened amid such excitement that it was hard to keep the spectators off the playing area. McCormick, who had taken four wickets in the first innings, showed he had at last struck form by taking three more, and catching Len Hutton off O'Reilly. English wickets fell fast, and when they had lost seven for 142 Bradman felt that Australia had a chance. But young Denis Compton, playing in only his second Test against Australia, stopped the rot. Hammond declared at 3.20 p.m. on the final day, at eight for 242.

Bradman's men once more had the seemingly hopeless task of making up a huge deficit. The only serious question was whether England could dismiss the Australians in the remaining 165 minutes.

Bradman saved the day again, with tactics totally different from those he used at Nottingham. He went in at 8 for one, forty-two minutes before the tea interval, and scored 38 before tea. At 18 he passed Jack Hobbs's aggregate of 3636 in Tests between England and Australia. He reached his century, including fifteen fours, in 144 minutes off 131 balls, and he was 102 not out when stumps were drawn.

His 102 provided exactly half the Australian total of 204 in the second innings, and secured another drawn game. His score also brought his aggregate for five consecutive Tests in England to more than 1000 runs.

His efforts did not soften the hearts of the Australian Board of Control. Soon after the second Test, Bill Jeanes told him of their refusal of his request that Mrs Bradman be allowed to join him at the end of the tour. Their reason was that it would 'create an embarrassing precedent', even though they had themselves created such a precedent when they allowed Woodfull's wife to join him in London in 1934.

The English and Australian press pounced on this gem of controversy with raucous delight. The *Daily Mail* telephoned Jessie Bradman in Sydney, where she was staying with Mrs McCabe, and reported that 'there was no mistaking a note of indignation in her voice, despite her assurances that she bore the board "no ill feelings".' Journalists besieged Bradman, but he would say only that he was 'very, very disappointed'. He refused to expand on this comment, although some

reporters predicted he would 'defy the Board', and even that he might withdraw from the tour.

Moyes cabled the *Sun* that the other members of the team were indignant at the refusal, and that they had asked the Board, 'in strong terms', to reconsider their decision.

Moyes also claimed that the incident had brought a spate of English offers to Bradman. He said the Lancashire League would virtually allow Bradman to 'write his own ticket' if he joined them, and that a leading newspaper was prepared to pay Jessie Bradman's fare to England, pay any fine the Board might inflict on Bradman, and 'fight the Board in the courts' on the legality of clauses 7 and 8. Subsequent legal decisions show there is little doubt that the Board would have lost such a case.

Moyes listed other offers: one of £4000 sterling a year from a manufacturer of sports goods, two from newspapers for Bradman to write for them, and another — a kind of foreshadowing of World Series Cricket — for him to organise a private team to tour England.

Bradman refused to add fuel to the fire and would say no more except: 'I have made my request and had my answer. That's the end

English and Australian newspapers published many mocking cartoons against the Australian Board of Control when they heard about the Board's refusal to allow Jessie Bradman to join her husband in London on the conclusion of the 1938 tour

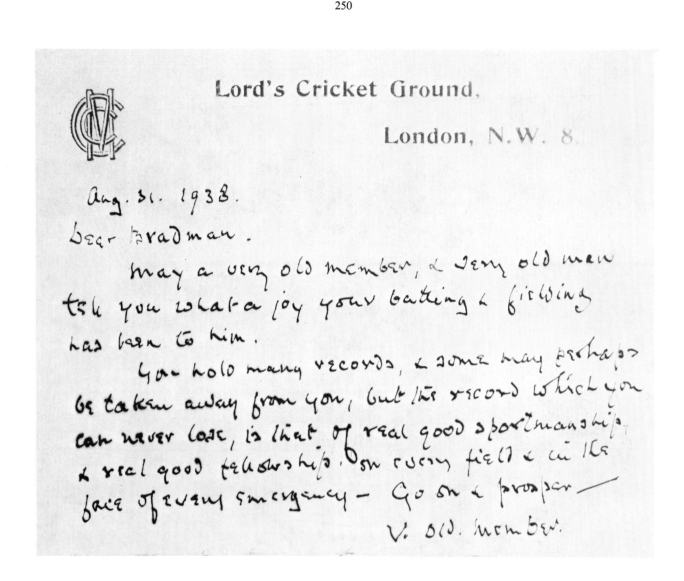

Lord's Cricket Ground,

London, N.W. 8

Aug. 31. 1938.

Dear Bradman.

May a very old member, & very old man ask you what a joy your batting & fielding has been to him.

You hold many records, & some may perhaps be taken away from you, but the record which you can never lose, is that of real good sportmanship, & real good fellowship. on every field & in the face of every emergency — Go on & prosper —

V. old. member.

A 'Very Old Member' of the M.C.C. wrote this note to Bradman in 1938 to applaud his good playing and good sportsmanship

of it.' But it was far from the end insofar as the press was concerned. It kept the story alive with everything from dignified comments in *The Times* to a *Reynolds News* article claiming that 'Don Bradman is not likely to play cricket in England after the present series of Test matches ... Bradman has lost part of his talent money — £150 per tour — on more than one occasion for kicking over the restrictive traces in which the Australian authorities place all cricketers playing under their auspices ... Mrs Bradman came to England in 1934 to nurse Don Bradman through a serious illness ... He is a partner in a firm of stockbrokers in Adelaide ... intimate friends believe he has always contemplated retiring from cricket in 1940.' Most of these comments were wrong, but Bradman was accustomed to journalistic inaccuracies and he still remained silent.

The newspapers varied their activities from simple abuse of the Board as 'Fascist dictators', 'sporting Hitlers', and 'Little Czars of Sport', to consultations with a Sydney barrister, who held that the controversial clauses were illegal because they were contrary to 'common policy'. A weird decision by the Australian Lawn Tennis Association, which allowed Mrs Harry Hopman to join her husband in New

York and play with him in mixed doubles provided that they did not sleep in the same hotel, set off a fresh clamour.

Bradman had no intention of breaking his contract — unfair though he deemed it to be — and publicly his attitude was above reproach. Privately, he was so upset by the Board's lack of sympathy and understanding of what he and his wife had endured for the sake of cricket that he seriously considered making an announcement that he would never play for Australia again after the 1938 tour.

He actually drafted an announcement to this effect and talked it over with Dr Rowley Pope, but the doctor's wise and friendly counsel persuaded him not to act on this impulse.

Bradman's team-mates, who understood the immense strain he was under, were intensely loyal to him, particularly at this time. Unknown to Bradman, they had a secret team meeting and forced Jeanes to cable the Board, virtually demanding that the request should be granted.

This union-like activity forced the Board to think again. The chairman called for another vote on the matter. By eight votes to five, the Board passed a face-saving resolution that any player's wife — including the manager's — could join her husband at the end of the tour.

The Board never explained why Woodfull, as an individual, was granted the concession which they at first withheld from Bradman.

At the end of the tour four wives took advantage of the privilege: Mrs Bradman, Mrs McCabe, Mrs Fleetwood-Smith and Mrs Jeanes.

The autocratic attitude of the Board in those days stands in sharp contrast to the present situation.

The fickle English weather had behaved reasonably well during the tour; but when the contestants met in Manchester for the third Test, they found the ground almost submerged and they had to abandon the match without a ball being bowled. The captains never even tossed a coin.

In Birmingham the Australians found a sodden pitch but Bradman won the toss and put Warwickshire in first, which gave the wicket a few hours to improve. But the wicket was still soft when Australia's

'Listening to the cricket' was a popular Australian pastime in the 1930s, when many Australians stayed up until the small hours to learn the fate of their Test team in England. This photograph shows Jessie Bradman and Don Bradman's employer, Harry Hodgetts, listening to a 1938 Test commentary over one of the large console radios popular in that era

turn came to bat. Bradman batted cautiously on the wet wicket but he still totalled 135.

The Australians reached Leeds on 21 July, with Test honours even and a crucial game ahead. The weather was threatening, but Bradman felt optimistic. Leeds was the site of two of his Test triumphs and historically the Headingley ground had been favourable to Australia.

His spirits dropped on the following day when Hammond won the

Cricketing weather in England, with a couple of optimistic spectators waiting for play to recommence. Don Bradman often had to play on English pitches badly affected by rain and still made impressive scores

toss and elected to bat first. The wicket seemed ideal for England, and
Bradman feared that they might again make an overwhelming first-
innings score. But 'Windmill' O'Reilly, as the English newspapers
called him, and Fleetwood-Smith, and McCormick despite his trouble-
some back and shoulder, raised Bradman's hopes again by dismissing
England for 223.

The Australians set themselves to chase this total, under a threaten-

ing sky that seemed about to deluge the pitch. The light became so bad that cricketers in the centre could see matches being lit in the grandstand, and pressmen complained that they could hardly see to write their copy. But Bradman believed his batsmen would score better in bad light on a dry pitch than in good light on a wet one, and he instructed them not to appeal.

He set the example and proved his theory with a magnificent innings of his own. Going in at 87 for two on the second morning, with the wicket moistened by some showers but the main deluge still stored in the clouds massed overhead, he batted confidently against Verity, Farnes, Bowes and Wright. After Farnes dismissed Barnett for 57, all Bradman's partners except Lindsay Hassett, who made only 13, fell for single figures, but Bradman 'batted with an ease which even for him was almost ridiculous'. C. G. Macartney wrote: 'He . . . was forced into a dangerous situation, and emerged from it with flying colours. He could not afford to take undue risks, but he punished the ball powerfully whenever opportunity offered and his placing was very exact.'

In the steadily darkening afternoon he reached his century, his twelfth for the season, after two hours fifty minutes, and broke Trumper's record for the most centuries scored in a season by any touring batsman in England. Eight minutes later, at 103, he lost his wicket to Bowes.

His total was largely responsible for Australia's meagre first innings lead of 19, and one English sportswriter said: 'This Don is now so firmly established as the greatest cricketer of all time that no matter what the situation is to-morrow morning we shall not be able to think of victory until he is back in the pavilion with his pads off.'

The Ashes now seemed to depend on the ability of the Australians to dismiss England quickly in the second innings. They responded nobly to the challenge and O'Reilly seemed to hurl himself down the pitch in his attack on Hardstaff, who looked dumbfounded as the three stumps scattered behind him. Immediately after that, off another ball from O'Reilly, Brown caught Hammond for a duck. It was the beginning of the end and England could muster only 123.

At first, Australia did not seem able to do much better. Verity, Farnes and Wright sent their wickets flying and even Bradman survived only thirty-five minutes before Wright caught him off Verity for 16.

With most of Bradman's good batsmen back in the pavilion he found himself, for the only time in his life, unable to watch the rest of the play. He stayed in the dressing room, where McCabe soon joined him. O'Reilly, with the pads on but praying he would not be needed, paced nervously up and down. Bill Jeanes actually left the ground and went for a walk among the crowds which had overflowed outside. Bradman wrote later: 'to prevent my teeth chattering in the excitement I was consuming copious supplies of bread and jam augmented by a liberal quantity of tea. We relied on our colleagues to give us a running commentary of the play.'

Amid breath-taking excitement the Australians held their ground, won by five wickets, and retained the Ashes.

Four weeks later, after a busy spell of travel and cricket in which Bradman scored a double century (202) against Somersetshire, the final Test opened at the Oval on Saturday 20 August.

The Australians, having lost every previous toss, gambled on winning this one. But Bradman lost it again — as he lost every toss in the series. They gambled also on leaving out McCormick, and the opening attack by Waite and McCabe must have been the most docile that any English batsmen have ever had to face.

An easier pitch could not be imagined, and the bottom seemed to fall out of Australia's hopes when wicket-keeper Barnett missed stumping Hutton outside the off stump when the batsman had scored 40 and was stranded half-way down the pitch. Barnett's mistake had

E. S. White (left) and
L. Fleetwood-Smith carry
Don Bradman off the Oval after he
suffered a flake fracture of the
ankle during the fifth Test at the
Oval, 1938

profound consequences and allowed Hutton to carry on to set an un-precedented batting record.

It was the irony of fate that Barnett had been included as one of the wicket-keepers largely because of his experience in 'keeping to Fleetwood-Smith for Victoria, in Shield games. But at the critical moment he failed to make the simplest of stumpings because he, like Hutton, was deceived by a wrong-un.

At the end of the third day's play, Bradman wrote in his diary: 'Continued Test. Hutton went on and broke my record. England made over 900 for seven and declared at 4.15 p.m. I busted my ankle bowling and was carried off. After treatment was taken to hotel. X-ray revealed a flake fracture. Bad night.'

For the next two days he wrote simply 'Day in bed', and on 26 August: 'Went to St Thomas Hospital for further X-rays and spent the rest of the day at the hotel. Plenty of visitors etc.'

The fracture occurred when Bradman took a turn at bowling, to relieve the other bowlers exhausted after more than two whole days in the field against the unrelenting Englishmen. (They ended with the staggering total of 903 for seven, including Len Hutton's record-breaking 364 for which Bradman was the first to congratulate him.) As Bradman made his run up, he turned his ankle in one of the holes worn by the bowlers.

Bradman's accident momentarily crowded the 1938 political crisis off the front pages of the newspapers, and it ended his cricket for the season. He spent the rest of the tour recuperating at the beautiful home of his friend Walter Robins, the notable English county and Test crick-eter of that period who had served as captain of both England and Middlesex. In some ways, Bradman was not altogether unhappy with this enforced spell of sick leave, especially since he was able to move about with the aid of crutches. The Test victory was won, he was very tired, and his back muscles were paining him after the prolonged effort.

He had plenty of time to think about the tour. One of the things which disappointed and puzzled him was the utter failure of 'Jack' Badcock, who played in every Test but could muster only 32 runs at an average of 4.57. Yet, for the rest of the tour, often against the same bowlers as he met in the Tests, he totalled 1572 runs at an average of 56. It was totally inexplicable because Badcock's temperament was undoubted.

Another interesting point concerns Bradman's philosophy on tactics for a touring team. He never concerned himself very much with the number of runs made by a county side, always believing his batsmen could do better; but he was very conscious of how long the opposition batted. The Australians were unaccustomed to playing cricket for six days a week, and Bradman considered it important for his players to spend as little time as possible in the field. Hence he placed great emphasis on the speed of wicket-taking.

He was well aware of the criticism of the selection of Ward instead of Grimmett. In retrospect, the best strike rate Grimmett ever achieved in England, on three tours, was one wicket every seven overs. In 1934 each wicket took him 8.9 overs. Frank Ward, in 1938, took ninety-two wickets at one wicket every 5.71 overs. Ward's selection had vindicated a theory which was of great importance to the tourists but completely overlooked by the critics. Ward did not play any direct part in winning

Opposite: Don Bradman (left) congratulates Len Hutton after the young English cricketer had made the highest individual score in matches between England and Australia during the fifth Test at the Oval, 1938

the Tests, but his value in other ways as a member of the team could be demonstrated beyond doubt.

Probably the 1938 tour, more than any other season, set the seal on Bradman's admiration for the bowling of Bill O'Reilly. His erstwhile colleague from New South Wales finished with 104 wickets at an average of 16.59, despite having to bear the overwhelming responsibility of containing the batsmen as well as dismissing them, often with quite inadequate support and on Test pitches which, apart from Leeds, were a bowler's nightmare. Excluding the Tests, O'Reilly's average per wicket fell to 13.6, truly a remarkable figure. Without his magnificent efforts the team could never have retained the Ashes — a fact which Bradman always graciously acknowledged and emphasised.

Despite Bradman's anxieties and tribulations, he had much cause for satisfaction when he looked back over the 1938 tour.

The team evened the series and so retained the Ashes, despite the handicap of losing every toss when batting conditions were so ideal that England's first innings totals at Notts, Lord's, and the Oval were respectively 8 for 658 declared; 494; and 7 for 903 declared, leaving the spectre of defeat or a draw as the outcome. Yet the Australians lost only the final Test, when Bradman could not bat because of his broken ankle and Fingleton was out of action with a ruptured leg muscle. A rather extraordinary facet of the last Test was that Australia took four wickets but 'No ball' was called each time. By such narrow margins may history be made!

The Australians were not defeated by any county and lost only one match other than the last Test. This was at Scarborough, to what was virtually an England eleven, when Bradman was not playing.

He had made a century in every Test in which he batted. His batting average of 115.66 — made under the new and much more difficult LBW Rule — was the first time any Australian had averaged 100 or more on a tour of England. In twenty-six innings (five not-outs) he made thirteen centuries, which was also a new record. To put it another way, 50 per cent of his innings were centuries.

In completed innings, excluding not-outs, his percentage rose to 61.9. The magnitude of that performance may be gauged when one realises that the next highest percentage achieved by any batsman during his career is 18.6 by Wally Hammond.

Bradman had proved himself a magnificent tour leader, and the responsibilities of captaincy had enhanced his ability as a player.

One performance which gave Bradman great personal satisfaction was that of Bill Brown. In 1934 Bradman had made no secret of his opinion that Brown would be a better choice for an England tour than Jack Fingleton. This was one of the reasons why Fingleton, in later years, waged a kind of vendetta against Bradman.

In 1938 Brown and Fingleton competed on level terms on a tour of England. Brown's Test average was 73.14. Fingleton's was 20.5. Bradman felt that his faith in Brown had been more than vindicated.

He thought about all these things as he relaxed in the kindly atmosphere of the Robins home, learned how to handle his crutches, and made the most of his last weeks in the 'Old Country'.

It was a strange time to be in England. Hitler, with his demands on Czechoslovakia, was mounting one of his giant bluffs against the democracies. Most people in Britain believed that war was inevitable.

Opposite: Newspaper writers frequently offered very definitive opinions upon the future of Don Bradman. This one, which appeared after his cricketing accident in 1938, proved to be as inaccurate as many others

Don Bradman in good company, resting at the home of his friend Walter Robins, noted English player of that era, after fracturing his ankle in the fifth Test. The smiling companions are Jessie Bradman (left) and Mrs Robins. The Bradman and Robins families still maintain their long-standing friendship

Bradman Won't Play Again In England

By THOMAS MOULT

DON BRADMAN, greatest run-getting batsman of all time, has played his last match in this country.

The accident which occurred during the final Test and turned the game into a fiasco will probably prove to have been the deciding influence in shaping Bradman's future.

He was forcibly reminded at the Oval that although he is physically sound, with exceptional stamina, his physique is by no means a giant's, and that the ordeal of another first-class cricket tour over here might be too exacting.

Consequently he has reviewed the numerous business proposals made to him since his arrival last April, and, unknown to anyone, may have already made his farewell appearance on an English cricket field.

He will continue to play in his own country, so that his Test career is not ended, but when he accompanies the next Australian side to England it is likely to be as a newspaper writer on the Tests.

In this he would follow the precedent of W. M. Woodfull, who was the Australian captain four years ago.

The Walter Robins' home where Don Bradman recuperated in September 1938

After the Board of Control lifted the 'wives ban' in 1939, Mrs McCabe (left) and Jessie Bradman (centre) made the voyage to England in order to join their husbands on the conclusion of the tour. This photograph was taken aboard the ship in Colombo, en route to England

The fleet was mobilised, conscription had become law, Air Raid Precautions squads practised in the streets of London, and labourers dug trenches in Hyde Park. Citizens lined up to be fitted with gas masks and administrators planned the evacuation of children from London.

Yet life continued under the shadow of war. London was still the biggest, richest and in many ways the most exciting city in the world, with a brilliant night life of theatres, restaurants, cabarets, pubs and night clubs. The Crazy Gang performed nightly at the London Palladium; Gracie Fields and Peter Dawson drew packed houses; C. B. Cochran's Young Ladies delighted their audiences; Noel Coward and Gertrude Lawrence put over their sophisticated jokes and songs; the Guards marched magnificently through the streets for the Changing of the Guard. Bradman enjoyed nights out in London and shopping expeditions to his tailor, and to Roote's to order a new Humber Snipe to be delivered to Adelaide. Jessie Bradman arrived in London — at about the time that Neville Chamberlain sacrificed Czechoslovakia and at the expense of Britain's honour bought a year of time to prepare for disaster.

London newspapers found space for photographs of 'the romantic couple' when Don and Jessie Bradman were reunited in London, and after a few days they set off for home. They ignored the advice of their travel agents by travelling across Europe to board the *Orontes* at Naples, and found the atmosphere in France and Italy to be very different from the cheerful confidence of Britain.

In Australia the problems of the northern hemisphere seemed so remote that the Board of Control was already talking about plans for the next Test series. Bradman barely had time to settle back into his work and home before he was launched into the 1938–39 cricket season, which was to prove particularly successful for the great batsman. Now aged thirty, he had achieved the maturity of style and execution which comes to every great athlete on the plateau of his career. In his seven first-class matches between 9 December and 25 January he scored at least a century or more in each of six innings: 118 when he led D. G. Bradman's Eleven against K. E. Rigg's Eleven at Melbourne; 143 for South Australia against New South Wales at Adelaide and 225 against Queensland at Adelaide; 107 against Victoria at Melbourne; 186 against Queensland at Brisbane; and 135 against New South Wales at Sydney. His only failure was in the final match of the season, against Victoria at Adelaide, when Fleetwood-Smith caught him off Thorn for five. But his steady flow of centuries helped to secure the Sheffield Shield for his home State, and enabled him to equal C. B. Fry's 1901 record of six consecutive centuries.

The winter of 1939 brought a welcome relief from cricket, which had involved him almost continuously since November 1937. It also brought the Bradmans the great joy of their son John Russell Bradman, born on 10 July — doubly important because of the loss of their infant son in 1936. They were at last a complete family.

The 'storm of the world' broke on 3 September 1939, when Prime Minister R. G. Menzies told the nation that it was his 'melancholy duty to inform you officially that, in consequence of a persistence by Germany in her invasion of Poland, Great Britain has declared war on her and that, as a result, Australia is also at war'.

Don Bradman, like most Australians of military age, began at once

Jessie Bradman and John Russell Bradman, born 10 July 1939

to consider how he might serve. Jessie Bradman, like most young wives and mothers in wartime, began to brace herself for the future. Cricket seemed of minor importance against the lurid background of war, but the Commonwealth Government thought otherwise. They asked that first-class cricket, apart from a proposed tour of New Zealand on which Bradman would have led the Australian team, should be played as usual for the sake of national morale.

This letter of 28 June 1940, congratulating Don Bradman on his decision to join the RAAF, was from H. H. M. Bridgman, one of Bradman's fellow-selectors for South Australia

> 5 Taylors Road,
> Torrensville,
> 28th June '40.
>
> Dear Don,
>
> It was with pride and admiration that I read of your joining up.
>
> Following our talk at the "Belle Vue", I fully realise the sacrifices you and your good wife are making.
>
> I am sure that your action will be an inspiration to all South Australian and Australian cricketers to fall into line.
>
> Congratulations Don, and all the best of luck.
>
> Yours Sincerely,
> Hugh Bridgman

Hitler's swift defeat of Poland was followed by seven months of 'phoney war', limited almost entirely to actions at sea, and the initial urgency faded away. For Bradman, that strange period in which the world seemed to hold its breath was one of cricketing dominance. In his fifteen innings of the 1939–40 season he scored eight centuries including three double centuries, and he joined Ponsford as one of the only two batsmen, until that time, to have scored 1000 runs in a season in Shield matches only.

Some of his innings in that season were among the best he ever played. On New Year's Day 1940 he scored a shattering 267 at Melbourne, and C. G. Macartney wrote in the *Sydney Morning Herald*: 'Bradman's phenomenal consistency continues. He is the supreme test for bowlers, and nothing yet devised by spin or swing, pace or slowness, seems to provide any unpleasant moment for him.'

Bradman was a national institution and his appearances drew enormous crowds. A total of 78 029 attended the Melbourne match; 75 765 saw Bradman play against New South Wales in Sydney. The government had been right in believing that 'cricket as usual' — or perhaps 'Bradman as usual' — was important for Australian morale.

His great scores were not only a triumph of batsmanship and of cricketing skill but, unknown to the public, a triumph over his worry-

A newspaper cartoon which appeared at the time of Don Bradman's decision to join the RAAF

ing physical problems that were gradually becoming more severe. In the same tantalising way in which his deepseated appendix infection had sometimes seized him, sometimes released him, for about two years before its eruption, he suffered repetitive bouts of muscular pain which defied any diagnosis except that of 'fibrositis'. There did not seem to be any definite cure, and on the whole the good days outnumbered the bad; but he never knew when he might be seized by an agonising muscular spasm.

THE DON UNDER ARMY ORDERS

One volume of Sir Donald Bradman's library of scrapbooks contains a cutting from a 1940 magazine or newspaper which describes some of his experiences, 'with 74 other athletic lads', at the Army School of Physical and Recreational Training, Frankston, Victoria.

According to the cutting, which does not carry a name or date, 'The training school is a pleasant place. It was the Church of England's Boys Camp before the war.'

The school was modelled on the British Army School at Aldershot, and the commanding officer, Major W. J. Dickens, was a product of the Aldershot school. The senior instructor, 'tall, dark, good-looking Sergeant-Major Bruce Cupitt', had also trained at Aldershot.

A number of the instructors were well-known Australian athletes, including Sergeant-Major L. O'B. Fleetwood-Smith. 'Chuck' Fleetwood-Smith was of course an old friend of Bradman's. They had known each other since the

cricketing tour of North America, and he played some part in influencing Bradman's transfer out of the RAAF to the army.

Some other instructors, also with the rank of sergeant-major, were the wrestlers Bonnie Muir and King Elliot and the international Rugby player Max Carpenter.

Carpenter was in England with his team when the war broke out. Instead of playing Rugby the team found themselves filling sandbags, and their only match of the tour was at Bombay on the way home to Australia.

The journalist wrote of the training programme: 'Work — physical jerks that limber up every part of the body, long jumps, high jumps, wrestling, boxing, medicine ball, shot put — all branches of athletics — begins at 9 a.m. and goes on until 4.30 p.m., with short breaks for rest and lunch.

'This is a school where energy is spelt with a capital E, but where students must acquire a good working knowledge of anatomy, physiology, and hygiene as well.

'They must also learn how to arrange and conduct every kind of sporting event, from a wrestling match to a sports meeting.'

The trainees also had to learn the art of dealing with injuries. This meant passing a St John Ambulance course, and with Don Bradman's usual thoroughness he topped the class.

The writer said that Bradman was one of the smallest, most lightly-built men in the school,

and that the skin was peeling off his sunburnt arms, face and shoulders. 'But he puts just as much pep into the exercise as the young giants twice his size . . . and he still wears his famous cheery grin.'

Don Bradman told the journalist of the instructors' claim that when the trainees left the school they would be fitter than ever before. But Bradman said: 'As a matter of fact, you have to be in pretty good nick before you come here. If you weren't, you would probably crack up by the third day.'

Bradman had to work hard to keep up with the programme and with his fellow-trainees, of whom a good many were younger than he was. They had been specially selected from their units and commands, and most returned to them as physical training instructors.

In Don Bradman's case, he certainly was not 'fitter than he had ever been before' when he left the training school. The rigorous exercises aggravated the muscular problems which troubled him and he had to be invalided out of the army.

Another 1941 newspaper cutting in Sir Donald's scrapbooks gives quite a detailed story of his life in the RAAF training camp at Cootamundra, New South Wales. Unlike the story quoted above, it was totally imaginary. Sir Donald carried out his preliminary RAAF training in Adelaide and was never in Cootamundra during the war. Some journalist invented the entire story.

He was also experiencing some trouble with his vision, which had first manifested itself after his 1934 illness and necessitated his wearing glasses for close work. He was beginning to suspect that twelve years of the tension and exertion of his cricketing career were finally exacting retribution.

Soon after the end of the 1939–40 cricket season, the battle for Europe began. France surrendered on 25 June, and the news sent countless thousands of Australians flocking to the recruiting offices.

Lieutenant Don Bradman (centre) at the Army School of Physical and Recreational Training, Frankston, Victoria, early in 1941. The officer at left is Major W. J. Dickens, commanding officer of the school

After some months in the RAAF, Don Bradman transferred to the army. This 1940 photograph shows him in the uniform of a lieutenant in the Australian Army

Bradman was among them, and on 28 June he joined the Royal Australian Air Force. Despite his apprehensions about his physical condition, the doctors passed him as fit for air crew duty, but he then had to endure the same frustrations as many other men who were anxious to serve in the air. The RAAF had more recruits than it could equip or train. Bradman attended preliminary training courses, but he had to wait until the slow-moving machinery could find a permanent place for him.

This delay allowed a rival service to look in his direction. The Australian Army felt he would be the ideal man, for both practical and publicity reasons, to act as a divisional supervisor of physical training with the army in the Middle East. They proposed that he should transfer to the army with the rank of lieutenant, learn his new job at the Army School of Physical Training in Victoria, spend some initiatory months in Adelaide, and then go overseas.

Disappointed by the RAAF delays, but eager to serve in any way possible for him, Bradman accepted the transfer with some mental reservations. On 31 October he entered camp at Frankston, Victoria.

The army course for physical training instructors was rigorous and demanding, and he soon found that its muscular exertions intensified

Don Bradman breasts the tape in one of the sports events at the Army School of Physical and Recreational Training in 1941. Vigorous exercise of this type aggravated his muscular problems and eventually caused him to be invalided out of the army

the physical problems which had threatened him for so long. Moreover, in December 1940 an ocular specialist confirmed his suspicions about his vision. The specialist was engaged in research connected with the vision of RAAF pilots, and he thought that the so-called 'eagle eyes' of the great batsman would give him some new data. To his surprise, but not to Bradman's, he found that the eyes which had defeated so many bowlers were beginning to falter. When Lieutenant Bradman obtained leave to play for South Australia against Victoria in December 1940, and in a Patriotic Match between D. G. Bradman's Eleven and S. J. McCabe's Eleven in Melbourne in January 1941, he found he could not pick up the flight of the ball. In four innings he suffered two ducks and aggregated only eighteen runs.

But he was determined to 'soldier on'. It was not the time for any man to give up easily, and Bradman felt keenly that he should do his utmost to conquer these afflictions and play his part in the war. A couple of weeks in hospital seemed to effect some improvement, and he returned to the heavy training programme. In February he led a team to victory in an Australian All-Services athletic meeting.

But this effort was the last straw that finished the batsman's back, and he had to return to hospital. It was a difficult period in the Bradman family because their second child, Shirley June, was born on 17 April 1941 and Jessie Bradman had to add the anxieties of looking after a new baby to her worries about a seemingly incapacitated husband.

By the middle of the year, Bradman knew that he would not be able to carry on. The army doctors could not ease the torture of the muscular spasm in his back, which had spread to his right arm. By June, after more hospital treatment, the nerves and muscles of his right arm were so badly affected that he could not raise the arm high enough to shave himself or comb his hair.

In June 1941 an army medical board invalided him out of the army and, as once before in 1935, he sought the peace and quiet of his father-in-law's farm at Mittagong, near Bowral, in the hope that relaxation in that quiet backwater would improve his condition. Mrs Bradman had her hands full, with a new baby, a little boy, and a sick husband to look after; but she met the challenge with her usual cheerful courage and practicality and even learned how to shave her husband.

It was a dark period for Don Bradman. At thirty-three, he felt himself to be 'on the shelf'. He did not even think about playing cricket again, but set himself to the long arduous process of rehabilitation.

He succeeded to the extent that the Bradmans could return to Adelaide early in 1942. He went back to his desk in Harry Hodgetts' business, and felt well enough to play a little golf in the winter; but he rejected the blandishments of those who wanted him to play cricket again if only for Kensington. On 11 May 1943 he was elected a member of the Adelaide Stock Exchange — a mark of confidence by its members because he was only an employee of Harry Hodgetts and not a partner in his business.

He busied himself with such war work as lay within his capabilities, and this included the task of Honorary Secretary and Treasurer for South Australia of the Gowrie Scholarship Trust Fund.

The purpose of this fund was to establish scholarships for members of the Australian armed forces and their descendants, in perpetual memory of men and women killed in action. It was named in tribute to Lord Gowrie, Governor-General of Australia 1936–45. As Brigadier-General Sir Alexander Hore-Ruthven, V.C., he had been a particularly popular Governor of South Australia from 1928 to 1936, and then of New South Wales. One of the scholarships was named after his son Patrick, who fell in action in North Africa, and others were named after Australians who died in the war. Bradman devoted a great deal of his administrative talent to the project, which raised £140 000 and benefited many young Australians.

The war in Europe ended and the Allies braced themselves for the great assault on Japan, which most people thought would take at least a year and be hideously costly in lives. But it seemed that final victory was at last in sight.

Bradman's health was improving steadily, and like everyone else he looked forward to an expansive new postwar world. But, in July 1945, his personal world seemed to collapse with devastating abruptness.

Unsuspected by any of his employees, Harry Hodgetts had been mishandling his business. Even in wartime, the news of his defections hit Adelaide like a thunderbolt. Hodgetts was a prominent member of the Stock Exchange, held in high regard by local investors and by the commercial community of South Australia, and he was ostensibly a very wealthy man. But he had over-reached himself, and used clients' funds in unauthorised investments. Like many another man in the same position, he had tried to cover his own losses by diverting funds paid in to him, until at last the whole shaky edifice collapsed. With debts totalling £102 926 he declared himself bankrupt and faced criminal proceedings. Overnight, Don Bradman found himself unemployed and forced to make urgent decisions which were vital for the future of himself and his family.

SCOREBOARD
1937–1940

In Don Bradman's sixty-six innings in first-class cricket between 5 November 1937 and 11 March 1940 he set another series of records in Test and Sheffield Shield cricket, some of which still stand. His records for that period include:

* The highest score ever made in matches between South Australia and Queensland: his 246 on 27.12.37.

* On 31.12.37, playing against Victoria, he passed Clem Hill's previous record Australian aggregate of 17 160 runs in first-class cricket. Hill took 413 innings for this total; Bradman 212.

* On 8.1.38, his first century in the match against Queensland broke Alan Kippax's record of twenty-three Shield centuries in ninety-five innings. Bradman scored twenty-four in seventy-five innings.

* In the 1937–38 season he exceeded 1000 runs for the ninth time in Australian seasons and for the third successive season for South Australia, which is still a record for that State. His seven centuries for the season broke his own 1936–37 record for a South Australian player, and his aggregate of 983 in a season's Shield matches is also a record for his home State. With five centuries in all matches for South Australia he broke Clem Hill's forty-year-old record of four centuries.

* His 258 against Worcestershire on 30.4.38 remains the highest score by an Australian against that county. It was then the highest innings ever played by a tourist on the first day of an English tour. No other batsman has made double centuries three times in succession in his opening innings of English tours.

* On 16.5.38, against the M.C.C., he completed his eighth successive innings of over 50 runs, then a record for Australians.

* Playing against Hampshire, on 27.5.38, he completed 1000 runs before the end of May for the second time in England. He is the only batsman to complete 1000 runs twice before the end of May in England.

* On 31.5.38, against Middlesex, he completed 1056 runs by the end of May: a record for any visiting batsman.

* In his forty-second innings against England, on 14.6.38, he scored his thirteenth century in Tests of England against Australia, and broke Jack Hobbs's record of twelve centuries in seventy-one innings.

* On 26.6.38 he passed Jack Hobbs's record Test aggregate of 3636 for England-Australia matches.

* In the match against Nottinghamshire on 19.7.38 he broke records set by Warren Bardsley and Victor Trumper. He made his twenty-eighth century in England in his eighty-fourth innings in that country and broke Bardsley's record of twenty-seven in 175 innings. It was his eleventh century of the season, in twenty-one innings, thus breaking Trumper's record of eleven centuries in fifty-three innings in 1902.

* In the third Test of 1938 he scored his twelfth century for the season and broke Trumper's record for the most centuries by a touring batsman in an English season.

* His batting average of 115.66 for the 1938 tour is still the record for *any* batsman in an English season.

* On 10.1.39, against Queensland, he made his fifth successive century for the season: a record for Australian batsmen.

* On 14.1.39, against New South Wales, he equalled C. B. Fry's achievement of scoring six centuries in successive innings.

* His average of 153.16 in the 1938–39 season is still the record for Australia; his five centuries in successive Shield matches were a record for South Australia; and his average of 160.20 in Shield matches only is also a record for South Australia.

* On 22.12.39 he completed his fifth century in five successive innings against Queensland. No other batsman has ever made five centuries in succession against another State.

* Playing against Victoria on 30.12.39, he completed his thirty-fourth double century and broke Wally Hammond's record of thirty-three double centuries. Bradman held this record until Hammond accumulated thirty-six double centuries, but Bradman then passed him again and now holds the lead with thirty-seven.

* His 1939–40 aggregate of 1448 for all matches remains a record for South Australia. For the tenth time, he had exceeded 1000 runs in all first-class matches.

14

THE 100th CENTURY

Don Bradman had worked for H. W. Hodgetts & Co., of which Hodgetts was the sole proprietor, for almost ten years. The association had been happy, useful, and profitable for both parties to the original six-year contract. Hodgetts, the big jovial extrovert with his finger in many commercial and social pies, had revelled in the reflected glory of Don Bradman. It brought new business to his firm and added substance to his personality. For Bradman the employment had provided a secure base, especially during the traumatic years of the early 1940s, and he had always worked hard to fulfil his contract in both its commercial and cricketing aspects. The association had given him a reputable profession while he continued to build up his mighty cricketing career. Without Hodgetts he might have had one or the other of these, but he would probably not have had both at the same time.

But now, at the age of thirty-seven, he had to reckon up his assets and liabilities and start all over again. He had accumulated some capital, but his principal asset was a supportive family background knit more closely together by the fact that his daughter had been born with cerebral palsy, and thus elicited even more loving care and attention than usual. Don and Jessie Bradman had grown together into an emotional maturity which withstood many strains.

His principal liability was his association with Hodgetts. Over the years, newspapers had occasionally referred to Bradman as 'a partner in a stockbroking firm', although, of course, this was done without his knowledge or consent. But some people believed that he was, in fact, Hodgetts' partner. When Hodgetts' firm collapsed, they thought that Bradman must be implicated in his employer's defection. Bradman had been as astounded as everyone else by Hodgetts' bankruptcy, but there was no easy way to convince the public that he had not been involved. On the contrary, he was one of Hodgetts' creditors. His former employer owed him £762. But Bradman had to make quick decisions as to his future business career, and he could not wait until all the evidence had become public property.

While the truth was emerging, Bradman received some offers which could have solved his financial problems at a stroke. The atom bombs on Nagasaki and Hiroshima brought an abrupt conclusion to the war, the newspapers were looking ahead to the resumption of first-class cricket, and the paper with Don Bradman as its cricket correspondent would have a big publicity advantage over its rivals.

But if he accepted one of the press offers, he would have to abandon both the active and the administrative sides of first-class cricket. Despite his indifferent health — and a prediction in the English journal *The Cricketer* that it was 'very doubtful' whether he would play in Tests again — he felt that his service to cricket was not necessarily at an end. The Board of Control wished him to resume his place as a selector, and the South Australian Cricket Association wanted him as one of that State's members of the Board — in place of Harry Hodgetts. Bradman felt a continuing responsibility towards the game; a need to repay all it had given to him; a moral imperative to help, physically and mentally, in rebuilding Australian cricket in the post-war world. If he became an employee of one of the newspapers he would simply become one of the camp followers of cricket.

He felt that his best move was to make use of the knowledge he had gleaned about the stock- and share-broking business and set up for himself. It was far from the ideal time to do so, because share-trading was still restricted by the government regulations designed to stabilise the wartime economy, and nobody knew what would happen next. Many predicted a post-war depression. When he discussed his idea with friends in the commercial world, they shook their heads. They gave him many practical reasons why he should not set up for himself and hinted at the unspoken reason: that investors might shy away from a man who had worked for Harry Hodgetts.

Bradman listened to their advice and made his own decision. He felt the surest way to proclaim his integrity and non-involvement was to establish his own business, Don Bradman & Co., and rely on public support. This he did in a small suite of offices in Cowra Chambers, 23 Grenfell Street, Adelaide, a building long since demolished. Sydney Deamer of the Sydney *Daily Telegraph*, who published a long article about Bradman on 26 October 1946, wrote: 'There is a subdued stable atmosphere about the office. It reminds one of a family solicitor's place, except that it is tidier . . . Bradman sits in a panelled inner office, facing the door. The sanctum is carpeted and quiet, and the desk immaculate.'

Bradman's advisers had been partly right. Some investors did steer clear of him to begin with, but a number of Hodgetts' previous clients knew and trusted him, and they were pleased that he could take over their affairs. He received invaluable moral and financial support from his bankers, and from certain institutions who knew the full facts and went out of their way to give him their utmost support. By simple hard work and meticulous attention to detail, he made a success of the new venture.

On 13 August 1945 the SACA elected him as one of their three State members on the Board of Control. He was by far the youngest member of that influential assemblage and it was strange for him to take his seat for the first time, on 6 September 1945, among men with whom he had been occasionally locked in public dissent. He was to serve on the Board for the greater part of thirty years, become perhaps its most distinguished chairman, and eventually become the elder statesman of Australian cricket.

When Bradman first sat on the Board, the immediate future of Test cricket seemed uncertain. But less than a month later, the Minister of External Affairs, Dr H. V. Evatt, took it on himself to further relation-

The South Australian Cricket Association was one of a number of Australian and English cricket clubs and associations which recognised Don Bradman's services to cricket by the bestowal of life membership

SOUTH AUSTRALIAN CRICKET ASSOCIATION INCORPORATED

SECRETARY
W. H. JEANES

TELEPHONES.
OFFICE : CENT. 1111
OVAL : CENT. 771

MANUFACTURES BUILDING,
14 PIRIE STREET,
ADELAIDE.

(S)

4th September, 1947.

Dear Mr. Bradman,

We have pleasure in advising that at the 76th Annual General Meeting of members held this day you were unanimously elected a Life Member of the Association in appreciation of the services rendered by you in the advancement of the game of cricket.

A gold medallion in token of such membership is enclosed herewith.

May we express the hope that you will long be spared in good health to enjoy the privilege which this election bestows upon you.

Yours sincerely,

President

Secretary.

D. G. Bradman, Esq.,
Holden Street,
KENSINGTON PARK.

ships between Australia and Britain by saying that a Test team would be welcome in 1946. The M.C.C. responded within a few days by saying they would send out a Test team, and the Board had to plan for their reception.

Bradman took part in this planning but was far from certain that he would take the field against the Englishmen. In October 1945 he had not even handled a cricket bat for almost five years. He was still tormented by the muscular spasms which could strike quite unexpectedly, especially when he was worried or tired, and they had occasionally affected his left arm as well as the right. A small but painful internal operation put him out of action for a few days, and he could not even be tempted to turn out for Kensington at the opening of the 1945–46 season. Some of his supporters believed he was a spent force as a batsman, and the general opinion was that Lindsay Hassett, who was leading an Australian Services team on a tour of England, India and Australia, would be the first post-war captain against England.

However, Bradman had often surprised all the commentators, and he did so again when he played for South Australia against Queensland on 24–27 December 1945. The spectators gave him a round of cheers as he walked out to the wicket, and applauded heartily when he opened his score by turning the second ball to leg for three. A strained leg muscle gave him a pronounced limp as the game continued, but he scored 68 in the first innings and carried his bat for 52 in the second. These totals were but a shadow of his giant pre-war scores against Queensland, but at least Don Bradman was back in cricket.

His second and last match of the season, as captain of South Australia against the Australian Services Eleven, brought him a comfortable 112 in 112 minutes before he threw away his wicket. He wrote later that he made the century 'by reflex action', but Harry Kneebone wrote in the Adelaide *Advertiser*: 'Don Bradman is fit, in cricket form and in physical condition, to resume big cricket . . . he did not make a mistake, played all bowlers with sublime confidence, made his runs in time which would bear comparison with any in his hey-day, and sprinted up the grandstand steps at the end of his innings.'

But he would not commit himself to the journalistic inquisition about his cricketing future, and said only 'A decision must wait until next season.'

The Board of Control sent a team to New Zealand late in the 1945–46 season, but Bradman did not feel fit to accompany them. He suffered another attack of searing muscular pain, and his selection committee colleague 'Chappie' Dwyer persuaded him to visit Ern Saunders, a Melbourne masseur noted for his treatment of injured athletes.

Saunders' advice and manipulation helped Bradman considerably as he built up his health during the winter of 1946, while he pondered the problem of whether he should or should not make himself available for the 1946 Test series against England. Jessie Bradman encouraged him to do so, and said it would be a pity if their son John grew up without seeing his father play in a Test match. The newspapers baited their hooks anew, with offers of big fees if he would abandon Test cricket and devote himself to reporting instead of playing. Friends and relations besieged him with well-meant enquiries.

The press continued its inquisition, to which he would reply only with 'a mysterious smile', and the sportswriters had to fill their columns with speculations. One journalist predicted that his reappearance on the squash court for social games meant he was building himself up for cricket. Bill O'Reilly, who retired from Test cricket after the New Zealand tour, wrote: 'Bradman is indispensable to Australia in the coming Tests. His presence, even if he finds that mammoth scores are physically beyond him, will be of infinite benefit to the many young fellows who are going to take part in their first Test series against England.' Norman Preston of Reuter's interviewed Bradman in the latter's office and remarked on how busy he was. Bradman told Preston he could not commit himself to the Tests because of this pressure of business.

Bradman's young and essentially personal business was certainly an important reason for deferring a decision. Participation in the Tests would mean leaving it in the care of others for several weeks during the series. And the state of his health still did not augur well for the future. Saunders had given him temporary relief from the muscular problems, but he was beginning to suffer from gastritis — perhaps as a result of prolonged nervous tension. In September 1946, feeling far from well, he went to Sydney for a Board of Control meeting and suffered gastric pains and upsets for most of the trip.

His doctor advised him not to play in the Tests and two specialists supported this verdict. They said he would be wise to abandon any idea of taking part in the series, but he asked 'Will I be risking permanent injury to my health if I try?' They replied that if he did not over-exert himself he would not, but that he should not expect to achieve anything like his pre-war form.

By that time some journalists, who could not seem to appreciate the complexity of his problems, were exasperated by what they thought of as mere procrastination. In England the sportswriter Paul Irwin wrote: '. . . Bradman is fostering much hard feeling in Australia by his curt refusal to discuss future plans . . . "I have nothing to say," is the Don's theme song. It is one the Australian sports public hears over and over again — and it is growing wearisome.'

But that many-headed monster, the public, could have no concept of the difficulties inherent in Bradman's dilemma. The easy solution was abandonment of cricket and enjoyment of fat journalistic fees, without the strains on mind and body inevitable in a Test captaincy. And yet, to Bradman, that seemed like desertion of the game which meant so much to him — and still needed him so badly. O'Reilly, Fingleton, Fleetwood-Smith, McCormick and McCabe had all retired from big cricket, Ross Gregory had been killed in action, and most of the men who had been making their names during the 1930s were now too old to be selected for their first Test series. Bradman felt he could not forgive himself if Australia lost the Ashes for lack of his support.

He compromised with an agreement to play in the two preliminary matches against the M.C.C., and for South Australia against Victoria, to see how he stood up to the strain. By way of a pipe-opener he turned out for Kensington on 19 October and made 42 not out in forty-three minutes. After the first match against the M.C.C., at Adelaide Oval on 25–29 October, he completed his Kensington innings with a total of 112.

Australia gave a heroes' welcome to the first post-war Test team from England. Victory over the Axis powers was little more than a year old, and most Australians retained a patriotic admiration for Britain's long wartime struggle. The team included the Test veterans Hammond, Hutton, Compton, Edrich, and Voce, together with the newcomers such as Alec Bedser and Jack Ikin. With an average age of thirty-three, they were a mature and well-knit team held together by a determination to show that English cricket was as good as ever after six years of war. Bradman was delighted to meet old friends from England at a reception in the Adelaide Town Hall.

In their opening sally against South Australia, the visitors batted first and showed their mettle with an innings of 506 for five declared. Bradman had a strained leg muscle as a legacy of two days' fielding, and when he went in to bat he was obviously not completely fit. Arthur Mailey wrote 'He lacked his old-time resilience, vitality, and aggressive suppleness', and the Australian cricket writer R. S. Whitington said more unkindly: 'The large crowd at Adelaide Oval yesterday watched but the ghost of a great batsman — and very few ghosts come back to life.'

Don Bradman and Wally
Hammond walk out for the toss
before one of the matches in the
1946–47 tour of Australia by
England

But the English journalists proved themselves more perceptive than
the Australians. The *Evening Standard* reported: 'Don Bradman is
likely to be England's chief cricketing adversary again on his showing
for South Australia', and the *Evening News* said: 'Write Bradman
down as a certainty to captain Australia . . . He nursed himself wisely,
as he is still short of full health, but he seems likely to be his old
dominating batting self by the end of November, when the first Test
is due.'

Bradman's 76 in the first innings was the best for his side, although
he made only 3 in the second. In Melbourne, as captain of An Australian Eleven against the M.C.C., he performed much better even
though his leg still troubled him. He made his century in three hours
thirty-five minutes, and threw his wicket away at 106. Two days later
he played his only Shield match of the season, against Victoria at
Adelaide, and showed many flashes of his old brilliance. In the first
innings he lost his wicket at 43 when he jumped out to drive, but in

'Tests were his tonic

Nov. 27, 1946, before the first Test in Brisbane, Don Bradman looked wan and anxious. Would his "come-back" succeed?

March 5, 1947 last day of the fifth Test in Sydney and Bradman had led Australia to victory, was almost (but not quite) his old self physically, had topped Test averages and hoped to play next season.

Newspaper photographs contrasting Don Bradman's physical appearance on 27 November 1946, when he had returned to Test cricket after an eight-year gap, to that of his cheery smile on 5 March 1947 after he had led the Australians to victory

the second innings his injured leg did not prevent him from completing 119.

Australia heaved a collective sigh of relief at the announcement that Bradman, after the long indecision, would play in the first Test. His captaincy was all the more welcome because Bradman, Barnes and Hassett were the only men of Australia's eleven with any Test experience against England, although the team contained some promising youngsters such as Keith Miller, Ray Lindwall, Ian Johnson and Colin McCool.

The first post-war Test opened on the hot and humid morning of 29 November 1946, with a crowd of 12 000 seeking shady spots on the 'Gabba ground, Brisbane. One writer, comparing it with the grounds in other capitals, said: 'It looks as bare as an unfurnished apartment.' Bradman, who had lost the toss on seven successive occasions against Wally Hammond, threw up his arms with pleasure when he won. In those days of uncovered Test pitches, captains were desperately anxious to bat first — a rather different attitude from that of today, when it is common for a captain to send his opponents in first. Barnes and Morris opened for Australia, and Bradman followed when Bedser dismissed Morris for two.

Jessie Bradman photographed among the spectators during one of the 1946–47 Tests

One newspaper, ignoring the passage of time, described Bradman as 'the young man who has arrived in our lives again to take our minds off post-war problems'; but he looked far from young as he faced Alec Bedser, the giant young medium-fast bowler. The pressmen noted that he seemed to be shaky and lacking in confidence as he played himself in very carefully against Bedser.

He had compiled 28 when Bill Voce, his old antagonist of bodyline days, sent down a ball 'near enough to a yorker'. Bradman attempted to guide the ball past the slip fieldsmen, but it touched the bottom of his bat, hit the ground, and ricocheted to Ikin at second slip. Ikin caught it above knee-height, but Bradman stood his ground because the ball had bounced into Ikin's hands. Ikin waited for a few uncertain moments, and then appealed 'Howzat?' But umpire George Borwick instantly replied 'Not out'.

The incident happened so fast that few people could be certain of the sequence of events. Radio commentators reporting the game told their listeners unanimously that it was not a catch, but pressmen had

Yet another generation of small boys swarms around 'The Don', hoping for his autograph

divided opinions. Harold Dale of the *Daily Express* claimed: 'The English team, and everyone else, believe the umpire made an honest mistake'; but Bruce Harris of the *Evening Standard* wrote: 'I must say I thought it was a "bump" ball. So did everyone else.' Hammond said after the match: 'I thought it was a catch, but the umpire may have been right and I may have been wrong.'

At the end of the day, Jack Scott the square-leg umpire was asked his opinion of the incident. He said unhesitatingly: 'The ball touched Bradman's bat, then the ground. It was not a catch and Borwick's verdict was absolutely correct.'

Years later, the 'Ikin incident' had a distasteful aftermath. In Jack Fingleton's book *Brightly Fades the Don*, he described the occurrence and then wrote: 'No harm is done in admitting to posterity that Bradman *was* out.'

But of course there was harm in this untrue 'admission to posterity': deliberate and intentional harm, with the implication that it could have altered the fate of that Test series. Fingleton had a long-standing prejudice against Bradman because of a time when the latter said that Bill Brown was a better batsman than Fingleton. Fingleton affected to scoff at the judgment of two umpires in his continuous attempt to undermine the integrity of Don Bradman.

At the time, the controversial incident seemed to settle Bradman down. Cardus wrote: 'In the first half-hour of his innings he committed more miscalculations and streakiness than memory holds of all one's experience of him ... Soon after lunch the miracle happened; Bradman's innings rose from the dead, a Lazarus innings.'

The heat-dazed crowd sat up and roared acclaim as Bradman struck out with much of his old authority. It was as though the calendar had gone back ten years: as though they saw Bradman giving one of the great performances of his prime. Apparently unperturbed by the stunning heat, he completed his first post-war century against England at 4.32 p.m., and at stumps he was 162 not out. Next morning he added another 25 before pulling a ball from Edrich onto his stumps. When he had made 160 he reached 4000 runs in Tests between England and Australia, the only batsman ever to do so, and his 187 was the highest score in Tests between the two countries at Brisbane. There was no more talk of 'ghosts' after he and his men put together 645 in their first innings.

Len Hutton and Cyril Washbrook had barely opened for England before a tropical storm hit the 'Gabba, and they had to resume later on a mud patch. The wicket did not have time to recover before another storm struck the ground with such fury that the cricketers were marooned in their dressing rooms. Hailstones bombarded the roof and the cyclonic wind blew a sight-screen over the fence. In less than half-an-hour the whole playing field was completely under water, and the stumps, left on the ground by the umpires, floated into the outfield. But the water drained away overnight and play began punctually next morning. Keith Miller and Ray Lindwall renewed the attack, with some of Miller's deliveries flying high off the sticky wicket and striking English batsmen on their bodies. A section of the press cried 'Bodyline!' but Arthur Gilligan described such reports as 'Utter tripe'.

England mustered only 141 in the first innings and did little better in the follow-on. Miller and Ernie Toshack were the destroyers who disposed of them for 172, and Australia won the first Test.

The sportswriters sprayed indiscriminate criticism, with some taking the attitude that Australia had won by good luck rather than good management. Even Bill O'Reilly wrote, for the *Daily Express*: 'England must be heartened by the fact that Don Bradman has moved so far down the batting ladder . . . he has now become just a normally good Test cricketer.' But another sportswriter, W. A. O'Carroll, said: 'Toshack and Bradman laughed last, and best, at the critics . . . there are too many captains in the pavilion.'

Bradman found the first Test needed all his stamina to see it through to the end, and he used all his cricket cunning to make the best of each moment without over-taxing his strength. At the same time, he had plenty of other things on his mind. He kept in touch with his business by telephone. Jessie Bradman, who worked as part-time bookkeeper in Don Bradman & Co. when he was away, kept him informed about events in Adelaide, and he was able to assure her that he felt fit to continue with the Test series.

One of the numerous theories expounded by the 'captains in the pavilion' was that Australia had succeeded only because Bradman won the toss and the weather turned against the Englishmen. But in the second Test, at Sydney on 13–19 December, Bradman lost the toss and the weather was not particularly favourable for the Australians; but Bradman's men won again.

Towards the end of the first day's play, Bradman repeated a mistake that he had made before. He tried to cut off a four by putting his foot to the ball, and strained a thigh muscle. Massage and hot fomentations helped a little, but he was still limping when England had been dismissed for 255.

Saturday's play ended badly. The Australian innings had been interrupted by heavy rain and the spectators had booed Bradman and Hammond when they went out to inspect the wicket. Three of the spectators decided to inspect the wicket for themselves, to see whether the delays were justifiable, and had to be fended off by police. Barnes repeatedly appealed against the light and Warwick Armstrong, whose newspaper comments in that season seemed to have an anti-Australian flavour, accused him of 'bad sportsmanship'. In fact it was so dark that an electric light in the pavilion, almost directly behind the bowler's arm at the members' end, had been upsetting Barnes's vision.

The newspapers made much of Bradman's physical condition, and a London report said he planned to retire from cricket at the end of the match. When local journalists quizzed him about this he replied: 'When I have made any decision I will announce it and not leave it to the press to make decisions for me.'

The controversial atmosphere attracted 51 459 spectators to the third day of the Test — the largest crowd ever to attend the Sydney Cricket Ground on a Monday. Bradman had suffered a gastric attack over the weekend, and the heavy strapping around his injured thigh made him walk stiffly out to the wicket when he joined Sid Barnes at 3.50 p.m., at 159 for four.

The pressmen doubted whether he could withstand Bedser's remorseless attack, and waited with pencils poised to write 'I told you so' criticisms of his performance. The press and public watched an obviously sick, tired man calling upon every ounce of his experience

Above: Not a collapsed cricketer, but Don Bradman snatching a brief rest in the outfield during one of the 1946–47 matches against Wally Hammond's men

Left: A scene in the second Test, Sydney, December 1946. Bradman, sick with gastritis and with an injured thigh muscle, batted in an historic partnership with Sid Barnes in which they made 234 apiece. At one point a ball from Bedser struck his injured leg

to protect his wicket, and he once uttered a loud cry of pain when a ball from Bedser struck his injured thigh. He took 115 minutes to score 52 not out, before returning to his hotel and going to bed early 'not feeling too well'. He had hit six typical boundaries and defeated all the English attempts to dismiss him, but the feeling was that his innings so far had been a triumph of the will and he could not last at the wicket very much longer.

Don Bradman and Sid Barnes leave the wicket for tea during their great partnership in the second Test, Sydney, December 1946

Opposite: Don Bradman returns to the pavilion after his dismissal in the third Test, Melbourne, January 1947

But on the Tuesday morning he rejoined Barnes and staggered all the critics with a historic innings. He and Barnes stayed together until seventeen minutes before close of play, with Barnes in his third day at the wicket. Their partnership of 405 broke numerous records for the fifth wicket and is still a world record for that wicket. Bradman completed his first century in two hours forty-three minutes, his eighth century in successive Tests against England, and then continued in the old relentless Bradman style. Against excellent English bowling and fielding he accumulated 234, and by a strange coincidence Barnes totalled the same number of runs. R. S. Whitington made amends for his earlier statement by writing: 'Bradman's batting convinces me that if his body was only hanging together by strips of adhesive tape, he would still score a century against any bowling the world can at present put against him.'

Bradman declared at 659 for eight, leaving England little hope of

making up the deficit. Australia won the second Test by an innings and 33 runs.

The English newspapers which had predicted Bradman's retirement were astounded by his performance, and they lambasted Wally Hammond for tactics which they believed had cost England the first two Tests. In fact, the Australians under Bradman's captaincy had pulled together into a formidable team and they were more than a match for the Englishmen. They proved this with drawn games in the third and fourth Tests and another victory in the fifth.

Bradman did not score another century in that series, which retained the Ashes for Australia, but he still scored more runs than anyone else on either side. His average of 97.14 remains a record for an Australian against England in Australia. He had maintained the characteristic Bradman consistency, with an innings of 50 or more in one innings or the other in all five Test matches, although he had a couple of failures. He scored a duck in the first innings of the fourth Test, bowled by Bedser with what Bradman later described as 'the best ball ever to get his wicket', and 12 in the first innings of the fifth.

The series had been particularly interesting because it saw the Test debuts of several Australians, including Miller and Lindwall, who were to become mainstays of Australian cricket in subsequent years; the debut of Alec Bedser who performed nobly for England; and the consolidation of men like Hutton, Wright, Compton and Edrich in the Test arena. The series also concluded the long Test career of Wally Hammond, who had suffered from muscular troubles similar to Bradman's and never struck form during the tour. He had been unable to play in the fifth Test.

The series had reintroduced Test cricket to Australia with all its old thrills, controversy and criticisms — including an ill-judged statement by Warwick Armstrong, who wrote: 'The Australian bowlers are particularly weak. Australia will have to find new bowlers if she is to succeed in England in 1948.' In the event, those same 'weak' bowlers were to prove England's downfall during the 1948 tour, and rank with some of the greatest in history.

Bradman could smile at such comments, especially since they were outweighed by those of people who passed more sober judgment. Dr Evatt, then the Deputy Prime Minister, sent a telegram to Bradman in which he said: 'Your own personal achievement adds another series to your imperishable record.' Robert Menzies, then Leader of the Opposition, wrote to him: 'As a highly interested onlooker I was constantly fascinated by the skill with which you controlled the game at all stages. There are very many of us who think we have never seen a better or more subtle exhibition of captaincy.'

Bradman had tested himself to the limit and come through with flying colours. Many people believed that the gay and gallant Don of pre-war years was back in full flight, but he knew all too well that he was no longer the 'run-scoring machine' who could face a full day at the wicket with youthful insouciance. From now on he must rely on shrewd knowledge and hard-won experience rather than computer-fast reactions. The boy from Bowral had become a seasoned veteran, scarred by the wounds of cricket but still a formidable antagonist.

He refused to answer any questions about his possible captaincy of the 1948 tour, especially since he was by no means certain whether he

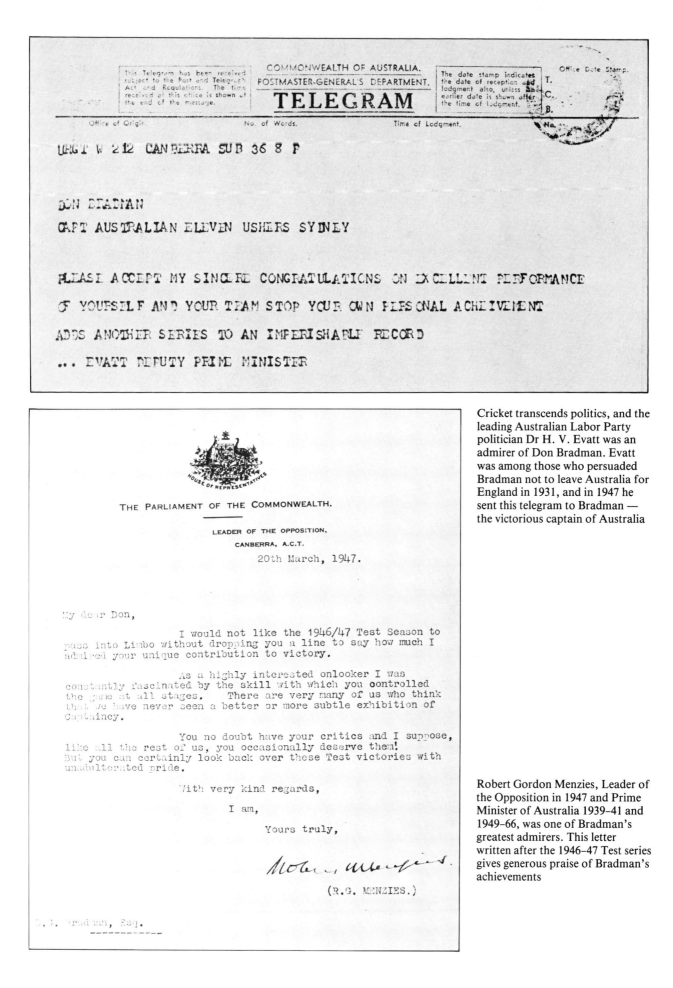

Cricket transcends politics, and the leading Australian Labor Party politician Dr H. V. Evatt was an admirer of Don Bradman. Evatt was among those who persuaded Bradman not to leave Australia for England in 1931, and in 1947 he sent this telegram to Bradman — the victorious captain of Australia

Robert Gordon Menzies, Leader of the Opposition in 1947 and Prime Minister of Australia 1939–41 and 1949–66, was one of Bradman's greatest admirers. This letter written after the 1946–47 Test series gives generous praise of Bradman's achievements

would take it on. He returned to the considerable demands of his business, then still in its infancy, and pondered on the future. The singular honour of Life Membership of the South Australian Cricket Association, bestowed on him by that body, was a measure of their appreciation of his efforts.

During the winter of 1947 the Board of Control concluded arrangements for the first visit of an Indian Test team to Australia, and Bradman felt he had a role to play in the historic event. His muscular and gastric problems still troubled him occasionally; but he had survived the 1946–47 season with an improvement rather than a deterioration in his health, and he gladly accepted the captaincy of the team to face India.

The Indian visit was preceded by a fresh spate of criticism against Bradman: in Jack Fingleton's book *Cricket Crisis* about the bodyline Tests, and in a *Sun* article by Whitington who commented on aspects of Bradman's captaincy. A Mr H. E. Dawson replied to Whitington in a letter to the *Sun*, in which he said: 'From all accounts, Bradman could have made a considerable sum of money by writing for the Press, but, unlike Whitington, he preferred to play the game rather than join those in the Press box.'

Clif Cary, sports editor for station 2UE, then entered the lists with a claim that Bradman had also profited by writing for the press. He said he had approached Bradman on behalf of the *Daily Express* with an offer of £1250 for four articles on the 1946–47 Tests, but that Bradman had turned it down and then written articles for another English newspaper.

Criticism has rarely evoked a reply from Don Bradman, but on that occasion he answered: 'It seems that the open season is here again, and that I am to be the "Aunt Sally" for certain people, who endeavour to draw attention to themselves by criticising me ... I think it proper that I should make public the true reason for my refusal [to write the articles].

'It was suggested that I should write on matters which were *highly contentious*, and that I should give my writing "that slightly provocative touch so welcomed by followers of international cricket."

'I refused the offer because no sum of money will ever tempt me to write "provocative" articles.'

The first Indian tour of Australia must have disappointed the scandal-seekers. It was perhaps the happiest and most pleasant Test tour in the history of cricket. Pankaj Gupta the manager of the Indians, and Lala Amarnath their captain, had both expressed the wish that Bradman would play 'because we want to learn from him', and Bradman proved himself a willing tutor. After each match he would visit the Indians in their dressing room and talk over the play with them, to give them hints on how they might improve their batting, bowling or fielding. Amarnath said: 'I love to play against him, and that goes for all my players, because he is such a great sportsman and a thorough gentleman.' In *Farewell to Cricket*, Bradman said that he found the Indians to be 'absolutely charming in every respect. They co-operated in all conceivable ways to try to make the games enjoyable, and the most wonderful spirit of camaraderie existed between the Australian and Indian players.' The tour was unusually free from controversy and notable for remarkable performances by Don Bradman — including his 100th century.

He made an unpromising start to the season in his first district matches for Kensington, with a duck in one innings and 11 in another, but he pulled himself back into form when the Indians met South Australia on the Adelaide Oval. After an almost chanceless 102, he hit out recklessly and totalled 156 before Sarwate caught him off Mankad. His century completed a trio of centuries scored in his first matches against touring teams from other countries: England, South Africa and India. No other Australian batsman has equalled this achievement.

The demands of his business restricted him to only one Sheffield Shield match for the 1947–48 season, on 7–11 November 1947 against Victoria. He made the ninety-ninth century of his first-class career, with a round 100 in 162 minutes, before Ian Johnson dismissed him two minutes later.

The world of international cricket now waited eagerly to see how and when he would complete his 100th century. He would be the only Australian batsman ever to do so, although a number of England's batsmen — who play many more innings each year than Australians — had scored more than 100 first-class centuries apiece. The Englishman with the ratio nearest to Bradman's is Denis Compton, who scored his 100th century in his 552nd innings. Bradman completed his 100th century in his 295th innings.

On 15 November, as captain of An Australian Eleven against Indians at Sydney, Bradman joined Keith Miller at 11 for one. Press speculation about his 100th century had attracted a large crowd, but at first he gave a rather cautious exhibition. He played himself in very warily and he was only 11 at lunch.

His performance changed dramatically during the afternoon. The crowd revelled in a display of classical cricket, with Miller and Bradman both in good form against the zestful and accurate Indian bowling and fielding. Tension increased steadily as he took his score up to 90, and then he had the crowd on the edge of their seats as the runs mounted by ones and twos. He wrote later: 'I turned a ball to square leg, ran one and then went for what the crowd thought was a risky second. One could literally feel them rise in their seats as they thought I might not make good my ground. Even in the most exciting Test match I can never remember a more emotional crowd nor a more electric atmosphere.'

At 99, in the last over before the tea interval, Amarnath puzzled Bradman by calling Kisenchand from the boundary and giving him the ball. Kisenchand had not bowled on the tour, and Bradman did not know whether the diminutive Indian was a demon bowler whom Amarnath had kept under wraps or a 'duffer' introduced to give Bradman a sporting chance of making his 100 before the end of the session. Bradman played the first ball carefully, but hit the second to mid-on for a single and the 'magic moment' had arrived.

The crowd cheered wildly, with some singing 'For He's a Jolly Good Fellow' as players rushed from all over the ground to congratulate Bradman on his 'century of centuries'. It had put him forty-seven centuries ahead of Warren Bardsley, the previous record-holder for Australia.

The Indians had a new ball after the tea interval, but all it did was to go faster off Bradman's bat. Having achieved his magic milestone, he determined to try to recapture some of the stroke-making of ten years earlier. In a glorious exhibition lasting forty-five minutes he added 72 runs, including a lofty six into the lower deck of the members' stand. The ball hit a girl named Norma Griffin so hard on the leg that she needed first aid.

Bradman became almost embarrassed by his virtual annihilation of the Indian bowling. He finally decided he had more than satisfied the playing public as well as giving the Indians a taste of 'vintage Bradman', and he deliberately gave a catch in the outfield.

Although they were on the receiving end, the Indians were actually delighted to be part of such an historic occasion. Pankaj Gupta said:

Bradman races for his 100th run in his 100th century in the historic match against the Indians at Sydney

'Bradman provided my players with their greatest cricket show.' His 100th century brought a flood of congratulations in the form of letters and telegrams from many parts of Australia and the world. The New South Wales and South Australian Cricket Associations and the Sydney Cricket Ground Trust made him handsome presentations.

The good-humoured Indian tourists next met Bradman at Brisbane on 28 November, but the first-ever Test match between Australia and India was not a good-humoured occasion.

Bradman won the toss, Australia batted first, and he went in at 38

for one. The Brisbane weather intervened during the afternoon, but he ran up his century in 171 minutes and then struck out at almost every ball in a race against the light. With storm clouds massing overhead he totalled 160 by 5.40 p.m., when the stumps were drawn almost in darkness.

The storm broke and a sodden wicket prevented play until 5 p.m. on the Saturday, but an exasperated crowd had demanded to see something for their money ever since lunch. They hooted, jeered and yelled at the captains and umpires each time they went out to inspect the wicket. Many demanded their money back, and a large number had left the ground in disgust before Bradman continued his innings at 5 p.m. In damp and unpleasant conditions he took his score to 179 before stumps, and batted again on the Monday after the wicket had received a further soaking from weekend rain. Angry crowds milled outside the ground, protesting against a decision not to honour 'rain checks' issued by the Queensland Cricket Association on the Saturday, while Bradman completed a total of 185 before he hit his own wicket.

The polite Indians were flustered by all this ill-temper and defeated by the wet wicket. They mustered only 156 runs in their two innings, and lost the first Test amid a storm of press and public criticism of the Queensland Cricket Association for their failure adequately to cover the wicket.

The bad weather followed the cricketers down the coast to Sydney, and ruined the second Test in which Bradman made only 13, on a very tricky wicket. After repeated attempts to play, the match was abandoned as a draw.

A few days later the Board of Control announced plans for the 1948 tour of England. For the first time a Test team was to fly to Tasmania for the pre-departure matches in that State, and the Board thought that post-war shipping difficulties might force them to fly the team home from England. The ban on writing articles during the tour had been retained, but Bill Jeanes said: 'If all the players want their wives to go to England they can do so. However they must not accompany the players on the tour.' *Truth* described the Board's change of heart on the 'wives ban' as an 'amazing somersault'.

But there was still one large gap in the Board's planning. Bradman had not yet decided whether he would captain the Australians. Many people believed he would retire at the end of the 1947–48 season and wondered how Australian cricket would survive without him. R. L. Jones, chairman of the Sydney Cricket Ground Trust, said: 'The Australian Board of Control is doing nothing to prevent the slump in big cricket that must follow the retirement of Don Bradman.' He remarked that Bradman had been responsible for enormous increases in cricket attendances since 1929, and the administrators of the game would have to find some way to fill the inevitable gap.

Journalists looked deep into their crystal balls in search of a clue to Bradman's future, and fished up some amazing predictions. The favourite was that he would enter politics. *Smith's Weekly* suggested jokingly that he would be 'the happiest choice for Governor-General'. The London news magazine *Cavalcade* said seriously that he had 'rejected an attractive offer by the Federal Opposition Leader (Mr Menzies) to join the Liberals, and has accepted an Australian Labor Party offer to stand for a Federal seat at the earliest opportunity.

Bradman has been learning politics under the wing of cricket-loving Doc Evatt, Australian Minister for External Affairs.' Another newspaper reported that the Liberal Party had urged him to stand for a metropolitan seat in South Australia. Bradman's answers to all these prophecies was 'No comment.'

In fact, he had been asked privately if he would accept pre-selection for a seat, but Bradman never seriously entertained the idea of a career in politics.

A crowd of 45 327, the largest to see the Indians play in Australia, flocked to Melbourne Cricket Ground on New Year's Day 1948 to watch the third Test. Bradman won the toss, went in at 29 for one, and once more dominated the Indian bowling. He completed his century in 159 minutes and carried on to score 132 before his left leg seized up with cramp. Play was held up for several minutes while he tried to ease the painful muscle spasm, and he tried to play on before he had recovered. The next ball, from the fast bowler Dattaray Phadkar, struck his pad and dismissed him lbw.

Australia totalled 394 in the first innings and the sportswriters began to predict an Indian victory, but the tourists could muster only 291.

The cover of the menu for a dinner tendered to the Indian cricketers in Melbourne, 3 January 1948. The Indian tour was lauded as one of the friendliest Test series ever played in Australia and the Indians praised Bradman for his continuous help to their players

The weather had changed again, recurrent rain gave India a sticky wicket, and Amarnath declared at nine.

It was a repetition of the situation that Bradman had handled against 'Gubby' Allen's men in 1938, and he used the same ploy. He put his tailenders in first, to hold the fort until the wicket had improved, but they fell fast and the Indians dismissed four for 32. One sportswriter said 'They batted like a lot of old hens on the brood', and condemned Bradman for his 'blunder'.

Bradman joined Arthur Morris and soon stopped the rot, on a wicket which had lost some of its venom. He opened carefully and took eighty-eight minutes to reach 50. After that, he sprang into action in the good old style. One sportswriter reported that 'he scintillated the longer he batted, and passed his century — a glorious knock — in 130 minutes . . . He drove, pulled, and hooked with the abandon of youth at picnic cricket, and gave the crowd one long thrill after he was properly set.'

It was a classic Bradman innings, against an Indian attack which Arthur Mailey described as 'On top of the world . . . Amarnath, particularly, gave a most impressive, sustained performance.' He remained 127 not out: the fourth time he had made a century in each innings. More rain overnight caused Bradman to declare at 255 for four.

India replied with a mere 125 in the second innings and Australia won the Test, but the sportswriters eked out only grudging praise. One of them, perhaps ignorant of the difference between Australian and English wickets, said that Bradman had 'missed his big chance' in his keenness to win the Test. He said he should have prolonged it in order to give his men practice on the kind of wicket they would encounter in England.

But the Indians would not entertain any criticism of Don Bradman. They had nothing but praise for his sportsmanship and co-operation. Gupta said: 'Our boys have a great respect for Bradman and are very fond of him. We wanted to see him in action, and are thrilled by his brilliant form.' Amarnath dismissed criticism of Bradman's tactics by saying: 'It was a Test match, not a festival game.'

The fourth Test opened in Adelaide under flawless skies and on a perfect pitch. Bradman won the toss and the Indian bowlers mounted a determined attack. They kept him in check for the first hour, in which he scored only 20. His partner, Barnes, was equally cautious, although Whitington wrote: 'Barnes was always sound, and batted far more impressively than his captain.'

After lunch, Bradman and Barnes got the measure of the bowling and gathered themselves together for an afternoon of steady scoring. Bradman completed his first century just before the tea interval and then forced the pace brilliantly. Despite a return of the cramp which had attacked him in Melbourne, he completed his thirty-seventh double century, the last of his career (and beat Hammond's record for the second time) in four-and-a-half hours. Two minutes later, with one more run on the board, he threw his wicket away.

Bradman's 201, Barnes's 112 and Hassett's 198 secured a convincing win for Australia and won the rubber.

Throughout the Test series, Bradman had had to endure the constant pestering of journalists about his cricketing future and especially about the 1948 tour of England. After the victory over India he was reasonably certain he could stand up to the strain of an overseas tour, but he would have to abandon his business for about eight months. He was strongly tempted to go, for his own satisfaction and for the sake of Australian cricket, but it would be a self-indulgent journey if his business and his family suffered for a final tourney against England.

Fortunately he had attracted a number of loyal clients, he had a most reliable chief clerk, and Mrs Bradman had proved herself to be a valuable deputy. He decided to take the risk, and announced that he would accept the captaincy. At the same time he ended further speculation by saying he would retire from cricket after the tour, and that the forthcoming fifth Test against India would be his last first-class match in Australia. (In fact, he was to play three more: the 1948–49 season benefit matches for himself, for Kippax and Oldfield, and for Arthur Richardson.)

In the eight months of first-class cricket he played between 25 October 1946 and 23 January 1948 he scored nine centuries and two double centuries and completed 6000 runs in Test cricket: an effective answer to the doctors who had said he would never regain his old form and the sportswriters who had regarded him as one returned from the dead. In those two post-war seasons he demonstrated a triumphant maturity in the face of great odds, which was even more admirable than his youthful successes.

The fifth Test against India, at Melbourne on 6–10 February 1948, very nearly made him change his mind about the tour of England. He

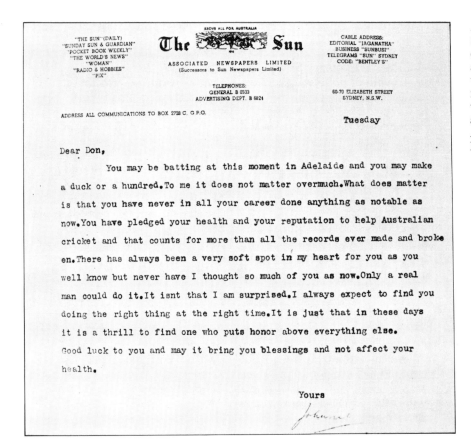

A. G. 'Johnnie' Moyes, the New South Wales cricketer and sports editor of the Sydney *Sun*, had been associated with Don Bradman since very early in Bradman's career in first-class cricket. Early in 1948 he wrote this letter to Bradman acclaiming his decision to lead the Australians on the 1948 tour of England

Jack Scott

won the toss yet again, went in at 48 for one, and after lunch showed himself to be batting at the top of his form. The crowd watched in happy expectation of another giant score, but soon after he reached 50 they saw him clutch his left side after attempting a drive off Ashok Mankad.

Concerned cricketers gathered around him, but after a few minutes he took his stance again. Refusing to surrender to the torture which gripped his left side, he tried to carry on but the pain was too severe and with his score at 57 he retired, hoping to resume next day. In the event, he was unable to resume batting at all.

A doctor examined him in the dressing room and diagnosed a torn muscle, or torn cartilage, under his left ribs. He wrote in *Farewell to Cricket* that 'it was one of those prevalent signs which come to men who continue to play vigorous sports when the time has come to make way for younger players'.

It was sad that Bradman's last Test innings in Australia had to be terminated by injury, and that the public, as he left the arena, did not know they had witnessed his last Test appearance on home soil.

He wondered whether it was a warning sign that he should not travel to England. He would be forty in August 1948, which was old for a Test captain although Blackham, Armstrong and S. E. Gregory had been slightly older in their final tours as captain. On the other hand, Wally Hammond had failed to reach form in the 1946–47 Test series because of physical problems similar to Bradman's.

He was very conscious that Australia was short of men with overseas Test experience; and he believed, justifiably, that his knowledge and experience might turn the scale. He decided to defy his reluctant musculature and do all he could to lead Australia to victory.

AN UMPIRE'S VIEW OF BRADMAN

During the second Test of the 1946–47 season, Umpire Jack Scott said that Bradman was a better batsman than Victor Trumper — and Scott's opinion carried a good deal of weight. In 1907, when he was eighteen, he captured the wickets of Victor Trumper and Monty Noble in his initial game in Sydney first-grade cricket.

Scott (1888–1964) was the best-known of Australia's Test umpires from 1936 to 1947. A wiry man of average height, he usually stood with George Borwick.

As a cricketer, Scott had played with or against most of the famous Australians in the first three decades of this century. Playing for New South Wales and South Australia, he was rated one of the fastest bowlers in Australia although he was never selected for a Test team. During his first-class career he took 227 wickets at 28.31.

Scott was also a useful batsman and an excellent fielder. Before the first World War he was a notable Rugby League player.

He tended to be a quick-tempered character and on one occasion he climbed the boundary fence to challenge a loudmouthed barracker. But as an umpire he was respected for his firm but fair handling of the game — although his decisions occasionally aroused press criticism.

He made his comments about Bradman during a discussion of the second Test in a Sydney tram, when he was returning home from the Sydney Cricket Ground. He said: 'I never thought I would see anyone better than Trumper or Macartney but Bradman is the greatest batsman Australia has ever produced. Some of Trumper's strokes were more brilliant but with Bradman you never know what he is going to do.'

The newspaper reporting Scott's statement remarked: 'Old-timers say you could not place a field to stop Trumper's strokes. On the fourth day of the second Test Bradman ... also demonstrated that he could unfold Trumperian strokes to bewilder the opposition.'

BAD LUCK
FOR AN OLDER BROTHER

Victor Bradman of Bowral was naturally proud of his young brother, with whom he had played cricket when they were boys. In 1948 he told a Sydney newspaper about one of the first times that the opposition 'couldn't get Don out'. He said: 'It was when we were kids at a Sunday School picnic. Don was about nine and we were playing cricket. The rule was that you had to get the boy who was batting out before you could have a go yourself.

'None of the kids could get Don out, and one of the kids went crying to the teacher. The teacher made Don give up the bat. Don was a bit wild. He reckoned he was within his rights.'

While Don travelled Australia and the world, Vic married and settled down in Bowral. He kept a menswear store, but followed the family farming tradition with a little primary production on the side. In 1939 he bought a piece of land for cultivation, but suffered a bad injury when he was working the soil with a rotary hoe. The implement hit a stone, threw him to the ground, ran over his leg, and cut it up so badly that the doctors thought he might not survive. The accident left him with a permanently stiff leg and forced him to abandon his favourite game — cricket.

Like Don Bradman in his earlier years, Vic played district cricket in the Berrima area. But he said he was 'never any good' by comparison with his famous brother.

Probably the last time the two brothers appeared on a cricket ground together was on Easter Saturday 1933. Don batted for a Bowral side captained by Alf Stephens, while Vic played for a Berrima District eleven. Don scored 71.

Victor Bradman told the newspaper he had never been lucky enough to see Don make one of his historic scores. He made a special trip from Bowral to watch the second Test against India, but the match was rained out and Don made only 13.

He said: 'I must be a Jonah. I've never seen Don make more than thirty runs in first-class cricket in my whole life. Once he got out as I was coming through the turnstile.

'We used to play in the Bowral district team when we were youngsters, but I never had any luck. I wasn't nearly as good as Don was, in fact I was never any good.'

At the time when the newspaper interviewed Victor Bradman, sportswriters were speculating about the impending 'retirement' of Don Bradman. Vic's reply was: 'I bet he doesn't give up big cricket while he's feeling well. Doesn't make sense to me.

'I don't really know what Don feels about giving up cricket, because I haven't had a chance to speak to him for about four years. I just come and watch him play and that's the only time I see him.

'I'm hoping to see him at Christmas time, though.'

Bradman's cricketing genius was not shared by any other members of the Bradman family. At that time Vic Bradman had a four-year-old son, but he said: 'The boy doesn't know one end of a cricket bat from the other. Not like Don. He was always playing, from when he was a little nipper.'

The 'whirlwind batsman' featured in a 1940s advertisement for Minties

SCOREBOARD
1946–1948

The first two years after the second world war found Don Bradman in poor health and deeply involved in the establishment of a new business, but he still succeeded in setting a variety of new records during the seasons 1946–47 and 1947–48. They include:

* In the first post-war Test against England he reached 4000 runs in Tests between England and Australia, the only batsman ever to do so. His 187 in that match was then the highest score in an England-Australia Test at Brisbane, and his third-wicket partnership of 276 with Lindsay Hassett remains a record for that wicket in Tests between the two countries.

* In the second Test, his 234 made him the only batsman to score double centuries in Test matches at Sydney, Melbourne and Adelaide, and on both grounds at Brisbane (the old Exhibition ground and the newer Woolloongabba ground). His fifth-wicket partnership of 405 with Sid Barnes, in the second Test, remains a world record for that wicket.

* His Test average of 97.14 for the 1946–47 season remains a record for an Australian against England in Australia.

* His 156 against the Indians on 25 October 1947 made him the only Australian batsman to score a century in his first matches against touring teams from three countries: England, South Africa and India.

* On 15 November 1947, playing for An Australian Eleven against Indians, at Sydney, he became the only Australian batsman ever to make 100 centuries. He scored his 100th century in his 295th first-class innings. Wally Hammond took 679 innings; Denis Compton took 552.

* In the third Test against India, his twenty-ninth run was his 6000th in all Test matches.

* His 201 in the fourth Test meant that he had scored three or more successive centuries nine times in first-class cricket: three times more than the next best, Wally Hammond.

* He is the only batsman to have made double centuries against four countries in Test matches: England, South Africa, West Indies and India.

* His aggregate of 715 is a record for all Tests between India and Australia for a batsman by either side. His average of 178.75 is the highest against India and far outstripped the previous record, Douglas Jardine's 73.66. His total of 1081 in all matches against India is the highest by any batsman against any India touring team.

* For the second time he returned a century-average for the season for both Test matches and all first-class matches: the only English or Australian batsman ever to do so.

15

THE FINAL TEST

The seventeen men selected for the 1948 tour of England comprised a mature and powerful team. Apart from Bradman, the average age was close to thirty. Neil Harvey, the Victorian electrician making his first overseas tour at the age of nineteen, was very much the 'baby' of the team. English sportswriters commented on its strength in all-rounders and worried about the ability of their own men to handle them. One wrote 'If only we'd a skipper like the Don', and Wally Hammond asked 'Who's going to get them out?' In Australia, Whitington wrote about Australia's 'wall of batsmen' but expressed doubts about the bowlers.

Bradman, then five months short of his fortieth birthday, began to feel some misgivings about his ability to stand the tour. His left side was still painful from the muscular injury and he wondered whether he was, after all, really fit for the long campaign. But when the tour assembled in Melbourne he quickly regained his enthusiasm. He felt confident in the choice of men, and the way in which they looked unquestioningly to him for leadership gave him renewed confidence in himself.

He believed the cricketing ability of his men outclassed that of any team with which he had ever travelled. He knew there were some weaknesses, but hoped these would rise to the challenges of the tour. The essential factor was morale, and in his first formal conference with the team he emphasised its importance. He told them that 'Happiness comes from within', and that if they determined to pull together, free from internal bickering and strife, they were bound to succeed.

He said: 'External influences can be important, but if we all resolve to be a happy and contented party, nothing can prevent it.'

Bradman was a good deal older in years and very much older in experience than the rest of his team, apart from the enormous superiority of his reputation. He was impressed by their close attention to his words, and encouraged by the knowledge that there were no men older than himself who might act as a focus of dissent against his judgment and decisions. He felt freer than ever before to use his leadership ability to the full.

He flew to Tasmania with his team but did not play in the matches there. He wondered whether he should nurse his injured side until arrival in England, but he took the risk of playing against Western

Australia in Perth, batted confidently, made his eighth century for the season, and totalled 115 before dismissal.

On the voyage to England he continued his process of moulding the team into a winning combination. He gave unstintingly of his wealth of knowledge about English cricketers and cricket grounds, discussed tactics, pointed out the elementary faults to be avoided by international cricketers, and helped them to believe in their own potential for victory. By the time the *Strathaird* berthed in Tilbury Docks, and the team made the brief railway journey to London through the dreary outer suburbs, they were all in high fettle.

The captain of Australia and the captain of R.M.S. *Strathaird* swap hats for the photographer during the voyage to England

The ten years since Bradman's last tour of England had wreaked enormous changes upon the nation that many Australians still called the Old Country. He had last seen London at a peak of power and prosperity, but in 1948 it was a drab and battered city. Great gaps in the buildings remained as memorials to the Blitz and to the bombardment by rockets and flying bombs. Everything was worn, shabby, long overdue for replacement, redecoration, or repair. The British had won the war but they now had to endure the long struggle back to economic security. The atmosphere was that of a nation close to exhaustion after its massive wartime endeavours, painfully seeking a way into the future. Rationing of all essential items was even stricter than it had been in wartime, and a symbolic gesture by the Australians created enormous goodwill. The tour manager, Keith Johnson, announced that they had brought some thousands of food parcels and tins of meat with them, donated by the people of Victoria, to be handed over to the British authorities. Johnson and Bradman waited on the Minister of Food to make the presentation, which brought warm acclaim from the British press.

The food shortages and the difficulties of transport and accommodation had discouraged all the cricketers except Sid Barnes from taking advantage of the Board of Control's reversal of the controversial

'wives clause'. Britain, at that time, was no place for a mere holiday visit, but Mrs Barnes had relatives in Scotland.

Despite all their difficulties, the British welcomed the Australians with as much cheerful friendliness as in pre-war years. Their reappearance after ten years was like a sign that life was slowly returning to normal. Stories, cartoons, jokes and articles about the cricketers brightened newspaper pages otherwise filled with reports about coal strikes, the rationing of food, clothes, petrol, and electricity, political upheavals, and the emergence of Russia as the great threat to the hard-won peace.

A book entitled *Cricket Controversy*, by Clif Cary, had just been published in England, and Cary said that Bradman was 'not revered as are many of the personalities who have delighted the crowds with bat and ball. He can be charming in any company, but he has never developed team mates to the same extent as the others. He has always been aloof, a personage unto himself.' One newspaper columnist queried this assessment, and wrote 'No aloofness showed in the Don at yesterday's Australia House reception to the tourists. He met the great ones present with the charm of an ambassador of the old school. And what do his team-mates call him? Why, just "Braddles."'

The sportswriters commented rhapsodically on the 'little man with keen and shrewd eyes under his trilby hat . . . the great Don Bradman,

The first Australian Test team to visit England for ten years, photographed aboard the *Strathaird* on arrival at Tilbury Docks. Newspapermen who met the team commented upon their high spirits under the leadership of Don Bradman the Don magnifico, the Don donnish, the Don feared, Don adored, Don glorious to watch, and Don leading those terrible fellows the Australian cricketers'. He charmed them all with his humour and affability, and his old friend and critic Neville Cardus wrote that his team was 'the most cheerful Australian side ever to visit this country'. Bradman's 'pep talks' during the voyage showed their effect as England responded delightedly to the happy band of Australians.

Journalists also noted the respect which Bradman's men showed towards their leader. One reporter watched the Australians practising at the nets, and wrote 'Anyone who has scored a century for Australia in a Test match against England could be excused for thinking he knew most of what there was to know about batting. But Colin McCool is learning differently.

'After he had batted during the Australians' first net practice at Lord's yesterday he was taken aside by Don Bradman and put on the mat.

'Don picked up a bat and showed the Queenslander where he had gone wrong. McCool listened meekly.'

The *Daily Express* wrote of Bradman: 'His remarkable run of Test team captaincies, his phenomenal scoring, his leprechaun fielding, his

A steady flow of spectators paid a shilling a head to watch the Australians practising in the nets at Lord's

tactical sense — all these point him as the cricketer of our time. Moreover his new ambassadorial look points him almost as one of the men of our time.'

Bradman had to cram many activities into the ten days in London before the first match of the tour. It seemed that everyone wanted to meet the Australians and they were guests at an Australia House reception (where Bradman had to shake hands with 200 guests); at the Coliseum Theatre to see 'Annie Get Your Gun' and at supper afterwards; at luncheons and dinner including those given by the British

INVITATIONS FOR THE AUSTRALIANS

Don Bradman and his men attended many receptions, luncheons, dinners, and other public occasions during the 1948 tour, and they could have spent all their time being entertained by the wellwishers who deluged them with invitations. One of Bradman's continuous problems was that of deciding which invitations to accept for himself and/ or his team, and which to turn down with a diplomatic refusal.

The first reception was on 17 April 1948, on the morning after their arrival. Organised by the Australian High Commissioner, Mr J. A. Beasley, it was at Australia House, on the Strand, London.

The *Manchester Guardian* noted 'the players were due at the nets in the afternoon, and their principal indulgence was in a jam-lined cake with a green top and wickets and sight-screens in icing sugar . . . Half-a-dozen clergymen were there and two middle-aged gentlemen whom one recognised as Mr Chapman and Mr Jardine . . . one noticed that although Bradman has not put on weight he has the firm bearing of middle age. His hair is receding a little at the temples, and his quiet manner expresses the self-assurance of the successful businessman rather than the correct shyness of the great athlete.'

British businessmen were

anxious to cash in on the publicity value of the Australians, but Bradman accepted very few of their offers. One exception was that of a firm of clothing manufacturers which presented the Australians with 'Elasta' cricketing trousers. They posed in them for a publicity photograph.

Outside London, the Australians paid goodwill visits to a number of large firms, including the Morris motor works outside Oxford. They were the guests of Lord Nuffield.

On one occasion a Lancashire newspaper reported that Bradman had 'disappeared' for three days, and then solved the 'mystery' by writing 'Rumours had ranged from a kidnapping to secret negotiations with a Lancashire League club. When the Australian captain arrived in Manchester to join his Team for the Test today he revealed the truth of the matter. He has been a guest of the mill-owner William Blackledge.'

Obviously the newspaper did not read the pages of one of its competitors, the *Chorley Guardian*, which reported the visit in full. Bradman later represented Blackledge's textile organisation in Australia. They remain the firmest of friends and correspondents and Mr Blackledge, now 90, is proud of their long and close association.

Apparently the Australians

were the only people in England to remember to place a floral tribute on the grave of W. G. Grace, at Elmers End, Kent, on the centenary of the great batsman's birthday.

Keith Johnson, manager of the touring team, placed a wreath on the grave with a card inscribed 'In memory of the great cricketer, from all Australians.'

At one of the London receptions, Don Bradman had a narrow escape.

He was among the guests invited to a dinner to meet Princess Marie Louise, a granddaughter of Queen Victoria, on her seventy-fifth birthday. The group assembled in the Grosvenor House apartment of Sir Norman Brooks, president of the Australian Lawn Tennis Association. They were going down in the lift to the restaurant when the lift attendant shouted 'Bend your knees — quick!'

He had lost control of the old-fashioned lift, which plummeted downwards until it was stopped by the safety brake.

The Princess was thrown to the floor and the Australian High Commissioner was knocked unconscious for ten minutes.

Reporters tried to wheedle a colourful story of the incident out of Don Bradman, but he would reply only 'It was of no consequence. I've nothing more to say about it.'

Sportsman's Club, the Royal Empire Society, the Institute of Journalists, and the Cricket Writers' Club, where the guests included the Duke of Edinburgh; at the Cup Tie Final at Wembley; and most memorable of all, the Silver Jubilee Service in St Paul's Cathedral to commemorate the wedding anniversary of King George VI and Queen Elizabeth. London might be shabby and battered but it still knew how to give a right royal welcome to its visitors.

Bradman's men could relax and enjoy themselves, but he was continuously conscious that he was — as he had told them before leaving Australia — their 'figurehead'. He spent countless spare moments in working out speeches for each occasion and in preparing himself to do this part of his job properly. He was rewarded by such press comments as that of the *Yorkshire Post*, which reported: 'Our cricket correspondent . . . is enthusiastic about the brilliance of his speechmaking at the Cricket Writers' Club dinner to the Australians.'

Bradman also had to find time to deal with an enormous quantity of mail. During the first fortnight he was never in bed before one a.m. The mail was to rise to a peak of 600 letters a day, and apart from letters it contained such items as books, cricket bats, and photographs, which the senders requested should be autographed and returned to them. Often they did not enclose return postage. Bradman had tried to prepare for the autograph problem by having his team sign their names to 5000 sheets of paper aboard ship, but these were snapped up in about a week.

Don Bradman had to deal with an enormous quantity of mail, rising to 600 letters a day, during his 1948 tour of England. Letters flowed in from many parts of the world and sometimes appeared to puzzle the postman, but Bradman was so well known that every letter reached him

When the Australians travelled by train to Worcester, for the opening match of the season, Bradman carried a large suitcase crammed with so many letters that he and two team-mates took the whole journey simply to open and read them. Many were requests for autographs, but more important letters were buried among the pile and Bradman had to give proper attention to every missive and make sure that no invitation remained unanswered.

England had greeted the Australians with weather as bad as that which Bradman experienced on the 1930 tour, but it did not deter a huge crowd from attending the opening match at Worcester. They endured rain, icy winds, and even a hailstorm in order to watch the Australian performance. The newspapers had whipped up interest by speculating whether Bradman, on his fourth tour, would open it with yet another double century at Worcester, and they had also written a good deal about 'Australian Bowling Doubts'. They claimed that the team lacked a bowler of the calibre of O'Reilly or Grimmett, and repeated rumours that the key bowler, Lindwall, had a bad habit of dragging his back foot over the bowling crease and incurring many no balls.

The *Evening News* wrote: 'There is no fear that he will be unsympathetically treated by English umpires. They are schooled in dragging-foot precedent, and they will surely treat and help Lindwall as they did Larwood, who was also a dragger.'

Bradman feared the effect of all this discussion upon Lindwall's morale, and that it would prejudice umpires against the bowler. He did his best to school Lindwall in keeping his back foot a long way behind the bowling crease, and told him not to bowl flat out until the problem was under control.

In fact the English umpires proved to be understanding and helpful. They saw that Lindwall did drag abnormally but they also knew their own limitations in watching hand and foot simultaneously and gave Lindwall a reasonable margin for error. He got through the tour with a minimum of no-balls.

There is little doubt that, with reasonable good fortune, Bradman could have completed his quartet of double centuries at Worcester, but he allowed commonsense to prevail over his desire to please the crowd. His injured left side still gave him twinges from time to time and he did not want to challenge it too early in the tour. Also he wanted to give his less experienced batsmen a chance to feel their way under English conditions, rather than occupy the limelight himself. He went in at 79 for one, and in company with Arthur Morris he batted comfortably until he had secured his century in 138 minutes. After tea he added another 7 runs and then, as he has done numerous times during his career, threw his wicket away. It still left him with the unprecedented record of three double centuries and one single century in the opening match of an English tour.

The tour continued along its usual course, with matches against Leicestershire, Yorkshire, Surrey, and the two universities, but Bradman 'rested' during the Yorkshire and university matches. He was confident his team could carry on without him and so they did — despite a very narrow squeak against Yorkshire. Bradman remained in London to catch up on his enormous mail and attend a number of the engagements pressed on him because it was his last tour of England.

Above: Bradman plays up to a very vocal fan — the ventriloquist's dummy 'Archie' of the long-running BBC radio show 'Educating Archie'. Peter Brough, the ventriloquist and creator of the show, is at right. His father, Arthur, was a great friend of Don Bradman

Right: Don Bradman has a box seat for the premiere of 'Annie Get Your Gun' in London, April 1948

He also found time for some relaxation. An executive of the Rank organisation took him to the premiere of the film 'Hamlet', followed by dinner at the Savoy. To Bradman's delight they were seated close to the famous dance band of that era: Carroll Gibbons and his Savoy Orpheans. Bradman had heard countless Carroll Gibbons records and he had admired the pianist for many years, and even attempted to copy his style of playing. He revelled in the opportunity to see and hear him at close quarters, and Gibbons rounded off the experience by introducing Bradman to his band and then engaging in some duo-playing with the famous cricketer in the band's dressing room.

When Bradman played against Surrey at the Oval, on 8–11 May, he was anxious to see how Alec Bedser would perform under English conditions. He suspected that Bedser might prove to be England's greatest menace to Australia, and later events were to prove him right.

Bradman himself was in excellent form during the Surrey match, and an English newspaper described the whole Australian performance as a 'Batting Orgy' when they totalled 632, but Bedser dismissed four of the tourists including Bradman and Hassett. Bradman scored 146, but as he wrote later 'Bedser finally bowled me with a glorious ball which pitched on the leg stump and hit the off — the same type of ball as that with which he bowled me for 0 in Adelaide in 1947.'

For England, Bedser seemed the only bright star on the horizon. When the Australians played Essex at Southend, on 15 and 17 May, they knocked up such an enormous score that the scoreboard on the Southchurch ground ran out of figures to record it. Their first innings score of 721, a world record for one day in first-class cricket, showed only as 21 on the board because there was no figure 7 on the hundreds reel. A club official said they had never expected to need it.

The match was played in perfect conditions, on a ground somewhat larger than average, against an eleven which included the fast-medium bowler Trevor Bailey who later played for England; Peter Smith, rated as the second-best slow bowler in England and one of Wisden's '5 Cricketers of the Year' in 1946; Ray Smith, a fast-medium bowler who bowled difficult in-swingers to a leg field; and the left-hander Price, who had headed Lancashire's bowling averages in 1946 and come close to Test selection.

Bradman's skilled indoctrination of his team bore splendid fruit as his batsmen handled these menacing bowlers with superlative ease. The Southchurch scorers had to work fast to keep up with them. Bradman went in twenty-two minutes before lunch, scored 42 before the interval, and then showed all his old relentless efficiency in a total of 187 in 124 minutes. The score brought his total of centuries against different English counties up to twelve, thus passing Warren Bardsley's previous record of eleven centuries against eleven different counties.

After this demonstration of effortless batting superiority, the Australians showed themselves equally dominant as bowlers. Miller, Johnson and Toshack dismissed the Essex batsmen twice in one day, for 83 and 187, to give Australia an astounding win by an innings and 451 runs.

The English newspapers gave the match as much coverage as if it had been a Test and wrote gloomy predictions for the future. Any Englishman who thought that Bradman's age and physical condition would favour England's Test chances had now been disabused. One writer described him as 'tough-looking, very bronzed, and just solid muscle and sinew'. Others mentioned his unfailing courtesy. The Southend *Newsman-Herald* mentioned that they had sent a reporter to interview Bradman in London, to 'bid him welcome to Essex', but the reporter had missed Bradman who had then written an apologetic letter to the editor. The editor remarked: 'The fact that he took the trouble to respond so politely shows what a great man he is, for all great men place first importance on simple acts of courtesy.'

The first match at Lord's, against the M.C.C. on 22–25 May, again proved that London cricket grounds were 'too small for a Bradman match'. A capacity crowd of 33 000 packed the ground and many thousands were turned away. Bradman went in on the first morning at 11 for one, and quickly delighted the crowd with a fireworks display which brought him 50 in sixty-seven minutes. He just missed his century when Edrich caught him at the wicket, off Deighton, for 98. Nevertheless he had broken yet another record: Bardsley's 7866 runs for Australia in England, in 175 innings. Bradman had now totalled 7927 in ninety-four innings.

The Australians gave another masterly exhibition, against a strong M.C.C. side, and won by an innings and 158 runs. Bradman began to feel that his men could more than hold their own against the best teams England could muster.

Earlier in the tour, in Bradman's speech at the Institute of Journalists luncheon, he had asked journalists reporting the tour to remember that the matches were friendly games between two brother countries. He said: 'We are a friendly lot and we wish to remain so . . . Let us make this tour one of friendly good will, free from unfortunate incidents and sensations.' Jack Hobbs replied in the *Sunday Express* 'And so say all of us.'

But newspapers thrive on sensation and they soon found 'incidents' of one kind or another. When the Australians played Lancashire at Old Trafford, on a typically wet and difficult Manchester wicket, nineteen-year-old Malcolm Hilton became the 'boy hero' of England when he

Sir Donald Bradman is an
Honorary Life Member of the
Yorkshire, Lancashire and
Hampshire County Cricket Clubs
of England. The clubs seized the
opportunity of his final Test tour to
extend the invitations for life
membership

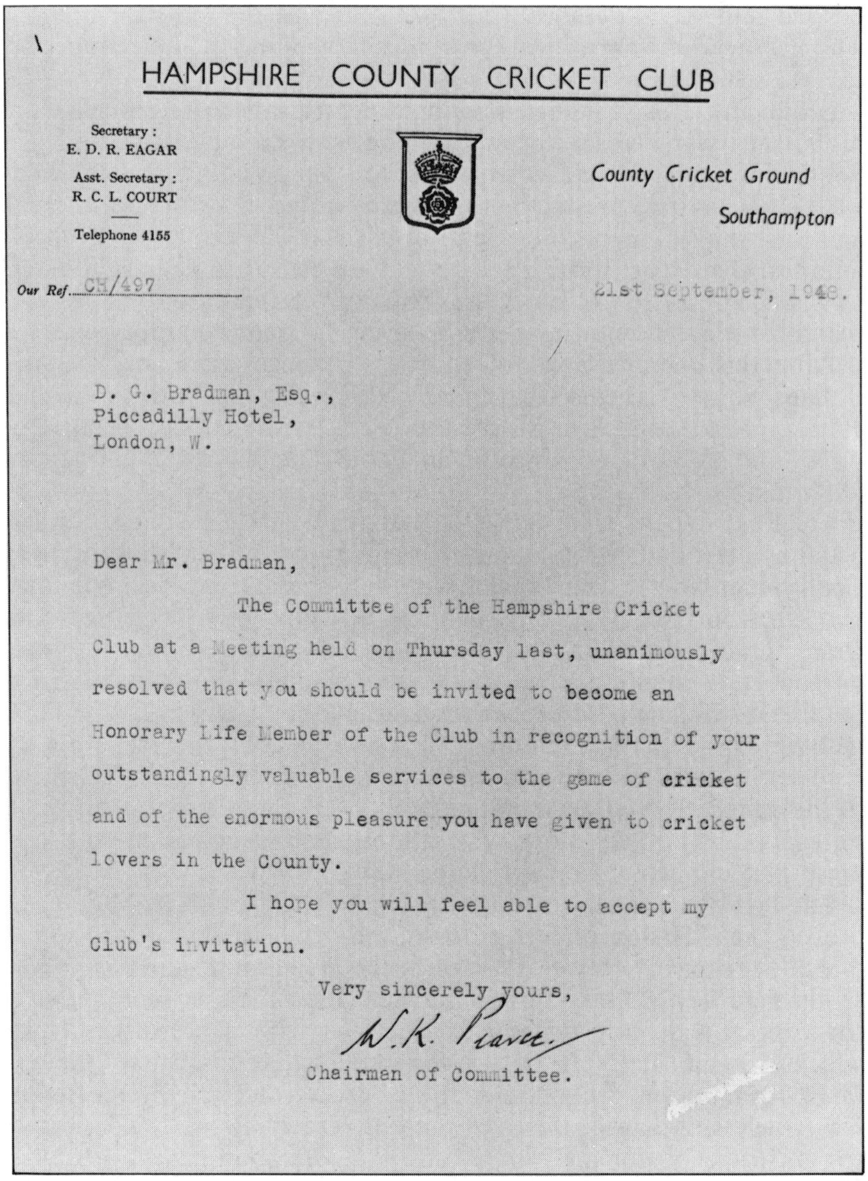

HAMPSHIRE COUNTY CRICKET CLUB

Secretary :
E. D. R. EAGAR

Asst. Secretary :
R. C. L. COURT

Telephone 4155

County Cricket Ground

Southampton

Our Ref. CH/497

21st September, 1948.

D. G. Bradman, Esq.,
Piccadilly Hotel,
London, W.

Dear Mr. Bradman,

The Committee of the Hampshire Cricket
Club at a Meeting held on Thursday last, unanimously
resolved that you should be invited to become an
Honorary Life Member of the Club in recognition of your
outstandingly valuable services to the game of cricket
and of the enormous pleasure you have given to cricket
lovers in the County.

I hope you will feel able to accept my
Club's invitation.

Very sincerely yours,

W. K. Pearce,
Chairman of Committee.

dismissed Bradman in both innings, for 11 and 43. The Australians did not equal their more recent performances, the match was drawn, and the newspapers blazoned Bradman's failure and the achievement of Malcolm Hilton.

At about the same time, the sportwriters Brian Chapman and David McNicoll stirred up further storms. Chapman accused Bradman of placing his fielders too close to the M.C.C. batsmen at Lord's; McNicoll said that Bradman had refused to see Lord Tennyson when the cricketing aristocrat called at the Australian dressing room. According to McNicoll, Lord Tennyson was 'furious' at such treatment. Other writers suggested that the noble lord had been imbibing in the members' bar and that Bradman had refused to see him for that reason.

The newspapers made much of several alleged 'bodyline' incidents when the crowds protested at bumpers from Miller or Lindwall. One of these occurred during the match against Nottinghamshire, another drawn game, in which Bradman scored 86. The Notts batsman Walter Keeton stepped in front of a shortish ball from Lindwall, and collapsed when it hit him over the heart. The crowd yelled 'Send for Larwood!' and when Bradman helped Keeton off the ground a number of spectators ran onto the field and crowded around them.

The Sussex match, on 5 and 7 June, was a lamentable demonstration by the English bowlers and batsmen. Lindwall made hay of the Sussex batsmen for a first innings of 86, and Bill Brown and Arthur Morris surpassed that total between them when they went in to bat. Bradman scored his century in 118 minutes and, at 109, threw his wicket away once again. For the thirteenth time, he had scored a century or more against different English counties.

The 'all-conquering Australians' threw the English sportswriters into such a tizzy that they doubted England's ability to stand up to the invaders in the Tests. Many, including Jack Hobbs and Neville Cardus, campaigned for a last-minute review of the English team and recommended the replacement of the captain, Norman Yardley. He had been vice-captain on the 1946–47 tour of Australia and he had a 'nice guy' image but the critics thought he lacked the iron determination essential to subdue the 1948 Australians. The usual tumult of press advice and speculation rose to a climax just before the first Test, when the selectors confirmed Yardley as captain of a team including Compton, Hutton, Edrich, Hardstaff, Washbrook and Bedser. Bill O'Reilly criticised it for being 'top heavy with batsmen' and an obvious attempt to secure a drawn game.

If that was indeed the selectors' intention they were to be sadly disappointed. Neither the batsmen nor the bowlers measured up to the Australians.

The first Test opened at Nottingham on 10 June, in fine weather and on a wicket which the groundsman said was 'full of runs'. Yardley won the toss, England batted first, and rapidly fell apart. None of the batsmen survived for long and even Compton and Hutton scored only 19 and 3 respectively. One newspaper lamented 'Let us weep.'

Bradman began his first innings at 73 for one, at 12.50 p.m. on the second day. England held him down by defensive bowling and fielding tactics and he was at first very cautious against Bedser and Laker, but he played steadily and soundly to accumulate 130 by stumps. Next morning, at 132, he completed his 1000 runs for the season before Hutton caught him off Bedser at 138.

Australia ended the first innings with a dominant 509, but England recovered some of their form in the second innings and totalled 441, including a 'fighting century' by Compton who played throughout the day in poor light. He totalled 184 before he hit his own wicket in trying to avoid a short-pitched ball from Miller.

But the recovery was not enough to stave off defeat, although Bedser and Hutton repeated the leg trap which dismissed Bradman in his first innings. It was more quickly successful on this occasion and he had not broken his duck before he glanced a ball off Bedser into the expectant hands of Hutton.

Australia won by eight wickets, and the tour had now generated such excitement that England regarded Bradman's next county match, against Yorkshire, almost as a 'mini-Test'. More than 40 000 spectators attended the Bramall Lane Ground, Sheffield, to see the pride of Yorkshire take on Australia, and it was in fact a very 'near-run thing'. Australian batsmen fell fast under the Yorkshire attack and Bradman had to fight hard for 54 in his first innings and 86 in the second, the best scores for his side apart from Bill Brown's 113. It was a rowdy match, with spectators booing Bradman for his frequent consultations with bowlers and Keith Miller for some of his alleged 'bodyline' bumpers. At one stage, Barnes and Miller turned to the crowd and affected to conduct the uproar of shouting and booing.

The match ended in a draw, and with a cloud over the immediate Test future of some of the Australians. Keith Miller had strained his left side, Ray Lindwall and Sam Loxton had strained leg muscles, and Colin McCool had a split spinning finger. The skin tended to split after very little work. The English newspapers showed a ghoulish glee in their reports of these injuries and seemed to see them as England's best hopes for the second Test.

It opened at Lord's on 24 June, with Loxton and McCool omitted from the Australian eleven. Spectators had queued all night to see the match although the ground had been swamped by rainwater two days earlier and there had been some doubts about the likelihood of play. Alec Bedser had 'eyed the wicket glumly' on the day before the match.

Bradman won his first Test toss in England, on a humid summer day which kept the wicket damp and green. As he said later, it was a dubious advantage because he wasn't sure whether to bat or field, but the end-result supported his judgment. The innings began badly when Hutton caught Barnes for a duck. Bradman walked out to join Arthur Morris, and the roar which acclaimed Barnes' downfall was almost repeated, but quickly throttled, when Bradman was nearly bowled first ball from Bedser.

Norman Yardley had once more set the leg trap which caught Bradman before, but he was very wary of it. For the first hour he played very cautiously, and he seemed to have settled down when he failed to time his leg glance properly off Bedser's bowling. At 38, he gave yet another catch to Hutton.

Jubilant English sportswriters claimed that Australia would now be 'lucky to make 300', but they mustered 350 and they dealt very decisively with England's batsmen. Ian Johnson, Bill Johnston and Ray Lindwall dismissed them for 215.

In Bradman's second innings he resisted the temptation to glance Bedser's in-swingers and thus kept himself out of the jaws of the leg trap, but the constant need for caution slowed down his scoring rate. In a long partnership with Sid Barnes — who compensated for his first innings duck with a total of 141 — he scored 50 in ninety-eight minutes before tea. After the interval he handled Bedser very competently and, at 89, appeared to be well set for his century. But then he gave a hard and low chance to first slip, where Edrich snapped up the ball with a magnificent catch.

It was Bradman's last innings in a Test match at Lord's, and some sportswriters expressed generous regrets that he had not been able to bow out with another century. One wrote: 'In spite of this it was an innings which worthily marked the close of an era at Lord's; and the crowd's ovation as Bradman left the field supplied appropriate recognition of his notable contribution to cricket there over the last eighteen years or so.'

Throughout the match, the cricketwriters had fluctuated wildly between hope and despair. They called Australia's first-innings dismissal for 350 'a triumph for the English attack' but then had to write 'Lindwall blasts England's hopes.' When Bradman declared at 460 for seven in the second innings, they wrote such comments as 'Only a miracle can rob Australia of victory.' The series was broadcast directly to Australia, and the lights burned late in many homes on the other side of the world as supporters listened tensely for the outcome.

By Monday 28 June it was almost a foregone conclusion. The Australian bowlers swept the English batsmen away like tumbleweeds before the wind. With Hutton out for 13, Washbrook for 31, Edrich for 2, Compton for 29, Dollery for 37, and Yardley for 11, the *Daily Mail* printed a banner headline proclaiming 'England's batsmen must score or go.' Sportwriters called for a complete revision of the Test team as England collapsed for a second innings 186 and Australia won by 409 runs. The *News Chronicle* said it was ridiculous that Australia, with a population only slightly larger than London's, should 'cut through the counties like a whirlwind and then carve up England in the Tests'.

The gross attendance of 132 000, and receipts of £43 000, broke all previous records for a Test in England.

On 30 June, immediately after the second Test victory on 29 June, Bradman's triumphant team took on Surrey's finest at the Oval. The Surrey side included Alec Bedser's twin brother Eric, who was a talented all-rounder, together with such notable players as Laurie Fishlock, Arthur McIntyre and Errol Holmes. Bradman won the toss but put Surrey in first.

They mustered 221, and then set the now very obvious leg trap in the hope of ridding themselves of Bradman without delay. But they did not have Alec Bedser to bowl to it and Bradman was too wise a bird to be caught yet again. He hooked freely through the fielders, scored 50 in fifty minutes, and was 84 not out, after ninety-six minutes at the wicket, at the end of the first day. Next morning he completed his century in a further twenty minutes and half-an-hour later, at 128, he threw his wicket away.

Australia won by ten wickets and Bradman gave himself a rest while his men travelled to Bristol to play Gloucestershire. Despite his absence, the enormous batting strength of Australia shone through as Arthur Morris (290) and Loxton (159 not out) led an avalanche of scoring to record Australia's highest total for the tour: 774 for seven wickets declared. Australia won comfortably by an innings. Bradman had mixed feelings about the forthcoming third Test, to open at Manchester on 8 July. He knew himself to be 'notoriously unsuccessful' at Manchester, but hoped he would do better on this final appearance. It would be good to secure the Ashes in the third Test and then carry on to enjoy the rest of the tour. Perhaps the weather, as so often in Manchester, would be the final arbiter.

Bradman and his co-selectors gave careful thought to their third Test eleven. They had to omit Bill Brown, because of a finger injured while fielding against Surrey, but they gave Neil Harvey his Test blooding as twelfth man. The sportswriters made a few comments about the selection but they were far more critical of the English side. The selectors' principal response to the cry for replacements had been the omission of Len Hutton and the selection of the comparatively unknown George Emmett. Bill O'Reilly wrote: 'The Australian prospects are even brighter than they have been for either of the two Tests already played . . . Emmett will find lots of trouble in dealing with the opening attack.'

O'Reilly's prediction came true when Emmett and Washbrook opened for England. Johnston dismissed Washbrook for 11, and Emmett survived only a few minutes of a partnership with Compton. Then Compton tried to hook a waist-high no ball but it flew off the edge of his bat to strike him on the eyebrow. The crowd gave some angry shouts as blood poured down his face and the Australians helped him off the field, but he was soon back again with two stitches in his eyebrow. He batted courageously on and totalled 145 not out.

Australia's fielding was somewhat below standard, with a number of missed chances, and they suffered a disaster when Pollard made a mighty swipe at a ball from Ian Johnson. He connected perfectly and the ball hit Barnes like a bullet, striking him in the ribs under the left arm. He collapsed in great pain and had to be carried off the field — to the cheers of a few unfeeling spectators.

Compton's performance was the best for the Englishmen, who mustered 363 but met a tempest of scorn from the newspapers. The *Daily Herald* wrote 'Compton saved England's face at the expense of his own', and the *Yorkshire Post* correspondent growled 'The batting was dreadfully poor . . . the most depressing experience I have ever had at a cricket ground.' Ray Robinson cabled to Australia '. . . the selectors, in their surgical treatment of a losing side, amputated the wrong leg.'

When the Australians batted, the jinx which haunted Bradman at Manchester exerted its influence once again. He went in at 3 for one on the second afternoon, in his fiftieth Test match, but he made only seven runs before Pollard dismissed him lbw with an in-swinger.

The English bowlers took speedy revenge on the Australians. Morris fell for 51; Hassett for 38. Barnes made a gallant effort to bat but his injury forced him to retire after twenty-three minutes with only one run. The first innings closed with a deficit of 141 and O'Reilly wrote: 'England's bowlers . . . set the stage for Australia's first defeat since 1938.'

On Saturday 10 July, England made an excellent start to their second innings. The Australians made another poor showing in the field. Hassett, at long leg, dropped two identical catches off hook shots from Washbrook, and Johnson missed a third catch from the same batsman. By the end of the day England had a lead of 316 with seven wickets in hand. The Sunday newspapers expressed hope of a sweeping victory.

But then the Manchester weather intervened. One of the endless flow of 'depressions over the Irish Sea' flooded Old Trafford and there was no play on the Monday. It seemed that another Manchester Test would be a literal wash-out, but Bradman and Yardley decided to recommence play at 2.15 p.m. on the last day. Yardley declared, at 174 for three, and the crowd watched tensely as Johnson and Morris opened for Australia 'on a wicket liberally poulticed with sawdust'.

Ian Johnson was soon back to the pavilion and Bradman went in at 10 for one. Pollard and Bedser bowled with an attacking field of six fieldsmen in a crouching cordon, and each ball made a pockmark on the sodden wicket. Bedser made the occasional ball buck and rear to head height.

But Bradman and Morris were playing for time rather than runs and they held their wickets in a grim defence, twice interrupted by heavy showers. When play was resumed for the last time some spectators jeered at Bradman for his defensive batting and one yelled 'Bowl him an underarm!' But Bradman placed each ball exactly where he wanted it to go. At stumps, Morris was not out for 54 and Bradman not out for 30. The match was drawn and the Ashes remained with Australia. Some sportswriters grumbled that England had been defeated by the weather rather than by the Australians, but it was all in the luck of the game. The attendance record had been broken yet again, with an aggregate of 133 740.

The Ashes were secure, but Australian delight was marred by controversy over the proposed Don Bradman Testimonial Match, to be played on his return home. The Victorian and South Australian cricket associations had arranged for the match to be played in Melbourne, but the NSWCA protested that this was a 'snub' for New South Wales. That State planned to stage a long-deferred testimonial match for Kippax and Oldfield in Sydney, and the NSWCA claimed that the Bradman match would 'divide interest and detract from both matches'.

Arthur Mailey said the New South Wales attitude was a result of Bradman having left that State to play for South Australia, but the NSWCA denied this. Bradman, in England, refused to comment on the argument flaring in Australia.

A match against Middlesex preceded the fourth Test and ended in an Australian victory by ten wickets, although Bradman batted only in the first innings and made a mere 6 runs before Compton, at backward short leg, caught him in the same old leg trap. The failure did not detract from Bradman's confidence as he travelled to Leeds, the scene of some of his greatest triumphs, for the opening of the fourth Test on 22 July.

Len Hutton was back in the English eleven, which was anxious to show they could win at least one Test. The Australian selectors omitted Barnes, who had still not completely recovered from his injury, and gave Neil Harvey his first chance in a Test. He had batted brilliantly in the county matches.

Fortune favoured Yardley in the toss and allowed him to put his men in first on a 'feather bed pitch'. Hutton and Washbrook made the most of it as openers. Edrich and Bedser followed suit, with the latter sent in as nightwatchman. O'Reilly wrote a scathing criticism of Australian bowling, which had allowed England to set a comfortable lead. But Compton fell for 23 and after that the English tail soon ceased to wag. However Yardley's men totalled 496 and their supporters lost some of their pessimism.

Bradman's massive achievements on the Headingley ground had made Leeds folk feel almost proprietorial towards him, and they greeted him with a prolonged roar of applause when he went out to join Morris, at 13 for one, only fifty-one minutes before stumps on the second day. He pleased the crowd with a display of explosive hooking against some short-pitched deliveries, and made 31 not out. He seemed to have made a good start towards another 'Leeds spectacular', but Pollard dismissed him, at 33, after only eight minutes of the third morning.

With Morris, Bradman and Hassett back in the pavilion the outlook was grim for Australia, but Neil Harvey's first brilliant Test century helped to raise the first innings aggregate to 458. Harvey totalled 112.

England responded with a day of aggressive batting and at the end of the fourth day had a lead of 400 runs with two wickets in hand. To most people's surprise, Yardley continued batting for five minutes on the last day, during which three more runs were added, before declaring. This gave Australia the huge task of scoring 404 to win, with only 354 minutes to play, on a worn pitch which took spin. The early evening editions of the newspapers predicted 'The best they can hope for is a draw.'

An immense crowd packed the ground or waited in long patient queues outside. The clouded skies which had given a gloomy start to the match had cleared, and much of it was played in unusually warm sunshine. In an atmosphere of electric tension, pressmen and spectators watched the Australians begin their seemingly hopeless battle.

No team in history had ever scored 400 runs in the last innings to win a Test and the odds against Australia were immense. But this match was to put the seal on Bradman's team and on his faith in their skill. He refused to think about a draw and told his men they were to aim for victory. This example of leadership was to win the game for Australia.

Alec Bedser, backed by the Lancashire fast-medium bowler Dick Pollard and the Surrey off-spinner Jim Laker, attacked with 'menacing determination'. Bedser hemmed in Morris and Hassett with an attacking field and the runs only mounted slowly as the minutes ticked inexorably by. After an hour there were still only 44 runs on the board.

Compton followed Laker at the bowling crease and soon dismissed Hassett for 17. The crowd, lulled out of their first tension by the long opening stand, sprang to life again as Bradman walked out to the wicket. They marked his last appearance on the Headingley ground with an enormous clamour of applause.

He had some unhappy moments off Compton's bowling, but scored 35 in the thirty minutes before lunch. In the afternoon, he and Morris launched into an historic assault on the English bowling. Morris punished Compton with a series of drives and square-cuts which brought him his century, and Bradman's hand-clasp of congratulation, in a few minutes over two hours. Bradman reached his 50 with an exquisite late cut off Bedser, and then proceeded to punish Ken Cranston the Lancashire dentist, a fast-medium right-hander.

Bradman reached his century at 4.10 p.m., after 145 minutes at the wicket. Just before tea, when he was 108, Evans missed a difficult legside chance to stump him. It was England's last opportunity to subdue his domination of the innings. Australia still needed 116 to win, with only 105 minutes to play, but the superhuman partnership continued until Yardley caught Morris when he had scored 182.

Neil Harvey hurried out to join Bradman but by that time there was little doubt of the outcome. Bradman remained not out 173, and Australia totalled 404, to win by seven wickets with fifteen minutes to spare. The superb second wicket partnership of 301 by Bradman and Morris showed conclusively that Australia could have retained the Ashes even without the drawn game at Manchester. Ray Robinson wrote that the Test victory at Leeds was the 'finest ever' in its conquest of seemingly insuperable odds.

WHO WAS AUSTRALIA'S TOP BATSMAN — BRADMAN OR TRUMPER?

From the moment that Bradman first sprang into prominence, cricketwriters compared him, in one way or another, with Victor Trumper. In the beginning such comparisons were usually in Trumper's favour — especially on the points of grace and style.

In that period, many of the writers were men who saw and idolised Trumper in their young and impressionable days. Others were players of the Trumper era who were growing old when Bradman burst on the scene, and did not live to see his final maturity.

But, as time passed, a certain number of critics of about the same age as Bradman — or even younger — continued to make these comparisons and often went to great lengths to prove that Trumper was the better batsman.

One of the notable exceptions was the great English cricketwriter Sir Neville Cardus, who once

One of the few surviving photographs of Victor Thomas Trumper (1877–1915) who was Australia's greatest batsman before the advent of Don Bradman

wrote: 'No batsman has equalled, or has come anywhere near to equalling, Bradman's power to amass vast runs day by day, season by season, quickly and absolutely safely.'

This point is unarguable, but it has not prevented the critics — perhaps impelled, in some cases, by jealousy of Bradman — from trying to prove that Trumper was somehow the better batsman.

Bradman himself has always remained completely aloof from the argument. He was only a lad of seven when Trumper died and obviously he never saw Trumper bat. His only knowledge of his great predecessor was gained from the lips of those who had seen Trumper play and from reading books and articles.

The only way to clarify the argument is by analysing the batting figures of both men and comparing the conditions under which they played, while first admitting that Trumper, by general consent, was the most stylish and graceful of batsmen.

The only Australians who appear to have approached his elegance were Alan Kippax (who was born in time to watch and be influenced by Trumper's batting); Archie Jackson, who in turn was influenced by watching Kippax; and perhaps Stan McCabe, although McCabe had a particular fluency of his own.

Style and grace are lovely assets and pleasing to the eye. They play a worthy part in the attraction of cricket for spectators. But, of course, they do not win matches.

To begin with, one should compare the vital rules as they were during the cricketing careers of the two champions.

The Ball. During Trumper's regime, the circumference of the ball had to be between 9 and 9¼ inches. During Bradman's career, it had to be between 8¹³⁄₁₆ and 9 inches.

This reduction in size must clearly have been of assistance to the bowlers — especially the fast ones — and the smaller ball must have been a more difficult target to hit.

Taking of the New Ball. Trumper's first-class career began in 1894. Up to and including the season of 1906–07, he had 268 innings. From then until the end of his career he had a further 133 innings.

For the first part, which comprised two-thirds of his innings, he batted under laws which only allowed one new ball per innings. The law allowing a new ball after 200 runs did not come in until after 1907.

Bradman played the whole of his career under (a) The new ball after 200 runs law, *or* (b) The more severe law which allowed a new ball after so many overs.

The latter was changed as experience showed what was appropriate, but when it was first introduced, in 1946, the number of overs was 55 and the new ball came into use well before the 200 runs had been scored.

In 1948, on Bradman's last tour of England, the new ball was frequently taken before 100 runs had been scored, because the requisite number of overs had been bowled before then.

The change was of enormous assistance to fast bowlers.

Trumper had a great advantage over Bradman, with regard to the taking of a new ball, in the need to cope with fast and medium pace bowlers.

Bowling Crease. In 1902, the width of the bowling crease was increased by one foot each side of the stumps. This was a distinct help to bowlers because it helped them to increase the angle of delivery.

Trumper enjoyed the benefit of the narrower width for his first 112 innings, or approximately 28% of those he played.

Bradman played under the wider crease for the whole of his career.

The Wicket. During the Trumper era, batsmen had to defend stumps 27 inches high and 8 inches wide.

In the late 1920s there was a decision, at first experimental but later mandatory, to increase the height and width by one inch, making the wicket 28 inches by 9 inches.

For all practical purposes, therefore, it may be said that Bradman, during the whole of his first-class career, had to defend a wicket more than 14% larger than the one that Trumper had to defend.

L.B.W. Law. Throughout the whole of Trumper's career, the ball had to pitch in a line between wicket and wicket — commonly called pitch straight — for an lbw appeal to be answered in the affirmative.

In 1935, an experimental rule was introduced whereby a batsman could be given out (providing the other conditions of the law were fulfilled) to a ball pitching outside the off stump. This became law in 1937.

It may therefore be reasonably said that Bradman had to contend with the offside law outside the off stump (which Trumper never did) for half of his career and for two of his four tours to England.

Significantly, Bradman's highest average on an English tour was in 1938, when the more difficult offside law was in operation.

The effectiveness of the new lbw law, and the added problems which it presented to the batsmen, may be deduced from the following facts:

In 1933, under the old law, eleven English batsmen averaged over 50 runs per innings. In 1934, fourteen did so.

In 1935, the year it was introduced, none averaged over 50. In that same year 1273 batsmen were given out lbw and no less than 32% of them fell under the new law.

In 1938, under the new law, Bradman averaged 115.66.

In 1902, in 53 completed innings, Trumper made eleven centuries — 20.75%.

In 1938, in 21 completed innings, Bradman made thirteen centuries — 61.9%.

Wet Wickets. This is perhaps the one area in which opinion must be formed on the evidence without the support of statistics.

A batsman may play on a wet wicket which is not difficult. If the soil is saturated, and there is no drying sun, the ball may cut through without much lift or spin. Or the wicket may be what is known as a 'pudding': slow and easy.

The same pitch, as it dries under a hot sun, may become a real sticky: a 'glue pot' on which a ball of full length will fly viciously and become almost unplayable.

One of the reasons for Trumper's great reputation as a wet-wicket player is that he made a century before lunch under wet-wicket conditions at Manchester in 1902.

But *Wisden* said of the match: 'The Australians derived great advantage from winning the toss as up to lunch time the ball did nothing on the soft turf. Trumper, Duff, and Hill made splendid use of their opportunities, but it must be said that the English bowlers did very poor work, pitching so short that it was often an easy matter to pull them.'

In the first 80 minutes, Trumper and Duff made 135. They could never have done this on a sticky wicket against fast bowling.

The most crucial argument in the whole matter concerns the covering of wickets and the ability to use fast bowlers on wet wickets.

In that 1902 Manchester match, the English captain could not use his fast bowler, Lockwood, until the score reached 129, because Lockwood couldn't get a foothold. The slow bowler Wilfred Rhodes had to open the bowling.

Prior to 1913, neither the pitch *nor the bowler's footholds* were covered. They were equally wet.

In the second innings at Manchester, the bowler's footholds had dried out and Lockwood opened the bowling. He quickly dismissed Trumper for 3, Duff for 4, and Hill for 0, and Australia were 3 for 10.

It is quite clear that batting on wet wickets after 1913 presented an entirely new hazard.

There is a vast difference between wet wickets in England and Australia. In Australia, they are infinitely more difficult and at times virtually unplayable. Probably this is why the Australian cricketing legislators were the first to experiment with covering the pitches, although England was always reluctant to follow suit. For a long period, in both countries, only the bowler's footholds were covered. The pitch itself was left exposed to the weather.

Even after Sheffield Shield wickets were totally covered, the wickets for international matches were left uncovered in Australia.

This meant that the wickets were never covered during Bradman's four tours of England and all his international matches in Australia. It made batting immeasurably more difficult, because fast bowlers could operate from firm and dry footholds and fire the ball at full speed into the sticky wicket.

In the 1936–37 Australian season, Bradman scored two successive ducks on sticky wickets. In Brisbane he was out second ball to Allen, and in Sydney he was out first ball to Voce. In the latter match, Voce got O'Brien, Bradman and McCabe for ducks in four balls. Allen and Voce were bowling from a firm foothold: the batsmen playing on a sticky wicket. It was impossible for them to play balls flying into their faces at 80 mph off a full length.

In the wet wicket comparison between Bradman and Trumper, one is not comparing 'apples with apples'. In Trumper's era, the fast bowler was disadvantaged and the batsman correspondingly advantaged. During much of Bradman's career, exactly the reverse applied.

Even when wickets are totally covered, as in Sheffield Shield matches since 1935–36, rain may seep under the covers and affect only a part of the pitch. Bradman had more than once to bat under such conditions, which are even more difficult than when the wicket is totally wet.

As to Bradman's own ability on rain-affected pitches, it is interesting to observe that B. J. Wakley, in his invaluable book *Bradman the Great*, devoted a special section to 'Bradman on Rain-Affected Wickets'. In this section, for statistical reasons and not for the purpose of comparison with any other batsman, he lists in detail all the innings by Bradman on pitches affected by rain.

According to Wakley, Bradman made altogether 1941 runs in England in 30 completed innings on rain-affected wickets at an average of 64.7. This compares with Trumper's career average, on both wet and dry pitches, of 44.5.

Wakley points out that Bradman certainly played some poor strokes on 'false turf' and had some disappointing failures on rain-affected wickets, and often appeared uncomfortable even when he was successful. But every other batsman in the history of the game, including Grace, has had trouble on wet wickets. Even Jack Hobbs, the master of sticky wickets, was not always successful on them. Bradman did at least as well on bad wickets as any of his contemporary Australians.

Naturally Bradman, like anyone else, preferred batting on good wickets to bad ones. Unlike anyone else, he was always expected to knock up a huge score and if he did not do so the critics immediately said 'He can't score on wet wickets.' But it is quite fallacious to suggest that he never made runs unless the wicket was in his favour. No-one could have averaged 96.44 on four tours of England, of which the first and last were particularly wet summers, unless he could make runs on both rain-affected and dry wickets. Bradman was perfectly capable of batting on a 'bowler's wicket' and, as will be seen, often did so with success.

Those who compare Bradman and Trumper often laud the latter for his performance in 1902, which they claim to have been a remarkably wet summer even for the British Isles. The figures, however, tell a different story.

The official weather records show that in the four principal cricketing months of the year in England, May to August inclusive, there were 285 millimetres of rain in 1902 and 299 millimetres in 1930. Bradman's first tour was in fact made during a wetter summer than Trumper's 1902 tour — and so, incidentally, was Bradman's 1948 tour.

During May to August inclusive, the average rainfall in Trumper's four tours of England was 259.7 millimetres. During Bradman's four tours, it was 265 millimetres. Obviously it cannot be said that Bradman enjoyed any kind of weather advantage over Trumper.

Another canard which does not stand up under examination is that Trumper's career, like Archie Jackson's, was cut short at an early age by illness, and that he would have gone on to even greater things than Bradman if he had lived to do so.

Trumper opened his first-class career in the 1894–95 season, when he was seventeen, and played his last first-class match in 1914, at thirty-seven. His career spanned twenty years.

Bradman's first-class career ran from December 1928, when he was nineteen, and concluded in 1949, at forty. From this period of twenty-one years one must deduct four years of the second world war, when no first-class cricket was played. His career was in fact three years shorter than Trumper's.

A comparison of their completed innings is:

	Trumper	Bradman
In Australia	186	218
In England	193	120
In South Africa	8	—
In New Zealand	14	—
	401	338
not-outs	21	43
completed innings	380	295

In Trumper's 380 completed innings he made 42 centuries, a ratio of 11.05%.
In Bradman's 295 completed innings he made 117 centuries, a ratio of 39.6%.
In Trumper's 81 completed Test innings he made 8 centuries, a ratio of 9.8%.
In Bradman's 70 completed Test innings he made 29 centuries,a ratio of 41.4%.

In Test matches, the following comparisons apply:

	Innings	n.o's	Runs	Average
Trumper	89	8	3163	39.04
Bradman	80	10	6996	99.94

Another yardstick to compare players is gained by calculating the number of completed innings a batsman played for each century he scored. This method shows that Bradman's figures are more than twice as good as any other player who ever lived.

Bradman scored an average of 39.6 centuries for every 100 completed innings. Next to him is Wally Hammond, with 18.6 per 100. Despite Trumper's advantages, mentioned earlier, he is well down the list with 11.05 per 100.

Some critics have been uncharitable enough to suggest that Bradman's career average is better than that of all other players solely because, after reaching 100, he went on to make huge scores.

This is rather absurd because Trumper also made many huge scores, including 300 n.o. v. Sussex, 293 v. Canterbury N.Z., and 292 n.o. v. Tasmania. Hammond made 36 double centuries, against Bradman's 37, including four scores over 300 against Bradman's 6.

But, if all of Bradman's 117 centuries were reduced to exactly 100, his average would still be 65.82: more than 10 runs per innings higher than that of any other player in cricketing history.

More detailed comparisons between Bradman and Trumper are as follows:

Trumper's first-class career:
401 innings 21 not outs 16 939 runs Average 44.57

Bradman's first-class career:
338 innings 43 not outs 28 067 runs Average 95.14

Trumper's four English tours

1899	48 innings	1556 runs	Average 34.57
1902	53 innings	2570 runs	Average 48.49
1905	47 innings	1667 runs	Average 36.23
1909	45 innings	1435 runs	Average 33.37
Total	193	7228	38.6

Bradman's four English tours

1930	36 innings	2960 runs	Average 98.66
1934	27 innings	2020 runs	Average 84.16
1938	26 innings	2429 runs	Average 115.66
1948	31 innings	2428 runs	Average 89.92
Total	120	9837	96.44

Trumper in Tests only against England in England

	Innings	Runs	Average	
1899	9	280	35	
1902	8	247	30.8	
1905	8	125	17.8	
1909	9	211	26.3	
Total	34	863	27.8	Average

Bradman in Tests only against England in England

	Innings	Runs	Average	
1930	7	974	139.14	
1934	8	758	94.75	
1938	6	434	108.50	
1948	9	508	72.57	
Total	30	2674	102.84	Average

The statistics show clearly that there is no comparison between the performances of the two men, especially when one considers the various advantages under the rules which Trumper enjoyed during his career. There can be no doubt that Bradman holds the position of Australia's greatest batsman.

In Bradman's six innings at Leeds during his cricket career he had totalled 963 runs at an average of 192.6. Yorkshiremen were as proud of him as though he had been one of their own and they would have been glad to show their pride and pleasure in his exploits, but he was already aboard a train for Derby. Immediately after the Test victory the Australians had had to pile into the train, hot, weary, hungry, and thirsty, en route to their next engagement. Bradman's side was paining him again and he was hardly in the mood for cricket when he batted against Derbyshire next morning. As he wrote later, he scored his 62 runs by 'reflex action'.

In the subsequent match, against Warwickshire, he managed only 31 and 13 in his two innings, but he showed better form in his second innings against Lancashire. The match was featured as the Cyril Washbrook Testimonial, and he pleased the capacity crowd with a brilliant 133. He made 108 before lunch, an extremely rare achievement, against the bowling of such men as Pollard, Ikin, and Cranston.

Bradman earned the plaudits of all Lancastrians by a wonderful gesture to Cyril Washbrook in this match. Instead of enforcing the follow on, when Australia led by 191 in the first innings, which could have ended the match in two days, Bradman batted again.

This had the double effect of making the match last three days and putting Bradman in again on the third day, thus helping to attract a capacity crowd. As a result, Washbrook's benefit realised over £14 000 sterling, then the highest sum ever earned by an English benefit match.

In the second week of August the Australians returned to London for Don Bradman's final Test, with the sportswriters excitedly discuss-

The 'old' ball (top) shows the difference in size from the 'new' ball. Victor Trumper made his great scores in matches using the old style of ball, whereas Bradman's were made with the 'new' ball

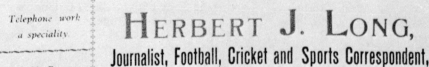

TELEPHONE: WOOLWICH **1514**.

Telephone work
a speciality.

Reliable Reports
and Comments by
Trunk Telephone.

Experienced
Telephone
Operators.

HERBERT J. LONG,

Journalist, Football, Cricket and Sports Correspondent,

23, THOMAS STREET, WOOLWICH, LONDON, S.E.18.

ESTABLISHED 1899.

Leading Provincial, Midland and Southern Newspapers Catered for.
Special Criticism for Morning Papers by Train.
Reports Telephoned to London Office of Provincial Newspapers.

Reports & Comments
promptly by
Press Telegram.

Special Cyclist
Messengers.

Cup-tie matter
a speciality.

D. Bradman Esq.,   16th August, 1948.
Captain,
Australia Cricket Team (in England) 1948.
Kennington Oval, S. E. 11.

     My dear Don,

          I am now nearly 70 years of age, and,
have been Reporting Test Cricket matches in England 43 years.
Next to Mr. Hubert Preston, Editor of "Wisden" my great friend,
and, at one time my Colleague on the staff of the Cricket Reporting
Agency, I believe I was the second oldest Pressman in the Press Box
at the Oval on Saturday last, 14th August:

          I feel I must write to you to say I thank
God I have been spared to witness the unforgettable scene at the
Oval on Saturday when you emerged from the pavilion to take your
place at the crease. First, the Surrey Members and, their Guests,
in the pavilion seats, stood up and set the cheering going. The
whole community on the ground were upstanding like a flash, Men,
Women, of all ages, Youths, young Girls, and Children, Boys and Girls,
who, through their Parents, had been privileged to be present on
this historic occasion, shouted and clapped their hands with an
enthusiasm that I, in my long lifetime, have never seen on a Cricket
Field before. And, I have seen all the old masters receptions
in their last Test match, Mc. Laren, Hobbs, Ranji, Hendren, Woolley
and the rest of them. Then the climax to your wonderful reception came.
The sight of the England team, spread out, but facing the pavilion
to greet you and clap you in right up to the crease. Then came Norman
Yardley, England's Captain, HATLESS, to go forward to you and, as I
saw through the powerful glasses, to give you a real PAL'S right
hearty grip of the hand of congratulation. Then suddenly, Yardley
raises his Cap and calls for THREE CHEERS for Don Bradman, and, the
whole assembly give it as I have never seen it on a First Class
Cricket Ground before.

          To me, an old man, it was an amazing sight.
I was thrilled to the bone, and, suddenly, I felt a **tear** trickling
down my cheek, and, I am not ashamed of it. The Oval crowd have always
been a great cricket public. The British crowd, as well as the
multitude of Australians, who were at the Oval on Saturday, were
keyed right up, and, how sincere was their shouts and hand-clapping
for Don Bradman. It was a wonderful day for them and, a wonderful
day for me. In this wonderful atmosphere Don, none of us, who witnessed it,
can exactly vision what your emotion could have been. We can just assume.
My greatest thrill on a cricket field was many years ago, when I bowled
out W. G. Grace, and, sent his middle stump spinning out of the ground.
My thrill at the Oval on Saturday was as great. It will remain with me
for the rest of my day's, short though they may be.

          Don, you are shortly going back to Australia.
And, in your mind will be the fact that, the Bristish public have
not only admired your cricket. BUT, also your sportsmanship. You, too,
have the consolation of knowing that the lads you have with you on the

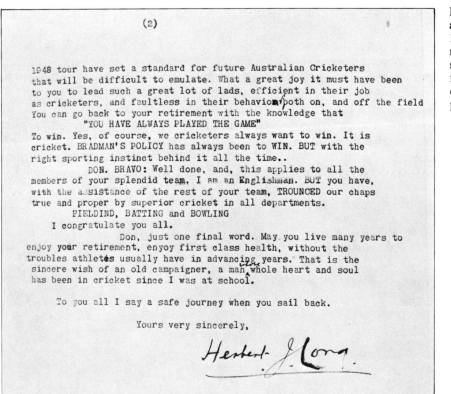

1948 tour have set a standard for future Australian Cricketers
that will be difficult to emulate. What a great joy it must have been
to you to lead such a great lot of lads, efficient in their job
as cricketers, and faultless in their behaviour both on, and off the field
You can go back to your retirement with the knowledge that
                "YOU HAVE ALWAYS PLAYED THE GAME"
To win. Yes, of course, we cricketers always want to win. It is
cricket. BRADMAN'S POLICY has always been to WIN. BUT with the
right sporting instinct behind it all the time..
            DON. BRAVO: Well done, and, this applies to all the
members of your splendid team, I am an Englishman. BUT you have,
with the assistance of the rest of your team, TROUNCED our chaps
true and proper by superior cricket in all departments.
        FIELDIND, BATTING and BOWLING
    I congratulate you all.
                    Don, just one final word. May you live many years to
enjoy your retirement, enjoy first class health, without the
troubles athletes usually have in advancing years. That is the
sincere wish of an old campaigner, a man whole heart and soul
has been in cricket since I was at school.

    To you all I say a safe journey when you sail back.

        Yours very sincerely,

        Herbert J Long.

Don Bradman's final Test appearance, at the Oval on 14 August 1948, was an emotional moment for all the cricketers and spectators. This letter to Bradman from an English sporting correspondent gives a graphic picture of the scene at the Oval

ing the English selection and the rain pouring steadily down onto Kennington Oval. The Surrey secretary said gloomily: 'Earlier we were rolling it with blankets, but all the blankets in the British Army can't help now . . . The pitch is like a sponge saturated with water . . . the constant rain has prevented us cutting the grass, and the outfield is like a hayfield.'

But the weather cleared and Bradman and Yardley decided to play. Yardley won the toss and chose to bat. As *Wisden* said later, this was 'An inevitable decision with the conditions uncertain and the possibility of more rain'. The grass was so slippery that Lindwall and Miller had difficulty maintaining their balance, and Miller actually fell after one delivery, but they and Johnston bowled superbly. Five men failed to score and when Hutton was last man out for a defiant 30, the whole side had only totalled 52. It was a record low for an English Test team on a home ground.

They had been conquered by superb Australian bowling rather than the state of the pitch, and perhaps by their own 'defeat mentality' after three Test failures and one drawn game.

In assessing Bradman's great record as a Test captain in England one should not overlook his misfortune with the coin. In his two tours he won the toss only once, and that on an occasion when it was of no advantage. On the contrary, the English captain had repeated use of a wonderful batting pitch. Even in the final, Yardley batted first because he thought it best for his team.

Barnes and Morris showed there was little wrong with the pitch when they opened for Australia, and passed England's score in less than an hour. They completed 117 in copybook style before Barnes stretched out at a leg-break wide of the off stump and Evans held a splendid catch.

Now came the historic moment when Don Bradman walked for the last time out to a Test wicket. Spectators, members, waiters, gatekeepers, groundsmen, and cricketers — every man and woman who saw him start his usual deliberate walk out to the wicket — erupted in a prolonged roar of acclaim. When Bradman reached the wicket the sound rose to a new crescendo as Yardley gathered his men around Bradman and led them in three cheers. The crowd joined each cheer in a crashing volley of sound, while the cricketers waved their caps and closed around the man who had set examples for every bats-

Don Bradman appears to look disbelievingly at his broken wicket when Hollies bowls him for a duck in his final Test innings

man to emulate. Gradually the demonstration died away as Bradman took his stance against the Warwickshire leg-break bowler Eric Hollies.

Bradman was deeply moved by the overwhelming drama of his final Test appearance, by the obvious sincerity of the English cricketers who had grasped his hand and wished him good luck for the future, and by the significance of this moment which marked the conclusion of his twenty years in Test cricket. He longed above all things to give the crowd a last great display of the batting which so many of them had come to see, so that in years to come they might say proudly: 'I saw Bradman make his last century at The Oval.' And he needed only four runs to give him a Test average of 100. To end with a 'century average'

STUMPS

BRADMAN OUT TO GOOGLY

Bradman, who had been beaten all the way when he played forward to a googly from Hollies, was grinning broadly as he returned to the pavilion.

The pitch was taking spin more sharply and Hollies several times beat Morris with well-disguised wrong-'uns.

With Hollies and Young bowling well, Morris and Hassett were content to defend their wickets, and scoring was slow! Then Compton relieved Young.

Scores:—

Morris, not out   77
Hassett, not out   10
Sundries   5
_____
Two wickets for 153

A newspaper 'Stumps' report of Bradman's last Test dismissal would be a wondrous conclusion to his Test career.

Tense and anxious, his vision blurred with emotion, he played the first ball from Hollies without making a run. Hollies ran up again and delivered a perfect-length googly. Bradman just touched it with the inside edge of his bat, and almost incredulously heard the crisp click as his off bail was dislodged. The crowd roared again, in mingled jubilation at this English triumph and sadness at the Don's defeat.

Keith Miller was in the dressing room when Bradman returned. He watched Bradman sit down to unbuckle his pads, and as he did so he said, 'Gee whizz, fancy doing that!' Miller wrote later: 'It proved that Bradman was as human as any other member of the team.'

Bradman's men won the match for him with 389 in their first innings, and England was not equal to the task of making up the huge deficit. The match ended with an overwhelming Australian victory of an innings and 149 runs.

Bradman had been grievously disappointed by the 'blob' in his final Test, but he now had a new target to aim at: that of leading an Australian tour which would return home without experiencing a single defeat. This could not necessarily be taken for granted. Five first-class and two second-class matches remained on the itinerary, and experience proved that the Englishmen had an uncomfortable habit of assembling what were virtually Test teams to combat the Australians when the battle for the Ashes had been decided.

But the Australians swept through the rest of the programme like a conquering army. At Canterbury, where the match attracted a record-breaking 42 000 to the ground, Kent mustered a total of only 175 in two innings, and lost by an innings and 186 runs. At Bradman's farewell appearance at Lord's, against The Gentlemen of England on 25–27 August, his team won by an innings and 81 runs. He compensated for his failure at the Oval by a faultless innings in classic Bradman style, reaching his century in 150 minutes and totalling 150 runs, including nineteen fours, before he threw his wicket away with a skier to mid-on. When he was 18 he completed his 2000 runs for the season, and thus became the oldest — as he had been the youngest — touring batsman ever to reach this total in an English season.

On 26 August, the day before Bradman's fortieth birthday, the members of the M.C.C. made him a birthday presentation because they feared the match might not last until the third day. The Earl of Gowrie, president of the M.C.C., whom Bradman had known when he was Governor of South Australia, presented him with a specially-bound copy of *Lord's* by Sir Pelham Warner and a big cake made in the form of an open book. One leaf bore the wording 'To Don Bradman. Many Happy Returns of the Day. From all at Lord's', and the other leaf bore a bouquet of sugar roses, a photograph of Bradman inset in the right-hand corner, and a marzipan kangaroo on each corner of the base.

On Bradman's last day at Lord's, the Australian players gathered around him as they entered the field and sang 'Happy Birthday'. At the conclusion of the match the public crowded in front of the pavilion to sing the same song and 'Auld Lang Syne', while Bradman and others waved good-bye from the dressing-room balcony.

And so it went on, with the Australians undefeated in every match and Bradman's admirers in the United Kingdom seizing the oppor-

tunity to render tributes of admiration and appreciation. They came from people in all walks of life. Great bundles of mail continued to arrive at his hotels along the itinerary and he was invited to a series of farewell receptions. The Yorkshire Cricket Club made him a Life Member and presented him with a splendidly engraved and inscribed silver tray, embossed in white enamel with the White Rose of Yorkshire. The newspaper *The People* inaugurated 'The Bradman Fund' in an unprecedented gesture towards an overseas cricketer. The subscriptions, limited to one shilling, flowed in to the newspaper in thousands from people of all ages.

Bradman's final first-class match in England was against Mr H. D. G. Leveson-Gower's XI at Scarborough. As usual, the eleven assembled by the diminutive stockbroker was practically a Test team. Nine of the eleven, including Hutton, Edrich, Robins and Bedser, were prominent English bowlers or batsmen. Bradman told 'Shrimp' Leveson-Gower that the Australians would fight every inch of the way to deny England a face-saving victory in this last match.

Bradman lost the toss, but on a pitch swept by North Sea winds and showers his bowlers gave 'Shrimp's' men a lively time from the moment Ray Lindwall dismissed Hutton with the fourth ball of the first over, for a duck. Lindwall accounted for five more of the Englishmen and Johnson and Johnston for the remainder, for a total of 177.

The birthday cake presented to Don Bradman by the M.C.C. on his fortieth birthday

Bradman went in late on the second evening, at 102 for one, and was 30 not out overnight. Next day he batted faultlessly throughout the morning, completed his eleventh century of the English season, and continued after lunch until he had reached 153. Then once again, as so often on that tour, he threw his wicket away.

He declared when Australia was 489 for eight, and the first-class section of the tour ended when he bowled the last over of the match. It ended in a draw, and Bradman's men had become the only Australian team ever to go through England undefeated.

A remarkable point was that Bradman's total of runs for the tour, 2428, was just one less than his aggregate in 1938. But whereas in 1930, 1934, and 1938 he had amassed no less than two triple centuries and ten double centuries, his highest score in 1948 was 187. He no longer had the stamina, and perhaps did not have the resolve, to match those earlier huge scores unless it had been absolutely essential. With such a strong batting array behind him, he was content to do just as much

The cover of a souvenir brochure sold on Bradman's last cricketing tour of Scotland

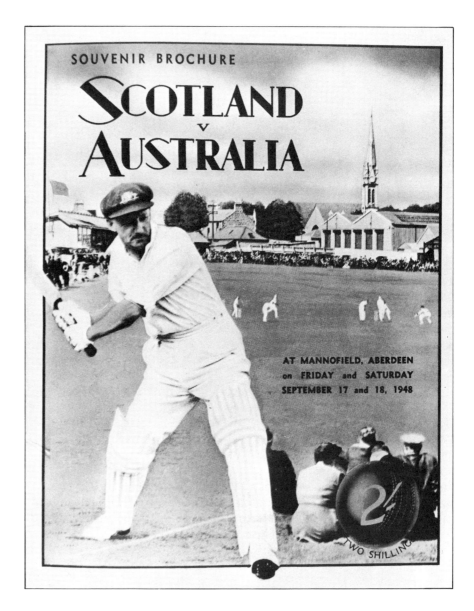

SOUVENIR BROCHURE

SCOTLAND
v
AUSTRALIA

AT MANNOFIELD, ABERDEEN
on FRIDAY and SATURDAY
SEPTEMBER 17 and 18, 1948

2/-
TWO SHILLINGS

as he thought was necessary or in the interests of his team. There is little doubt that he could have gone on to double-century figures had the need arisen.

A visit to Scotland, to play at Edinburgh and Aberdeen, showed that interest in Don Bradman was just as strong north of the border. His last game in Britain, at Aberdeen, attracted the record crowd of 10 000. On 18 September 1948 he played his last innings on British soil and 'went out in a blaze of glory'. He treated the Aberdonians to a whirl-wind display of Bradman batsmanship, reaching his century in 80 minutes. He scored 123 not out and chalked up the last 23, including two sixes, in nine minutes.

It was a pity that Jessie Bradman, with her Scottish descent from Clan Menzies, could not have watched this great performance in Scotland. Ian Johnson, later to become secretary of the Melbourne

Afternoon tea at Balmoral was a memorable occasion for the Australian cricketers in Scotland in September 1948. Don Bradman and Queen Elizabeth talk to Princess Margaret, who wears the 'New Look' fashionable in those post-war years

Cricket Club, shared in most of Bradman's final partnership with a splendid innings of 95, and said later that it was one of the proudest moments of his life.

In Scotland, the Australians received the honour of an invitation to afternoon tea at Balmoral. King George VI, Queen Elizabeth, the Duke of Edinburgh and the two Princesses received them in a homely friendly manner, and on this relaxed occasion the press photographers snapped Bradman chatting to the King with his hands in his pockets. In fact Bradman was not the only man with his hands in his pockets, but the press published only a part of the photograph and singled out Bradman for criticism over the informality. In reply to the taunt of discourtesy, Bradman pointed out that it was a completely informal event and that His Majesty also would in all probability have had his hands in his pockets, if he had not been wearing a kilt.

The story prompted a humorous editorial in an Australian newspaper, pointing out that Bradman at least did not have his hands in someone else's pocket. That privilege was reserved for the tax collector.

The last formal occasion of the tour was a luncheon at the Savoy Hotel, London, arranged by *The People* for presentation of the tribute purchased with subscriptions to the Don Bradman Fund. This was a solid silver replica, twenty-one inches (53.34 cm) high including the base, of the famous Warwick Vase: the huge white marble vase of Roman origin discovered and restored by Sir William Hamilton in 1774 and later presented by him to his nephew George, Earl of Warwick.

Two hundred people, including ten young lads as representatives of the thousands who had supported the fund, attended the luncheon. The Earl of Gowrie presented the trophy to Don Bradman, Norman Yardley supported the toast to Bradman, and he replied in words with which he tried to express his gratitude to the English people, his devotion to the game of cricket, and the principles he had followed throughout his career.

The sum of money raised by *The People* was greatly in excess of the amount required to purchase the vase, but Bradman refused to accept the balance in cash. Instead, he requested that it should be used for the purpose of laying down concrete pitches in English parks for the benefit of under-privileged children.

Recently, he donated the magnificent silver replica of the Warwick Vase, together with the unique Royal Worcester porcelain vase presented to him in 1938 when he scored his third double-century against Worcestershire, to the State Library of South Australia. In the summer of 1982–83 they formed the central features of a display of Sir Donald Bradman's memorabilia, including bats used in his famous exploits and other trophies. It is hoped that a permanent display of these mementoes will eventually be mounted for posterity. The Warwick Vase replica and the Royal Worcester vase, perhaps two of the most valuable cricket trophies in Australia, are now held in perpetuity by the State Library for the people of Sir Donald's adopted State.

The 1948 tour had been an enormous success for Bradman and his men, not only in its cricketing triumphs but also because of the cheerful confidence which impressed and encouraged so many English people in that dark year after the war. Philip Noel Baker, the British Minister of State, wrote to Bradman from the Commonwealth Re-

Opposite: Newspapermen used this photograph in order to accuse Don Bradman of 'discourtesy' because he had his hands in his pockets while chatting with King George VI. In fact the whole photograph, from which this portion was cropped and enlarged, showed that Bradman was not the only man with his hands in his pockets on what was a very informal occasion

The English newspaper *The People* opened a fund, with subscriptions limited to a shilling apiece, so that English cricket lovers might pay tribute to Don Bradman on his final tour. The newspaper used a portion of the subscriptions to purchase a silver replica of the Warwick Vase, which was presented to Bradman by Lord Gowrie at a function in the Savoy Hotel. Bradman asked that the remainder of the fund to be used to establish concrete cricket pitches for under-privileged English children

Don Bradman's last tour of England was the most successful, and probably the most popular, of any Australia Test tour of the 'Old Country'. The tourists did not suffer a single defeat, and they received universal acclaim as the 'happiest team' ever to tour England. This official letter illustrates the English attitude towards the Australians

> COMMONWEALTH RELATIONS OFFICE,
> DOWNING STREET, S.W.1.
>
> 25th September, 1948
>
> My dear Bradman,
>
> I said to you at the Savoy lunch on Monday that I was going to write you a letter to tell you what I think of the work which you and your team have done for Commonwealth relations during your present tour.
>
> No team from Australia has had such an unbroken and astonishing measure of <u>cricket</u> success. But your success has not only lain in victories on the field. No visiting team at any Game has ever been so popular as yours has this year. No team has ever done so much to stimulate and to create good feeling. Both the United Kingdom and Australia owe you a real debt of gratitude, and I hope you are very proud of what you have done.
>
> Believe me, with warm congratulations and sincere good wishes to you all,
>
> Yours ever,
>
> Don Bradman, Esq.　　　　Philip Noel-Baker

lations Office: '. . . your success has not only lain in victories in the field. No visiting team has ever been so popular as yours this year . . . Both the United Kingdom and Australia owe you a real debt of gratitude, and I hope you are very proud of what you have done.'

Despite the magnitude of Bradman's personal contribution towards the success of the tour, he was the first to recognise that victory had been achieved by a team effort. As a token of his gratitude he presented each member of the team with a silver ashtray, suitably inscribed with 'From your Admiring Skipper'.

The Australian success also prompted the Board of Control to depart from their usual rather parsimonious attitude. They paid tribute to an unprecedented tour by presenting each member of the touring party with a beautiful inscribed silver cigarette box.

Bradman felt both pride and sadness during the homeward voyage. His last tour would go down in cricketing history, and he could feel he had done his utmost for Australia as both captain and batsman. But there was sadness in the thought that it *had* been his last tour: that he was leaving so many good friends in England and that it might be a very long time before he saw that beloved country again. Bradman, like many Australians of his generation, regarded Britain as a second home.

As the ship neared Australia the newspapers provided a little light relief with a cable enquiring about Bradman's intention to enter Australian politics. He had not expressed any interest in the political arena but rumours were flying so profusely that a question was asked in Federal Parliament. A distinguished politician telegraphed Mrs Bradman, asking her to keep her husband out of politics lest he be reduced to a 'political stooge', by people who wanted to 'exploit the affection and respect that is held by all Australians for your husband'. When Bradman landed at Adelaide a wharf labourer bellowed: 'If you're going into parliament, Don, you'd better stand for the Labor Party!'

The argument about the Don Bradman Testimonial Match had been settled before he reached home, with the NSWCA consenting to its being played in Melbourne, and although he had announced his retirement from first-class cricket he could hardly refuse to play in his own testimonial match.

It opened on 3 December, with Don Bradman leading an eleven against Lindsay Hassett's Eleven. Most of the men on both sides were those who had played in the recent tour with Bradman and the others were notable Sheffield Shield players. Some of the tourists were still suffering from various cricket injuries but they would not miss the opportunity to turn out on the great occasion.

A day of rain in Melbourne seemed likely to postpone the match, but the weather cleared in time and the game started in near-perfect conditions. Newspaper publicity, which had irritated Bradman so often in the past, now did him a favour by attracting huge crowds to the four-day match. Journalists prophesied that it would return him £5000 to £10 000 or more. The millionaire John Wren promised to pay Bradman a pound for every run he scored, with a minimum of £200. He said 'I hope he scores 500.'

The twenty-two cricketers were exhilarated by the mass of spectators in the Melbourne Cricket Ground, who applauded each side with equal favour but reserved maximum acclaim for Bradman. Jessie Bradman, knitting calmly, watched from the wives' reserve.

Lindsay Hassett won the toss and his men gave a crowd-pleasing batting exhibition, for a total of 406. When Bradman went out to bat, at 3 p.m. on the Saturday, 52 960 spectators rose in their seats for the greatest demonstration ever heard on the MCG. One sportswriter reported: 'The Don, his head sunk in his shirt collar, edged his way down the aisle to the arena, faced a battery of cameras, and with his bat clasped under his arm as if he were afraid of losing it, fidgeted with his batting gloves as he made his way to the wicket.'

He responded to the occasion with a magnificent innings in which he faced some of Lindwall's fastest bowling. He reached his 50 in the hour before tea, and after the interval 'carried on majestically towards his 100'. At 97 he skied a ball from Johnston to wide mid-on, where Colin McCool got his hands to the ball, juggled it, and then dropped it. Bradman wrote in *Farewell to Cricket*: 'Whether Colin could have held that catch or not is something I did not ask nor shall I ever do so, but I have never been more grateful to see a catch grassed.'

At 123, including thirteen fours, he threw his wicket away. He had batted for two hours thirty-four minutes and made his 117th century.

On the Monday the cricketers were in light-hearted mood although they still gave the crowd more than its money's worth. Sid Barnes threw down his bat, produced a tiny toy bat from under his sweater, and blocked a ball from Johnson before throwing the little bat to umpire Wright in mock disgust. Shortly after this he bumped into Doug Ring while going for a run, wrestled him to the ground, and then hurried on with the game. He scored a dashing 89.

Bradman's eleven accumulated 434, but Hassett's men replied with a second innings of 430. The crowd enjoying this feast of cricket displayed as much excitement as though it had been a vital Test match, and groaned with despair when Johnston dismissed Bradman for 10 in his second innings. Other wickets also fell cheaply, but Don Tallon saved the day with a brilliant performance. He made 91 out of 100 scored in the last hour and 'stole' a century when it seemed that Hassett's men had the game sewn up. With 13 runs needed to win, and the last two batsmen at the wickets, Tallon maintained his stand until there was but one ball to go and three runs required. Tallon pulled the last ball hard to square leg and snatched two runs, but the last run was impossible and so the match ended in a dramatic tie.

It had been a sensational contest, with an aggregate of 1672 runs and a total attendance of 94 035 spectators. Bradman went into the press room to thank his old friends and critics for their help in creating such a brilliant success.

As a token of his appreciation, Bradman presented each player who participated in the match, together with the umpires and managers, with specially-made gold sleeve links of a cricket bat and cricket ball linked by a chain. No doubt these unique souvenirs will be treasured heirlooms, to be handed down through their families for generations to come.

After taking in donations and adjusting for expenses, the final cheque handed to Bradman was something in excess of £9000. This was a handsome amount for a genuine amateur player and to some extent it compensated him for the long years of endeavour and for the many absences from his family which he had endured over the previous twenty years.

But it was only a fraction of what he could have made by forsaking the cricket field for the press box, and some modern cricketers earn far more than that amount each year from playing fees, provident funds, and endorsements. Even a speech at a function is likely to bring a substantial fee to a modern player, whereas Bradman spoke on hundreds of occasions during his nearly fifty years of association with the game and never accepted as much as an honorarium for doing so.

Moreover, Bradman continued to serve Australia and South Australia as a selector and administrator, entirely honorary posts, for a quarter of a century after he had retired from first-class cricket, and gave the type of service which few players are able or willing to volunteer for the sake of the game.

On paper, Bradman's testimonial appeared to be the largest so far in Australia. In terms of purchasing power it was a good deal less than the £3000 which Trumper received in 1913, and it was not much more than half the total that Bradman helped to raise for Cyril Washbrook, a fine but far less distinguished player. It was dwarfed by the recognition of Dr W. G. Grace, who in 1895 was awarded a national testimonial of over £9000. The modern purchasing power of this amount would be over $400 000.

One should also remember what Bradman's magnetic drawing power had meant to the finances of various State cricket associations. Irving Rosenwater, in his splendid biography of Bradman, analysed the effect on the gate takings for New South Wales home matches when Bradman left that State for South Australia. Rosenwater showed that receipts for *only* the major home games fixture, the Sheffield Shield match against Victoria, fell from £2480.11.7 in 1933–34 (when Bradman was playing in Sydney) to £498.12.3 in 1935–36 after he had gone to South Australia, and thereafter declined to £98.15.0 in 1936–37 and £130.0.4 in 1937–38. From a surplus of £3167 in the financial year ending 30 June 1934, the New South Wales Cricket Association fell away to a loss of £3460 in the first year after Bradman had left them.

In Test and Sheffield Shield matches Bradman always received the same fee as that paid to all other players: no more and no less. This was a very different situation from that of the other great batsman, Dr W. G. Grace. On occasions, Grace received special consideration in regard to his medical practice and his fees for a match or tour. When the English team toured Australia in 1891–92, Grace had had a poor English season in 1891 and made only 771 runs at an average of 19.76 — but he was paid all expenses for the tour plus a special fee of £3000, worth about $140 000 in 1983.

The 1891–92 tour was the one financed by Lord Sheffield, who also donated the money to buy the prestigious Sheffield Shield: the focus of Australia's main internal cricket competition ever since then. The payment to Grace in that season was twenty times the cost of the Shield.

Bradman Helps Old Test Star

Don Bradman chats with Arthur Richardson (1888–1973) the right-hand opening batsman who played for South Australia from 1919 to 1927 and for Australia in 1924–25 and 1926. Bradman's last first-class match, the Sheffield Shield match against Victoria in Adelaide in 1949, was made into a Testimonial Match for Richardson . . . and ended badly for Bradman when he injured his ankle

FROM SIR DONALD'S SCRAPBOOKS

Newsprint was still in short supply in the post-war Britain of 1948, and editors had more than enough news to fill their columns. The exuberance of victory in 1945 had faded away in the anti-climax of the cold war, when Russia turned against her previous allies. Housing shortages, rationing even stricter than it had been during the war, post-war inflation, the continuation of conscription, and difficulties in obtaining all the comforts and necessities of life from coal to whisky made for a drab existence in Britain. The 1948 Test tour was one of the brighter spots of that difficult year and the newspapers made space to cover it in full. Several of Sir Donald Bradman's scrapbooks are devoted to the tour, and the following extracts, of which some are not accredited, give some glimpses of the British reactions to Don Bradman and his men.

Don pleased pressmen and photographers alike with his courteous readiness to pose and answer questions, and altogether the visitors created a splendid impression with everyone who went to the docks in the early hours to welcome them. — *Western Morning News*

The Australians had their last home-side meal of bacon and eggs and sausages before they left the steamship at Tilbury today. From now on they are pledged to live on British rations.

Bradman calls himself, as skipper, a 'decrepit old man.' By request he doffs and waves his hat and calls to the camera man: 'See, I'm pretty nearly as bald as you are.' The Antipodean accent is as marked as his grin.

Don Bradman will play in the first match of the Australian cricket tour, against Worcestershire. An unusually flippant Bradman, he joked merrily and posed comically for photographers on the quayside. In a message to England's cricket public he said: 'We will play the best cricket we are capable of giving.'

Here come the Australians to resume the cricket battle begun in 1876. The shooting war tore a gap in the records. But here is the mighty Bradman to link them together again, and to shed on our days the lustre that Grace, Ranji, Hobbs, and the other giants stamped on the cricket fields of the past.

Comedian of the party is mock serious Buster Keaton-ish Lindsay Hassett, the vice-captain. Music is supplied by pianist Don Bradman. He also bats.

England's cricket stock just now is very low. We have not yet recovered from our wartime losses, and the demands of economic recovery have necessarily hindered our team building. The young player to-day has to do his share of national service in the Forces or the mines, and release for full-time cricket is not easily obtained. — *Yorkshire Post*

People who have heard Don Bradman's public speeches since he arrived have been commenting on what a witty and pointed speaker he is. — *Sheffield Telegraph*

Don Bradman, Australian cricket captain, presented 17,000 food parcels from Victoria State to the Lord Mayor of London, Sir Frederick Wells, at a Mansion House dinner last night. The parcels are for needy people in all parts of Britain. — *Evening News*

Worcester gave an enthusiastic welcome to Don Bradman and his men when they arrived in the cathedral city . . . a local girl was nearly run over when she rushed across the road to throw a bat made from flowers through the window of Don Bradman's car. — *Daily Mirror*

Rumor, which more than once has declared Bradman to be old or ill or failing, was utterly discredited. — *Birmingham Post*

The Don . . . is a very different man. As late as two years ago in Australia he was always rather aloof, unsmiling, even a little grim. But now he is joking and laughing on the field, even during his own innings. Off the field he is going out of his way to meet people. At hotels he is making a point of personally thanking the staff for their attention to his team. — *Daily Herald*

When Alec Bedser bowled Bradman, the master batsman paused on the way out to tell the England bowler what a good ball it was. — *Daily Graphic*

There was great fun with a little brown and white dog who did his best to distract the Australians' concentration but only succeeded in upsetting Umpire Skelding, who refused to take it from Barnes as part of a player's equipment. Bradman sat on the grass and roared with laughter. — *Sunday Graphic*

We expect there will be acute analysis of batting, bowling, fielding, and captaincy, but we do not think the game should be used as a vehicle for distortion or exaggeration of events. — *Don Bradman in a speech to the Cricket Writers' Club*

Came the Don — a smiling, carefree cavalier of the crease, less sedate and cheekier than ever in his run-getting, especially with the late chop through the slips . . . Typical of Bradman's new look in Australian skippers was his mid-wicket handshake for Barnes as he made the run which gave him the century. — *Empire News*

All the obligations of fame surround Don Bradman at the present time. His daily post must be beyond the hopes of any film star; he makes numerous speeches, and it is not to be supposed that their excellence is achieved without time and thought; he is so genial and easily accessible that he can have singularly little time to himself. Yet he seems to thrive on exertion. — *The Field*

Don Bradman was seeing something new this afternoon, after lunch with the committee of the Stock Exchange. On the House floor a full-sized pitch was chalked out, and here a comic match was played . . . as, amid wild cheering, Bradman appeared, he was handed a toy bat. It broke at the first ball. Handed another, he proceeded to sky the next two balls to the dome. — *Daily Telegraph*

It's not all fun being a cricket celebrity. Don Bradman is harassed by clamouring fans wherever he goes. On Saturday he appeared almost unrecognised. By Monday he had to be brought to the ground by car, with two policemen hanging on each running-board to repel boarders. — *Essex Chronicle*

The first feature which strikes one about the Australians, and a feature they have amply substantiated to date, is the strength of their batting . . . Of their great earlier batsmen, Bradman stands out still as the finest run-getting machine in the world. He is a master at moving quietly and smoothly out to the pitch of the ball, and it is almost impossible to bowl a length to him. — *Country Life*

I was a guest over the week-end at a luncheon given to members of the Australian cricketing side by the Brighton and Hove Golf Club . . . I asked Bradman 'Isn't it easier to hit a stationary ball?' to which he replied with invincible logic 'It would be if it was as big as a cricket ball.'

My own memories of 'The Don' are of a captain, unlucky in the toss, half-doffing his blazer as he approaches the pavilion, a broad grin on his face, to let his men know they are fielding; of a skipper sitting in the open doorway of his dressing room during a 'bad light' period, a thoughtful expression on his face, autographing cricket bats; of a 'god' shaking hands with one of his worshippers — a nine-year-old boy, trembling with excitement — and chatting encouragingly to him. — *Nottingham Guardian*

An old lady in Australia was sitting up at night listening to the broadcast commentary of one of Bradman's early double centuries against England in this country. 'What a remarkable batsman,' she exclaimed suddenly. 'I wonder how many he'd get if he played in the daytime.'

First wicket down — and the small boys, the camera addicts and a controlling line of policemen form a corridor through which Don Bradman passes to the wicket. Neat, almost birdlike, he walks lightly, always with the collar of his shirt turned straight up and with his green Australian cap shielding a sun-rosy face but never throwing into complete shadow those sharp eyes. — *John Arlott in John Bull*

A horse named after Don Bradman won at 25-1 at Newmarket yesterday. But none of the Australian cricket team backed it. They did not even notice that it was running. The horse was Bowral Boy, owned by Mr B. Kerr, Irish cricketer. 'It's sire was Willow Knight,' said Mr Kerr. 'I knew Bradman was called the "Bowral Boy" because he first became famous at Bowral, New South Wales.'

In 1948, Don Bradman's old friend A. G. Moyes published a book entitled 'Bradman', which covered the batsman's life and cricket career until that year. Arthur Gilligan, the notable county cricketer and England captain, provided a foreword for the book in which he wrote:

. . . Don Bradman has always played cricket according to its highest traditions and he deserves the thanks of cricket lovers throughout the world.

Future generations will regard him not only as a very great batsman, but also as a brilliant captain and, above all, as one of the truest gentlemen who ever wore flannels.

THE LAST SCOREBOARD

Bradman's last first-class cricketing seasons, 1947–48 in Australia and 1948 in England, enabled him to add yet another series of records and achievements to the long list he had compiled since 1928. They included:

* The century in his first match against the Indians, which meant that he was the only Australian to have scored 100 in his first matches against touring teams from England, South Africa and India.

* His 100th century, scored against the Indians on 15 November 1947, made him the only Australian ever to reach this landmark.

* His 201 in the fourth Test against India was the sixth time that he made 200 or more runs in a day's play in a Test match. The closest competitor was Wally Hammond, who achieved 200 in a day in four Test matches. Bradman is the only batsman to have scored 200 against England, South Africa, the West Indies and India in a Test match against each of these countries.

* His 187 against Essex on 15 May 1948 was the highest score ever made by an Australian on the Southend ground. It was the fastest innings of his career, averaging 90 runs an hour.

* In the fourth Test match he completed 5000 runs against England. He is the only batsman ever to have done so, and the only Australian or English batsman to have completed 5000 runs in Tests between the two countries.

* In the 1948 tour he scored more than 2000 runs for the fourth time in succession on tours of England, and beat Warren Bardsley's record of 2000 in each of three tours.

16

KNIGHTHOOD
AND BEYOND

Sir Donald Bradman's collection of cricket memorabilia includes a unique tribute to the life and work of a world-famous Australian. It is a set of fifty-one splendid albums, each measuring twelve by thirteen inches and bound in green leather, assembled by the State Library of South Australia by way of a permanent reference to the life of the great batsman from his youth in Bowral until his retirement from first-class cricket. There are two sets of the albums, one in the State Library and the other in the possession of Sir Donald.

The library compiled the albums from Sir Donald's personal archives, but even though they are extremely comprehensive they contain only a portion of the material he collected during his career as cricketer, journalist and businessman. The extracts used in the albums include copies of newspaper cuttings, personal and press photographs, letters, telegrams and similar material, together with descriptions of each of his first-class matches based on the summaries given in B. J. Wakley's indispensable book *Bradman the Great*.

Three complete volumes of the set contain copies of the letters and telegrams which poured in from many parts of the world in January 1949, when the New Year Honours List included the creation of Donald George Bradman as Knight Bachelor, in recognition of his services to cricket and to Commonwealth sporting links.

The story flashed around the world and the messages of congratulation came from old friends, from cricket clubs and associations in Australia and overseas, from politicians, businessmen, umpires, and groups and associations of many different kinds; also from men, women and children in every cricketing country. Eight-year-old Gouranghadar Rajkowhra wrote from India and ten-year-old Dudley Tickle from New South Wales. Many of the messages were addressed simply to 'Sir Donald Bradman, Adelaide'. The manager of Slazengers Ltd summarised the general feeling when he wrote from London: 'I think I can say, without attempting to flatter you in any way, that this is one of the most popular of the New Year Honours among all the people in this country, and I am sure the same applies in Australia also.'

On 14 February 1949, a letter from the Official Secretary and Comptroller to the Governor-General invited Donald George Bradman to receive the accolade from the then Governor-General, Mr W. J.

The knighthood of Sir Donald Bradman, announced in the New Year's Honours List of 1949, received wide publicity and brought a deluge of letters and telegrams of congratulation from many parts of the world. Numerous English and Australian newspapers marked the occasion by special articles or by cartoons such as that reproduced here

McKell, in Queen's Hall, Parliament House, Melbourne, on 15 March. On that date, Bradman sat with 201 recipients of honours and decorations in the great hall with its towering statue of Queen Victoria, while Lady Bradman sat among the 500 invited spectators.

When an aide called 'Donald George Bradman, Esquire' he rose and walked forward with what the newspapers described as 'a half-smile on his face' to kneel on the red plush cushion. An officer handed a shining military sword to Mr McKell, who touched it lightly on Bradman's left and right shoulders and told him to arise. Both men smiled as Mr McKell shook hands and said 'Congratulations, Sir Donald'.

By that time, Bradman had at last played his final matches in first-class cricket. The organisers of two testimonial matches, for Kippax and Oldfield in Sydney and for Arthur Richardson in Adelaide, had asked him to play in those games, and he agreed to do so for the sake of those notable Australian cricketers.

His presence at the wicket was a virtual guarantee of success for the Kippax-Oldfield testimonial. A crowd of 41 575, including the Governor-General and the Prime Minister, waited impatiently for his appearance and then roared the greatest welcome he had ever received on the Sydney Cricket Ground. They applauded every step of his progress to the wicket, fell briefly silent when he took strike, and roared again when he pulled the first ball past square leg for two. As the players returned to the pavilion for the tea adjournment, a small boy burst from the crowd and ran towards Bradman with an autograph book. He laid his arm around the boy's shoulders and led him through the players' entrance.

The newspapers acclaimed his innings, of 53 in sixty-five minutes, as 'sweet batting' and 'entertaining cricket'. He played the fast bowling of Miller, Walker and Johnston with a deadly precision reminiscent of his most triumphant years, until he mistimed a slower ball from Miller. To the dismay of the spectators, Meuleman, at mid-on, just reached the catch with outstretched hands.

By comparison with the Sydney testimonials, the Adelaide match was something of an anti-climax. The crowd was not as large as the organisers had expected, and in his first innings he disappointed them with an uncertain performance which totalled only 30 before he chopped a low ball onto his stumps. Later in the match he suffered a fielding accident when he caught his foot in a sunken watertap as he ran after a ball. He twisted his ankle so badly that he had to retire from the game.

The incident marked the end of his active career in first-class cricket, but it was far from the end of his service to the ancient game. He was still an Australian selector and a member of the Board of Control and he was closely associated with the South Australian Cricket Association. He was a member of the Cricket Committee of the SACA from 1938 to 1965; vice-president of the Association 1950–65 and president from 1965 to 1973, when he retired to make way for a younger man; State representative at the Interstate Conference of Sheffield Shield States from 1945 to 1975; and from time to time a member of various sub-committees. He was one of the State selectors until 1965, and he is still a trustee of the Association.

He had to make time for all these obligations amidst the demands of his business life. The firm of Don Bradman & Co. had become well established but it required an enormous amount of his time and attention, especially since the post-war boom was accelerating and the share market was busier than ever before. Six-day weeks and twelve-hour days were not unusual for the proprietor of the firm. His work gave

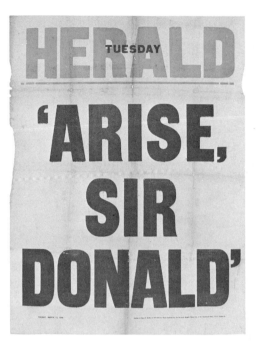

Above: The Melbourne *Herald* poster of 15 March 1949, the day on which Sir Donald Bradman was knighted by the Governor-General of Australia

Below: A champion's farewell. Leaving the field after the last innings on the Sydney Cricket Ground on 26 February 1949

Sir Donald Bradman in 1950

him such a solid reputation in the commercial world of South Australia that numerous companies offered him a seat on their boards, but he accepted only some of these. Sir Donald Bradman would never be content as a mere 'letterhead director', and when he joined the boards of various prominent companies he worked for them as devotedly as he did for his own firm.

He found relief from the demands of business life by turning to his old occupation of writing about cricket. As a non-player, he was no longer under the dictates of the Board of Control. He wrote a series of articles for the London *Sunday Chronicle*, which were also printed in the Melbourne *Herald*, and embarked on a much more comprehensive work of cricketing literature.

On 13 May 1948, early in his final Test tour of England, the English sportswriter Denzil Batchelor wrote a letter to Bradman commencing:

'Messrs Hodder & Stoughton are very keen to produce a book bearing your name as author, dealing with your life in cricket and your views on the game, to mark the occasion of your retirement from first-class cricket.' Batchelor's letter suggested that he should do 'the main part of the work' as co-author, and that terms should be negotiated by the literary agent David Higham. He enclosed with the letter an article he had written for the *New English Review*, which he described as a 'valedictory paean' to Bradman.

Bradman replied that he could not understand why Hodder & Stoughton had not approached him directly, as many other publishers had done. He said also that Batchelor and Higham would have to produce good reasons why he should engage them as agent and collaborator.

As for Batchelor's 'valedictory paean', he criticised it for using the phrase 'world-weary Bradman in 1948' and for repeating some of the objectionable comments in Clif Cary's book.

Despite this unpromising start, Bradman later agreed to meet David Higham and to sign a contract with Hodder & Stoughton, but he did not use Batchelor, or anyone else, as a collaborator.

The book was *Farewell to Cricket*, published in June 1950 and partly serialised in *The People*. It was Bradman's cricketing autobiography,

Sir Donald Bradman's third volume of reminiscences, published in 1950 as *Farewell to Cricket*, became a bestseller among cricket lovers in both hemispheres. This English bookseller made a gala occasion of the book's publication

with some sidelights upon other aspects of his life and many comments upon the game and the cricketers of that period. The book carried his story up until March 1949, and concluded with a series of articles on Bradman's philosophy of the game as it applied to such matters as captaincy, umpires, cricket grounds and critics of cricket.

Like Bradman's earlier books it was written with urbane good humour, precise and descriptive, without any attempt to emulate the florid prose of the best-known sportswriters of that period. He gave generous praise to a number of the cricketers of several countries with or against whom he had played, but said comparatively little about controversial issues. He devoted no more space to the 'bodyline' Tests than to other Test seasons.

Who better to write *The Art of Cricket* than the internationally famous batsman, captain and cricket administrator? The publishers, justly, called it 'The Classic Book of Cricket Instruction' and it received glowing reviews in every cricketing nation. Many bookshops, like this one in England, featured window displays of the book on publication

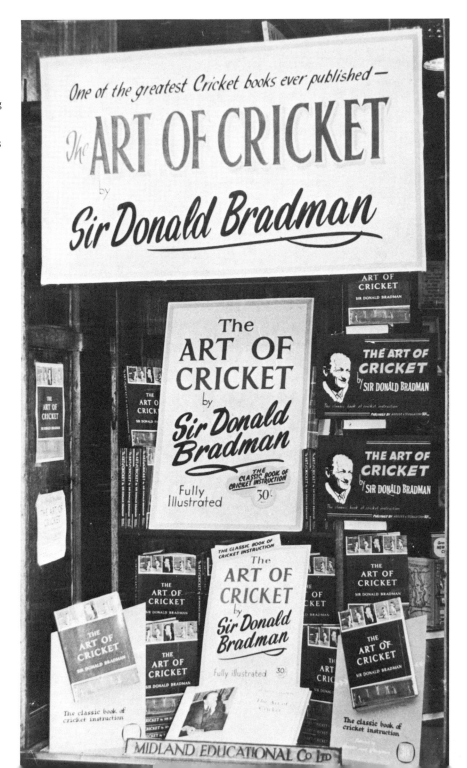

And, as in his earlier books, he tended to dismiss his own achievements rather casually, with such comments as '. . . it is remarkable that I played only one innings over a century in Sheffield Shield cricket that season. It was against Queensland. In making 452 not out, I managed to obtain the world's record score in first-class cricket. It still stands.' The comments made many years earlier about the modesty of the 'Bowral wonder' were still relevant. (In the 1958–59 season, the Pakistani champion Hanif Mohammed beat Bradman's record when he made 499 for Karachi v Bahawalpur. His 499 took 970 minutes: Bradman's 452 took 415 minutes.)

English reviewers gave the book a mixed reception but the great historian of cricket, H. S. Altham, wrote: 'It is a remarkable book, and by virtue of its range, penetration and authority must rank as one of the classics on the game.' In the prestigious London *Sunday Times*, Ian Peebles wrote that it was 'one of the most comprehensive and absorbing books yet published on an extremely well-documented subject'. Cricket lovers rendered the final verdict by making the book into a bestseller.

Despite blandishments from many British and Australian publishers, Sir Donald Bradman has written only one more book. It is *The Art of Cricket*, published in 1958. The book is an encyclopaedic volume of particular value to young cricketers, both as a treasury of information

---

THE HISTORIAN'S VIEW

One of the most comprehensive books ever published on cricket is *A History of Cricket*, by H. S. Altham and E. W. Swanton, published by George Allen & Unwin Ltd, London.

On page 310 of the second volume of the history (1962 edition) the writers provide a splendid summary of 'The Bradman Style' in the words: 'Not since W. G. in the '70's has any cricketer so dominated his generation. And when we remember the remorseless glare of publicity that attended his every innings and the strain of living permanently on a pedestal and ranking with Sydney Bridge and Harbour as the wonder of a continent, we may well marvel at the measure of self-control and simplicity which he preserved. Genius defies analysis, but no one could watch a long innings by Bradman without realizing some of his outstanding assets: a quite abnormally quick reaction, commanding immediate obedience from a perfectly co-ordinated body to the message of an icily concentrated mind: eyes, feet, and wrists that see and work just a fraction quicker than the "ordinarily great" player's, and enabled him to meet with ease the most delayed threat of speed or swing and to force ordinary length bowling almost where he willed through the gaps in the field: a repertoire of strokes so elastic that those gaps always seemed to be there, and yet so subordinated to his judgment that he could for hours cut out any that might involve unwarrantable risk. Add to this immense determination, seemingly inexhaustible physical endurance, and a genius for adapting his play to the changing tactical situation.

'It may be that Bradman had not the sheer grace of Victor Trumper, the versatility on all wickets of Jack Hobbs, the annihilating unorthodoxy of Gilbert Jessop, but for sheer ruthless efficiency no cricketer in the post-Grace era could compare with him.

'In the many pictures that I have stored in my mind from the "burnt out Junes" of more than half a century, there is none more dramatic or compelling than that of this small serenely-moving figure in its big-peaked green cap coming out of the pavilion shadows into the sunshine, with the concentration, ardour, and apprehension of surrounding thousands centred upon him and the destiny of a Test Match in his hands.'

and practical hints and for such philosophic comments as 'it is essential that a captain should enjoy the respect and confidence of his team. Not only should his cricket record be such that he is looked up to as a player but also his private life should be beyond reproach.'

In the interval between publication of the two books, Sir Donald returned to journalism as a special writer for the London *Daily Mail*, on the 1953 and 1956 Australian tours of England, and also devoted much love and effort to a problem of his family life.

In 1951–52 South Australia was subject to a particularly virulent epidemic of poliomyelitis. The Sabin and Salk vaccines had not yet been introduced and many young people fell victim to the crippling disease. They included twelve-year-old John Bradman. He had to spend the best part of a year in a steel frame, undergoing daily therapeutic treatment. It was an anxious period for patient and parents because complete recovery was by no means assured.

However, he progressed so well that he eventually returned to school and successfully completed his studies. In sport, he made a century in the Inter-Collegiate cricket match and became his school's outstanding hurdler. On the Adelaide Oval he set a new South Australian record for the 120-yards hurdles.

At one time John Bradman was seen as a potential Olympics hurdler, but a very bad knee injury ended his career in that sport. In cricket he reached district first-grade standard, but he did not long pursue his activities on the pitch.

John's recovery enabled Sir Donald to accept the *Daily Mail* invitation to spend two months or so of the 1953 Test season in England, to cover the Tests for that newspaper. The invitations for the 1953 and 1956 seasons were welcome for more than one reason. Sir Donald has always been attracted to journalism, he writes strongly and fluently, and he relished the opportunity to write for one of the world's leading national dailies. The fees were useful to a man who had to rely on his own hard-won skills to make his way in the world, and the two visits were wonderful opportunities to renew old acquaintances and to see England again. Above all, they gave him an unexpected chance to enjoy all the old thrills, tensions and comradeship of a Test tour — without having to bear the weight of a captain's responsibility.

In June 1953 Sir Donald and Lady Bradman made their first international flight and arrived in England in time to attend the first Test of that Coronation Year. England was a happier and more hopeful place than it had been in 1948. Most essential items were still 'on the ration' as a part of Britain's prolonged sacrifice for the sake of her European neighbours, but the nation was poised on the brink of two decades of prosperity. In a welcoming article, the *Daily Mail* staff writer Tom Clarke said that Sir Donald was 'incapable of dipping his pen in venom', and predicted that he would write informed and intelligent reports which would be in refreshing contrast to the 'gladiatorial gush and poetic piffle' indulged in by many cricketwriters.

Clarke's prediction was accurate. Sir Donald certainly did not write in the flowery and ornate style of some other cricketing journalists and, unlike some of these, he did not seek for controversies with which to spice up his articles. He wrote clearly and straightforwardly, with occasional flashes of humour or vivid phrases to illuminate some event, about the game he knew better than any of the other writers. In his description of play, discussions of tactics, and comments about the strengths or weaknesses of various players, he took his readers into the heart of the game. His articles, which were also syndicated in some Australian newspapers, were extremely popular. The circulation of the *Daily Mail* increased during that English summer and the rise was attributed to the interest aroused by Bradman's articles.

Shortly before his 1956 visit to England, after his retirement from business, there was a good deal of discussion about him acting as manager for the Australian team, although he never took any part in this. Sid Barnes wrote in the Sydney *Daily Telegraph* that Australia needed Bradman as manager if they were to recapture the Ashes lost in 1953. Barnes believed that had management had been responsible for that defeat, and that the team needed 'a little martinet like Sir Donald' to 'handle firmly the collection of prima donnas, schoolboys, and playboy types he is likely to have under his control'. In fact there was never any official suggestion that he should manage the team and he would have rejected the appointment if it had been offered to him.

But Barnes may well have been right. Sir Donald followed the tour simply as a journalist — together with Lady Bradman and their two children — and Australia failed once more. If he had offered to manage the team there can be little doubt that his Board colleagues would have accepted him, and it is interesting to speculate on the possible difference that it could have made to Australia's fortunes.

Perhaps Sir Donald felt that his position as an Australian selector attracted enough criticism, some of it vituperative, without taking on the burdens of a tour manager as well. A selector's task is a thankless one under almost any circumstances, and as he once remarked, 'The only difference between being a player and a selector is that as a player you can sometimes be right.' No matter what team the selectors may announce, there will be vociferous supporters of those omitted. If the team loses, it is the selectors' fault. If it wins, then a disgruntled minority will claim that the victory should have been by a larger margin.

In 1957 *Truth* called Bradman and his co-selectors Jack Ryder and 'Snow' Seddon 'The Terrible Trio', because of their omission of Queenslanders from a team to tour New Zealand. The newspaper accused the selectors of regarding Queensland as 'a big bit of nothing', and that any Queensland cricketer who thought the three men would choose him was 'trusting enough to sleep with a taipan'.

Nevertheless, history shows that in Sir Donald Bradman's term of service as an Australian selector, which stretched from 1936 to 1971 with an interruption only during his son's illness, the majority of Australian sides were successful. He played a part in selecting teams for 151 Tests played against six different countries, and of this number Australia won 68, drew 50, tied one, and lost 32. This record speaks for itself, but many critics tended to treat the failures as though they were the personal responsibility of Sir Donald Bradman.

All of Sir Donald's activities, whether in the boardroom or on the Stock Exchange, at the typewriter or on the golf course — and even in the occasional 'fun' game of cricket such as the sharebrokers v the brokers' clerks, in which he knocked up 85 in good style on the Railway Oval — were carried out under the threat of those muscular problems which had tormented him since the 1930s. A period of ease from pain could be followed by a sudden attack, especially when he was

After Sir Donald's retirement from cricket he made two trips to England to report the Tests for the London *Daily Mail*. In 1956 he travelled to England for the last time aboard an Orient liner with the Test team, and retained this 'race meeting' programme as a souvenir

overtired or overworked. He was a periodic victim of such muscular spasms until the 1970s, when modern methods of manipulation seemed to ease their frequency and severity.

If such methods had been developed earlier they might have changed the pattern of his life. Medical science of nearly thirty years ago was only just beginning to understand the effects of interwoven physical and nervous tensions on the musculature of the body. The advice he received in June 1954 was that he must relieve himself of some of these tensions or face even worse consequences. He followed it by a decision to retire from his active role in stock and share broking. He transferred control of his business to the man who had started with him as his chief clerk and risen to be his associate. Don Bradman & Co. ceased to exist, and the new firm, Len Bullock & Co., came into being. Bradman's only connection with the new firm was that of a consultant.

Withdrawal from the daily drama of the stock market did not mean total retirement from public life. He was still on the boards of a number of companies, and deeply involved with the affairs of the Board of

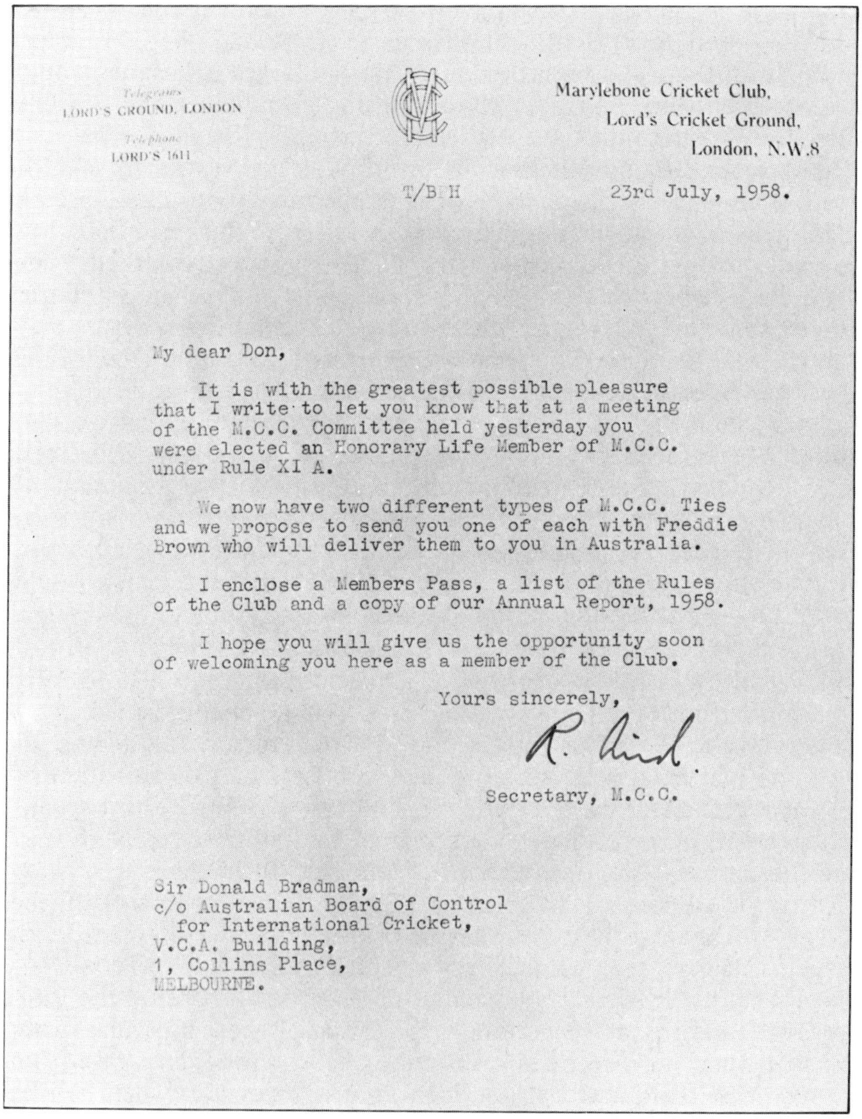

Honorary Life Membership of the M.C.C., bestowed in July 1958, is one of the many cricketing honours received by Sir Donald Bradman

Telegrams
LORD'S GROUND, LONDON

Telephone
LORD'S 1611

Marylebone Cricket Club,
Lord's Cricket Ground,
London, N.W.8

T/B H   23rd July, 1958.

My dear Don,

    It is with the greatest possible pleasure
that I write to let you know that at a meeting
of the M.C.C. Committee held yesterday you
were elected an Honorary Life Member of M.C.C.
under Rule XI A.

    We now have two different types of M.C.C. Ties
and we propose to send you one of each with Freddie
Brown who will deliver them to you in Australia.

    I enclose a Members Pass, a list of the Rules
of the Club and a copy of our Annual Report, 1958.

    I hope you will give us the opportunity soon
of welcoming you here as a member of the Club.

                    Yours sincerely,

                    R. Aird.

                    Secretary, M.C.C.

Sir Donald Bradman,
c/o Australian Board of Control
  for International Cricket,
V.C.A. Building,
1, Collins Place,
MELBOURNE.

Control and the South Australian Cricket Association. In 1958 his continuing service to cricket, added to his magnificent record in the game, led to bestowal of the honour of Life Membership of the Marylebone Cricket Club. He is also a life member of the Yorkshire, Lancashire and Hampshire county cricket clubs and of various other cricket clubs and associations.

In 1959 he was appointed chairman of a Select Committee on Throwing, established to deal with the knotty problem of 'suspect' actions on the part of various bowlers. It caused great anxiety because of a feeling that English and Australian umpires might not see eye to eye on the matter. There was a burgeoning controversy which some people believed might 'wreck international cricket', and in 1960 the Board of Control sent Sir Donald to London, together with their chairman Bill Dowling, to represent them in the relevant discussions at the International Cricket Conference. The two men were the first to represent Australia at the ICC. In the past, the Board had always appointed notable figures in the English cricket world to act as their proxies at the conferences.

Members of the conference watched films of bowlers in action in their attempts to determine what was, or was not, a 'fair delivery'. They threshed out a new experimental definition of Law 26, re throwing, and the Board of Control assured the ICC that they would do everything possible to eliminate the problem.

On 13 September 1960 the Board of Control unanimously elected Sir Donald as their chairman. He was the first Test cricketer to hold that position. He served the statutory three years until 1963, continued as a member of the Board, and was again elected chairman for 1969–72.

Three days after Sir Donald's first election as chairman, the Board released a press statement on the throwing controversy. It was to the effect that the Board could not guarantee that the action of every Australian bowler touring England in 1961 would 'meet with the complete approval of English umpires'. In order to ensure that the tour would proceed harmoniously, the Board was sending a proposal to the M.C.C. for consideration.

English newspapers promptly erupted into an assault on the 'proposed truce on throwing', which they saw as an Australian attempt to introduce bowlers with 'suspect actions' — especially Ian Meckiff and Gordon Rorke. The terms of the 'truce' were that the English umpires should not no-ball any 'suspect' Australian bowler in the matches prior to the first Test, but simply make a confidential report on him to the respective authorities. The latter would then have an opportunity to confer with the player to iron out the problem. He would be liable to no-ball calls if he repeated the same action during the Test matches.

The West Indies were touring Australia in the 1960–61 season and the newspapers soon dragged them into the controversy by asking for their opinions. Critics were quick to blame Sir Donald for what they saw as 'a disaster to the game', but he remained as imperturbable as ever during the long process of settling the dispute in the best interests of cricket. It so happened that none of the Australian players selected for England had their actions queried by English umpires, and newspaper threats of a blow-up came to nought.

As a Board member, Sir Donald played a part in organising the 1960–61 West Indies tour of Australia, the first for nine years. It was

A famous batsman tries his hand at a new sport — indoor bowling

enormously popular and successful. The great all-rounder Gary (later Sir Garfield) Sobers was the hero of the tour, and Sir Donald was one of those who persuaded him to join South Australia for three seasons. He made a startling impact on the Shield matches.

During the 1960s, it might be said that there were three different Bradmans. Firstly, there was Sir Donald Bradman, almost continuously in the public eye, knowing that whatever he said or did was liable to be picked up by the press and publicised as far afield as India and South Africa; by far the most famous citizen of South Australia and probably the most influential figure in international cricket, chosen to sit next to Queen Elizabeth II at a banquet during the 1963 Royal Visit, while Lady Bradman sat next to the Duke of Edinburgh; the company director with a seat on the boards of such prestigious local companies as Kelvinator Australia Ltd, Clarkson Ltd, F. H. Faulding & Co. Ltd, S. A. Rubber Mills Ltd, and Argo Investments Ltd.

Secondly, there was Don Bradman the family man and the friend of many people in many walks of life. His former employer Percy Westbrook, in an address to the Moss Vale Rotary Club in January 1964, said of him that one quality in his personality was 'his fondness for his home, and to those of us who know, it is one of the biggest things in a man's make-up'. Bradman never forgot old friends and he made many new ones. Westbrook had visited him in his Kensington Park home, Alf Stephens had accompanied him on his 1948 tour of England, and the people of the old days in Bowral were still as important to Don Bradman as all the famous figures he had met since he left the Southern Highlands. Lady Bradman told a New Zealand newspaper in 1971: 'He has never looked on himself as a celebrity, and so his knighthood never made any difference to us.'

Thirdly, Bradman was — and is — 'The Don': the adored hero, almost demi-god, of the cricket field, against whom all other batsmen have been measured and found wanting. For countless ordinary men and women he represented the splendour of human achievement and was a kind of living symbol that a man born with few worldly advantages could rise to great heights without losing his essential humanity. More than thirty years after he stepped down from the pinnacle of fame, his fan mail is still enormous: much larger than is received by the usual public figure. A revealing point is that countless letters arrive from people who were not even born when he was playing first-class cricket. The legend is so potent that it continuously renews the world's curiosity and interest.

In February 1963 Sir Donald Bradman made his 'positively final' appearance at the wicket. He had frequently laughed off invitations to play, usually with some such comment as 'My hands are too soft now. They'd be covered with blisters in about fifteen minutes'; but he agreed to captain the Prime Minister's Eleven v the M.C.C. in a one-day charity match at Canberra. It attracted almost as much publicity as one of his Test matches, a record crowd of 10 000 filled the stands at Manuka Oval.

The M.C.C. batted first and declared at 253 for seven. The Prime Minister's Eleven had scored 108 for three, with Don Chipp still holding his ground, when Sir Donald walked out in his cream flannels and green Australia cap to the plaudits of the crowd.

Before the match, the umpires and players (apart from Sir Donald)

One of the phenomena of Sir Donald Bradman's cricketing career is that many young people who were not even born during his great days as a batsman still regard him as 'the greatest'. These young cricket fans sought his autograph after he played for Stockbrokers v. Brokers' Clerks in Adelaide, after his retirement from first-class cricket

had consulted together and agreed that, come what may, he was to make at least fifty runs. But, as though to prove that cricket matches cannot be 'faked', the Nemesis of cricket decreed otherwise.

After Sir Donald had faced a mere four balls and scored four runs, he took strike to Brian Statham. He played a good length ball in the middle of his bat, but was a fraction late. The ball trickled off the bat between his feet, and Sir Donald accidentally kicked it onto the base of the stumps and just dislodged a bail.

The umpire could not see the ball and had no chance to play his part in the conspiracy by calling 'No ball'. Sir Donald was legally out and he promptly, but sadly, departed the scene, never again to face a bowler in the middle in a match.

As the elder statesman of cricket and a prominent public figure in his own right, Sir Donald attracted publicity throughout the 1960s whenever cricket was in the air and found himself obliged to make press and public statements more frequently than ever before. Some occasions were happy ones, such as receptions for M.C.C. teams or a retirement dinner for Les Favell. Others, such as the argument whether Australian Rules football should continue to be played on the Adelaide Oval, were controversial. (An English newspaper said that Australian Rules football 'is about as important as lacrosse'.) The fierce light of publicity showed no signs of fading. When he was ill in 1970, it was reported as far away as the Lahore *Pakistani Times*. When the English Test team arrived in Adelaide in October 1970, the Adelaide *News* celebrated the occasion with a series of articles entitled 'The Bradman

John and Shirley Bradman photographed in the early 1950s

Magic', by Ray Barber, as a potted version of Sir Donald's career. In 1969 he was invited to be Father of the Year, but courteously refused.

This interminable publicity was a great burden on the Bradman family life. John Bradman felt it was an invasion of his own individuality. The name of Bradman was so famous that, even when he visited Britain, he could not avoid questions about his father. Whenever he was introduced to somebody new, the first question was likely to be 'Are you Sir Donald's son?' By 1972, when he was a lecturer in law in the University of Adelaide, he had had enough. He decided he must retain his own individuality by changing his name by deed poll; and the newspapers naturally gave as much publicity to this decision as they did to everything else connected with Sir Donald Bradman. But John achieved his aim and continues to avoid the publicity which his father will never be able to evade.

Lady Bradman and John Bradman in London in 1956, when the whole Bradman family accompanied Sir Donald to England on his last tour with an Australian Test team — as a newspaper correspondent instead of captain

The last great cricketing controversy to involve Sir Donald was that aroused by the Board's invitation to South African cricketers to tour Australia in 1971–72. The Board had issued the invitation in the interests of international cricket and for the benefit of countless Australians who hoped to see the South Africans in action again. They had toured in 1952–53 and 1963–64, attracted huge crowds, and played entertaining cricket, although they did not quite manage to achieve victory in either series.

But by 1970, the attitudes of some sections of society had hardened towards South Africa. Some members of all political parties and of the trade union movement, the dignitaries of most churches, the majority of academics, and many ordinary citizens expressed disfavour of the Board's invitation. Another large body of opinion was in favour of the tour. According to a poll by the *Australian* newspaper, seventy per cent of Australians wanted the tour to proceed.

One of Sir Donald Bradman's dominant characteristics is that of 'doing his homework'. As soon as the lines were drawn for the impending confrontation he began to collect evidence for both sides. His archives contain a substantial file of newspaper cuttings dealing with

A LETTER FROM A FAN

Out of all the millions of words written about Sir Donald Bradman since the 1920s, the comments made in fan letters are sometimes the most illuminating. They show the significance of Sir Donald's achievements to the ordinary cricket lover, who writes from the heart with no thought of publication.

One such letter arrived from a South Australian supporter in February 1963. In parts of his six-page letter, this fan said: 'When I was on the "Hill" in Sydney last week the comments in the crowd were enough to convince any man that you are on a pedestal that is so high no one will ever reach you. In quiet patches of play, or at lunch, drinks, etc., the little groups fell to reminiscing about "Don". Everyone hooted and laughed when one chap said "Would Don Bradman ever get stuck into this mob? He'd make 'em give up cricket!" Others said "Could we do with him now!" or "He shouldn't be mentioned in the same breath as these blokes."

'I was born in the slums of Port Adelaide and my most vivid recollections are sitting up listening to you play cricket. Everybody knew there were 10 others in the Test side but Don Bradman was the idol of the poor. In the depression years when comfortable living was non-existent I suppose Sir Donald that you were a shining symbol that success could be achieved and not be just a dream. At Primary School so many boys (including myself) wrote compositions on Don Bradman that the best marks were given to a boy who was "original" and wrote about the King!

'After I finished High School I worked in the S.A. Public Service and when the cricket fever gripped everyone Don Bradman was discussed every time. The same happened when I was in Korea and Japan. In *every* instance no person was ignorant enough to suggest that any other batsman would equal you.

'Never feel that the rabble who throw mud at you are *ever* speaking for Australians. Korea made me aware of my love for Australia and it is because of great men like you that our country means so much to us.

'Whenever cricket is discussed you will always come to mind Sir Donald. Personally I always think of you as being so valuable to Australia that when a Test is played we have 12 men out on the field. In the centuries to follow long after we pass on, I will be forgotten but you will be like Drake's Drum of cricket.

'In the office they call me "D.G." and men in their 40's and 50's unashamedly admit that you are their idol. There's not a cricketer to compare with you Sir Donald — "You could eat them without salt." Great should be used very rarely but you are a *great* man.'

various aspects of apartheid and with international moves against South African sportsmen. One of the first was that of the English Cricket Council. At the request of the Home Secretary, they cancelled the proposed 1970 South African tour of England.

Sir Donald also had to study a mass of letters and telegrams, many addressed to him personally and others to the Board, from organisations and individuals taking one side or the other. The majority were against the tour. Most of these communications were couched in temperate terms but a few were rather strangely worded. These included a letter which began 'I thought I would drop you a note' and then continued for twenty-two pages plus a three-page appendix.

Sir Donald and his colleagues on the Board soon realised that the controversy was going to be argued out on the basis not of reason but of emotion. In the winter of 1970, a Springbok rugby team visited Australia and encountered violent abuse and opposition from the moment they landed. Opponents of South African racial policies subjected the tourists to many kinds of harassment on and off the field.

Sir Donald's retirement from cricket did not check the flow of his fan mail, which still pours in from many parts of the world in many different forms

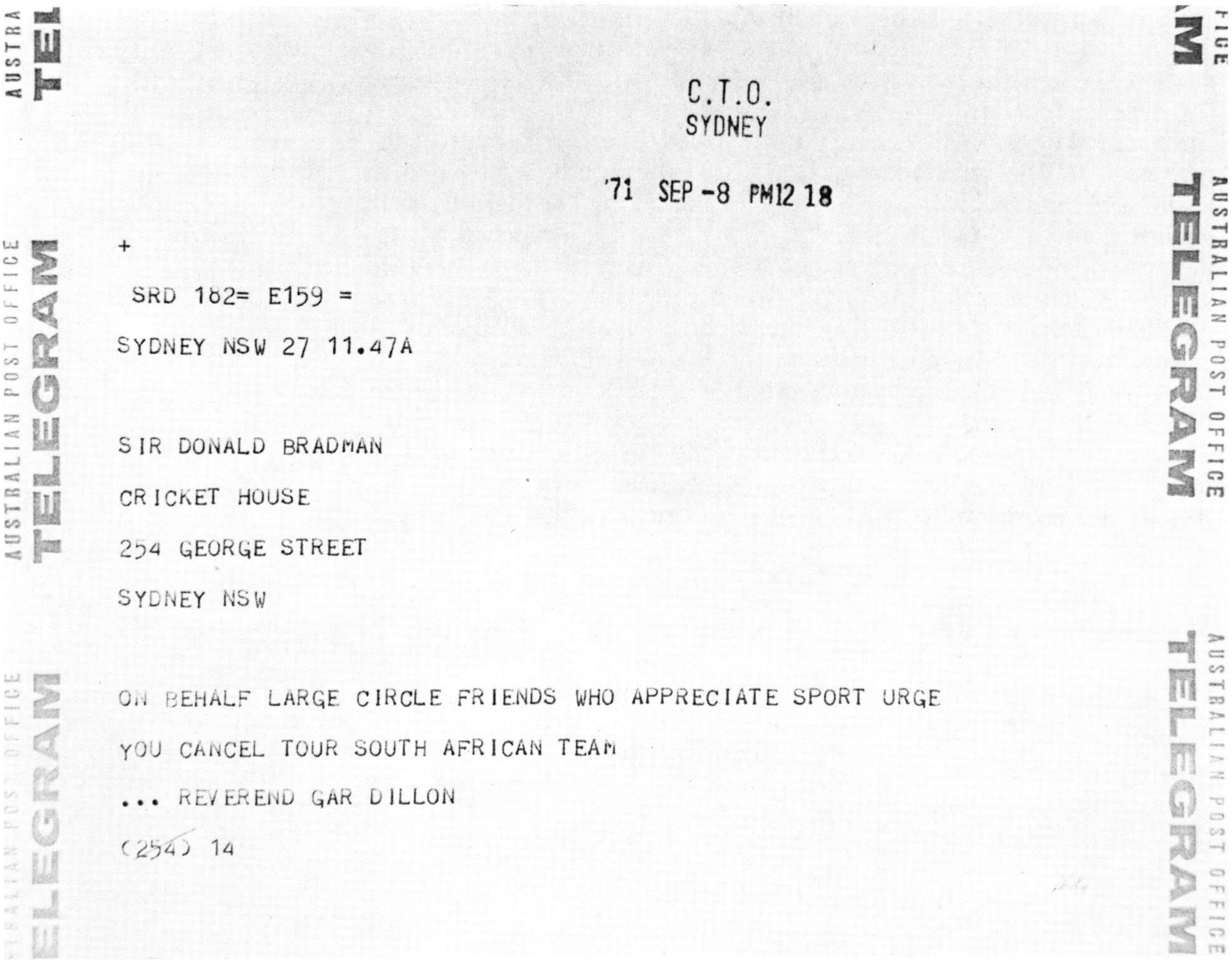

```
                              C.T.O.
                              SYDNEY

                         '71  SEP -8  PM12 18

   +

   SRD 162= E159 =

   SYDNEY NSW 27  11.47A


   SIR DONALD BRADMAN

   CRICKET HOUSE

   254 GEORGE STREET

   SYDNEY NSW


   ON BEHALF LARGE CIRCLE FRIENDS WHO APPRECIATE SPORT URGE

   YOU CANCEL TOUR SOUTH AFRICAN TEAM

   ... REVEREND GAR DILLON

   (254) 14
```

As Chairman of the Australian Cricket Board in 1971, Sir Donald was drawn into the controversy concerning the proposed tour of Australia by a South African cricket team. The Board's decision to withdraw the invitation to South Africa was applauded by many Australians. During and after the controversy, Sir Donald received many letters and telegrams either urging him to cancel the tour or praising him for having done so . . . together with messages from supporters of the tour

In order to gain first-hand knowledge of the situation, Sir Donald went to watch one of the rugby Tests at Sydney. There, in company with the South African ambassador, he saw visual evidence of the physical problems. The ground was ringed by barbed-wire barricades; holes had been dug in the outfield, with piles of sand alongside, to extinguish the flares and smoke bombs thrown over the fence; and a cordon of police was on guard inside the boundary fence. But even these precautions did not prevent protesters from bursting onto the arena, where they were arrested and taken away in relays of police vans. Hundreds of police mingled with the crowd and had their hands full quelling the riots between protesters and anti-protesters, while the air was rent by a continuous screaming cacophony of abuse.

That night, Sir Donald dined with the manager of the South African team at their motel, and again saw the massive police protection required to guard the players on every step of their tour. It was obvious that a cricket tour could not take place against such odds.

Nevertheless, Sir Donald and his colleagues continued to seek a rational solution. For the sake of a possible 'silent majority' who simply wanted to watch the Australians match themselves against the South Africans on the cricket pitch, they felt themselves obliged to study every angle of the potentially ugly situation. They sought the

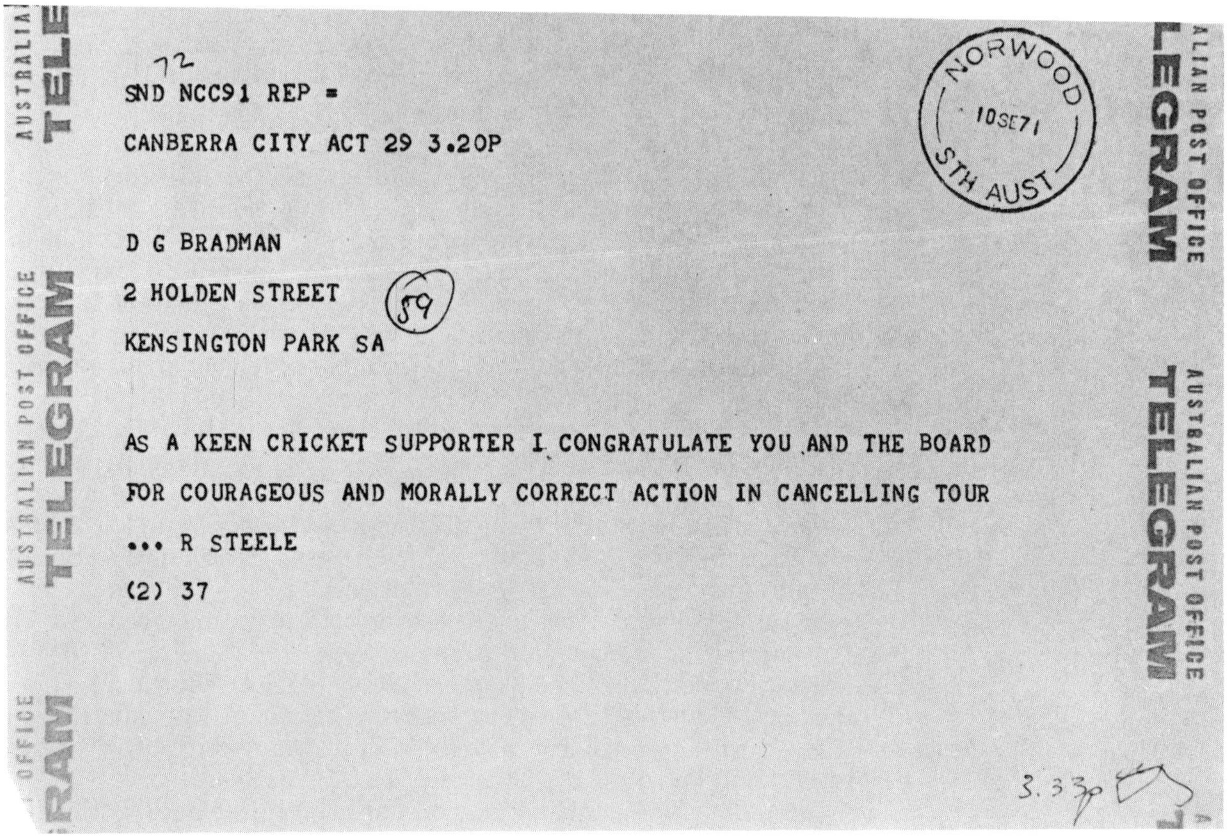

```
            72
   SND NCC91 REP =

   CANBERRA CITY ACT 29 3.20P



   D G BRADMAN

   2 HOLDEN STREET   59

   KENSINGTON PARK SA



   AS A KEEN CRICKET SUPPORTER I CONGRATULATE YOU AND THE BOARD

   FOR COURAGEOUS AND MORALLY CORRECT ACTION IN CANCELLING TOUR

   ... R STEELE

   (2) 37
```

advice of police commissioners — who said they could not guarantee
to prevent invasion of the cricket grounds — and of groundsmen and
State cricket administrators. Sir Donald personally waited on the
Prime Minister and every State Premier. The inevitable conclusion was
that any attempt to proceed with the tour would end in chaos and
degrade Australia in the eyes of the world. An ironical aspect of the
controversy was that the South African Cricket Association actually
opposed its government's policy of apartheid in sport.

On 9 September 1971 the Board met in Sydney and decided that their
invitation to South Africa must be withdrawn. Sir Donald, as chairman, had the unenviable task of informing the press.

He did so with a heavy heart and the utmost reluctance. South
Africans included some of his dearest friends, and he knew that the
players were in no way responsible for the political policies of the
South African Government.

However, his duty was clear and he made a lengthy press statement
in which he said that, no matter what decision the Board arrived at,
they would face the displeasure of a large percentage of the population.
But they had not let this knowledge influence their deliberations. They
had withdrawn the invitation in order to avert the bitterness and violence which the tour was certain to attract.

One of those who approved the decision said it revealed that Australian cricket had 'a moral conscience worthy of the dignity of the
game'. The Adelaide *News* remarked: 'Prudently, the board resisted
the impulse — and it must have been potent — to slap down or attack

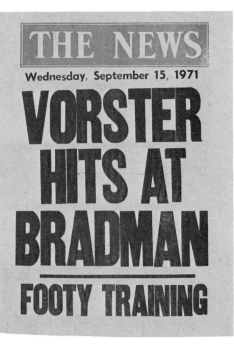

An Adelaide *News* poster which appeared during the controversy surrounding the proposed South African cricket tour of Australia in 1971

opponents of the tour . . . the board's decision must go down as one of the utmost wisdom and sagacity — and a great personal victory for Sir Donald.' The *Australian* said it was 'an example of dignified commonsense in trying circumstances'.

Those who disagreed with the decision agreed with the South African Minister for Sport, who said it was 'a victory for anarchy'. They said the Board had been bulldozed into the decision by the threat of violence against the cricketers of both sides, and that the State and Federal Governments should have been prepared to use equal violence to protect them. This argument ignored the fact that each cricket match played under such conditions would have been a shambles, and that the tour would have developed into an extremely divisive force in Australian society.

Many people wrote congratulatory letters to Sir Donald and praised his influence on the Board's decision. The Sydney *Bulletin* published a satirical article on the South African affair, which contrasted Sir Donald's handling of the problem with the dithering of the Federal Government. The *Bulletin* recommended that Sir Donald should be installed 'at once' as Prime Minister, with a cabinet of other sportsmen, because 'Australia is a sportocracy and the people we love best are our sportsmen'.

The cancellation of the proposed South African tour left a void in the Australian first-class programme. The Board immediately gave thought to the possibility of organising a composite tour, by a team to be known as Rest of the World, to take its place.

Inevitably, Sir Donald became primarily responsible for working out the plans and bringing them to fruition. He had retired from the Australian selection committee but his immense knowledge of world cricket and its players was essential for the success of the tour. He was co-opted to assist and his voice became dominant in the choice of players.

Eventually a magnificent array of international players accepted invitations to tour. Leadership was entrusted to the great West Indian, Gary Sobers, with Intikhab Alam of Pakistan as vice-captain. Bill Jacobs, a prominent Victorian cricket official, was appointed manager.

The other members of the team comprised a wealth of talent. They were Rohan Kanhai and Clive Lloyd of the West Indies; Hilton Ackerman, Graeme Pollock and Tony Greig of South Africa; Zaheer Abbas and Asif Masood of Pakistan; 'Sunny' Gavaskar, 'Rooky' Engineer and Bishen Singh Bedi of India; Norman Gifford, Richard Hutton (the son of Sir Leonard Hutton) and Bob Taylor of England; and Bob Cunis of New Zealand.

The visitors arrived at different times and from various directions. Tony Greig and Hilton Ackerman flew in direct from South Africa and Sir Donald Bradman and Phil Ridings met them at Adelaide airport. The visitors were very tired and a little deaf from the long flight, and after Sir Donald had introduced Phil Ridings and himself he asked them if they would like some coffee and toast.

Greig and Ackerman accepted with alacrity, and soon after they sat down Greig looked at Sir Donald and asked 'Have you two chaps got something to do with Australian cricket?'

Obviously he had neither recognised his hosts nor heard Sir Donald's introduction. His monumental gaffe must stand as one of the most humorous in cricket and Tony Greig never tires of telling the joke against himself.

Apart from sundry matches, the team played five times against Australia. Two matches were drawn, Australia won one, and the World Eleven won two. In the third of these games, Sobers played an innings of 254 in Melbourne which Sir Donald still thinks was the greatest ever played on Australian soil. It became the subject of a special film for which Sir Donald did the commentary.

A Royal occasion. Sir Donald Bradman, as one of South Australia's leading citizens and one of the most notable figures in Australian sport, with Queen Elizabeth II and Prince Philip on Adelaide Oval during a Royal Tour of Australia

The tour was a triumphant success, especially in the way in which players from several countries, of different races and backgrounds and with varying political opinions, mingled in perfect harmony under the banner of cricket.

At the conclusion of the tour the team held a farewell dinner in Adelaide. They invited only one guest: Sir Donald Bradman. It was a wonderful tribute to the one man who had made the tour such a great success.

He described the dinner of that night as his most emotional cricket function, supremely memorable because it demonstrated the way that cricket could transcend racial barriers.

Apart from various minor mentions in the newspapers, Sir Donald next occupied the news columns and the TV screens on a different type of occasion: the opening of the new $1½ million Bradman Stand at the Sydney Cricket Ground, on 5 January 1974. The crowd gave him a thunderous welcome when he walked to the centre of the oval during the lunch interval of an Australia v New Zealand Test match. To please the cameramen he pulled a stump from the ground and played two of his famous cover drives off an imaginary ball, showing that his movements were identical with those of the 1930s.

Mr J. B. Renshaw, chairman of the Sydney Cricket Ground Trust, said in his official address that the stand had been named 'as a tribute to the greatest batsman the world has seen'. Sir Donald in his reply said: 'This is a somewhat traumatic occasion for me. I am the only person here who has had a stand named after him. They usually leave that sort of thing until after you're dead. But I am pleased to be alive and to be here today, and I hope to stay that way for quite some time to come.'

Two months later, Sir Donald and Lady Bradman were in London on his last 'official' overseas tour. It was to attend one of the social and sporting highlights of the London year: the annual dinner and function of the Lord's Taverners, a body devoted to raising funds for charity, of which H.R.H. Prince Philip, Duke of Edinburgh, is permanent 'twelfth man'. They had persuaded him to deliver the traditional annual address, and in 1974 he took the podium to address an eminent audience. Many notable men had spoken at this function over the years but none had been listened to more eagerly and appreciatively than Sir Donald Bradman. As a token of their admiration, the Taverners presented Bradman with a cut glass decanter with a silver label hung around its neck, inscribed 'To Sir Donald Bradman for his unique and unforgettable contribution to world cricket. London Hilton Hotel Monday 13th May 1974.'

Another traditional event, the annual fund-raising auction, followed his address. Sir Donald had donated one of his blazers to be sold at the auction, and the famous comic Tommy Trinder 'knocked it down' to an enthusiastic bidder for some £750.

Prince Philip expressed his appreciation in a letter which is now one of Sir Donald's treasured possessions.

Before setting out for home, Sir Donald visited friends in Norway. But illness forced an early return to London for medical attention, and he was still unwell when he flew south again. Nevertheless, he kept faith with an engagement to return home via South Africa and stay for a few days with his old friend Jack Cheetham, who had captained South Africa against Australia in 1952–53.

He also took the opportunity of having an audience with Mr J. Vorster, Prime Minister of South Africa, to see if there might be any way out of the cricketing impasse with that country.

Sir Donald's illness persisted, but as he said farewell to Jack Cheetham at Johannesburg airport he could not foresee that his fellow-cricketer, twelve years his junior and apparently in the full bloom of health, was shortly to contract a serious ailment from which he did not recover.

Home again in Adelaide, Sir Donald sought immediate medical advice and was hospitalised for tests and treatment. The resultant advice was that he would be taking a grave risk if he did not curtail future activities, especially those involving any mental or emotional stress. He resolved at once to reduce his work load and to refuse further invitations to speak at public functions of the type which constantly poured in.

Eight years later this stream of invitations is still as heavy as ever, but Sir Donald has stuck to his resolve apart from three notable exceptions which he felt could not be refused.

The first was in September 1976, when the citizens of Bowral decided to hold a cricket match to mark the opening of their new cricket ground. They had named it, naturally, the Bradman Oval.

Bowral folk welcomed Sir Donald and Lady Bradman back to the scenes of their childhood, on an occasion which generated much pride and publicity. The whole Bowral district had changed enormously in the forty-nine years since young Don Bradman had moved to Sydney to work for Deer & Westbrook Ltd. Some of the grand old houses built by wealthy Sydney folk had fallen into disrepair, although the house built by George Bradman in 1924 still stood as sturdily as ever. The population had grown, and there were new roads, new homes and new businesses among the other signs of post-war prosperity. But there was no change in the warmth of the welcome extended by all those Bowral folk who remembered Sir Donald and Lady Bradman simply as Don and Jessie.

The wheel turns full circle. In 1976 the people of Bowral gave the name of Bradman Oval to their sports oval on which Sir Donald began his cricket career more than half-a-century earlier

Sir Donald's parents had long since passed away, as had his uncles George and Dick Whatman. His brother Victor had died, aged only fifty-five, and those two Bowral identities Alf Stephens and Percy Westbrook, who had done so much for him in earlier years, also had departed. But a surprisingly large number of friends, former schoolmates, and relations attended the celebrations to pay homage to 'Our Don', as they did also to Lady Bradman. Her relatives and friends were there in even greater abundance.

The guests at the opening ceremonies included Sir Donald's old friend and cricketing antagonist Bill O'Reilly. The Bradman Oval stands on the same site as the 'old' oval, where the two had first faced each other some fifty years earlier. After the formalities, Sir Donald took block on the pitch which stands in almost exactly the same place as the one where the bowler and batsman first came to grips on a cricket field. Bill O'Reilly, seventy-two in 1976, had not lost his old skill. He sent down a delivery outside the leg stump, and the crowd burst into cheers and friendly laughter as Sir Donald tried to hook it but missed. That light-hearted moment was his last appearance on a cricket pitch.

The second invitation for which Sir Donald decided to break his rule was tendered by the Australian Cricket Board, for him to speak at their dinner given to mark the Centenary Test between England and Australia at Melbourne in March 1977.

For every cricket lover the dinner was of course the occasion of the century, and Sir Donald felt he could not refuse the invitation. He held his audience spellbound with a splendid speech, which somehow en-

A MATHE-MATICIAN'S ASSESSMENT

During Bradman's cricketing career his name was often used as a standard of excellence. One who did this was the famous English mathematician G. H. Hardy. In a foreword to the 1967 edition of Hardy's book *A Mathematician's Apology*, the English novelist C. P. Snow wrote: 'Mathematicians not intimate with Hardy in his late years, nor with cricket, keep repeating that his highest term of praise was "In the Hobbs class". It wasn't; very reluctantly, because Hobbs was one of his pets, he had to alter the order of merit. I once had a postcard from him, probably in 1938, saying: "Bradman's a whole class above any batsman who ever lived; if Archimedes, Newton, and Gauss remain in the Hobbs class, I have to admit the possibility of a class above them, which I find difficult to imagine. They had better be moved from now on into the Bradman class." '

compassed and did justice to 100 years of Test cricket in a mere forty minutes. As he sat down the guests burst into tumultuous applause, and the chairman of the Board summed up their feelings when he said 'Thank you, Sir Donald. Nobody else could have made a speech like that.'

Fortunately the speech was recorded on tape and is available for posterity.

His third, and last, major address was given when a Sydney charitable organisation, The Primary Club, decided to hold a reunion dinner for the cricketers who had played in the 1948 tour of England. Again, Sir Donald felt he was obliged to accept the invitation. As captain and 'figurehead' of the 1948 Australian Test team, he was the one essential personality to ensure the success of the function. Once again he set aside personal problems and gave an address which enraptured and amused a vast audience — including Norman Yardley, the English captain in 1948, who paid everyone a great compliment by flying out from England especially for the occasion and paying gracious tribute to the Australians in his speech.

In between these occasions, Sir Donald's health problems had become more severe and Lady Bradman also was in poor health. She had developed angina pectoris to a degree which greatly restricted her activities.

The somewhat vague symptoms which had surfaced on Sir Donald's 1974 visit to England became sufficiently well defined for his medical advisers to recommend an internal operation. Fortunately the condition did not turn out to be as serious as might well have been the case, but it was severe enough to cause much anxiety until the problem was located and cleared.

At about the same time, Lady Bradman's heart condition deteriorated to the point where she faced the choice of having open-heart surgery or of being a permanent invalid. She did not hesitate for a moment in deciding upon surgery; but in those days, and especially for a woman of her age, the likelihood of success could not be guaranteed.

The operation was performed at the Royal Adelaide Hospital. After three very anxious days and nights the main danger was over. Thanks to the great skill of the surgeon and nursing staff, together with her own sturdy constitution and indomitable will power, she not only survived the operation but also became restored to excellent health. Today she is a living example of this modern medical miracle.

Since that traumatic period she has persuaded many sufferers not to shrink from the inevitable, and has comforted friends and strangers alike in their understandable fear of the future.

Such experiences make it easy to understand why, over the past few years, Sir Donald continued his deliberate withdrawal from the public eye. Media questions along the lines of 'What do you think, Sir Donald?' received an even more emphatic 'No comment' than in the past. When publishers approached him for another book from his pen, he rejected very substantial offers with his customary firm diplomacy. He consented to write forewords for a number of books about cricket, but only after he had had the opportunity to study the authors' material. Publishers, editors and other media folk try vainly to lure him back into the limelight by asking him to give interviews, launch books, appear on radio or television, write articles, or comment on some cricketing controversy. Some media personalities, with an inflated idea of their right to invade the privacy of others, react angrily to rebuffs.

He could earn large fees by writing articles on almost any aspect of past or present cricket, but he always refuses. On one of the very rare occasions when he did agree to an interview, for a newspaper article to be published on the fiftieth anniversary of the bodyline Tests, he found himself obliged to write to the Adelaide *Advertiser* to correct the omission of some vital facts.

His insistence on privacy for himself and his family has now continued for more than fifty years. It is not a struggle he enjoys. He is fully aware that the media have played an important part in his life and he takes no pleasure in repelling those who work for them, but he is also aware that it is all too easy for a public figure to become a mere puppet of the media. He knows, too, that his determination to preserve his privacy and individuality has given him the reputation, in some quarters, of being aloof and arrogant. However, countless friends would testify to his warmth and consideration.

Over the years, many people have commented on the difficulty of interviewing Sir Donald Bradman. The difficulty, if it exists, stems simply from the fact that he is not prepared to expose the privacy of his inner feelings. Perhaps this seems strange in an era which invented the phrase 'in-depth interviews', with the implication that a subject should submit himself to dissection by the media; but it is not remarkable for a man of Sir Donald's background and character. He was brought up in a period when a man was judged by his actions rather than his emotions and when a good sportsman preserved the same demeanour in victory or defeat.

On 16 June 1979, he received what one may reasonably suppose to be the final accolade to his career, when Governor-General Sir Zelman Cowan invested him with the appointment as a Companion of the Order of Australia. This is the second highest civil Australian award, ranking six places higher in the order of precedence than that of Knight Bachelor. It is a rare and precious award, reserved for those who have rendered very special service, and it indicates in full measure how well Sir Donald Bradman has served his country in sport and in public life.

Sir Donald and Lady Bradman still live in the house they built nearly fifty years ago. It is a solid, comfortable family home, with most of the souvenirs of the cricketing years confined to the billiard room and to Sir Donald's study. The struggle to protect their privacy from the outside world, apart from friends and relations including two adored grandchildren, still continues. Recently, Sir Donald had once again to change his unlisted telephone number because too many outsiders had somehow ferreted it out. Even the overseas media had got hold of it and an optimistic employee of the British Broadcasting Corporation telephoned him from London, in the middle of the night, for a comment on the bodyline anniversary. A Sydney newspaper used it to check up on one of the rumours which still proliferate around the Bradman name. Shortly after Christmas 1982, the newspaper rang for confirmation of a story that Sir Donald Bradman was dead. He took the call, and answered 'I can give you first-hand evidence that he's not.'

The comment was typical of a mind which functions as fast as ever,

LORD BRADMAN?

Newspapers and others frequently canvassed the possibility of Don Bradman entering politics, although most of the reports and predictions were incorrect. Bradman did receive one direct approach from a political party, and feelers went in his direction on other occasions, but the prospect did not appeal to him.

However it is not generally known that Prime Minister Sir Robert Menzies, who was a great friend and admirer of Don Bradman, once contemplated the appointment of Sir Donald Bradman as Australian High Commissioner in the United Kingdom.

Sir Robert broached the subject privately with Sir Donald one evening as they departed together from a late cricket gathering, and there can be little doubt that the appointment would have been an extremely popular one in Great Britain.

But the possibility did not come to fruition.

It is of course customary for such appointments to be regarded as 'political plums', to be bestowed on men who have had a long association with a political party or served a faithful apprenticeship. In Sir Donald's case, the reason why Sir Robert did not pursue the matter must remain a matter of pure speculation. Perhaps his colleagues dissuaded him from such a departure from tradition.

Governor-General of the Commonwealth
of Australia and
Chancellor of the Order of Australia

To

DONALD GEORGE BRADMAN

Greeting

WHEREAS with the approval of Her Majesty Queen Elizabeth
The Second, Queen of Australia and Sovereign of the Order of Australia,
I have been pleased to appoint you to be a Companion in the General Division
of the Order of Australia.

I DO by these Presents appoint you to be a Companion in the
General Division of the said Order and authorise you to hold and enjoy the
dignity of such appointment together with Membership in the said Order
and all privileges thereunto appertaining.

GIVEN at Government House, Canberra, under the Seal of the
Order of Australia this sixteenth day of June 1979.

By His Excellency's Command

Secretary of the Order of Australia

Sir Donald Bradman's appointment
as a Companion in the General
Division of the Order of Australia

just as the body, after three-quarters of a century, moves with the agility of a much younger man. Sir Donald takes the stairs of his home as briskly as though he were going for a catch in the outfield. His reflexes show the same old computer-fast reactions: the small feet move quickly and certainly; the small, shapely hands are as dexterous as they ever were. Most of the fair hair which once brought him the nickname of 'Goldie' has vanished now, but the blue eyes are as shrewd as ever and his conversation is crisp and definitive. Shakespeare's phrase 'Old men forget' certainly would not apply to Sir Donald Bradman. He seems to have a precise memory of every match he ever played.

The impression now is of a compact, vigorous personality, totally integrated, fully in command of himself, as quietly confident as when he first faced the bowling on the Sydney Cricket Ground. And yet, despite all the decades of publicity and hero-worship, he remains a sincere, unassuming and kindly man, just as Lady Bradman remains a serene and charming woman. Her influence on this remarkable partnership, which has already lasted more than half-a-century, cannot be overestimated. In some miraculous way they have retained all the homely virtues of their upbringing in a little town in the 'old' Australia.

Don Bradman is forever a part of the history of Australia, and as with most historic figures there is a certain mystery about him which cannot be solved. There are no words to define genius. Don Bradman was the genius of the cricket pitch, and we shall not look upon his like again.

APPENDIX 1

Batsmen Who Have Made 1000 Runs in England Before the End of May

Player	Year	Innings	Runs	Average
W. G. GRACE	1895	10	1016	112.88
T. W. HAYWARD	1900	13	1074	97.63
W. R. HAMMOND	1927	14	1042	74.42
C. HALLOWS	1928	11	1000	125.00
D. G. BRADMAN	1930	11	1001	143.00
D. G. BRADMAN	1938	9	1056	150.85
W. J. EDRICH	1938	15	1010	84.16
G. M. TURNER	1973	18	1018	78.30

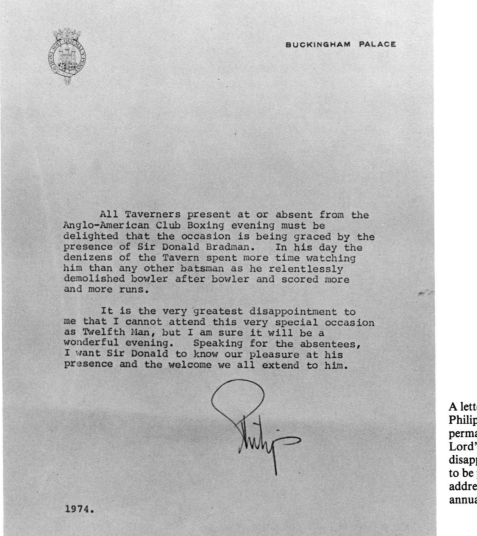

BUCKINGHAM PALACE

All Taverners present at or absent from the Anglo-American Club Boxing evening must be delighted that the occasion is being graced by the presence of Sir Donald Bradman. In his day the denizens of the Tavern spent more time watching him than any other batsman as he relentlessly demolished bowler after bowler and scored more and more runs.

It is the very greatest disappointment to me that I cannot attend this very special occasion as Twelfth Man, but I am sure it will be a wonderful evening. Speaking for the absentees, I want Sir Donald to know our pleasure at his presence and the welcome we all extend to him.

1974.

A letter from H.R.H. Prince Philip, Duke of Edinburgh, the permanent 'Twelfth Man' of the Lord's Taverners, expressing his disappointment that he was unable to be present when Sir Donald addressed the Taverners at the annual function

APPENDIX 2

Batsmen Who Have Made Over 100 Centuries

Wisdens Cricketers Almanack for 1982 lists the batsmen who, up to and including the English season of 1981, had made 100 or more centuries in first class cricket. The list is set out below.

It shows the total number of innings played including those in which the batsman was not out. The percentages shown are therefore slightly lower than they would be for completed innings.

For example Hobbs was not out 106 times, so that he had 1209 completed innings, on which his percentage would rise to 16.2. Hammond's figures would change to 1005 minus 104 = 901 — percentage 18.5, and Bradmans would change to 338 minus 43 = 295, percentage 39.6.

The percentages show that Bradman's centuries scored to innings played is more than twice as high as any other player of all time, Hammond coming second. The comparison becomes more marked in test matches where Bradman made 29 centuries in 70 completed innings, or 41.4%, to Hammond's 22 centuries in 124 completed innings, or 17.7%.

Player	Innings played	Centuries	Percentage
J. B. HOBBS	1315	197	14.9
E. H. HENDREN	1300	170	13.0
W. R. HAMMOND	1005	167	16.6
C. P. MEAD	1340	153	11.4
H. SUTCLIFFE	1088	149	13.6
F. E. WOOLLEY	1532	145	9.4
L. HUTTON	814	129	15.8
W. G. GRACE	1493	126	8.4
G. BOYCOTT (a)	827	124	14.9
D. C. COMPTON	839	123	14.6
T. W. GRAVENEY	1223	122	9.9
D. G. BRADMAN	338	117	34.6
M. C. COWDREY	1130	107	9.4
A. SANDHAM	1000	107	10.7
T. W. HAYWARD	1138	104	9.1
J. H. EDRICH	979	103	10.5
L. E. AMES	951	102	10.7
E. TYLDESLEY	961	102	10.6
G. M. TURNER (b)	771	98	12.7
ZAHEER ABBAS (c)	613	88	14.3

(a). Boycott is still playing and has now scored more than the 124 centuries listed up to 1981.

(b) & (c). Turner and Abbas are both still playing and each has now exceeded 100 centuries. They are the only two non-English players (except Bradman) to have scored over 100 centuries but of course both have played county cricket in England for many years.

ACKNOWLEDGMENTS

The principal sources for this book are the newspaper and magazine cuttings, photographs, letters, telegrams, and other printed or holographic material collected by Sir Donald Bradman and/or his friends and relations from about 1910 to 1980, but mainly during the period 1926–76. A good deal of this material is contained in scrapbooks or albums compiled by Sir Donald and others, but a quantity of photographs and documents is in separate form. Copies from a selection of this material have been assembled into the fifty-one Sir Donald Bradman Scrapbooks compiled by the State Library of South Australia, of which one set is housed in the library and a duplicate set is in Sir Donald's possession. The author has referred both to the bulk of original material and to the State Library scrapbooks, which were particularly useful because they contain copies of documents and photographs, details of matches, and other data assembled in chronological sequence.

In many instances the newspaper cuttings, photographic prints and other material do not carry any evidence of their origin. For example, a number of newspaper cuttings do not show the titles of the publications from which they were extracted. Wherever possible, the sources of newspaper reports, magazine articles, etc are given in the text. When sources are omitted it is because they cannot be traced.

Similar comments apply to illustrative material. Many of the newspaper and other photographs do not carry any accreditation, but when it has been possible to trace the origin of illustrations the appropriate captions have either been given in the captions or they are believed to be as follows:—

Sport & General Photographic Agency, London: Photos of Bradman executing cricket strokes, pp. 63–7; Bradman being presented to King George V, p. 90; Bradman at Leeds, July 1930, pp. 95, 96; Bradman and Jackson, pp. 103–4; and Test match photographs on pp. 201, 203, 205, 255, 257, 320.

Punch Publications Ltd: Cartoon on p. 91.

Sydney Sun: Cartoon on p. 118 and possibly cartoon on p. 148.

Allen's Music House: Song-sheet 'Our Don Bradman' on p. 130.

Adelaide Sunday Mail: Cartoon on p. 216.

Melbourne Age: Bradman with fellow-selectors, p. 230.

Planet News: Bradman with Peter Brough, p. 304.

Photographic News Agencies: Bradman with members of the Royal family and with King George VI, pp. 325, 327.

Adelaide News: Bradman with autograph hunters, p. 347.

Associated Press: Bradman with Babe Ruth, p. 156.

The photographs of the bats and balls used by Sir Donald, and of some of his other cricketing memorabilia, were taken by Marcus Brownrigg, Adelaide.

Reproductions of original documents, newspaper cuttings, photo prints, etc were made by David Wilson, Adelaide, for use in the book.

For the reasons given above it is not possible to give any more precise or extensive accreditation for material reproduced in the book. Should any person feel that any such accreditation is incorrect, and/or that a matter of copyright is involved in any illustration or any part of the text, then he or she is invited to contact the publishers.

The following books have been of great assistance in tracing the chronology of events, in checking statistical data, and in providing some supporting details:—
Sir Donald Bradman's *Don Bradman's Book* (Hutchinson, London, 1930) and *Farewell to Cricket* (Hodder & Stoughton, London, 1950); *Bradman's First Tour* (Rigby, Adelaide, 1981) which is a 'scrapbook' of 1930 newspaper reports; Harold Larwood and Kevin Perkins' *The Larwood Story* (Bonpara Pty Ltd, Sydney, 1982); Christopher Martin-Jenkins' *The Complete Who's Who of Test Cricketers* (Rigby, Adelaide, 1982 edition); A. G. Moyes' *Bradman* (Angus & Robertson, Sydney, 1948); Irving Rosenwater's *Sir Donald Bradman* (B. T. Batsford Limited, London, 1978); Jack Pollard's *Australian Cricket: The Game and the Players* (Hodder & Stoughton (Australia) Pty Ltd, Sydney, and the Australian Broadcasting Corporation, 1982); B. J. Wakley's *Bradman the Great* (Nicholas Kay, London, 1959); and *Wisden Cricketers Almanac* of various dates.

Grateful acknowledgment is made to all those writers and photographers who recorded Don Bradman's feats for posterity, and thus enabled this book to be derived from their efforts.

'Our Don Bradman' by Jack O'Hagan; reproduction of the song sheet has been made by permission of the publishers Allans Music Australia Pty Ltd.

INDEX